THE COURAGE TO GO

THE COURAGE TO GO

A MEMOIR OF THE
SEVEN THOUSAND MILES
THAT HEALED ME

EMILY DOBBERSTEIN

First paperback edition published in the United States of America
by Creating Space for Wonder, an imprint of the publisher,
Emily Dobberstein, in 2020.

Publisher's Cataloging-in-Publication Data
Dobberstein, Emily, author.
The courage to go: a memoir of the seven thousand miles that healed me /
Emily Dobberstein —1st ed.
ISBN 978-1-7356653-0-6 (paperback)
ISBN 978-1-7356653-1-3 (ebook)
LCCN 2020917911
1. Dobberstein, Emily—Travel—West (U.S.).   2. Christian Biography.
3. West (U.S.)—Description and Travel.   4. Grief—Religious Aspects.
5. Travel writing.
DDC 277.308

Printed in the United states of America
Set in Adobe Garamond Pro with Bebas Neue Pro
Edited by Jasmin Morrell, mikemorrell.org
Interior design by Emily Dobberstein
Cover design ©Santo Roy
Cover photograph ©Benjamin James Roberts

emilydobberstein.com

For those who need help living into the hope
that healing is possible,
For those who are questioning
the "one right way" they were handed
and feel isolated and alone,
For those who wish to feel seen
in the midst of their grief,
For those who have lost or needed to leave
something that once defined them,
For those who have been hurt
by the worldview they were handed,
And for those who don't understand
how their worldview could ever hurt people.

CONTENTS

AUTHOR'S NOTE

To write this book, I used modified excerpts from the detailed journals I kept during this period of my life, my memories from my perspective of these past events, and my consultations with many people who appear in this book. With the exception of Ethan, every name mentioned in this book is a pseudonym, and I changed many identifying details to preserve anonymity. I researched facts whenever possible. Aside from tweaking some minor chronological details, inserting a few fictitious conversations, and eliminating events that did not contribute to the main storyline, the events and conversations in this book have been set down as faithfully as possible.

This book is about seeking mystery, not debating theology.
This book is about making peace with ambiguity, not resisting it.
This book is about the questions, not the answers.

I can only hope that this book leads us all back to the fundamental truth that vulnerability breeds vulnerability, and we all know this world could damn well use some more authenticity.

This book is a part of my story.
I invite you to find yourself in it somewhere,
And may it take you wherever you need to go.

THE COURAGE TO GO

{1}

THE GOING

"I'm not sorry.
I'm not sorry.
I'm not sorry."

I OPENED MY EYES TO MY HEART POUNDING. IT FELT LIKE fists on the walls of my chest, pleading for escape as I awoke. Moments before, I drowned in a sea of darkness. My mind realized it was just another nightmare, but my body didn't know it yet. Cold sweat still clutched to my brow, and my breath remained shallow as I rolled over to my back and stared at the ceiling. I coaxed myself into a series of breaths as deep as my longing for a night's sleep that didn't leave me more tired than I was the day before, and my heart began to relax. If I reached back far enough in my memory, I could find vague whispers of peaceful, happy mornings, when waking up felt like a gift instead of a curse, when rested, rejuvenated, and excited to get out of bed were states of being with which I was familiar instead of feelings I could only dream of. Those mornings felt like they took place in another life, and the person that lived them was a stranger to me now.

I blinked away the fog of sleep as I watched the first rays of July sun peek through my window, as if they were checking to make sure I was okay. I knew I wasn't, but I had become a professional pretender. The sun, like most people in my life then, would never know.

I thought the day I left would be different. I thought I would feel excited, or invigorated, or at least something close to happy, but I found myself wrapped in a familiar blanket of heaviness even as I remembered that today was the big day. It was a normal summer morning in my quiet home in Boone, tucked away in a pleasantly old-fashioned valley in the Appalachian Mountains of North Carolina, peppered with old buildings, where farmers, vagabonds, and young professionals roamed the same small streets. This place had held me for the two years since I moved from Georgia to go to college at Appalachian State University, and although part of me wanted to pull the covers over my head and pretend like I never decided to change anything, I knew I had to get out.

Thank goodness for the sunshine, for the light helped lift some of the melancholy. Depression had made its bed in my chest for months, and though leaving in the rain would have felt more appropriate, part of me was glad the sunny skies seemed to hold an invitation, though to what, I couldn't tell.

I had become used to my house being eerily quiet for the four weeks since my roommates left for summer break, but as I walked back and forth from kitchen to bedroom to bathroom and back again, trying to remember the last things I needed to pack, I noticed the old floorboards creaking under my feet. The floor's groans sounded louder and more pronounced on this particular morning. Maybe it was because I became aware that after I left that day, I didn't know how long it would be before I would hear that familiar sound again. I had few set plans. By the time I came back, would I step lightly? Would my soul feel less creaky, old, and tired?

My dream of taking a long road trip accross the United States was finally manifesting in reality, even if my present circumstances didn't line up with my dreams for this day. I'd dreamt of leaving in happiness and health, with the love of my life sitting beside me. We'd take turns driving and fight playfully over what song we would listen to next on the stereo. We'd stop wherever we wanted to explore and adventure together. We'd find new swimming holes, meet new friends, and talk about life and love and everything we hoped to change about the world. It's funny how we create these idealized images of what the future is supposed to be like, as if we never learn that it can set us up for heartache when that future never comes. The future trip had finally reached the present, but because of the events of the past months, I was going alone. Grieving, depressed, and anxious, I was particularly aware of the contrast between the ideal and reality.

I wasn't confident that I would enjoy this road trip without Cam. Remembering him every day would be searing. After almost five years together, his sudden absence carved a gaping hole in my chest, and I didn't know how to fill myself back up again. He had emptied me.

I chose to leave my little house above the red-painted scuba shop in Boone anyway, clutching to the small hope it would be good for me. I would make my way West. Just me. Myself. And all of my insecurities, trauma, rage, doubt, and fear. Everyone's ideal travel companions.

When I said my goodbyes to my friends and family the day before, I had held my head high, smiled, and spoke confidently, telling them how excited I was to travel solo across the country and see where the wind would take me. I presented the poised, strong, independent mask I always wore—fooling them again and buying me a little more time so I could leave before I had to tell them the truth.

I'd been hiding for months. Standing in front of the bathroom mirror one last time, I felt exposed. My light green, 35-liter hiking backpack weighed heavy on my shoulders. I hadn't told anyone the full story. No one knew exactly why I was leaving. Maybe, I still didn't know myself. I locked my door, threw my last few things in my trunk, and started my car.

"GO BACK! This is a terrible idea! Don't leave! It's too scary!" Every voice in my head begged me to stay, but something in my gut made me go.

I pulled out of my driveway. I wanted to go back to the safety of my bedroom, where I had places to store all of my emotions—underneath overturned picture frames, in boxes of Cam's things in my closet, tucked in the pages of neglected journals, books, and Bibles that no longer had a purpose in my life besides slowly collecting dust on my shelves.

To combat my shaking hands, I gripped both sides of the steering wheel. Then, with resolve, I pressed the gas pedal down, whipping my black Jeep Liberty around the curves of highway 321 North toward the Tennessee line. I had submitted to my fear for far too long, and I knew that continuing to let it govern my actions would not take me where I needed to go.

I wanted to be myself again. I wanted to be happy again. I wanted to be whole again. I wanted to feel alive again. I wanted to hope in something again.

Not only did I attempt to resist the normal fears that came with the idea of a twenty-year-old female driving across the country and sleeping in her car by herself—like serial killers and rapists and sketchy truck stops—but I also tried my best to ignore the more subtle fears that began rising to the surface.

Will I be brave enough? Will I have to bail and admit failure? Will I find some way to fill this hole in my chest and heal? The memory of what it felt like when the dirt caught the weight of my knees that night flashed quickly in my mind. I watched myself try to stand and fail as I slammed my fist into the ground. I felt so broken then, when my whole world crumbled. Even though it all finally ended that night and I was now physically driving away from that place, part of me was still back there, crumbled in that dirt. I shook it away.

Will I be found out after all of this hiding? Will I be able to finally face the entirety of myself—my thoughts, my darkness, my pain—that I've repressed for so long?

It is terrifying to accept the possibility of having all our theories about ourselves and about the world disproven. I knew by going on this trip, I would have to accept that possibility. Some days I was fully confident in the Emily I believed I was, but I knew there was so much of myself I kept below the surface because I feared what I might find in the depths. It could be too much to hold. I wanted to believe I was strong and confident enough to set off on the open road with nothing but a few pairs of clothes, some gear, a tent, and an assortment of granola and canned tuna, but I knew that this trip would expose parts of me I had been ignoring and hiding. I didn't know if I was ready.

It had been months since I'd let anyone close to me. I had not told a soul about the toxic internal space I inhabited most days—the anxiety, the panic attacks, the nightmares, the seemingly never-ending spiraling thoughts. No one knew the constant internal turmoil that took place in my self-prescribed isolation. How could I have begun to explain? I survived only by doing my best to avoid it all. I distracted myself with constant school and work and gym and friends. I pretended to be a worship leader in my Christian community—putting on a mask to convince people I still believed it all when I actually didn't know what to do with the idea of God anymore. I knew that leaving meant I had to leave behind the distractions. Leaving meant that I had to tell the truth, and I feared that I could not bear it.

I drove in silence for a while to let my mind settle, slowly working through panicked logistical questions. My stomach sunk to my toes a few times for reasons that ranged from worrying I forgot my rain jacket, or I didn't bring enough underwear, or I didn't bring enough blister bandaids, and everything in-between. I tried to give myself permission to be frantic for a couple miles while I was still close enough to turn around if I forgot something dire, but I hoped that I wouldn't find anything forgotten. I feared that if I had to go back to my house, my wave of courage would fizzle out, and I would be tempted to stay.

Prayer had not been a part of my life for quite some time. I'd resisted all things regarding God for months, but for some reason, in this moment I was drawn to pray.

Once I abandoned my identity steeped in a specific form of conservative, fundamentalist, evangelical Christianity, every attempt to pray felt foreign and awkward, or like I was lying. Or worse: it was as if I was being lied to. My Christian faith had been one of the most important aspects of my life for almost twenty years. However, once I was forced to look at all of the questions I'd been repressing about Christianity, God, and the evangelical Church as a whole, the idea of God became only a source of pain and confusion for me. When I approached any thought or conversation about faith, I found nothing but anger and feelings of betrayal, so I decided it was easier and less painful to just not believe anything anymore. But why is it in moments of significance, or uncertainty, or fear of facing the unknown that the human spirit is often drawn to speak or release something out into the Universe—in hopes that it is caught and held by something larger and beyond ourselves—a wish, an intention, a prayer?

As the distance between myself and comfort became greater, despite the lack of prayer or belief in my life, I prayed. Maybe it was because there was a part of me that desperately wanted to hold on to the belief that God could somehow still exist, but mostly it was because I was overwhelmed with a lot of emotions, and I didn't know what else to do.

Attempting to pray was like walking through thick mud up to my knees, awkwardly pulling up each phrase like a heavy, muck-soaked foot. I plunged forward trying to keep my balance. Though past attempts had been unsuccessful, I tried to walk through praying without getting stuck in anger, resentment, or pretentiousness.

God, Divine, Universe, Father, Mother, Spirit, Friend,
Whatever he? she? it? they? you? might be,

I do not know who or what you are, or what you could be, if you are conscious to be able to hear this prayer, which I doubt, or more so, if you even exist. At some point over the last year I lost myself, and with that I have lost the ground of my being that led me to find light and purpose, and I am left in nihilism, in meaninglessness. I feel scared, numb, and confused. Something deep in my soul craves some aspect of the Divine again, but I don't know how to find it. I don't know where to start. I used to see the sacred that flowed in all things, and now I look upon myself and this world and see nothing but darkness and pain. I know that the person I have been lately is not my true and full self, but I don't know how to find myself again, or maybe how to find myself for the first time.

I want to believe that there is something out there, that there is still a sacred dance to enter into, that it is possible to be led by something higher than myself. But I don't know how to find it. I don't know where to begin. I don't have language to speak of any of this anymore. I want to believe that I need you somehow, if you can even be a you, but I don't know how to get through the wall around my mind. It seems to get thicker and taller every day, and I feel myself spiraling further into depression daily. Even now I hear the voice that rebukes my ignorance to ever think that God could be real, that anything within spirituality is worth pursuing, that there could actually be a world where the Divine is as close as breath, where there is a stillness that is constantly available to me.

I have been searching for life, but all I see is wasteland, desert, dust. My mind and heart are so disconnected that I don't know how to experience reality anymore. Each one works in isolation, my mind spiraling into toxicity, my heart barely beating with a thirst for life.

God, whatever God means, I am filled with rage. I don't trust you. I don't trust religion. I don't trust anyone. I don't believe that you are good, and I don't know why I am even praying this, but I don't know what else to do. I'm terrified that I will always feel like this, and that the hopelessness will get worse. I don't want to continue spiraling, but I don't know how to stop. This is my prayer, my outcry, my projection of my best intentions out into the Universe, and I hope that there is something there to catch them. And if you're not out there, to the consciousness and love that fills this body I live in, may I find hope again, and most of all, may I find the courage to heal.

I didn't try to force any deep or profound revelation. I was, after all, only twenty miles down Highway 321. Maybe if God was real and could intervene like people claimed, God could have moved mountains in just twenty miles, but I wasn't expecting to suddenly become a different person simply because I said a prayer and my journey had officially begun.

I couldn't find God in the Church anymore. (When I use Church as a capital noun, I mean it to represent evangelical Christianity as a whole. When I use the word without capitalizing it, I mean it to reference a specific church community I have been a part of in my life). I was fed up with the diluted, hypocritical, judgmental, homophobic, exclusive Christianity I saw in so many Christian circles, where it seemed like no one told the truth of their lives; where the marketed "Jesus that saves" didn't actually save people from their abusive and toxic cycles; where the claim that "all are welcome" often looked more like an exclusively "suburban Christianity." In my experience that kind of Christianity was made up of privileged communities who excluded the poor, sick, hungry, and marginalized when those were the very people Jesus actually spent most of his time with. I had tried to stay in church after my faith had crumbled internally, hoping to salvage something of my relationship with this institution that had been my foundation for twenty years. I always left church with more anger and constriction than what I already carried.

As the six months leading up to my trip counted down, I drowned in questions with no answers. It was easier to just become an atheist out of anger, but I think often after leaving one form of fundamentalism it is easy to react by immediately attaching ourselves to another form of fundamentalism. I figured if the God that fundamentalist, evangelical Christianity gave me was not a God I wanted to believe in, then God just must not be real. End of story. Choosing not to believe in God helped me retain some sort of sanity while everything else in my life felt like it was falling apart. If it was all meaningless anyhow, it made my pain a little more bearable.

The image of God that once was the foundation of my life had been ripped apart and now seemed unsalvageable. However, I still sensed that there was some part of me that could not fully let go of the possibility that God—in some way—could be real. And if God were real, perhaps God was much more vast and abstract than the small, strict God-box I'd been handed in my Christian experience, where I'd been told over and over again that the only way to God was "our" way, and everyone that doesn't follow that way goes to hell.

I hoped, if nothing else, I might be able to start over on my trip by finding God outside and seeking the sacred in the whispers of the wind, in the warmth of the sun, in the rattling of leaves, in the rush of a river, in the wet of the rain, in the gloom of the fog, in the dark of the night. I wanted to find God inside of me, within the fluttering of my heartbeat and the whispering of my spirit. I wanted to find God in my interactions with both friends and strangers alike in love and kindness and compassion.

The six months before I left had been the hardest and most isolating months of my life, and I knew that just because I was leaving my external circumstances in Boone, all of the shadows of my trauma which I had not yet found the courage to confront would not stay behind. I knew I would have to face them, but I wasn't ready yet.

To distract myself I inserted *Aeolian*, an album by an artist called Benjamin James, into my CD player—a practically ancient gadget. Even though the album had been in my car since a friend from church gave it to me, I had only listened to it once in passing, not really paying attention to the lyrics. I knew the artist was not explicitly Christian though, so I knew there was less of a chance that the music would be triggering. I had over thirty-five hours of driving ahead of me before I reached the Pacific Coast, with only my thoughts, music, and podcasts to keep me company. So if there was any time to intentionally listen to an album all the way through for the hell of it, it was now.

I rested into the beginning melody of brass instruments stacked in flawless harmony as I slowly twisted and turned through the hardwood and pine-covered Appalachian mountains that surrounded me. I passed the mirror-like water of Watauga Lake, signaling that I had crossed over from North Carolina into Tennessee. One state down. I wondered how many states I would cross by the time I re-entered North Carolina. With no set itinerary or return date, only time would tell.

The lyrics continued to build with more volume and intensity, and the chorus of the first song broke the slightest crack in my hard outer core.

> *"Come back to the river*
> *I will take you to the sea."*

I hoped that if God existed and I had an opportunity to sit across the table from him or her or them and talk all of this out, that he or she or they would say something similar to those lines. *"Come back to the River; I will take you to the sea."*

I used to live in the flow of that River constantly and effortlessly, and I trusted that it would always take me where I needed to go. But then my life-raft of beliefs was shredded. I tumbled through rapids without the raft for a while, just trying to survive. At some point in the spring semester before I left, I couldn't afford any more cuts and bruises. I became too tired to fight anymore. In order to survive, I had to find a way to get out. I had to leave the River I had always known. I didn't know how to exist in it anymore without drowning.

I crawled up on the bank of the River and started walking blindly, with no idea where I was going or which way led to safety. And after walking without a compass for so long I reached a desert where I got lost, and I no longer knew the way home. I was far away from the River, but I wanted to believe that if I found my way back to it, that it could somehow lead to a deep, expansive, powerful sea instead of a dry creek bed. I hoped this trip would give me some tools to build a new raft—a new spiritual foundation—to carry me through the River's flow, if I found it again. Maybe one day it would lead me to a new life, a new love, a new heart, a new soul, a new sea.

At some point in my contemplation I felt a foreign sting in my eyes. It almost felt like tears beginning to form. After everything happened with Cam, I had been physically unable to cry, no matter how much I desperately wanted to. This unexpected sensation caught me off guard so much that it was hard to remain in my body long enough to feel the emotions attached to the sensation. No tears actually fell, but it was encouraging to feel the slightest bit of emotional response for the first time in months. Since the final year with Cam trained me to be emotionally unresponsive, I knew it would take a long time to relearn how to feel.

I took a deep breath, and despite my apprehension about leaving, a slight grin spread across my face. I was really doing this.

There are seasons where comfort and certainty are necessary to help us feel safe enough to enter into growth, but sometimes seasons come where we must enter into the paradox found in leaving comfortability and certainty so that we might find something to hold onto in the paralyzing ambiguity, in letting ourselves be broken open so that we may be filled up again, in giving into the death, hoping that in the deep dark, light will finally break through.

The only certain thing in my being that day was that my heart was beating, and its rhythm was enough assurance to help me embrace the uncertainty wrapped up in my leaving. I was a twenty-year-old woman travelling alone for the first time, driving across the United States, living out of my car or tent in towns I had not yet decided. I had no idea who I was, what I believed, where I was going, or when I would come back. But I was going, and that was all that mattered.

I eventually reached I-40 West, the road I would get to know well the next few days. Time passed slowly and relatively peacefully, chipping away at the six hours of 350 uneventful miles between Boone and Franklin, Tennessee, where I would sleep that night. The Appalachians have their own inherent beauty, with their rolling, smooth ridgelines and unique blue haze, but I wondered about the landscapes that would meet me as I moved West.

These mountains felt so familiar to me, so normal, to the point where it was hard to see them in their full light anymore. I needed a different external reality to help reground myself in the physical world. In the past weeks my episodes of depersonalization had gotten worse. I didn't know it was called depersonalization then, but one of the psychological symptoms of my response to trauma was that reality had started to become hazy. Some days I felt so detached from my internal and external experience that I started to struggle to identify what was real and what was a figment of my imagination. I often felt like I was observing myself and my life from a dream. My emotions were so distant from me some days that I wasn't sure if they even belonged to me or if I was actually feeling them. I felt like I was going insane. I was scared of what I was experiencing. I was scared of my own brain. And I had told no one.

Franklin is about thirty minutes south of Nashville, and my decision to stop there first was not because I had any personal desire to be in the Nashville area, the hub of country-music-lovin' folks and all things

Southern, during Independence Day weekend. If I could write up a social nightmare for myself during this period of my life, it would look quite similar to what I was about to walk into.

I was stopping in the Nashville area because my cousin Ryan lived in Franklin with his aunt and uncle, Lynn and Chip, who offered to let me stay at their place on my way out of town. I had seen Ryan often in the past year, but I hadn't seen Lynn and Chip since before college. When they reached out to me, I figured it would be a convenient place to stop my first night before the real unknown began. Additionally, despite my apathy about Independence Day in America, I did think that if there was any ceremonial way to mark the beginning of a great American road trip, it was celebrating the Fourth of July in one of the most patriotic and nationalistic cities in the country. Even if I hated it the entire time, I figured it would at least bring plenty of opportunities for interesting anthropological observation.

Ryan is my oldest first cousin, and until the previous winter, we were not very close. This was mostly because he was six years older than me, and our age difference was a little too far apart for friendship while we were growing up, but I also attributed our distance to Ryan's extreme adolescent phases. He'd switch frequently from extreme skater boy to tough jock to put-together prep, all of which intimidated and confused me when I was a child. The gauges in his ears and his nose ring and dyed hair tips freaked me out, so I avoided any prolonged conversation at family gatherings to prevent the chance of things being more awkward than was already necessary. Though we were around each other a lot, I never felt like I actually knew him.

This all changed though, when Ryan randomly texted me one day the fall of 2014 saying he had unexpectedly been offered a job near Boone and would be moving up right away. It was exciting thinking about having an opportunity to get to know Ryan, now that I was older and could hold a conversation with the twenty-six-year-old, grown-up, businessman Ryan instead of the awkward, ten-year-old me failing to relate to the sixteen-year-old Ryan with spikes on his shoes.

We hung out a few times as autumn turned to winter, having dinner together and slowly catching up through the years we hadn't been involved in each other's lives. For me, that involved catching him up on the long and complicated saga of Cam.

I told Ryan the story from the beginning. It started in the first months of my sophomore year of high school, the fall of 2010, when this new guy that always seemed to be climbing on top of something dangerous caught my attention at a youth group retreat. He often toted a book of poetry under one of his perfectly sculpted arms, rarely wore shoes, regularly pushed against whatever boundaries he was given, and consistently talked about exceedingly intelligent, abstract ideas for a sixteen-year-old, which captivated me the most. We started dating that fall, and he quickly went from being the odd guy I stayed away from to becoming my everything. Cam and I fell in love hard and quickly, so caught up in emotion and expectation that "Cam and Emily" became one merged identity in our minds and in the minds of most of our peers. We had no intention of ever separating that identity again. That's how life works at sixteen.

Cam and I became the dream couple, the classic picture of high school sweethearts. Cam was a perfect combination of Romeo, Tarzan, and Aristotle. He was kind, loving, caring, wise, adventurous, romantic, intellectual, *and* he was a Christian. I'd been told my entire life that being a Christian was the most important thing to look for in a partner. I believed it. I was safe. A Christian guy would never hurt me.

Cam fascinated me. He exposed me to philosophical ideas and existential questions I had never thought of before. He challenged me. He encouraged me to grow. He became my role model and my teacher. I was totally consumed by this beautiful human that had entered my life and turned it upside down in the best of ways.

We did everything together. We would spend hours walking through the woods talking about philosophy and religion, which I craved because I hadn't met anyone my age that would have the kinds of conversations I was interested in. Cam saw past the shallow, pretentious, materialistic life so many people in our hometown were caught up in. He was my best friend and the consummate romantic. He would show up at church with a handful of wildflowers he'd picked on his walk that morning. He would surprise me with candlelit dinners underneath star-dotted skies. I'd stumble upon notes and letters he hid in my room or under my windshield wiper when I got out of softball practice. He was always making grand gestures. One day he ran out in the middle of a pep rally performance, snatched the microphone from the person speaking, and asked me to prom in front of the entire school. The entire stadium erupted in cheers and applause.

Two years later, halfway into our senior year, Cam made the decision that he was going to enlist in the Army instead of going to college. Though we were wary of how that would affect our relationship, we decided we were ready to conquer whatever challenges came with a long-distance, military relationship. We had it all planned out. I would go to college in North Carolina, graduate a year early, move to wherever he was stationed, and we would get married and live happily ever after. Even though we were eighteen then, life still seemed really straightforward to us, not having seen any other side of the world beyond the simplicity of our adolescence.

We did everything we could to stay on the 'one right path to a happy, healthy adulthood' that was handed to us by our families and churches. The main checklist included things like: don't drink, don't do drugs, be a good Christian, stay away from people who will lead you 'astray,' go to church, pray, and—especially—don't have sex. Then: graduate high school, go to college or into the military, get a good job, make sure you save your virginity until marriage (because if you don't your life will be ruined forever), get married to the person who is supposed to complete you, have a couple kids, make sure they become Christians and don't sin, and everything will be okay and you will live happily ever after. Easy, right? We were doing what we were supposed to. We were checking the boxes. We would be fine. I didn't know how damaging my attachment to these expectations of how life was *supposed* to work would be later on.

We graduated in May, going on three years of being attached at the hip. We spent the summer in a fantasy land, not ready to acknowledge the drastic change coming in August, when we would both leave. We spent almost every day together. I couldn't see it then, but we were entirely codependent.

Eventually summer came to an end. I moved to Boone to attend college at Appalachian State University. Cam went to basic training shortly after that. Though communicating only through letters for a few months was hard, it felt romantic. It felt exciting. It felt like we were healthier and more committed to our dream than we had ever been.

I found out at Cam's graduation that he decided to pursue more regimented training to apply to the Army Special Forces and become a Green Beret, one of the most challenging, dangerous, and elite roles in the Army. I wasn't surprised, as Cam always seemed to have an insatiable thirst for an adrenaline rush, but I was worried about what scenarios that position would lead Cam into. It seemed like he hadn't given the implications of the stress and danger of the job much thought. Since he said he was excited about it, I tried to be excited for him too.

Over the course of my freshman year of college, Cam was trained under intense pressure to become an unreactive, numb, human robot. At least that's what he seemed like to me. Things between us became unhealthy quickly, and I couldn't do anything but sit back and watch the man of my dreams turn into someone I barely recognized. He changed from romantic to passive, loving to cold, and passionate to apathetic. Where he was once encouraging, he was now controlling. He'd been a dreamer, but now he was a human machine. His letters and phone calls got darker—he hated the Army and wanted to get out, but he was trapped. If he didn't keep his contract for four years, he would be given a dishonorable discharge, which would negatively affect his job opportunities in the future. He said he feared how the Army was changing him. I feared it too, but I didn't know what to do or how to help.

Cam couldn't tell me many specifics about what he was training for because it was classified information, but he said his schooling was often more mental and emotional than physical. To me, it seemed like his training mostly involved disconnecting himself from his emotions so he could focus in the high-stress situations Green Berets might be sent into. Over time, not only did he bring that mindset into dealing with his own emotions outside of the Army, he expected me to behave the same way. I was expected to match his nonreactive countenance and lifestyle, which was extremely confusing when only months before we had been hiking and laughing through the French Alps, talking about all of our hopes and dreams for our lives. Only weeks before, Cam had sent me emotion-filled letters in which his passion for life was evident. In every letter, he said everything was going to be okay, and he pleaded for me to hold on to *"our dream."*

I learned quickly that my emotions were not to be expressed, and if they were, they were to be expressed at a designated time at a designated level.

"God, you're so sensitive!" I remember him huffing if I couldn't hold back my tears on our Facetime calls, even if I was trying to communicate that something he did or said had been hurtful to me. "You need to learn how to control your emotions better, Emily. You need to practice non-reacting, Emily. It's more mature. Can't you just have a *rational* conversation?" He acted like he had mastered emotional control, and because I still felt my emotions deeply, I was somehow less than him. He would often communicate these things non-verbally as well, with a certain look in his eyes that made me feel like the dumbest person in the world for feeling.

Cam became extremely depressed and terribly angry. He despised everything about the military and desperately wanted to get out. He couldn't control anything about his situation, so he started to control me instead. He dictated what was okay and what was not okay, what I should and should not be doing in all areas of my life. Since I had always believed Cam was more wise and mature than me and saw him as a role model, I believed that he knew what was best for me. When he said that I felt too much, I believed him and decided I should be more rational. When he said I was too touchy, I took it to heart and trained myself to be less sensitive. When he said I was too needy, too extreme, or too much, I decided he was right and learned to keep my mouth shut and shove down my need for emotional connection with my partner. To avoid frustration, anger, or belittlement from Cam, I learned to repress, repress, repress.

Because I started to believe the stories he told me about myself, over time, without realizing it, I allowed my internal voice to become Cam's voice. I would rebuke and shame myself for speaking up for myself, for feeling too much, for needing too much, for being too much, because that's what Cam said about me, and since he knew me the best out of anyone, I thought it must be true. I wanted to do whatever I could to keep Cam happy so that we could make it through his military contract. Unfortunately, I was so deep in the belief that it was up to me to save Cam from being brainwashed by the Army that I couldn't see the ways he'd become emotionally abusive.

Once I trained myself to keep my emotions within Cam's acceptable boundaries—in order to avoid conflict and keep him from getting angry and berating me—our Facetime calls and letters became a little more stable and calm. I self-sacrificed daily, and though I didn't realize it then, I was slowly killing myself for the sake of saving *"our dream."* *"Because we had a plan, right? It was in God's will, right? We were doing everything we were supposed to do, right? We were going to get married and live happily ever after, right? We've been planning this for years, right? He loved me and wouldn't do anything to hurt me, right? It wasn't his fault, right? He didn't mean to hurt me, right? I was happy, right? He would get better, right? Things would change eventually, right?"*

The few times I visited him, I only caught glimpses of the person I fell in love with. Most of the time I spent talking or being with Cam in person I felt inadequate, ignorant, and incompetent. I didn't realize that it was the way he interacted with me that caused these feelings. I believed that because Cam made me feel incompetent that I was incompetent. This cycle perpetuated the idea that I needed to look to him for answers and truth. I did whatever I could to justify staying together. *"He may be unhealthy now, but it is just a phase. He'll get over it. He'll be himself again once he's out of the military, and things will be back to the old us."*

I put off my need for connection and lived for the day that Cam got out of the military, when we would have space to dream again, when we would be able to get married and start the life we had always planned for, when I would be able to remind him of who he used to be. I lost myself a little more each day in the process, submitting to Cam's authority, letting him be the one who was always right, even if I didn't agree with him, and accepting that whatever random thing he blamed on me was my fault to avoid conflict. I did my best to just survive around the controlling, condescending, harsh person he was becoming in hope that the loving, gentle, caring person that I knew was inside of him somewhere would surface again.

I was so unhappy. I became depressed. I went to sleep every night anxious, knowing that our relationship was unsustainable and that something had to change, but I was addicted, and I was consumed with figuring out how to save *"our dream."* I think I knew deep down that I needed to leave, but love is irrational, and I was so wrapped up in a toxic form of it that I truly believed that sacrificing my dreams and happiness to save Cam was justified and what I was called by God to do. I told no one except Ryan that things were even slightly unhealthy because I thought I had it under control.

I was given a chance to get out in August of my Sophomore year of college, four years after we started dating. Cam randomly called me in the middle of the day, which he never did because he was normally in training. I answered hesitantly, with a slight sense of dread bubbling up out of nowhere in my chest.

"Emily, I can't do this anymore. It's too much. I just can't be what you need me to be, and I don't know what else to do."

That was it.

Phone call ended. No explanation. He left me crippled with nausea and the weight of a million unanswered questions.

He cut contact with me, and I did not speak to him again for four months. That time was spent trying to heal and move on, but I had no closure to move on from, no reasons or discussion from Cam that would help me emotionally let go of a person and relationship in which I had invested so much time and energy. I felt as if I was suspended in open air, trying to run but not having any sort of ground to push off of.

Ryan moved to Boone a month after Cam had cut things off, which was when I began to tell him this story. He was a helpful person to process with throughout the start of winter, and he assured me that it seemed like a good opportunity to get out of a relationship that was so dysfunctional and that had caused so much pain.

However, at the beginning of December I got another curveball phone call from Cam. He told me the news that changed everything:

"I'm getting out of the Army."

My heart skipped. *Maybe this was our chance to finally be able to have "our dream."*

He told me he figured out a plan to break his contract and get out of the military without a dishonorable discharge or going AWOL, which he had seriously started to consider. He had begun to fake symptoms a while back to see if he could convince his doctors and supervisors that he had a certain condition that made him unfit to stay in the Army. He said he couldn't tell me all of the details in order to protect himesef, but the scheme had worked. He was being discharged from the Army in a week, which meant he would be home for Christmas.

"I just wanted to let you know, and I thought maybe we could meet up while I'm home and catch up." He said it so casually, as if it was perfectly normal and okay for him to call me out of the blue and expect me to be fine with it after randomly breaking up with me and refusing to speak to me for four months with no explanation.

Out of the military? I was completely caught off guard. Knowing how much Cam despised being in the military and how much it was killing him inside, I was happy for him, but how was I supposed to respond? I was trying so hard to get over him and move on with my life, but I thought this might change things for us.

I blamed all of his and our dysfunction on the military, and I wondered if things would be different if Cam had more time and space to remember who he was, if the man I fell in love with would resurface from the depths in which he had been repressed. Even if we didn't get back together, I knew I would not be able to move on unless we had an in-person conversation to have a tangible sense of closure to move on from. I was so tired of our relationship being tucked in Cam's back pocket, taken out to enjoy and use whenever it was convenient for him, as if I was disposable. I wanted to be free from the manipulation.

I told Ryan about the phone call, and he asked me during our last dinner in Boone before Christmas how I felt about seeing Cam again when I went home. He wondered if I thought it was a good idea.

While I had no contact with Cam, I had started to detox from my addiction to him and began to see how toxic most of our interactions were. I told Ryan I knew deep down that getting back together would be insane, so I planned to go home at Christmas and simply have a conversation, acknowledging that things were different now, that we needed to go our separate ways and figure out who we were. Over. Done.

But then came the third curveball.

I swallowed hard as I walked up to Cam's mom's front door, trying to quiet my heart rate that was so loud in my chest I swore Cam could already hear it from inside.

Just say you want closure. All you have to do is have a short conversation. We're breaking up for good. I don't want to drag this out when we both know it's over. I tried to give myself a pep talk and rehearse what I wanted to say to him as I nervously awaited a response to my knock on the door. I didn't want to back down. I wanted to be free of it.

My heart sank as I turned the corner from the entryway into the living room, where Cam was playing with his little brother. He looked normal, the same old Cam. He looked so gentle in the warmth of the living room compared to the numb person I spoke to on the phone four months ago. When I made eye contact with him, I could not hold on to my anger as it melted out of my clenched hands.

We spent the evening in surface-level conversation with his family about what college had been like and Cam's experience in the Army. I could tell that Cam and I were both tiptoeing around, trying to avoid disturbing the elephant in the room, fearing getting trampled and hurt. Eventually, once his little brother went to bed and his parents went upstairs, I made myself bring it up. I wasn't going to leave and pretend like everything was okay like I'd done too many times before.

"Look, Cam. We both know why I'm here." My heart pounded.

Cam gave a deep sigh. "Yeah, I know."

I tried my best to hold back tears as I told him that I was ready to be done with the back and forth, the seemingly never-ending cycle of pulling close and pushing away.

"Don't you agree that we should just end things here?" I asked him.

"Em, I've been going crazy these months without talking to you. It hasn't been easy, and I think I made the wrong decision when I made that phone call. With some time apart and time to reflect, and especially being with you tonight, I think I'm falling in love with you all over again. I swear I'm different. And tonight confirmed that I'm going to move to Boone to work things out with you."

WHAT? Move to Boone? I tried to keep the explosion of confusion that happened in my mind from expanding to show on my face. Cam's response was the last thing I expected to hear. *We're supposed to be breaking up, and now he said he's going to move to Boone? For Me? I don't understand.*

"I don't trust you," I told him. "My family doesn't trust you. In fact, my whole community doesn't trust you."

A wave of genuine concern washed over his face. "I know you don't. And you shouldn't. And I'm so sorry. But I'm ready to prove to you that I'm serious about this, about being with you." He put his hand on my arm, the first touch we had shared since I saw him during my visit six months before. "About our dream."

He did seem serious. He seemed genuine. He seemed almost, happy. He seemed like he had changed, like he wanted to be different. Throughout Christmas break, Cam was romantic again and made even larger gestures to win me back. He even took my dad to dinner one on one to explain himself, knowing my dad was the most skeptical of him out of anyone, which made him seem even more serious to me. He apologized to me and my family for the way he had treated me in the past and explained why he was going to move to Boone to pursue things with me again. He promised that he was seeking God and promised to respect and honor me.

We had been longing to be in the same place since we graduated high school, and I couldn't help but wonder if we could make it work. I told him I didn't know how to feel, but I couldn't control whether he moved to Boone or not, and maybe, if we took it slow, I would give him a chance.

That was the last thing that Ryan heard about Cam and I, that Cam was suddenly out of the military and was moving to Boone to try to work things out with me, because at the beginning of January, Ryan got relocated to another branch of his company back in Tennessee, and we hadn't talked about it since.

I was excited about spending time with Ryan again, but I was nervous about the inevitability of having to tell him the rest of the story that led me to this moment, driving across the country, without Cam.

I was supposed to get to Lynn and Chip's house earlier than I did to have time to settle in, but by the time I took the exit off of I-40 toward Franklin, there was only forty-five minutes before Ryan and I would have to leave. Ryan bought us tickets to the men's USA vs. Guatemala soccer game a few days before, and not knowing how to tell him that the idea of a whole stadium filled with thousands of people screaming at once made me want to retreat to a dark closet for a week, I sent him an emotive text saying that I would absolutely love to go with him.

As I exited the interstate, I didn't feel prepared to see them. There would be hugs and *"I've missed you's"* and *"how are you's,"* and I was saddened by the fact that I would not be able to answer truthfully. I would have to look into Aunt Lynn's sweet blue eyes and give a half-hearted *"I'm fine,"* because how do you even begin to tell your very evangelical Christian extended family that you are actually in an extreme existential crisis? How do you tell them the traditional Christian worldview in which you grew up suddenly does not work anymore? Worse still, how do you tell them your spiritual house has crumbled to the ground, and you don't know what to do about it? How do you tell them you don't know if God is good, much less if God exists? How do you tell them that sitting inside church fills you with rage because you hear people claiming that Jesus is there, but you can't find him? How do you expose the hidden mask of depression behind your smile when you don't know if they will reject you or embrace you? How do you explain that you have felt numb for months after the most intense betrayal you could have ever imagined?

I knew I had mastered projecting the "I'm okay" image that people expected to see. I didn't show people what was really going on inside of me, so I wasn't too fearful of the outcome of our meeting. I just hoped my improvising would not fail me—without it this weekend had the potential to be pretty awkward.

I took a final deep breath before I knocked on the door. I was welcomed by the warm smile and booming voice of my glorious Aunt Lynn.

"Hellooooooooo my darlin'!" Lynn exclaimed with wide eyes as her curvy frame appeared from behind the big front door. She embraced me in her special way, and my body morphed into her plush chest as if I'd lived there forever. The perfume she wore screamed grandma, but something about the powdery scent was familiar and comforting.

"Ryan! It's so good to see you." I extended my arms. "I'm so glad this worked out!"

"It's good to see you, Em. Glad you're here," he welcomed as he hugged me.

Chip pulled me in last with a big squeeze. "Been a while, darlin.' You sure have grown up! Come in and get you some dinner! We have it all ready since you and Ryan gotta get out the door soon."

"Thanks so much for making dinner, and sorry I'm late! It took a little bit for me to get out the door this morning, just making sure I had everything I needed."

I left out the part about spending a lot of time staring at myself in the mirror trying to convince myself that I could be brave enough to leave.

"Oh sweetie, don't you worry." Lynn replied. "We're just so tickled pink that you could come stay with us on your grand adventure!"

I sat down to my plate which was already set, steaming with simple and sweet Southern comfort food. Baked chicken, mac n' cheese, baked beans, and potato salad. I was starving and dug in. My fork, filled with creamy mac n' cheese, had almost reached my mouth when I realized that everyone was staring at me. Like a dog waiting for a treat, saliva almost dripped off my tongue. With their hands extended in prayer, my family's facial expressions might as well have said, *"Put your fork down you ravenous heathen. It's time to say grace."*

Oh, whoops. I forgot this was a thing. I smiled apologetically, set my fork down, and followed by grabbing hands, bowing my head, and closing my eyes. Chip said a short and sweet prayer, thanking God for the food and for bringing me there safely.

Did he though? Did God bring me here safely? I resisted his words, as I often did when I listened to someone pray. *I may look okay on the outside, but my heart does not feel very safe or protected by this God.*

After the amen, Lynn asked, "So Em, tell us, what in the world made you want to take a trip like this all the way across this big ol' country all by yourself?" She looked with wide blue eyes peeking through her small, red, circular reading glasses.

The classic question followed by a half-true answer.

"Well, road tripping across the country has been a dream of mine for quite some time, and with me taking the fall semester off of school, it made sense to do it this summer since I didn't have to be back for anything. I was intimidated to commit to going because I've never traveled by myself before, but I figured that I might as well take a risk and push myself out of my comfort zone."

I tried to give only enough details so I could answer the question without having to explain much of the why.

"Oh you're not going back to school in the fall?" Ryan asked as he leaned forward on one elbow. "Why not? Need a break?"

"Well, sort of. School isn't really a source of difficulty in my life; I've made straight A's every semester so far, still beating dad's record of only making one "B" in college." I winked.

"You've always been such a great student," Lynn affirmed.

"Oh I bet your daddy is all bent outta shape about that. I know how competitive he is," Chip chuckled, his broad shoulders shaking up and down as he laughed.

I laughed and agreed. "I'm taking the fall off because of a scheduling complication with my classes. My next sequence of nutrition classes isn't offered until the spring, and I don't have any more general education classes that I need to take, so my options were to either pay a lot of money to take fall classes that I don't need to graduate or take the fall off of school, save money, and re-enroll again in the spring."

Though all of what I said was completely true, I left out what was underneath all of it. My scheduling complication was a free ticket out of a system I didn't know how to buy into anymore. Once there was no option to continue school in the fall, I was able to consider for the first time that my current reality was not actually working for me, that maybe school wasn't right for me anymore, that maybe I had to figure out how to look all of my problems in the eyes and not back down until they no longer ruled my life.

I held back my rant about how I was so frustrated with the way the American education system shoved information down our throats only to be regurgitated for the test but never sustainably remembered. I did not tell them how alienated I felt from the people around me. I did not tell them how I walked away angry from classrooms where professors spoke apathetically to a room full of students on their phones, scrolling through Instagram, comparing their picture perfect lives they portray on social media to the edited versions of the lives of those they follow. I didn't tell them I didn't believe in the American dream, in climbing the capitalist success ladder, even though my whole life I had been told something along the lines of "do more so you can buy more" was the point of education, work, and life in general. I didn't tell them how anxious I felt when I was forced to talk about my future, what I was going to do with my life, or what career I wanted to pursue. Nothing in me wanted to continue to buy into a system that would put me in never-ending debt so that I would have to work constantly in the same job for the next forty years just to pay off loans, making money that I did not want, buying things that I did not need, making the life that my culture was telling me that I needed to be happy while feeling empty and unfulfilled on the inside.

Lynn's excited voice jolted me back to reality. "Oh well that's nice that you are taking advantage of this time! Who are you going to stay with? Friends along the way?"

Knowing that I needed to make my trip sound as safe as possible, but not knowing how to make sleeping in my car sound comforting to them, I just decided to be brutally honest.

"Um, I actually don't really know. I'm eventually going to get to San Diego. I have a friend there I could stay with for a night, and I have a mutual friend in Texas, but beyond that, I have no plans. I'm going to decide as I go and sleep in my car the rest of the time."

Chip furrowed his brow and chimed in after a hard swallow. "Sleep in your car? Where? Do you have a bed in there, or will you just recline your seat and sleep up front? And what about your windows? Will people be able to see in? Aren't you scared of child molesters or somethin' like 'em?"

Their facial expressions were almost audible: *please tell us more, you insane human.* In an attempt to ease their anxiety I told them that I had slept in my car in Walmart and hotel parking lots plenty of times before, that it was super common, and it was completely safe. That was not true, though I had heard of people doing that and being fine, so I guess it wasn't a total lie. Still they did not seem to understand or agree.

Lynn changed the subject. "Well that's great I guess, as long as you feel good about it! Ryan said you were meeting up with some friends at some point or somethin'? Is that true?"

"Well, the original plan was to go solo the whole time, but about a month ago I met my friend Sydney, and when she heard that I was going on this trip, she said that she has wanted to do something similar for a while but has never had the chance to. I told her I was open to her coming, but she said she could only do two weeks, so we worked it out to where she will fly to San Diego on the 16th, a little over two weeks from now, and I'll be alone until then."

"Oh I bet you two will have a beautiful time!" Lynn chirped as she leaned back in her chair and crossed her legs, revealing her feet, clad with white, fuzzy puppy slippers that looked exactly like her toy poodle, Milly. I wouldn't have been surprised if she had them custom-ordered with how much she loved that dog. I glanced across the dining room at Milly curled up and fast asleep in her pink embroidered pillow on the living room floor.

"Yeah, it should be great," I replied, though I barely even knew Sydney, and I was actually a little nervous about her coming. "Oh, also, something that only happened this week is that another one of our friends, Will, decided to tag along as well. Sydney and I mentioned it to him a while back, and he said he couldn't go, but he decided to join us last minute as long as he can make it a work trip and get some video footage for a project he's working on. He wants to be a professional videographer."

"That works out nicely. Now you get your own personal photographer as you hike through the national parks," Ryan joked. "You're going to be on the cover of the next edition of National Geographic!" He nudged my arm like an older brother would do to a younger sibling.

I raised my eyebrows. "Um, I don't know about that," I chuckled.

"How do you know these folks?" Chip asked as he stood up and reached over Lynn to grab the pitcher of sweet tea.

"I know them from my church, actually." I felt hesitation in my voice as I said it. I knew that detail would be comforting to my family, but I wasn't sure how I felt about it. Will used to lead worship at my church for years and had quit before I joined the worship team the previous year, and I always wondered why that was. I'd never known him well enough to ask him. Sydney still attended most church events and services as far as I knew, so I had no way to tell where she was at internally. I figured church and Christianity still worked for her, which made me anxious about where conversation might go with her during the trip.

I shook my thoughts and continued, "We've only had a few conversations here and there, so it will be interesting travelling with them.

I don't know what to expect, but I'm sure after two weeks alone it might be nice to have some company. Thankfully Will was able to get on the same flight as Sydney, so I'll pick them both up in San Diego on the 16th."

"How fun! I was worried about you being all by yourself the whole time. Y'all are going to have a blast. You'll have to take lots of pictures while you're gone!" Lynn gushed and quickly fluffed the white hair on top of her head with her fingers, something she did frequently throughout the conversation.

"And I'm sure bein' crammed in your car with 'em both will bring y'all pretty close pretty fast," Chip chimed in, laughing. "Where exactly are you goin' again? You mentioned somethin' about Texas and California, but what about once you're with your friends? Y'all won't all sleep in your car will you?" He raised his big eyebrows, which were more speckled with gray hairs than the last time I saw him.

"Definitely not," I giggled. "That would be suffocating, and I think we might kill each other, especially since we are all pretty introverted and need a lot of space to ourselves."

"Also suffocatin' because y'all are probably goin' to stink with being outside all the time and not showerin,'" Chip laughed. "At least I'm assumin' there won't be too many places to shower out there," he trailed off as if anywhere West of the Mississippi was some far-off, unexplored land only fit for the bravest class of adventurous folk. My family, including Lynn and Chip, didn't travel much.

"Umm, I'm not sure," I admitted. "I think some campgrounds will have showers, and if not we'll be around lots of rivers to rinse off."

"Whoo-wee that is not my kind of hygiene," Lynn piped.

I laughed. "Back to your question, Uncle Chip. As far as my itinerary goes, I think I'll stay fairly south on the way to San Diego. Maybe stay with that mutual friend in Texas to get a shower."

"Oh that will be good I'm sure. I can't go a day without showering, so I would have to stay with someone every single night! I just don't know if I could do it. You're impressing me, Emi!" Lynn smiled and shook her head. 'Emi' was the nickname that most of my family called me by.

"We'll see. I'm pretty fine with being dirty. Boone is a hippie mountain town, and it has rubbed off on me the past two years I guess.

After Texas I'd like to drive through the desert in New Mexico and Arizona, and then once I get to California I was just going to figure it out until Will and Sydney get there."

"Girl you are just so adventurous!" Lynn enthused, affirming that the requirement for adventure in my family was going to the next state over.

"And once you pick up your friends at the airport?" asked Chip.

"We'll camp every night until we get back to North Carolina, whenever that is. First to Yosemite National Park, and then head back south to backpack to the bottom of the Grand Canyon."

"You're going all the way to the bottom of the Grand Canyon? And then you have to hike out of it? That's intense!" Ryan exclaimed.

"And hot," Chip added.

"Yeah, we'll see. I'm feeling a little out of shape, so it might be terrible, especially with the July heat. If we survive there, I don't know where we'll go. See where the road leads, I guess," I shrugged.

"So when you say backpack, what does that mean exactly?" Lynn questioned. "This is all very new to me."

"Oh, yeah. Backpacking generally is where you carry all of your food, cooking equipment, and camping gear with you on your hikes, and then you make camp along the way, sleep, wake up the next day, and hike from there to the next camping spot."

"Shoo-wee! And that is supposed to be fun? I'm afraid that is something I could never do. We could maybe do an RV, couldn't we honey?" Lynn grabbed Chip's arm. "But I don't think we could ever do the tent thing, much less walk and have to carry all of our stuff with us. I think I would be plum worn out and lay down on the trail and not be able to get up!" Lynn cackled. "Have you done much of this backpacking before?"

"Actually, never. I hike a lot in Boone, but I have never carried all of my stuff on a hike to then set up camp out in the woods. I don't really know what to expect, or if I'll even like it. I'm sure this will be an eye-opening and probably blister-opening experience for me, but I have plenty of band-aids, so I should be good." Everyone laughed.

"So I take it you have enough campin' gear for y'all in your car?" asked Chip, seeming to be the most interested in making sure we had all of the logistics sorted.

"Yep I have a tent for Sydney and I, and Will gave me his tent before I left so he wouldn't have to carry it on the plane," I explained. "I can show y'all my car setup at some point tonight or tomorrow if you want. It is definitely nowhere close to those fancy camper vans totally decked out with whatever you could possibly need in neat, organized shelves and drawers. I have some cardboard boxes and a food bin for organizing. There are more established ways to do it, but I didn't plan much of this out, and I'm just hoping it will do."

"Yeah we would love to see how you're gonna manage all this," Chip replied. "This is all just so interestin' to us. We have never known someone that has done somethin' like this. When all our friends travel, they might go to the beach in Florida or somethin' but never across the entire country alone sleepin' in their car for goodness' sake! You sure are brave sweet girl. I know your mama is going to be worried sick about you, but I know she and your daddy want you to be able to do what you want to do."

I felt a twinge of pain. My parents were worried, I thought. About my physical safety, yes, but Lynn, Chip, and Ryan had no idea the extent to which my parents were worried about me. Being conservative, evangelical Southern Baptists, they had pretty rigid beliefs. To them, if you weren't a "Christian" that believed exactly the same things they believed, you wouldn't end up in heaven. My parents were worried about my eternal safety, ever since I finally came out and told them I didn't know if I would call myself a Christian anymore. And if it were another universe where I might feel comfortable telling Lynn, Chip, and Ryan where I was actually at internally, I knew they would respond in the same way as my parents. They would feel fear, because I would be put in a box. I would no longer be on the "us" side. I would now be a "them." An outsider. The one who left the tribe. They would view me as having a sickness that needed to be healed, needed to be prayed out of me, as if all I had to do was just pray a little harder or read my Bible a little more and all of this would make sense. I tried that. God didn't show up. Nothing changed. I already felt like I was isolated enough. I didn't need it to be reinforced now, so I kept my thoughts to myself.

"Well you two better run upstairs quick and get ready while I do the dishes," Lynn encouraged. "Chip, honey, help me get these plates."

I thanked them excessively for letting me stay with them and for feeding me such a welcoming dinner.

I walked outside to grab some clothes out of my "closet," which was a small cardboard box pressed up against the right side of my trunk, next to my "bed," which was a yellow foam twin mattress topper that stretched out over the length of the carpet that faced up when my back seats were folded. My cardboard box closet held a couple pairs of hiking shorts, a couple tank tops, bras, underwear, hiking socks, and one sundress, because sometimes you just need to feel pretty, even if that means putting on a dress over a dust and sweat-covered body. I figured that a soccer game did not call for anything fancy, so I dug out a white tank top from the bottom of the box. I looked in the reflection of my car window to see if my hair measured up to Nashville standards. Considering the lack of brushing it had been receiving lately, I decided it probably wouldn't, but it would just have to do for today.

In high school I did my hair and makeup extensively each morning before school, not necessarily because I consciously believed that I could only be beautiful if I was in full make-up, but because that was the culture of my hometown. All the other girls did it, so to fit in, I played along, trying to make myself look more Barbie than human.

However, upon entering college, being in a long-distance relationship, and being surrounded by a more natural Boone culture, I had stopped wearing makeup except on special occasions. The most I usually did to my hair was put it in a French braid after I got out of the shower so that my hair would dry wavy. It was a healthy step back from my supposed *need* for make-up and helped me realize that I actually really liked my natural hair and skin.

Unfortunately, once I became depressed in the midst of my relationship and deconstructing my faith, the pendulum swung in the other direction regarding my appearance. I grew apathetic. I absolutely did not care what I looked like, how tidy my hair was, how well my clothes fit, much less how well they matched. I rarely looked in a mirror. Most of the time I wore a baggy flannel over a tank top with the same hiking shorts because it allowed me to not have to think about my body if I wore the same thing every day. I felt like my femininity ran off in my grief, and though it might have still been alive somewhere, searching for it and rediscovering it felt like too big a task.

I did not love myself most days, much less feel beautiful or worthy of love. Completely disregarding my outward appearance was my way to deflect attention away from my body, to make myself smaller. I learned how to take up less space so that I would not be a burden on anyone, especially when I wanted to keep myself safe from being yelled at or scolded by Cam. Even though he was gone, I had played the part for so long I didn't know how to take on any other role.

I'd lost my grounded sense of self on the inside, of identity, of Emily-ness, and when you don't love yourself, you don't have a desire to put effort into things for yourself, especially your outward appearance.

"Emily, time to go!" Ryan called from downstairs.

I looked in the guest room bathroom mirror at the same timid blue eyes I saw in my mirror before I left that morning. Dark bags lay under them, telling of exhaustion and restless nights haunted with nightmares. I splashed some cold water on my face, and as I dried it on my towel, I mentally put on a mask full of more confidence than the fragile shell I had started to break down during my time driving in the car. *I can't let them see me. I can't let them know. I have to hide.*

"Be right there!" I yelled back in my best cheerful voice and took a deep breath before running down the stairs and hopping in the car.

Between the screaming and cheering and blow horns and obnoxious Fourth of July costumes and people bumping into me, I had a hard time interpreting the soccer game. Since I never played soccer when I was a kid, watching soccer had always been like watching people running around like ants with no intention. I found it quite difficult to lose myself in the excitement of the game.

Ryan, however, was psyched and enthralled most of the game and didn't create much space to talk. I was thankful because I could just stand, observe, and stay inside my head, though I still had not managed to find an internal space to inhabit that was anything but heavy.

From our perch in the box reserved for Ryan's work friends, I looked down at all of the people in the stands below us. It seemed like everyone around me had a people, a place, an identity in relationship to the tribe they belonged to, a common purpose to get excited about together, regardless of where they came from. There were matching jerseys and face paint. There were hats thrown and beer cans chugged. People were hugging, kissing, handing out high fives, giving toasts, and laughing—all of the things people do when they feel like they belong and feel loved, seen, and valued by the people surrounding them. I wish I could say that I looked around and was happy for the joy that I saw, but I only felt longing. What do you do when you had a tribe that provided these things your whole life, but then you were forced to leave it?

I couldn't help but see the joy of community in those stands as a juxtaposition to the abrupt and significant loss of my own community I experienced through having to leave the Church. Christianity had given me a people, a tribe, a place of belonging in relation to a higher purpose. Once I started deconstructing my faith, my place in that tribe began to dissolve.

Once things with Cam got really bad, I clung tighter to my faith that was slipping through my fingers faster than I could process, but it was proving to be a useless tool to help me navigate my experience. The tighter I grasped it and pleaded for it to make sense, the more I became aware that it had been suffocated and died out a long time ago. As things came to an end with Cam, I quickly realized that my faith wasn't real enough to save me, even though for so many years I had thought it was infallible. I could no longer repress all of the questions and doubts I had about the Christian Church as a whole, much less my place inside of it. The more my doubts and confusion surfaced, the further I was separated from the people and tribe I had found in my personal church community. The more I tried to reach out for God to save me from the toxic space I inhabited internally, the more I realized that the God I thought I knew was nowhere to be found.

Growing up in a specific faith community and coming to the realization that you must leave it is traumatic and confusing for anyone involved in organized religion, but it wasn't just that I attended church and sat in the audience every week. I was on stage, with a microphone. I played piano and sang in the worship band. I was part of the church leadership team. I even preached sermons occasionally for our campus ministry. Though I was healthy and authentically believed in God and Jesus and salvation when I stepped into those roles when I first got to Boone freshman year, once I couldn't look past my questions anymore,

I became so disconnected from the whole thing that I eventually was leading people into a spiritual experience I didn't even believe in every single week.

I hadn't found the courage to step down from my position in the worship team until only a few weeks before I left on my road trip. My church community was my only community, and even though I had been silently deconstructing my faith since the previous winter, I waited to quit because I feared that if I quit, I would have to tell people why I was leaving. If I was honest about the fact that I identified as more of an atheist than a Christian most days, my relationships with all of my friends might change, possibly permanently. I didn't know if I was ready for that. The other students, leaders, and I had made so many memories together, both inside and outside of church, and I loved them dearly.

For a while, I believed the possibility of losing my community was too risky. I thought everyone would feel betrayed if they found out I had been faking it, and I definitely didn't know how to tell them the truth, so I kept silent and pretended.

I sang about a man named Jesus when I wasn't sure if he was even a real person, or if the stories about him were true. I sang about the power in his resurrection which I wasn't sure it even happened, and if it did, I wasn't sure that the blood he shed on the cross meant anything to me. I sang about a God that stood with the powerless while not being able to reconcile how that could be true within a religion that had been used throughout history to justify powerful people exploiting the powerless. I sang about God being a good father, but I was filled with anger toward this father. How could he sit back and let his children go through so much meaningless suffering all around the world, and then punish them with eternal torment if they happened to never hear the Gospel and convert to Christianity? But I could never say any of this aloud. My friends, my co-leaders, my pastor—they would be horrified if they found out.

Every week lyrics flowed out of me that I consciously didn't agree with. I would look out into the audience during worship and meet the gazes of dozens of dear friends who trusted me and listened earnestly as I spoke or sung words that used to be the foundation of my entire world but meant nothing to me anymore.

I watched them raise their hands while I felt angry about the God language in the song lyrics not making sense to me anymore. I watched tears stream down their faces as they worshiped genuinely while I felt completely numb on stage and faked emotion. I watched them smile and dance and feel connected to a God I once knew but no longer could find or hear or see. I was completely surrounded by people who I considered friends, and I had never felt so unseen and alone. I felt like a puppet trapped in a puppet show, following a script that someone else had written, desperately wanting to disconnect the strings of tradition and expectation that I let dictate my actions and run free, but I was too scared to leave.

I lived in a state of constant cognitive dissonance, and it broke me apart with intense feelings of isolation. I had created a mask painted with the healthy, happy, "okay" version of Emily that was excited about the fact that *"Jesus saves! The Lord is good! We offer God our thanks and praise! The Holy Spirit is here and inviting you into a life of freedom!"*

I made sure I never took the mask off, especially on nights when I had something to attend at the church, because how could I tell them? How could I admit I wondered if the Bible was the ultimate truth, or if creation happened in only seven days, or if purity culture was healthy, or if God's will was truly real? I wondered if heaven and hell even existed, or if homosexuality truly was wrong. Was science and discussing evolution dangerous? Was Christian mission work closer to white colonialism than something that actually helps people? Doesn't Western Christianity often perpetuate the harmful systems of racism and patriarchy that Jesus seems to be against? Why would I want to be a part of a family with this image of God as the father, when often the God talked about in the Bible seems like someone I'd never want to be like? How was I supposed to tell anyone that I was falling apart when so many people expected me to be the one that had it all together, when so many people expected me to have answers?

Before I started deconstructing my faith and fundamentalist evangelical Christianity still genuinely rang true for me, I frequently wrote essays about what God was "speaking to me." At my church, we called these "words from the Spirit." I would share them in church, and they always meant a lot to the audience. I would get so much positive feedback that friends and church members began to expect that same level of greatness and connection to God whenever I shared anything, which added extra pressure to always confidently have it together. When I spoke, people listened. Every time I stood on stage and gave a sermon or shared an essay or poem I had written, I would look up from my notes occasionally and meet dozens of eyes beaming with the expectation that I would say something true and valuable.

Once my views about God started changing, and I felt like I had nothing more to say which they would want to hear, I had to find ways to avoid speaking. If I couldn't avoid it all together, I had to edit my language to fit into the Christian box of acceptable answers, where I still used phrases like "maybe it's just God's will" and "the Lord will guide you" or "I'll be praying for you," when there was no heart or belief behind the words.

I started turning down invitations to speak at our campus ministry meetings because I was "too busy," but in reality I just didn't really believe in God anymore and had nothing to say that wasn't filled with anger and resentment. I stopped attending prayer nights because of "homework," but in reality it was because I thought prayer was pointless and the outcomes were only confirmation bias. I skipped outreach and ministry nights in the community because I didn't believe going out and trying to convince people that believed other things about God that they should believe in this one, strict, narrow, exclusive image of God, that they could only be saved if they confessed that Jesus died on the cross for their sins.

Before I stepped down from the worship team, I made a few attempts in conversation with friends or other church leaders to bring up some mild aspects of Christianity that didn't make sense to me. However, any time I tip-toed into conversations where I hinted at the thoughts that plagued me, like not knowing if I believed the Bible was the only literal, complete truth from God without flaw, being uncertain of what I thought about sin, prayer, or salvation, not knowing what to do with the fact that a lot of Western evangelical churches seemed to market Jesus as an emotional drug that would fix all of your problems and bring you prosperity, or not understanding why so many Christians I knew seemed scared or judgemental of every category of people that Jesus calls Christians to be around the table with, I would walk away from those conversations feeling frustrated and unheard.

Some people responded avoidantly by either not acknowledging whatever I said or just saying "I don't know" and changing the subject immediately when I asked a hard question. Others would respond to my questions or thoughts with a quick and certain, *"Look, Emily. Here is the one *right* answer found in, [insert specific Bible verse, taken completely out of cultural context, that was supposed to immediately eradicate all of my doubt],"* with no room for discussion.

The worst though was when people would respond like Kate, one of my best friends, often did when I tried to be honest about what I was thinking.

"Emily, I don't know what to say to you anymore. You're just too *deep*."

Responses like these were the most invalidating to me. I received most of my conversations like this as a message that my questions were too much, I was too much, and that me in my entirety would not be welcome if I was my true self. This belief led to the first level of the walls I began to build between myself and the people around me. I thought that is what I had to do in order to keep myself safe.

I was so tired of the "right" answers and churches claiming they were a safe space to process life while completely avoiding most hard but real things that people actually deal with every day. I wanted to talk about sexuality and addiction and greed and materialism and porn and grief and loss and over-consumption and racism and anxiety and depression and poverty and abuse and mental illness, but those seemed to be off-limits in the Church. I was sick of surface-level Christianity, and in any conversation where I tried to point to the thoughts I had under the surface-level Christian mask, I walked away dissatisfied and unfulfilled. I thought no one would ever understand me. I figured if my questions on the surface were already too deep, there was no way I could ever be honest about the questions that were deeper, like if hell was real, or hell, if God was real.

When I realized I wasn't going to be able to have the conversations I wanted to have without scaring people or getting passive answers, I tried to keep pretending and play along for a while. I felt like a total hypocrite, and it killed me, but I didn't know how to leave. I felt like if I left the Church, I would have had no one. I figured I would rather lead worship without believing the words of the songs and still have people around me than leave and spend Sunday mornings alone, grieving the fact that not only was Cam suddenly out of my life, but it felt like God had abandoned me too.

Although it would have been painful regardless of whether I stayed or left, eventually the inauthenticity became so isolating that I thought it would be less painful to leave it all behind.

"Why are you leaving, Em?" Kate, who was also on the church leadership team, asked after I announced that I was stepping down from the worship team during our weekly meeting.

I remember looking under her furrowed brow into her beautiful blue-green eyes, the eyes that had cried many tears of laughter and joy and sadness and heartbreak since we had become best friends freshman year. I had spent almost every weekend of my entire college experience with her, hiking and exploring on Saturdays, church on Sundays, leading campus ministry events during the week. I didn't want my answer to separate us. I didn't want her to think differently of me, and I especially didn't want my answer to hurt her, much less anyone else in the community. I remember the moment where I had to decide which of my two answer options I would say. Both were true, but the one which was the most significant factor in my quitting worship team was much more risky, for if I chose to say that one, the stability of my world would be compromised even more than it already had.

"The break-up has just been really hard," I replied in a monotone voice. This was true—I had not been handling the break-up well, but I still felt myself crumbling on the inside as I said it. In my mind, this meeting was my last chance to ask for help and invite someone into the troubled space inside of me, and I chose to hide. Choosing not to say that I was quitting because I didn't believe in God anymore was choosing to go on this journey to figure out what I believed alone, outside of the Church, which was completely uncharted territory for me. The weight of that reality made my knees weak, but I tried my best to stand tall.

"And I've just been so busy with school and work that I don't have enough time to be present here anymore." I remember that I couldn't hold eye contact with her as I said it, in fear that she would see the tears building in my eyes, in fear that she would ask what deep well they were coming from.

I had been hiding for so long, and even though I desperately want-ed to be honest, I didn't know how to take off the Christian mask.

Kate and the rest of the leadership team were understanding. They said the "right" things. They said that the Lord had a plan and that I should draw close to him during this time, that they had some scrip-tures that might be helpful, that they would pray for me. Little did they know, each of these statements added another level of bricks to the invisible wall that had already begun to separate us.

I was there, a crucial part of the community, and then suddenly one day I wasn't. My entire community was centered around a place I didn't know if I would ever be able to go back to, and I felt completely alone.

So, in addition to grieving the loss of the main person I had done life with for almost five years and the loss of my entire spiritual founda-tion, I also had to grieve what felt like the loss of my entire social web, my entire support system, my entire tribe, and it was all too much to know how to bear. I wasn't sure if there was anything more lonely than not feeling I had a place anymore, like I didn't belong, like I no longer had a people. Leaving was the only choice I seemed to have.

While all of these thoughts were stuck in my throat, the soccer game roared around me. Goals were scored. Chants were screamed. Beers were chugged. And again, I played the part. On the outside I faked the smiles. I cheered when everyone else did. I pretended I was part of the pack. I edited what I said so I could be safe and not really expose who I was on the inside. I still felt too raw to be honest, especially with strangers, so Ryan's work friends walked away thinking I was simply a nice girl taking a pretty rad adventure. That's all I was ready to let them see, and maybe it was okay to embrace that part of it. I was taking a pretty rad adventure. I wanted to feel the power in that reality, but I thought it might take a few days for it to fully sink in.

As we walked to the car, I assured Ryan that I had fun and repeated that again to Lynn and Chip when I crawled through the front door completely exhausted.

I laid awake for a long time in the guest room king-sized bed, pierced with loneliness. I knew I was running away from everything because it felt like too much to bear, but I didn't know what I was running toward. Most of the time I couldn't see beyond nihilism, beyond the belief that everything must just be meaningless, that suffering is unjust and unexplainable, that love is a lie because there is no way for it to be unconditional, that people would always hurt me.

Day one had already brought up so much in me, and I worried that I was in way over my head. I didn't know if I would be strong enough to endure weeks of this, but I knew I had to be. I had to find a way to keep walking, and I went to sleep, hoping that the going is what would eventually save me.

{2}

THE ALARM IN MY HEAD

I WOKE UP THE NEXT MORNING WITH FOURTH OF JULY excitement nowhere to be found in my being. However, despite my lack of psych, I was interested to see how the day, which included dropping in to Nashville's Annual Hot Chicken Festival in the morning and attending the largest fireworks show in the country that night, would unfold.

The Fourth of July used to be such a day of sweetness and tradition in my life. It was joy. It was light. It was family. It was closeness. But this Fourth of July was grief. It was heavy. It was solitude. It was far from feeling close to anyone.

My phone vibrated next to me on the bed. I looked to find a text from my mom.

"Happy Fourth of July sweetie! Just wanted to let you know that your dad and I were thinking about you and are praying for safety as you continue your trip! I know God has you in his hands!"

I noticed my heart rate rise as I read it. Every time I heard from or talked to my parents, I felt the ever-present tension which had been growing between us since the day I told them I didn't know if I believed in Christianity anymore. I didn't tell them because I necessarily wanted to, but I think sometimes what we want to say is really under the surface. I think it was a cry for help when I didn't know how to ask for it.

We were eating lunch at a local Indian restaurant in Boone. My parents had come up to visit on Easter Sunday. I pretended at church for them, sang along and acted like I was paying attention while I ranted in my journal about not knowing what to do with the crucifixion and resurrection of Jesus, how it had anything to do with me and my supposed sin, or the state of my salvation.

Cam was with us. Things were really toxic then, but my parents had no idea. We were trying to have a cordial lunch of all you can eat dal and naan, and then the argument began.

"And that's what Easter is all about," my dad finished his story about how great it was that a woman had gotten "saved" during the Easter church service by praying with the pastor at the end. "Jesus's resurrection calls us all to be saved, so that we can then go and bring others to the cross to be saved as well. Now she's one of us, part of the Kingdom. Praise God!"

"One of us? You see, it's people saying things like that that really piss me off," Cam huffed. "No one cared about that woman two seconds before she raised her hand when the pastor was leading the sinner's prayer. Hell, most people probably didn't even notice her before she raised her hand. And now, all of the sudden, just because she supposedly found God today she is someone noteworthy? She was a sinner this morning, but now she's a celebrity because she got saved and she's in the club? Some man dying on a cross to create yet another us versus them or in versus out mentality in the world doesn't sound like a healthy religion to me."

"Well Cam, you've got it all wrong," my dad replied cautiously. "The Bible says—"

Cam slammed his hand on the table. "Fuck what the Bible says!" He interrupted my dad loudly enough to make multiple people throughout the restaurant turn their heads. My dad's eyes grew wide under his sharp brow. My mom looked horrified but didn't say anything. I immediately felt sick to my stomach.

I grabbed Cam's thigh under the table and shot him a sideways glance. "Not now, Cam. Come on," I urged, My heart pounded against my chest.

"God, I'm just so tired of Christian bullshit!" Cam shook his head.

"Okay, that's enough!" my dad spewed as anger washed over his face.

"Cam," I squeezed his thigh tighter, desperately wanting reality to be anything but this.

"No!" Cam brushed my hand away. "I'm done playing the game. It's an abusive system that I don't want any part of anymore. It creates all of these unnecessary barriers between people, convinces people that they don't have agency to help themselves, and they have to rely on some Jesus who died on the cross in order to change anything about their life." Now everyone in the restaurant was staring at us.

My dad continued to try to defend Christianity to Cam, but Cam wasn't having it. Things continued to get more heated. I was getting more and more frustrated. Neither my dad or Cam would back down. I didn't know what else to do.

"Honestly, dad," I quickly interjected. "If you really want to know the truth, I don't know if I believe any of it anymore either." The words clawed through my throat as I spoke them and fell into a heaping pile on the table, laying out in the open while we all stared at them in silence, even Cam. None of us knew how to reply to the last thing any of us expected me to say.

In that moment, I completely dissociated from my body. I felt like I was removed from reality, as if my physical body was sitting in the booth but I was looking down and observing our conversation from somewhere above us.

Mom immediately started crying. Dad was speechless. At first they were silent once they realized I was serious, and then they responded in panic, in terror, in tears, as if I had blatantly betrayed them.

"What do you mean you don't believe any of it anymore?" my mom choked.

"The whole thing, mom. Christianity. Jesus. God. It doesn't mean the same things to me anymore."

"Well, honey, maybe you're just confused," mom urged as she wiped a tear from her cheek. "You know Satan can grab a hold of you when you spend too much time in intellectual pursuits."

"Emi, you probably just aren't praying and reading your Bible enough," dad urged. "That is where the Lord meets us, in our quiet time, and that is where He makes everything make sense. I have a book that you should read. It has all of these Bible verses laid out with proofs and explanations, and it always helps me when I struggle with doubt. I promise, if you just give Him more time, the Lord will reveal Himself to you and remind you who He is."

I sat completely still, and I couldn't open my mouth, for I feared that if I did, I would scream and wouldn't be able to stop. I had barely even scratched the surface. I still hadn't told them about how abusive things with Cam had become, or about the depression, panic attacks, scary depersonalization episodes, or the anxiety. If they could barely handle this, how was I supposed to tell them anything else? On the inside the reel of anger spun viciously. My mind was filled with a rant I wished I could scream, but I couldn't bring myself to open my mouth.

Really? I'm not doing enough to keep God around? God will be found again if I turn my brain off and stop my "intellectual pursuits," right. Well those "intellectual pursuits" have been me pouring my entire being into trying to understand, nose-deep in Christian books and spending hours desperately seeking answers in podcasts, since no one is going to help me explore my questions in the Church without giving me a Bible verse to look up that is somehow supposed to make everything make sense. Do people seriously think God is something that you have to do something for in order to have access to or understand? Isn't that the exact opposite of the Gospel you claim to believe in? How is that good news? You will never understand.

That day, in my fear and anger, I shut down and decided that talking about my experience with my parents was no longer safe, that even my family would reject me if I was honest. I decided I was alone and no one would ever understand. My parents viewed my deconstruction as if I had a sickness that could be healed, as if my questions about God and the Church could be prayed away, but the last thing you want to hear when the world feels like it is falling out beneath your feet is someone close to you saying that you are in pain because you are just not doing enough, that it is somehow your fault, that you brought this upon yourself, and it is up to you to fix it.

Since Easter, my parents hadn't brought our conversation up again, but I knew they were still terrified. Dad occasionally sent out-of-the-blue emails with seven-page research articles "proving" that certain evangelical beliefs were true, while mom sent texts with prayers and Bible verses, but I rarely acknowledged them. To them, if I did not believe exactly what they believed, I was now "other." I was no longer on the "us" side. I now belonged to the "them." The lost. The ones that must be saved. Deconstruction was already traumatic but feeling like I could no longer be open and honest with my family added to that trauma.

I untied my fingers from the knots of tension preventing them from typing and forced myself to send a reply to the text that said thanks and that I loved them. I wanted to believe that somehow they meant well, that they were just doing what they thought their faith instructed them to do, that they didn't know how hurtful the way they responded was to me. I knew they loved me and that they wanted me to be safe. I just wanted to help them understand so they weren't so scared.

I decided to wear my one sundress that day. It was simple. Royal blue, strappy, solid, almost t-shirt material, the kind that is a close excuse for getting to wear something similar to pajamas in public while looking semi-put-together. I was lacking in the shoe department, though, as my cardboard box closet was only so big. I wore the only shoes I had besides my hiking and running shoes—Chacos, my strappy, black outdoor sandals that fall somewhere between tacky grandma and adventurous vagabond. I had become accustomed to living in small-town mountain culture where anything goes regarding fashion. I wore my Chacos with everything, and my sundress was no different. I figured some Nashvillians would be horrified by my fashion choice, but they would just have to get over it.

I came downstairs and offered 'good mornings' to everyone, and after a giant spread of biscuits, bacon, eggs, and bad coffee, Ryan and I headed out to go to Nashville's Annual Hot Chicken Festival, another surprise plan made by Ryan.

Sure. Hot Chicken Festival? Why the hell not?

Ryan and I left the house early to go pick up Mike, one of Ryan's friends from college, who would be joining us in our gastronomic excursion. I'd been preparing myself for the inevitable question since the night before, and Ryan finally asked it while we were riding in the car.

"So I didn't ask you last night, how are you and Cam doing?" Ryan asked.

I stumbled over my words trying to find the beginning of a response. "Oh. Yeah. Um. I guess I never told you how things ended up after you left North Carolina."

"Yeah the last time we talked, Cam was in Boone and y'all were trying to work things out."

I didn't know where to start, so I started with the short answer.

"Well, we're over for good, and it ended in the worst way possible."

"Oh no. Em, I'm so sorry," Ryan consoled. "What happened?"

"How much time do we have before we get to Mike's?"

Ryan looked at his GPS. "About fifteen minutes."

I took a deep breath. "I'm just going to tell you everything because there's no way to talk around it, but it's kind of a lot, and I'm going to have to get personal, so as long as that isn't uncomfortable for you..." I trailed off.

Ryan shook his head. "No, that's fine with me."

"Okay. So you knew that Cam moved to Boone to work things out with me, and I told you how I didn't know how I felt about it because of how back and forth things had been last fall and how things started to get unhealthy."

"Right." Ryan nodded his head. "You said you didn't trust him, and your friends were worried about how it would turn out knowing how negatively he had already affected you, but you were going to give him a chance to show that he was serious."

"Correct. He moved to Boone the second week of January, so we went from being 600 miles apart with no contact to him living a mile down the street from me with a mutual friend."

"Dang. That is such a drastic change. What was that like for you?" he asked as he turned on the interstate.

"Well, I stood by what I initially told Cam for a while, that we would take it super slow and build trust again before we jumped right back into a serious relationship. In the meantime, he cooked dinners, he wrote love letters, he was super intentional and showered me with affection. I saw the faintest glimmer in his eye that made me wonder if things could be different. He seemed like his old self. I thought we might be able to be healthy again. I held on to the man I believed Cam could be because I had seen that person and believed he would come back and stay.

"Soon I was spending all of my time with him. Well, any time I had outside of working three jobs and leading worship and taking eighteen hours of class that semester. We spent most evenings together, and eventually I was spending almost every night at his house."

I paused. "And this is where it gets more personal, but I'll tell you because there's no way around it."

"Whatever you're comfortable sharing," Ryan affirmed.

"Okay, well just let me know if it's too much."

"No, go ahead. I'm here for it." Ryan looked at me as we stopped at a red light and nodded in affirmation. I knew Ryan grew up in church, but I didn't know exactly how much he identified with Christianity, so I hoped what I was about to tell him wouldn't be too uncomfortable because I knew that most Christians weren't okay talking openly about anything to do with sex.

"So for context, Cam and I decided early on in our relationship that we were fully committed to waiting to have sex until we got married, because we thought that was what we were supposed to do, according to all of the fear and shame-based propaganda we were handed growing up that was attached to God and the Bible. We had been pretty intimate in other, um, ways," (this conversation was already hard, and I wasn't about to talk to my cousin about oral sex) "but we had never had vaginal sex because we were saving our virginity. We, like most people who grow up having purity culture constantly preached at us, were told that virginity was the only option for healthy sexuality, and anything outside of that framework was sin and would scar you and your partner forever. So in our minds as long as penis did not enter vagina, we could do anything else. As if we could trick God or something I guess? I don't know." Ryan raised his eyebrows and nodded. I hoped it was okay that I just said vagina out loud with my male cousin. I could feel my slight embarrassment in my cheeks, but I took a deep breath and continued.

"For a while being back together was great and seemed to be fairly healthy, or at least I told myself it was. We both were caught up in how great it was to have a companion, but we were mostly riding on memories of the past. Eventually the present caught up with us, and soon I started to see the reality that Cam was still in a really negative place.

"Once I was sucked back in and committed to figuring things out, we quickly spiraled into toxicity again. Cam was already controlling and invalidating before he got out of the military, but it got even worse after he got out. He would constantly make pointed, harsh, or degrading comments toward me or laugh about my behavior, about my emotions, about my body. He would say things like, *'Oh sorry, I was just laughing at the way your legs jiggle when you walk. God, why do you react so much? You should have more control over your emotions. You're crying, again? You're making this a way bigger deal than it actually is.'*

"Jeez. I'm so sorry." Ryan shook his head.

I nodded. "Thanks. Cam was really angry about a lot of things. I mean, he was going through a lot himself. There was all of the military stuff, and he had also begun questioning everything, but from a really dark and angry place. He brought up conversations that I was too over-whelmed to have because I was so focused on trying to save my ideal dreams about our relationship that were crumbling.

"He had always smoked marijuana, but he started smoking so much and so frequently that he was rarely sober. He started talking about experimenting with more serious drugs, which scared me know-ing that he was already unstable, and any time I tried to have a con-versation about it he would get frustrated about my "ignorance" and "closed-mindedness" and belittle me.

"Then sex became a huge thing for him. He suddenly was fine with having vaginal sex after years of being totally against it, and he didn't want to wait anymore. Whether he did it consciously or not, he constantly put this subtle pressure on me to agree, but I was too overwhelmed with feeling confused that I refused, and refused, and refused. And I continued to refuse while he continued to disconnect and withhold love, and I continued to try to "put out" enough to keep him satisfied so he wouldn't leave." Ryan was shaking his head again. I continued.

"He continued to get more harsh and degrading toward me, re-inforcing the message over and over again that my emotions were too much, and my body was not enough unless he could have all of it. This went on for months as winter turned to spring, and I spent most nights crying myself to sleep next to him after trying to connect sexually and still feeling so incredibly alone and scared that our relationship was ending, and I didn't know what to do with that possibility.

"Things got worse, with more yelling from Cam, more crying from me, which would then elicit more anger, frustration, and invalidation from Cam. I knew that none of my needs were being met, that this relationship was not good for me, and that Cam had a lot of stuff he needed to figure out before he could be healthy in a relationship, but I didn't know how to leave. We were back in the same familiar, destructive pattern. Cam setting the boundaries of what was and wasn't okay, and me desperately trying to fit myself into his strict expectations, failing, and getting punished for it.

"Eventually we were both so empty inside that we could no longer pretend like there was a way for our relationship to be saved. I had been so attached to the idea that the old us would return, but that us was long gone. One morning in April, Cam looked at me numb and emotionless, and slow tears fell from my cheeks as we acknowledged that this had to end. We were breaking up, for good, and I knew we needed to.

"That morning I was upset and sad because it had been such a long and dramatic four and a half years, but I felt a sense of relief because it meant that things would finally change. But that wasn't the end of the drama."

"Goodness, Emily." Ryan's brow furrowed. "There's more?"

"Yep. So we went our separate ways that Saturday morning, and didn't talk at all that night. I went to church the next day because I didn't know what else to do, and then right before church started, Cam walked in with his roommate and a curly-haired girl I had never seen before and sat in a row of chairs on the other side of the room."

"What the hell?" Ryan let out. "I thought you said he didn't want anything to do with God?" I looked out the window to see that we had gotten off the interstate and were entering some suburbs, so I figured we were getting close to Mike's house. I continued quickly to try to finish the story before we got there.

"Right. I knew that Cam would never come to church because he wanted to. I rarely could get him to come with me. I remember thinking, *'Why the hell is he here, of all places, the morning after we broke up?'* Knowing him, something about it seemed really manipulative.

"He came up to me afterwards and was acting super weird, not keeping eye contact during our conversation which I assumed was just because he was processing a lot and wasn't very good at dealing with his emotions. He asked if I could come over later, to talk for a second and to get the rest of my stuff, since I did laundry at his house the day before and still had clothes in the dryer.

"I was like, *'oh, right, sorry, I forgot about that.'* I didn't really want to talk to him, but I told him I guessed I could come that night after dinner to grab my stuff. So I sat in nausea all day, having a gut feeling that something was off, wondering why he was being so weird, what more he could possibly want to say to me. With Cam, it could have been anything.

"I went over that night, apprehensive because I had no idea what to expect. I walked in, and Cam was finishing cooking dinner, so I went into the laundry room to get my stuff out of the dryer without saying much besides 'hello.' Then he came into the laundry room, jittery and anxious, and asked if we could take a walk outside."

I could feel myself becoming triggered. I hadn't told the whole story aloud to anyone yet. My heart rate was elevated, I felt nauseous, my throat became tight, and my palms were sweaty. I kept going.

"I didn't know why we had to go outside just to have a conversation, but I figured it was just a weird Cam thing. We walked out the back door and into the field behind his house. We walked in silence for a while in the dark. I didn't ask for this, so I just kept my mouth shut and waited for Cam to start talking. He walked over to a wooden stairwell that led up the hill to the street, went up a few steps, and then turned around to face me.

"Cam finally spoke and said, *'I don't really know how to say this, but I know I should tell you.'* And then he paused, looked me in dead the eyes for the first time that day, and he said, *'Charlotte and I had sex last night.'*"

"*NO. WHAT?*" Ryan gasped and looked at me with wide eyes. "The night you broke up?"

"Yep. So. We didn't have sex for going on five years, and after all of the investment and loyalty and commitment and putting up with the emotional manipulation and being whipped around, after pouring my entire being into saving our relationship, we broke up. And we should have. But then, less than twelve hours later, Cam fucked a stranger." I felt bad that I said fuck out loud. My voice was getting louder now. "A STRANGER. AFTER FOUR AND A HALF YEARS. AND TOLD ME ABOUT IT THE NEXT DAY, KNOWING WHAT THAT WOULD DO TO ME." I quieted my voice again. "And you know why he asked to go for a walk outside? Because she was there. Charlotte, this random girl he met that week and had sex with the night we broke up was there, in his room, where they had sex, waiting for us to be done talking. He pointed her out to me through the window from the staircase like a prized pony." I took another deep breath and shook my head. "I'm sorry for yelling."

"Oh my God. Do not apologize. I want to scream too!" Ryan began ranting. "I don't even know what to say. Em, I am so sorry. I am so angry for you! Why the hell would he tell you like that? Why would he invite you over knowing she was there? Did he organize that on purpose?"

"I don't know for sure, but it felt completely manipulative," I muttered, "as if he wanted to see how it would break me."

"Ugh! Thinking about that makes me sick. I can't imagine how hard that must have been for you to hear. How could he do that to you? It's disgusting."

"I don't know. And the worst part is that he made sure to let me know that he wasn't sorry."

"Wait, seriously? What do you mean?"

"Well, the first thing that came out of my mouth after he told me was 'Fuck you.' That was the first time I had ever said the word 'fuck' out loud. I've said it quite a few more times since then, though." I smiled slightly.

"Um, I hope you said that!" Ryan affirmed. "I can think of a few other choice things I would have said to him too. What did you do next?"

"I tried to walk away, but as the reality of it all set in, my body felt really weak. My knees buckled, and I fell to the ground. I think I became so overwhelmed with grief that I couldn't stand up anymore. I cried and cried." I looked out the window, but I wasn't really seeing anything that we passed. All I saw was myself back in that memory, sitting with my hands in the dirt. "I thought I would never stop. I just watched my tears fall next to my hands in the dirt, and that image is branded into my mind."

"What did Cam do after he told you?"

"He just sat on the steps and watched me unravel on the ground, not moving or saying anything. And then when I eventually tried to walk away to get to my car, he grabbed my arm and asked if we could talk more. I asked him what more he could possibly need to tell me after that, and our brief follow-up conversation was mainly so that he could say that he didn't think it was a big deal, that the sex wasn't even that great, as if that made it any less horrible, and most of all, he made it clear that he wasn't sorry and that he didn't feel bad about it. He kept saying that throughout the conversation. 'I'm not sorry.'" I let out a long sigh. My heart was racing and my breath was short.

Ryan sighed. "That is the shittiest thing I have ever heard."

"It would have been shitty regardless of our history, but because of how I understood sex in my brain from what I was handed by the Church, because of the fact that we had chosen not to have sex for so many years, because it was this sacred thing we were saving between us, and because Cam knew me more deeply than any other person in the world, the fact he would choose to have sex with a stranger the day we broke up was the absolute worst form of betrayal I could imagine at this point in my life."

As the words came out, I knew there was emotion somewhere inside of me that went with them, but my tone was void of feeling. I spoke bleakly, for that night blew apart all connection between my thoughts and my emotions, and I had not been able to reconnect them since. Cam's betrayal caused the most intense pain I had ever experienced, and I believed that feeling it again would finish me.

I could see we were pulling into what was probably Mike's apartment complex, so I finished by saying, "So yeah. That's why Cam isn't doing this trip with me."

Ryan sighed. "I don't know what else to say besides I'm sorry, and I hate that that happened to you. I can't imagine how it has affected you. Are you okay? I mean, I'm sure you're probably not, but how are you dealing with it all?" he asked.

"Thanks. I don't need you to say anything. Honestly, I'm not okay. I'm not really myself these days, and I have a lot of shit to work through before I can find a new normal. So if I seem a little off, that's why." I took a deep breath.

"That is so valid, and thank you so much for telling me. Seriously. That was really brave. I'm so sorry again," he grabbed my arm reassuringly, "and obviously if you need anything or someone to call while you're gone please don't hesitate to call me." He parked the car. "This is Mike's place, and he'll be out soon. Is there anything else you want to share right now before he gets out here?"

I gave a weak smile and said there wasn't, that I was just grateful for the fact that he was here to listen and that he cared.

I was surprised at myself, for telling him the whole story. I did leave out the deconstruction of my faith part of the story which was just as significant, but what I shared with Ryan was the most I had shared with anyone. I had told some people that Cam and I had broken up, and I told a few of my closest friends about our conversation the night after we broke up, but I hadn't told the whole story at once yet because I was scared to. However, something about naming it aloud, something about putting language to what happened in detail fully for the first time made it a little less scary, as if somehow it had a little less power over me, as if I was a little less defined by it.

The sound of someone squealing came through the window, and I looked to my right to see who it was.

"Hello beautiful people!" Mike's voice floated across the parking lot. Walking our way was a smiley, jovial, almost too-happy guy in his late twenties, and I felt on edge. I did not do well with too-happy people at this point in my life.

"Soooooo, how are you guys doing? What a beautiful day, right?" Mike spoke in harmony, each word with a higher dose of pep and joy than the average human at 9:00 a.m. I gave him a weak smile and went through a quick, polite introduction.

"You ready to go eat some hot chicken?" Mike asked excitedly.

"Um, I don't think I actually fully understand what we're going to," I chuckled.

"Nashville is famous for its hot chicken." Ryan informed, "It's a huge cultural thing here. There's a never-ending contest of which fancy restaurant or hole-in-the-wall chicken shack has the best hot chicken, and there's always debate over what kind of sauce is the best and stuff like that. I found out about the festival from a co-worker of mine, and who can say no to fried chicken?"

After a morning of ingesting way more spicy chicken than my stomach could handle at the festival, we met Lynn and Chip for the most gourmet all-you-can eat Southern food for dinner. My skin felt like it was crying deep-fried oil, and my dairy-phobic stomach swelled from the punches of heavy cream and cheese. Though my body felt terrible, I tried to soak up the extra calories before the canned tuna and granola days to come on the road.

We waddled with our stuffed stomachs up an alley away from the main drag of downtown to get a better view of the fireworks, which I was fine with because it meant I was able to escape the suffocating crowds. I had little patience left after walking around the crowded streets with Ryan and Mike all afternoon. I wasn't very hopeful for the supposed grandiose nature of the fireworks show, for rain now trickled down steadily, and as the night air cooled, a dense fog had begun to hover over the city.

The first explosion startled us, but when we looked up the sparks barely made their way through the fog. More followed in rapid succession. We could see the clouds lighting up, but it looked more like white lightning than colored fireworks. I bet the folks who worked for the city and spent thousands of dollars on the show were not feeling very excited, but it seemed like the diverse group of spectators around us still enjoyed it. Along the street, couples stood hand in hand, pulling each other close. An old man sat in a lawn chair on top of the hill by himself, the smile on his face lit up by the occasional flashes. Children were running and squealing at every pop.

Everyone looks so happy. I felt a pang of sadness. Now that the day had slowed and I had thirty minutes without talking or being talked to, I felt the lingering heaviness of my doubt and unknowing. As the sparks continued, my thoughts drifted.

I gazed up into the haze of rain and fog and light, occasionally catching a glimpse of a red or blue firework that was able to escape the thick wall of mist, smoke, and fog, and it seemed like an accurate metaphor for my deconstruction experience. For the most part, everything regarding the idea of God in my mind was like a dense, foggy mist full of doubt, questions, ambiguity, and unknowing, but occasionally light would show itself for a brief moment.

It happened randomly and unexpectedly, always catching me off guard, as if someone had tapped me on the shoulder when I wasn't paying attention, but I could never turn around quickly enough to see who it was. It happened most when I was on a hike alone in the woods, when I would hike for so long that my thoughts would run themselves out, and some deep knowing of peace would brush by me as subtly as a slight summer breeze, one you have to be facing a certain way in order to feel it on your cheek. But it was not the same kind of peace I found when I used to worship or pray before I deconstructed. That peace was certain, systematic, attached to a static idea of God. This kind of peace felt different, but not necessarily in a negative way. It hung somewhere just out of sight, flashing quickly before me, only soon to retreat back into the haze once more, and I couldn't find it again no matter how desperately I called for it to come back. It was those moments of stillness and peace that made me want to believe that I was still capable of seeking some idea of God, but I felt helpless to dissipate the fog.

Who are you, God? What are you? Are you separate from me? Are you inside of me? Are you conscious? Do you hear me? Do you know me? What is the higher power that I think I feel at the inner core of my being sometimes, yet from which I feel so distant and separated? How do I find you? How do I know you and believe in you with full confidence when the idea of you makes absolutely no sense to me? How can my heart sense your presence but my mind reject and deny you?

I don't know what to do or where to go from here. I sit in tension, for how do I know what I should devote my heart to and what direction to take in life when I no longer know what I believe or who I am? You can't exactly be part-Christian and part something else. Or can you? I want to believe consciously that human experience in separation from spirituality leads to a world void of much meaning, but my spiritual house has been bulldozed to the ground, and what used to be familiar and comforting is unrecognizable now. Do I leave it all together? Or do I dig through the rubble and try to build something new from the pieces?

There have to be deeper levels of reality beyond the existence of the species of man alone. But how do I live in harmony with a world of which I am a part but do not know the truth behind its maker and what he or she or it has to do with me, or if there is even a conscious maker at all? Is there a personal relationship to be had with God, or is God distant energy that is uninvolved in our personal lives? I have felt and sometimes still feel a spirit moving inside me and leading me, and whether it is Divine or the "Holy Spirit" or not, I do not know. But I know that it is something, and there is some innate knowing in the midst of my unknowing that draws me to a place of reverence. Even in the midst of my hardest days of depression, there is still a part of me that holds onto a thread of belief that this life is extraordinary and beautiful and worth living, and for that I want to continue the pursuit of finding out more about the source from which that thread of belief comes, even in the midst of my despair. I still don't trust my emotions though. They are unpredictable and scary. I don't know what is me and what is not me anymore. I need help sorting through the chaos. I need help crossing the chasm to truth.

"You okay?" Ryan's voice jolted me back into reality. I heard the explosions of the fireworks again, and I noticed that I was still uncomfortably full of chicken.

I sighed. "Okay is the goal." I attempted a half smile.

"I just wanted to check in and see how you are holding up since our conversation this morning," he noted softly.

"Oh, yeah. I mean, most days are pretty hard, but it has just become normal now. Cam is still one of the first things I think about when I wake up in the morning, but the grief is not always as intense now as it was in the beginning. At first I could barely think about anything else. Every time I would close my eyes, I would see him on that staircase, telling me he wasn't sorry. I feel embarrassed sometimes about how often I think about him, but maybe that's just how grief is in the beginning.

"I've always heard people talk about grief like it's just this clear path that everyone takes in the same direction, and I feel like a lot of people think grief is something you move through quickly. There's these five stages or certain steps, as if they are just boxes you can rush through checking off so you can be done grieving. Maybe it's true, but right now I think grief is more like an alarm that constantly goes off at first, and it's so loud that I can barely function sometimes. I want to do whatever I can to shut it off so I can rest for a moment without thinking about it, but I also want to resist just finding whatever turns it off because I don't want to numb myself. I'm trying to view the alarm when it gets triggered as a reminder to pay attention, to name it, to give my grief room to take up space instead of repressing it. I numbed it at first. And it didn't do anything but make it worse and cut me off from myself. Maybe over time the alarm gets quieter and we can function better, or maybe it gets triggered less frequently and less intensely. Maybe it goes from constant to going off just once a day, or once a week, or once a month, or maybe even once a year, but I think it will always be there, and it comes up in waves."

"Wow, I've never heard it put that way before. I can totally resonate," Ryan confided. "That's how it felt when I decided to break the engagement with Lindsay last year. It was like an alarm that was always going off. And everyone around you has no idea how loud it is in your head, and there's no way to let people fully know what it's like inside of you. It's really hard."

"Yeah, exactly. That's where I'm at. The alarm is still going off multiple times a day, and it's triggered by such random things that bring up memories or reminders, so it's impossible to prepare myself for it." I sighed. "Thanks for asking. And I know we talked about it a lot last year, but I'm sorry again about Lindsay."

"Of course. And thank you. I hope this trip gives you what you need, Em. I'm sure it will be helpful to have a chance to breathe for the first time in a while. Plus, it sounds like you're going to be doing some really cool stuff out there. I'm jealous. Make sure you come back though," he warned.

I smiled. "Thanks, Ryan. For everything. The soccer game, the festival, showing me around today. It's been fun, at least much closer to fun than I imagined." We both laughed. "It's hard to push past the heaviness and enjoy myself most days. Though I have noticed that I have felt less heavy since our conversation this morning. Thanks again for listening and understanding."

"Of course, kid," he said as he extended his arms out to hug me.

We were suddenly startled by the increased rapidity of violent sounds coming from the sky, which signaled the beginning of the grand finale. The epic, expensive tubes of gunpowder were exploding in a harmonious rainbow array of dancing color and light and sound, which I'm sure would have been more spectacular if we could have seen any of it. Instead it was an anticlimactic sequence of sounds that told of the presence of such a sight that was just beyond reach. The unpredictable rates and volumes of the explosions continued to emanate from behind the clouds for a few moments until all was silent. People still clapped and cheered.

"Wasn't that fireworks show beautiful?" Mike roared sarcastically as he walked over to us.

"Most colorful one I've ever seen," I replied sarcastically, and everyone giggled.

We said our thank you's and goodbyes to Lynn and Chip since they were staying in a hotel downtown for the night, and it was finally time to leave. After so much poultry and people and patriotism, I longed for sleep.

{3}

STUNNED

THINKING I WAS SURELY THE FIRST ONE AWAKE, I WENT downstairs to fix myself some coffee and be alone for two seconds. As I walked down the stairs, I felt like I was six months pregnant. I was still bloated from our culinary endeavors the day before.

I grabbed a mug out of the cabinet, but not quietly enough apparently. Lynn's head immediately popped out of the master bedroom door.

"Good morning beautiful! What a lovely day!" she sang.

"Jeez, you scared me!" I stammered. "I thought you wouldn't be home from the hotel until later! It's pretty early!" I looked at the clock. It was only 8:00.

"Oh yes sweetie, well church is at ten o'clock and we wanted to come back in time to eat and get ready before we go. I figured we'd all go together, and then after we'll go take you to lunch before you hit the road. Sound good?" Lynn chirped with a smile that stretched to her ears.

The split second before I opened my mouth, my brain was filled with a flash flood of thoughts. *Oh. Right. Church. It's Sunday. Shit. Of course.*

I did not think all the way through the timing of stopping at Lynn and Chip's on a weekend, because a weekend includes Sunday morning, and Sunday morning in my family is always, and I mean always, spent at church.

She didn't really ask if I wanted to go. She just said we're going. Like that was the only option. They have been so hospitable and gracious in paying for all of my food this weekend so it would probably be weird if I said I wasn't going to go, but thinking about going to church makes my blood boil and what if I have a panic attack and what if I depersonalize or get trapped in a toxic thought cycle I can't pull myself out of...

Despite my panic, *"sounds great"* dropped out of my mouth through a forced smile before I could reel it back in.

"Perfect. We'll leave about 9:30 or so," Lynn replied with that same smile. I smiled and turned to walk up the stairs. My apprehension still hung in my throat, and the caution alarms going off in my head blurred my vision.

Why did I say yes? I took this trip to get the heck away from church. Now I'm just supposed to roll up in a pew and pretend like I'm fine? I haven't been inside a church since Easter with mom and dad, and the idea of going makes my brain feel like it's going to explode. I can't say no without explaining why, so I guess I'm just going to have to embrace it somehow.

The service was less traditional and conservative than I expected, though there were subtle charismatic notes woven in that were triggering because they reminded me of my old church community. Much like the way I'd led worship in Boone, the worship band at Lynn and Chip's church stayed on one lyric during the bridge and repeated it over and over again, building the music each time to heighten emotion and help people "feel" the Holy Spirit. More hands went up, and more people began swaying and dancing.

As I looked around the room, I saw the ghost of who I used to be raising my hands next to them, connecting to the music as naturally and easily as breathing, but my hands in reality were like lifeless weights hanging next to me. Holding my old religious self and pretending religious self and current angry who-knows-what self all in one space was so confusing.

During my months of pretending while I was still leading worship at church, I spent the time during sermons journaling. Mostly it was me vehemently scrawling all of my angry judgments of how frustrated I was with Christianity and why I could never be a part of it again, but it was also a way to drown out whatever the pastor was saying so that I wouldn't have more things to add to my rant. From the outside observer though, it looked like I was passionately taking notes about how good the sermon might have been, which helped my agenda of remaining an in-the-closet semi-atheist trying to keep from drowning in the "I'm okay" fundamentalist ocean.

So that's what I did again while sitting next to Lynn, Chip, and Ryan that day. I hated myself for pretending again, but I didn't know what else to do.

07/05/15, Day 3 -

The hardest aspect of being in a spiritual environment similar to the one I used to be a part of is not the anger. It is the envy. I long to be able to close my eyes and feel and connect to God like I used to. I long to enter into prayer and actually believe that it changes things. I long to add my voice to the flow of harmony and emotion during communal worship without getting caught up in lyrics I don't believe in.

Why does all of this work for them? Are they just totally content to remain on the surface of all of this? Why did my brain turn against simplicity and cause me to see things in a way to where I can no longer un-see everything that is wrong with the Church? Am I insane? Do other people feel like this? Why is it fair that I was pushed out of the tribe because I wanted to explore my mind, but so many people get to stay in the tribe because they're fine with leaving theirs turned off? What is wrong with me to make this not be a place I can be a part of anymore? Why do they get to remain in their neat and tidy spiritual houses, with their cookie-cutter Gospel that supposedly saves everyone, but from the outside seems to only save people who make themselves look, act, and speak like them?

I once lived in a spiritual house like that. It had a foundation of faith and walls built on theology that I never necessarily gave consent to take in as my own. My spiritual house was built for me by my parents, by my Sunday school teachers, by my pastors, by the text-book answers that were given to me my whole life. For years it was a very structured and safe spiritual home. It certainly helped me stay within certain moral boundaries during my youth, it taught me how to be a "good person," but it didn't give me the tools to handle the hard questions of my transition into adulthood.

Once I started paying more attention to the stuff that my spiritual house was composed of, I realized that I had very little part in the building of it, and even further, I realized I was never separate from the Church enough to choose it for myself. I've been steeped in a very specific form of Christianity since the day I was born. Over time, it became me, and I became it. Eventually, my identity couldn't exist separate from "Christian."

When you are born into certain forms of Christian culture, I think it is hard to separate what is true and what is not because the way of life you are given is just simply the way things have always been done, no questions. For most of my life, since it seemed like no one else around me was questioning it, I figured I didn't need to question it either. I believed with everything in me that if truth was given to me by the Church, if it was said from the pulpit, it must be ultimate truth, and I must follow it exactly. Everything I heard at church immediately got added to my spiritual house, even when it seemed contradictory to the way of life I thought Jesus was pointing to. I now know how harmful that can be.

I eventually began comparing my beliefs and how I lived them out to what Jesus actually calls for—standing with the oppressed, fighting for the marginalized, advocating for the poor, and inviting ALL people around the table to be their full and authentic selves. I realized many of the ways my supposed Christian faith informed my life actually prevented me from living like Jesus.

Following this certain form of Christianity has kept me separate from anyone who isn't white, privileged, heterosexual, cis-gendered, able-bodied, educated, conservative, and Christian.

There has been much more exclusion than inclusion, and I never questioned it until this year. My entire community growing up has consisted of people that are exactly like me, and most churches I have been to throughout my life have been the same. I realize now that if there is one thing that Jesus definitely did not preach about establishing, it was separateness, but separateness is the story I've lived out. I feel shame when I think about the fact that in the past I've been the very Christian hypocrite I now feel anger toward. Admitting these things is hard, but I know it is the only way toward reconciliation and healing.

As I critiqued my faith further, my spiritual house began to not seem like home anymore. I started to see cracks in the walls I hadn't noticed before. The paint was flaking off, and all of the metal was rusting. The air started to get musty from lack of use. Mold started growing and eating away the life and joy that once filled the rooms. It became uninhabitable.

At first I just tried to avoid going in my spiritual house, because if I didn't think about God or church or Christianity, I wouldn't have to face the fact that my supposed steadfast faith was actually crumbling and decaying. I wouldn't have to face the possibility that my religion often did way more harm than good, to me and to the people it affected, inside and outside the Church. I wouldn't have to face the fact that what I thought was the source of my life was actually dead at the roots.

Then, the night that Cam told me he had sex with Charlotte, after months of toxic manipulation and control, a final tornado of trauma ripped through my spiritual house. The cracks, which I refused to look at until then, splintered and shattered until the whole house was torn apart. The structure in which I lived and through which I understood and experienced God and the world was left in a heap of rubble strewn about, unrecognizable.

I was so focused on Cam that I hadn't fully looked at the questions and doubts I'd been repressing, but once things ended, the veil was cut from my eyes, and once you see you can't unsee. For the first time, I felt the full reality of my existential angst, and with no tools to handle the emotions I found there, I was sent into absolute existential crisis. A cleft was made between *emotion and logic, between faith and science, between my humanity and my spirituality. I feel like I can no longer merge the two sides.*

None of my pre-deconstruction beliefs can be accessed without bringing intense skepticism, doubt, and confusion along. Most days I feel like my mind is my worst enemy, but it is a part of me, and I know I can't build a new, healthier spiritual foundation by silencing it. Maybe letting it speak is not as scary as I think.

Sitting in Lynn and Chip's church, I felt like someone held a mirror up to me, but my reflection was distorted and jumbled. I didn't know how to bridge the gap I felt between me and the people around me. I shook hands and smiled politely through introductions, but I was desperately looking forward to getting on the road and being alone. Surface level conversation all weekend had totally drained my introvert battery. I needed time to recharge and attempt to process all that had come up in me so far.

After lunch, Lynn offered, "You are more than welcome to stop back by here if you need a place to stay on your way home sweet girl. All you need to do is call me. Even if we're not here, I'll leave the key under the mat for you."

"You're so generous, and it has meant so much to me to have been able to catch up and spend time with you," I sighed. "Thanks for feeding me and providing me with a bed. Soon I'll only be sleeping outside for a couple weeks." I smiled and hugged her tightly.

"Remind us where you're heading now?" Chip asked.

"Making my way toward Waco, Texas for now. Probably going to stay with that guy I told you about. I looked up the drive this morning and saw that it was eleven and a half hours, so I think I'm going to break it up. Little Rock, Arkansas is about half-way. I've never been and know nothing about it, so I figured it might be a good place to stop. We'll see!"

"And you're sure you're going to be fine sleeping in your car?" Chip questioned, obviously still uneasy about my traveling approach.

"Yep, it will be fun! So it begins!" I said and gave him a hug. I turned to Ryan.

"Thanks again. I'm so glad I got to see you. Good luck settling into your new job. I hope to see you soon."

"You're welcome, kid." Ryan smiled. "Be safe out there."

I stuffed my clothes back in my cardboard box closet and got in my car. I was glad Chip reminded me about staying with Isaac, because I realized I had never let him know what day I would arrive in Waco. Whoops. I sent him a text saying I would be there tomorrow evening sometime depending on what I did in Arkansas.

I pulled out of the driveway. I waved to my hosts standing by the front door, and even Milly was waving via Chip moving her tiny paw. Another deep breath. Back into the abyss filled with thousands of miles of potentials and possibilities.

The subtle sound of my phone vibrating in the passenger seat brought my attention back to the physical after driving for a couple hours. After not-so-safely balancing the steering wheel with my knee, I leaned over and grabbed my phone to see who it was.

Ugh. I sighed. *Mom.*

If you ever want to give your helicopter parents a chance to up-grade to a new advanced model of helicopter parent, programmed with heightened surveillance modes, take a road trip across the country by yourself. Before I left I tried to communicate to my parents that I un-derstood that they would be worried about me while I was gone but that I also needed some space. However, the consistent thread of "just checking in" texts every couple hours since I left Boone were sending the message that my wish was not going to be as respected as I would have liked. I exhaled hard, hoping some of my negativity would flow out with my breath.

"Hi Mom," I sang with as much excitement I could muster.

"Hey babe. How goes it so far?"

"Well Nashville was," I hesitated, "interesting. It was good to see Lynn, Chip, and Ryan, but I'm excited to be alone again."

"I know they were so happy to have you, and it makes me feel bet-ter knowing that you were under a roof and taken care of," she trailed off. There was a terribly long pause, as if she was waiting for me to say something, but she was the one that broke a boundary I had asked for.

I had nothing to say to her, so I waited for her to continue on with whatever she felt was so necessary to call me about.

"Well, I know you are driving, but oh honey you will never guess who came into dad's office today! That's the main reason I called. I was at the front desk helping with some paperwork, and then this salesman walks in to talk with me, and you will never guess what he was selling. Tasers! Disguised as flashlights!" My eye twitched. "I don't know if they're even legal, but I took it as a sign from the Lord because I have been worrying and praying about your safety, and I thought a taser would be so perfect to have for your trip! You know, in case something happened. So, long story short, I bought you one, and I'm gonna send it to your friend in Texas! So could ya get me his address, and I'll express ship it there so you can have it once you get to his house?"

Though I rarely can guess where conversation will go with my mother, her purchasing a device for me to electrically shock another human as a means of safety was probably in the fifth percentile of what I could have come up with.

"A *taser?!* Seriously mom?" I was beside myself. "What the heck am I going to do with a taser? I don't even know anything about tasers. I don't think you can just casually walk down the street with one, can you? How big is it?" I shook my head in disbelief as I imagined myself beep bopping down a trail with a giant taser strapped to my belt, as if I was trying to say to the world, *"Hey look I don't have a big dick, but I'll sure shock yours right off if you bring it near me!"*

"Oh no no no, sweetie. Listen, it's smaller than the normal flashlights we have at the house. And it even has a carrying case!" *Oh good. A fashionable taser.*

"Is it pink with shiny sparkles and diamonds?" I asked sarcastically.

I could feel her roll her eyes. "Ugh, no, it's just simple and black. And," she paused, "I can vouch that it works." She started laughing.

"Wait, what do you mean?"

"Well, I was taking it out to show your dad, and I was trying to figure out which way turned the safety off for you to do the taser, but apparently the safety mode was already turned off because when I turned the flashlight over to look for the button..." she was laughing more now, "...I tased myself."

"MOM! What? You tased yourself?! How? Were you okay?" My jaw hung open, and I felt my eyes widen and brow furrow.

"I know. Isn't that hilarious?" she cackled. "I yelled *my word* right away. I couldn't help it."

Now by referencing *"my word,"* I knew my mother did not mean she literally said the expression, "my word," which some Southern women tend to use to express surprise or to highlight the intensity of any emotion they are feeling. Any time she referenced herself using 'her word,' it was her subtle way to say that she responded to a situation with a certain exclamation of profanity, also known as the word *"shit."*

After referencing her shit-saying, mom continued, "And then once your dad and I realized what happened, we died laughing. It didn't hurt as much as it scared me. And I barely touched the on button, so it was a short shock, but just from that I can tell how it would definitely make anyone stop whatever they were trying to do if you held that button down and didn't let go!"

I couldn't help but laugh at the insanity of it. "Well I'm glad you're okay. Also, if it is just one where you press a button and it sends out a shock at the end, I'm pretty sure it's called a stun gun, not a taser. But regardless, I barely even know this guy that I'm staying with in Texas. What am I supposed to say? *'Hi, can I have your address so that my mom can send a shocking device to your house that I may or may not zap you with if you come near me while I sleep?'* He's going to think I'm actually a crazy person."

"Oh sweetie, it's not that big of a deal. You don't even have to tell him what's in the box. He will never know!"

"Mom, I think that's even more sketchy if I tell him that there's a mysterious box being mailed to his house that he is not to open…"

"Oh hush. It will be fine. Just ask for his address and send it to me please."

"Okay look, you do you. But I think sending a stun gun is a little excessive. I can't promise I'm going to carry it with me," I said hesitantly, "but do whatever you want. I gotta go. I'm pulling off the highway to stop in Memphis for a little while."

"Oh. Okay. Well, Love you. Stay safe. Have fun in Memphis! Say hi to Elvis for me!"

"I know mom. Thanks. I love you too."

I was baffled. My mother bought a stun gun from a random stranger, somehow accidentally shocked herself with it, and intended to wrap it up in a box and ship it a few states over to the house of a person I had spoken with no more than fifteen minutes in my whole life. Further, she expected me to casually unwrap said stun gun at said person's house and take it in its fancy carrying case to ward off the serial killers and rapists that are apparently so significant in concentration in my mother's perception of reality, that she felt it necessary to carry a weapon on my hip.

I think there is a healthy awareness level of danger, and my perception of danger during this period of my life was probably more ignorant than I would like to admit, but despite that, I could not imagine being in a scenario where I would feel the need to carry a stun gun with me. However, if my mom was so worried about me traveling alone that she felt the need to ship a stun gun to me, I guessed I could live with giving her the opportunity to do something to give herself a sense of comfort and control in the midst of her fear.

Sometimes we all need that—an embodied action where we are either consciously or subconsciously trying to process the fact that we have zero control over the outcomes of our circumstances.

I sent Isaac a text asking for his mailing address since my mom needed to mail me something for my trip. He didn't ask any questions and sent the address shortly. With apprehension, I forwarded it to my mom, hoping that I was not setting myself up for an incredibly awkward interaction once I arrived to Isaac's. If nothing else, it was a good time to practice radical acceptance.

I decided to stop in Memphis like one decides to eat a whole bag of chips. Not because I really wanted it or needed it, knowing I would probably be unsatisfied and would possibly feel a little sick afterward, but did it anyway just because it was conveniently there in my lap. I had zero intentions of what I would do once I got out of my car, but I figured it would be an opportunity to practice the road trip thing of stopping in random places along the way just because you can.

I parked and embarked on an unexpectedly sweaty walk down Beale Street as the chill of my air conditioned car was quickly melted by the blazing, 95-degree heat of the day. After passing the giant Elvis Presley statue, I walked straight up the street, mostly empty on a sleepy Sunday afternoon. There were colorful shops and bars that continued down the street as far as I could see.

The heat already made my walk hard to enjoy, but then my lack of excitement for Memphis quickly turned to disdain. As I walked down Beale Street, I was met with eyes that looked everywhere but my face and muffled "damn's" and "hey girl's" offered to me as I walked by the few men hanging outside the one open bar. I was wearing hiking shorts that fell to my mid thigh and a racerback athletic tank-top, but they made me feel as if I had been stripped down to my underwear and forced to prance through the street just for their pleasure.

I wish I could tell you that I looked them in the eye and stood up for myself. I wish I could tell you that I made an empowered comment calling out their objectification of my body that was completely uncalled for. I wish I could tell you that I responded by standing taller, but I said nothing. I wanted to implode. I made myself smaller. I walked faster and took the discomfort and shame, as I did every time a man catcalled me, because I felt as if somehow it was my fault.

I put my head down because I had grown up my whole life hearing in church that my woman's body was bad and dangerous, that it was something that would make men lose control if I let them see too much of me. My first thought was that maybe I was asking for it, that my clothes must not have been modest enough, but I realized I was doing it again. I was playing a part in a game I didn't want to take part in anymore. Even though throughout my deconstruction I had started to become aware of how toxic the Church's beliefs about women's bodies were, those beliefs were so ingrained in me. I had been taught it was up to me to make sure men didn't make me feel like those men on Beale Street did, but I was starting to realize that when I blamed myself for the objectification I received from others, especially men, I perpetuated the system of violence against my body. I reinforced the lie that my body was bad and should be blamed, which was also not okay.

I tried to remind myself as I walked away that what those men made me feel was not my fault, and it was not okay, even if I didn't have the courage to stand up for myself. I was so angry. My belief that objectification and sexual harassment toward me was my burden to bear was only one of the dozens of ways my religion had been negatively affecting my life, and I felt sad for the thousands of women in the same place as me. I wanted to believe my body was good, that it was something to take up space with, that it did not need to be hidden or feared. I wanted to tell a different story about my body and what it means to be a woman, but I had to learn a different story first, and I didn't know where to go to be able to do that. It surely wasn't going to be in the church settings I had experienced.

I tried to walk out some of my anger along the Mississippi River for a while. As I looked across the slow-moving water, I remembered that the other side of the bank belonged to Arkansas, which marked the beginning of the real unknown for me. Besides a family ski trip to Colorado in sixth grade, Tennessee was the furthest West I had ever been. I would enter into every new town a stranger, an outsider. I felt the tension between the ache of loneliness and the invigoration of freedom that comes with the realization that you are tied to nothing and no one in the space in which you find yourself. I found relief remembering there would be no expectations of who I was supposed to be, and maybe with the distraction of expectation out of the way, I might be able to find the true Emily somewhere in the unsettled space I embodied.

I avoided Beale Street on my way back to my car since the sour taste in my mouth from earlier still lingered. As I neared the entrance to the parking deck, a nickname for Memphis surfaced in my mind. When I first heard it from a friend I thought it was a little harsh, but after my asshole-ish first impression of the city, I felt it to be quite fitting. I started my car and said farewell to Memphis, Tennessee—*The Butt Crack of America.*

About an hour outside of Little Rock I saw that my fuel level was low, so I pulled off I-40 to find a gas station. As I stood there staring at the fuel screen with its rapidly changing numbers, my thoughts fell on the concept of time.

Before I left Boone, every second of my life felt pre-planned. Time was something that was always running ahead of me, and it seemed like I could never quite catch up to it. I defined myself by my constant doing, and I didn't know how to be still. I had been so caught up in the culture of performance and productivity, and trying to pour out of an empty cup for so long had left me at a new level of fatigue.

I noticed how different being at this gas station felt compared to the hundreds of times I had stood beside a gas pump in Boone. There was nothing to rush off to. I wasn't tapping my foot staring at the fuel gauge, hoping that I could make it speed up with my mind. I wasn't anxious about everything I had to get done that day. I did not feel annoyed at how inconvenient it was that I had to pull off the highway. I had no responsibilities to fulfill and no obligations to meet. There was much about traveling alone that I was uncertain of, but I was excited about the fact that each day I would wake up without being tied down to a plan or an expectation of someone else's desires.

I hoped that each new day on the road would slowly begin to fill my cup with life again. The constant anxiety in my chest which used to make me feel like I had electricity running through my veins had settled to a subtle pulse that I now only noticed occasionally. I no longer had chills from my never-ending to-do list always breathing down my neck. I didn't feel as dizzy from my racing thoughts that used to paralyze me. I had begun to feel the first touch of rest, and I craved more of it.

The last hour to Little Rock passed quickly. As I got off the interstate, I realized I hadn't thought much about how I would get ready for "bed" while I was sleeping in my car. Brushing your teeth outside is super normal when you are camping in the woods, but I didn't exactly know how one discreetly brushes one's teeth in a hotel parking lot without drawing attention. Plus, I really had to pee, which I also couldn't do in the hotel parking lot.

I decided to route to the Little Rock Walmart to do my business without getting questioned. I packed my toothbrush and toothpaste in a small bag I had in my car, and I walked in, hoping I looked like a casual shopper not about to get ready for bed in the bathroom.

A wave of relief washed over me when I saw that the bathroom stalls were empty. I peed quickly and washed my hands so that I could possibly squeeze in a brushing before someone walked in. Halfway through, when my toothpaste foam was like clown lipstick around the entire rim of my mouth, a young girl walked in. I gave a foamy smirk as I met eyes with her through the mirror, trying to give off the air that this was totally normal and socially acceptable. She raised a questioning brow but thankfully didn't say anything and went about her business.

This is definitely a first. I laughed to myself, spit, and rinsed quickly. I tidied my disheveled hair and scooted out the door.

Though I had never slept in my car before, finding a hotel parking lot and choosing a spot where I would make my bed for the night came naturally. I saw a lit-up sign for the Best Western Hotel, which was my least sketchy option. I chose a spot off to the side of the building, away from most of the parking lights. I hoped that I would not wake in a few hours to the blinding flashlight of a security guard telling me that I had to move.

Good thing I'll have a taser soon. I shook my head. *I can't believe mom is sending that thing to me.*

It was only a little after 9:00 p.m., but I was exhausted from five hours in the car. It was dark now, and I had little desire to fill my time with anything but sleep once I parked. I was too scared to open and close the door in fear that someone would see me and report me, so I crawled back from the driver's seat to my "bed" in the trunk. The exposed section of the foam mattress topper was just wide enough for my body to lay down, wedged between my cardboard box closet to my left, my gear box to my right, my food box toward the trunk door to the right of my feet, and the tents and sleeping pads to the left of my feet. I had my sleeping bag for warmth, but it was so hot that I didn't think I would need it. I thought about stripping to make the sticky heat more comfortable, but I figured a woman sleeping naked and alone in a dark parking lot would not attract the most desired of guests. I closed my eyes as the darkness settled around me.

Before I fell asleep, I had a crisis of not knowing what to do about the windows. I could either leave the windows cracked and risk bugs and peeping Toms, or I could leave them closed and risk oxygen deprivation. I chose the glorious option of oxygen deprivation. I hoped the air inside my car would continue to hold the appropriate amount of oxygen I needed to wake up in the morning.

To turn my thoughts away from all of the chance things that could go wrong and how scared I was of getting in trouble for doing something against the rules, I thought about what it might be like to stand in the Yosemite Valley or at the rim of the Grand Canyon in less than two weeks, gazing out into peaceful wilderness. I wondered what it might look like, what it might smell like, what it might feel like to be in the presence of so much space that you could never touch all of it in one lifetime. Somewhere in that expanse of wonder, my thoughts settled, and sleep came easily.

{4}

DOING THE SCARY THING

U PON WAKING, FOG FILLED MY EYES AND WINDOWS, AND
through the haze, my trunk bed reality slowly came back to
consciousness. I surprisingly slept without waking during the
night, and though I could not remember their details, my dreams were
light and happy. It was odd that I didn't have a nightmare. I occasionally had nights without them, but those nights were rare. I wondered if
the change in environment was already helping.

During the night it had become chillier because at some point I'd
pulled my sleeping bag up over me. Now I pulled it up tighter toward
my face, finding comfort in the silky cocoon. I couldn't help but smile
at how normal it felt to wake up like this. Though it was new, it somehow felt familiar, as if some part of me that had been dormant for a
lifetime was awakening.

I don't know how long I laid there staring at the ceiling, soaking
up whatever this far-off sense of belonging was, but it was not long before the gurgling sensation of hunger brought me back into my body.
I shook myself out of my sleeping bag so I could reach toward my feet
to get something out of my food box. My small eight-ounce portioned
bags of granola were still lined in two neat rows: one cinnamon raisin
row, and one chocolate row.

Before I left Boone I made a gallon of each because I knew granola would keep well and wouldn't require any preparation. I'd never made granola before. All the prep work and time it took to make two gallons of it felt like it had aged me a year, but from what I could tell it turned out alright. It wasn't too heavy, and it was high in protein and healthy fats from the nuts, seeds, and coconut oil. There was plenty of sugar from the honey to help me stay energized on hikes, or to help me wake up when I felt like I was going to fall asleep at the wheel, but I hoped I wouldn't have to use it for the latter. I plucked a bag of the chocolate kind, flipped over on my stomach, and nibbled while I figured out where I would go from my hotel parking spot home.

I remembered my dad had mentioned some mountain in the Little Rock area that I could hike if I ended up here. Although I knew that one hike would not reverse my sedentary neglect of my cardiovascular health throughout the past few months, I figured hiking at least once before I showed up in California to hike at high altitude while carrying thirty pounds on my back might make me feel slightly less unprepared. Thankfully there was only one mountain in Little Rock, so my vague Google search took me directly to the website of Pinnacle Mountain State Park. I read that there were two trails that reached the summit— one strenuous and one easy. Strenuous sounded California-like.

I hadn't planned out what I would tell someone if the legality of my sleeping habits was questioned, but thankfully it was still before eight o'clock, so there was no one in the parking lot to inquire about my disheveled emergence from the depths of my trunk. As I walked to the driver's seat, I shook the granola crumbs out from their hiding place in my bra (I'd never been good at eating while laying down). I said farewell to my first parking spot home and routed to Pinnacle Mountain.

Large oaks loomed over the roads inside the state park. Their crowded branches and deep green leaves left shadows dancing along my face as I drove the winding curves. Simply being in the midst of lush greenery again was a breath of air that my soul needed, dusty from having spent so much time in concrete cities and on interstates the past couple days.

I was giddy to be back in the woods. The woods were my place of solace since I couldn't find rest and belonging in the Church anymore. There was something about the vastness of a forest that provided a sense of safety for me. Being in the woods reminded me the earth is constantly moving and adjusting to chaos and complexity, is constantly bursting with life and decay, birth and death in every space, and it would only make sense that we, as part of the earth, would carry that in us as humans as well. Something in me was dying, and I knew I had to let it so that some sort of life would be able to grow from it.

The consistency of stillness in the midst of the chaos of food chains and the dance of predator and prey in the wild provided stability when I felt like everything I had known to be true was imploding inside of me. No matter what happened in my small human world, the woods would go on doing their thing like they have for millions of years, and something about that was comforting.

The woods became what I wished church would be. The woods never ran out of space to hold me and all of my anxieties and pain and questions. The God I had been told about in church was supposed to be that big, but I found the opposite when I was inside church walls. I found that wild spaces were the only ones where I could let my guard down anymore. I could take the mask off and be my full self. I could just exist and sit in my unknowing without the need for language. In church, I needed to know what I believed and why, with concrete language and Biblical evidence to back it up, and for someone whose foundation of identity was now mush, I needed the freedom to just be.

Alone in the woods, there was no expectation for me to be anything for anyone, and I didn't have to have answers. The trees didn't need me to be anything for them. The birds knew who they were without me explaining it to them. The mushrooms modeled the beauty of finding life in decay without me needing to remind them. There was no need for me to have it together and know what I believed. There was no need to argue about theology or the afterlife or salvation. Divinity was everywhere, in all and through all, and I didn't understand why it had to be any more complicated than that.

The outdoors were the only source of inspiration I had left. The only flutters of healing I had caught a glimpse of since Cam and leaving the Church had all happened outside. I knew that if I was going to heal, and if I was going to somehow find space to hold a semi-concrete idea of God again, it would probably start in a sanctuary made of dirt, under a canopy of oaks and evergreens, through the harmonious praises of birdsong.

I found the trailhead to the summit, and the sight of only two other cars in the parking lot was pleasing for someone desperately wanting to avoid other humans. The early morning breeze brushed cool against my face as I searched through my gear box to locate my hiking boots. I heaved them up from the bottom, reminded of how heavy and bulky they were.

I bought this pair of stiff, high-ankle, brown leather boots with waterproof lining and rugged traction to help me survive the ice and snow of Boone winters. However, even though I knew they would probably be too heavy and stiff for summer hiking, new boots were not in the trip budget (generated by three minimum wage jobs squeezed between classes). The boots weren't terribly uncomfortable per se, but they were not made to bend with the steep inclines and ninety-degree temperatures that awaited me. I could only hope that I didn't have a trail of blisters waiting for me in the near future, but good thing I remembered my blister Band-Aids.

My fingers danced the memorized movements that tucked my thin blonde hair into the tight French braid down my back, a look I wore so often those days. I laced up my boots quickly, antsy to get on the trail and sweat a little after sitting for hours in my car. I heaved my left boot onto my bumper, and while I hooked my laces through the last eyelet, the little patch of my grainy blue ten-pound dumbbells showing through the pile of tents caught my eye.

I don't remember what logic led me to decide that two ten-pound dumbbells should make the limited list of necessities for this trip. It had been ages since I had done a bicep curl, and choosing to revamp one's workout routine in random parking lots across the country doesn't seem sensible to me now. I guess I was consumed with preventing the continued "loss" of my firm body that had been melting away by the emotional eating I used to combat my grief. I ended up finding a great way to put them to use, or so I thought.

I wonder if I could carry those in my backpack to make it heavier. I'm going to have to carry at least thirty pounds when we backpack into the Grand Canyon, and probably in Yosemite too if we find a permit, so it would be good training, right? Like adding weight when you do squats?

Having full confidence in my brilliant idea, I tucked not one, but both ten-pound dumbbells in the bottom of my small day pack. I threw my full water bottle on top of them for extra weight, closed the car door, and walked to the trailhead. I started off down the trail, my head high and breathing in the bliss of being in the woods again.

However, not long after I began tromping down the trail, amateur backpacker me realized that not only was the weight distribution in my pack extremely disproportionate, for there was a dense twenty-plus pounds resting at the very bottom of my pack with nothing to counter its awkward force on my shoulders, but the two bottom heads of the dumbbells also felt like they were carving out holes in my lower back. I could feel the friction on either side of my spine with every step. I figured the wise thing to do would be to walk back to the car and ditch them, but I was already about two hundred yards down the trail, and thinking about walking back to my car was not an appealing option to me. It was already getting hot, and I just wanted to keep walking. I shoved the warning signs aside and continued my trek with my oddly shaped backpack.

My little red and black day pack had been through so much. At this point, every memory associated with it had been with Cam. It used to be his, and at some point along the way of taking trips and sharing backpacks and having our stuff divided and lost somewhere between our parents' houses, either he gave it to me, or I just claimed it.

It was old and battered. The pad on the back had lost its stitching, so it would fall out if I was not too careful. I could only zip it one direction, or the zipper track would get messed up, and everything inside would fall out. Its smell reflected its age just as much as its tattered appearance, for gallons of sweat had leaked from my pores into its pores over the past four and a half years. We were family, a part of each other in that weird way that you can get attached to gear from significant trips, even though regarding functional use, the pack was not that practical. Its one large pocket created a soup of my belongings, where it was guaranteed that I could always find every single item except the particular one I was looking for at that moment. However, despite its fray, its smell, and its impracticality, it had been my companion for so long. It was home for me. I feared that if I gave up all of the parts of me woven into the memories associated with it, there would be nothing left.

Once I was stable enough to drive home after my last conversation with Cam, I thought about burning the pack, along with everything else associated with Cam, but every time I tried, I ended up not being able to go through with it. It held too many good memories inside, and even in all of my anger, I couldn't bring myself to destroy it. Burning it would require being at a place where I could fully let it all go, and though I longed to be, I wasn't there yet.

My grief didn't make any sense to me, but I was learning that it went far and wide, and the ways it manifested were unpredictable. Though it was easy to judge myself for being overly sensitive, as Cam had told me hundreds of times, or to feel shame for being attached to a dumb backpack associated with someone who had hurt me, I tried to find grace for myself. I felt like everything in my life was attached to Cam, and I would slowly have to replace the Cam-associated memories with me-associated memories. This was the first trip I had taken without him in almost five years. His absence was ever-present in my mind, but it was time to make memories with the pack alone. It felt like a small way to begin to reclaim my life.

I continued down the winding path woven with knobby roots and bright moss. The recent rain created a sweet earthy aroma that soothed me. I looked around, admiring the various trees as I passed them, their roots intertwined, a vast system of interconnectedness, a community that communicated by pH levels and hydration content, a family that spoke a language that I did not understand but was somehow connected to. I extended my arm and let my skin brush the bark of the closest trees as I walked. The smoothness of my fingers met their sandpaper trunks, shaking hands with all of the age and time and death and life they'd experienced as they gained their rings.

I followed the trail to what seemed like a dead end. Just before I turned around to head back and see if I missed a trail marker, I saw a faint arrow painted on an old, weathered piece of wood pointing up a wall of boulders.

Seriously? I looked up the cascade of boulders, and from where I was standing, I couldn't see the top. I definitely drove into Little Rock with outdoor superiority about there being a "strenuous" trail on a baby hill that I figured was only called a mountain because all of the land around it was completely flat, but I had to tip my hat.

I began the climb alone, but dozens of one-legged squats and lots of butt sweat later, a guy who looked to be in his late twenties was suddenly by my side. He sent me a peppy 'hello' as he passed. Red faced, sweaty, and a little dizzy, I choked out a quick 'hi' and gave him a smile that probably looked more like I was grimacing in pain.

Oh don't mind me, I'm just drenched in sweat and may pass out at any moment. I felt self-conscious. He bounded up the wall of rocks like it was nothing. His feet danced along the crevasses as if they knew the most efficient way to the top from memory. I watched, huffing and puffing, in adoration, hoping that by the end of this trip I could bound up a mountain without feeling like I was going to have a heart attack. He was a mountain goat, with agility and lightness in every step and jump, and I was an elephant, stumbling over my trunk, barely able to pick my giant thighs high enough to reach the rock above me.

I crawled up the last step to the summit. My hair was dripping with sweat. My legs were burning, and the skin on my back felt like it had been scrubbed with steel wool for an hour from the dumbbells.

Okay, Pinnacle Mountain, I take it back. You can keep your strenuous trail title.

I walked up behind the guy that passed me earlier on the trail, looking for a rock to sit on.

"Do you come here often?" The mountain goat's voice caught me off guard.

"Oh. Um, no. I'm not from here actually. I was just passing through and decided to stop and hike. Do you?"

"Yeah I try to come here once or twice a week. It keeps me in shape, and it gives me a way to get out of the city."

That explains how you just sprinted up that wall of rocks. "Yeah I'm pretty impressed. I didn't expect it to get so steep. It gained quite a bit of elevation all of the sudden, and this view is beautiful." I looked out across the valley. Rivers and lakes were intertwined throughout the sea of summer green. My body felt invigorated, giddy on endorphins.

"My name's Stephen," he said as he walked over and extended his hand. Startled, I extended mine, clammy and hot, to his.

"Emily."

"Would you like a picture of you with the view in the background?" he asked.

"Oh, that's nice of you to offer," I extended, though I wasn't sure that my sweaty hair slicked back in my braid would be the most glorious first hiking picture of my grand adventure, but at least it would be telling the truth. I felt bad giving an excuse, so I told him that would be great.

I handed him the little orange camera my mom had bought as a gift that past Christmas. It was a water-proof, shatter-proof, break-proof camera that surprisingly took fairly good quality photos for its small size. I turned and walked toward some boulders on the edge of the cliff, hoping that he wouldn't ask what the strange lumps were at the bottom of my pack. I posed, holding the straps of my backpack. My giant hiking boots extended like clown feet from my thin shins, and my small eyes hid in the shadows between my round cheeks and strong brow bones like they have in any photo ever taken of me.

"Thanks," I offered as I walked over to retrieve my camera. "Do you happen to know if there's another way down? I mean, I'm fine with going the way I came I guess, but my knees would probably be more grateful for something a little less," I paused, "harsh."

"Oh yeah, you can go down this way; I'll show you." He pointed me in the direction of the trail markers on the other side of the summit from where we were. "This trail is a little bit longer than the way we came up, but it's really nice and enjoyable. I'm also going down this way, and you're welcome to walk with me."

"Oh, yeah, okay," I hesitantly agreed, feeling my male suspicion triggered, but he seemed harmless. As we descended, I found out that Stephen was in pharmaceutical school in Little Rock, but his real dream was to study herbal and natural medicine in Asia.

"Do you not like pharmaceutical school?" I asked.

"It's not that I don't like it; I just support the philosophy of naturopathy more so." He sighed. "I'm in pharmacy school because it's supposed to be a stable career, not because I necessarily agree with everything about it. It doesn't really give me life or inspire me."

"So what's keeping you from quitting?" I asked.

"Because going to Asia is scary. There's no guarantee that it will lead me to success, and there's no guarantee that I would make money if I became a naturopathic doctor. My parents wouldn't support it, and they've contributed a lot financially to my schooling, so I would feel bad leaving. If I become a pharmacist, I'll always have a job, and I'll be able to support myself."

"Is it successful to have money and comfort but hate your life?" I asked him.

Stephen paused and took a deep breath. I was surprised by how much I needed to hear that question too. "You're right," he began. "On paper I agree that financial success doesn't mean anything when you're not happy and not doing something you enjoy. I just don't know how to up and leave without knowing where going to Asia will lead me, if it will lead me anywhere at all. I know I'll be unhappy if I stay with pharmacy school, and I think I'll regret it if I don't make it to Asia, but I already have so much student debt…" he trailed off.

"I feel ya there," I agreed. "Debt is a huge part of my questioning if I should even go back to school next spring. Debt has become the norm in our country, and I don't get it. I've heard people justify their ridiculous loans by saying everyone else is in debt, as if somehow the fact that everyone spends money they don't have makes it okay and normal. I don't get why students aren't encouraged to question it before they sign up for four years of school straight out of high school, forking out thousands of dollars in hope that the random major they chose at eighteen is going to lead them to something they like doing, much less to success and happiness."

"So true," Stephen agreed.

"I for sure didn't think twice about going out of state for college when I was eighteen," I continued, "even with the loans for out of state tuition being four times as much as in-state. But now, already having over twenty thousand dollars in debt, I'm like, do I really want to double that without knowing what I want to do for a career and be trapped in the system when I graduate because I can't afford to do anything but work full time right away?"

Stephen nodded. "Yeah I didn't think twice about loans either, and now I feel stuck."

"It sucks! A bunch of my friends are there too. I've heard so many people say they'll take a year off to do the non-school things they've been waiting to do after finishing their bachelor's degree, but often they have to go straight into work with little vacation time because they can't afford their loan payments once they graduate. But what I'm wondering is why not wait to go to college until people have done what they want to do outside of their career pursuits? Saving money to travel is way easier to do without debt, even working a low-wage job, as long as you live pretty simply and don't buy excess things you don't absolutely need."

"Jeez. You said you're twenty, right? I wasn't even close to thinking like this when I was your age. Are you not worried about not going back to college?" Stephen asked.

"There's a negative cultural stigma about dropping out which I'm a little worried about, and people for some reason look down on folks working minimum-wage jobs, but why would I not delay finishing college until I'm ready to make the investment in something I care about, instead of doing it just to get the piece of paper that society tells me I have to have by twenty-two in order to have a chance of success? I think for some people, taking time off of school, or not going to college in the first place, is the right choice if that is where the life is for them. And in your case, leaving pharmaceutical school might be the right choice if naturopathic medicine is where the life is for you. Life is too short to not do what you care about, even if there's no chance of it ever making you six figures." I shrugged.

Stephen chuckled. "You hit the nail right on the head. I really needed to hear that," he confessed. "Where did all of these thoughts come from for you?"

"I just never felt like I was supposed to go to college," I continued, "but I went anyway because that was what was expected of me. People thought that just because I had a 4.0 GPA that I had to go to an expensive, fancy school to reflect my talents or whatever. But it's hard to stay in something when you constantly wonder what it would be like to do the scary thing you're being nudged to do. I think sometimes doing the scary thing is the only right next step, even when it's risky, even when there's no guarantee that the step will lead you in the direction of the monetary and material success that capitalism tells us we need to be seeking. That's what taking time off school and going on this trip feels like for me."

"I love the way you phrased that—when doing the scary thing is the only right next step," Stephen repeated contemplatively.

"What do you feel in your gut, Stephen?"

He sighed. "That I'm supposed to do this."

"Sounds like a nudge," I shrugged and grinned.

"A nudge?" He looked confused.

"Yeah," I nodded, "a nudge that points us to the next thing, the feeling we get deep in our bones when truth comes to us, the whispers in our gut that guide us, the gleam in the distance that draws us to what's next. I've heard people describe it in a lot of ways, but I think they're all pointing to the same thing."

"Okay, yeah. I got you. I guess it feels kind of like that. I don't know how to just go for it, though."

"I don't know either, but what I do know is that not following the nudges is how we end up becoming the very versions of ourselves we've always feared." I raised my eyebrows expectantly. "Worst case scenario, you go to Asia and decide to come home and stay in pharmaceutical school, but then you won't have to sit in torment forever wondering what it would be like to leave like you are now. I think so many people are starting to wake up to the fact that the institutions and systems we've bought into our whole lives aren't as straightforward and faultless as we thought. It looks different for all of us, but like I said, eventually we have to give ourselves the gift of trying the scary thing so that we don't have to be tormented forever by the what if's…" I trailed off.

"I think I have a lot to think about," Stephen admitted, and we both laughed.

I noticed the trail had changed from the gradual, gravel-covered incline to a slow rolling wooded trail that wound its way along the circumference of the base of the mountain. We seemed to have walked for quite some time, and our conversation was helpful because it distracted me from the bruises the dumbbells continued to pound in my back. It was refreshing to have a conversation that mattered with someone who didn't think I was crazy for questioning the supposed one-right-way-to-be-an-adult-in-America that so many people blindly buy into. Stephen had no preconceived notions of who I was or wasn't, and it was nice not feeling like I needed to edit or filter or apologize for what I was saying. I just wished that it was easier to be that genuine with my family and friends who I thought would never understand if I tried to be honest.

The concrete of the parking lot began to show itself through the trees in front of us.

"Well, Emily, it was nice to meet you, and I wish you the best of luck on your travels. I'm so glad I ran into you today. Thanks for challenging me."

"Likewise! And thanks for the guidance down. My knees are thankful. I hope you get to Asia one day."

"I will try my best." He smiled, waved, and turned his back on me as he made his way to his car.

I hid my grimace while I adjusted the position of the weights in my pack from behind and waved goodbye when Stephen looked back at me once more before he got in his car. I hurried over to my car so I could take the dumbbells out of my pack.

Yeah, Em, definitely not your brightest idea. I shook my head and laughed to myself as I placed the two weights back in their home under the tents. I took my hiking boots and socks off, and I changed out of my sweat-drenched clothes right next to my car. I did a quick hop to yank my fresh pair of underwear up to my waist quickly, hoping no one was in the woods behind me to see my bare cheeks. I finished dressing and laid my salty clothes on the hood of my car in the sun to dry while I fixed a quick lunch.

I took a can of tuna, a handful of nuts, an apple, and one of my mini bags of granola and hobbled barefoot through the gravel to a picnic table in the grass across the parking lot. I chewed slowly. I closed my eyes and turned my face toward the sun, rubbing my sore backside as the breeze cooled my body, the drips of sweat down my neck becoming less frequent. I breathed deeply, grateful for such a glorious morning.

I don't know who to thank anymore for weather like this. If not God, do I just thank the Universe? Are they the same thing?

As I sat there soaking in the bliss of sunshine on my skin, I tried to give myself a pep-talk in order to feel excited about driving for the six hours between Little Rock and Waco. I felt sleepy, but a road trip where you are the only one in the car means that you are responsible for 100% of the driving, and car naps don't happen without the likely possibility of death. The longest solo drive I had ever taken before leaving Boone was only four and a half hours, so anything above that felt daunting. Since leaving I had only driven around twelve hours and 690 miles total, which meant roughly 1700 miles and twenty-four hours of driving as the crow flies still stood between me and the Pacific Coast. I was only one-third of the way across the country, and I was already feeling a lack of excitement about interstates.

I did the math, and I was pulling an average of five to seven hours a day on the road, and in order to stick to my plan to reach Temecula, a small town outside of San Diego, in five days I had to keep up an average of six hours on the road every day. A lot of time in the car. A lot of sitting. A lot of time to be in my head. A lot of time for more things to arise that I didn't want to look at.

The only requirement left to satisfy before my departure was an empty bladder, so I snuck behind a tree and completed the awkward sequence of events that are involved in a female peeing in the woods. First you have to decide which approach you are going to take, which typically depends on the style of pants you are wearing. If you are wearing pants or leggings, you have no option but to completely strip, pulling your pants and underwear down to your ankles, squatting close to the ground, and peeing between your legs as you pull your pants forward and out of the way, with all cracks and orifices 100% exposed to any bystanders. You are probably going to soak the sides of your shoes and calves with a hefty amount of urine splatter bouncing back from the ground, and then there is always the chance you will have to duck walk in some direction while peeing because somehow the pee stream always seems to run in the exact direction of one or both of your feet.

The other approach requires a little more skill but is extremely convenient to use when you are wearing loose shorts, and if you are in the presence of more people or less trees to hide behind. If you can get the angle right, you can literally just pull your shorts to one side of your crotch and pee directly down, kind of like they teach you to pee when you're wearing a one-piece bathing suit so you can avoid the extremely frustrating task of putting a curled up, wet one-piece back on again. No one can even tell you're peeing unless they see the stream of liquid falling down. No exposing orifices, no shaking legs, no hurting knees, no splatter on your shoes, just standing urination bliss.

There are apparently these plastic penis-looking pee funnels you can buy to stick up between your legs. They are supposed to calmly transport your urine through a tube that will deposit it safely away from your body, but buying one always felt like cheating. The challenge of being stealthy and clean was more exciting to me. This time I did my business using the stealth-mode-pull-your-shorts-to-the-side method, and I walked away with dry shoes and ankles, feeling emptied and ac-complished. I got in my car and continued on to Waco.

Oh shit. The taser. My stomach dropped as Isaac and I walked into his apartment building in the center of downtown Waco after a cordial dinner of small talk over enchiladas. The entire ride up the elevator, Isaac was saying something to me about his work, but all I could think about was the box that was chilling somewhere in his apartment con-cealing the fact that it contained a weapon.

We walked in the door and there it was, a shipping box on the counter, addressed to me.

"Well, this is my place," Isaac gestured. "You'll sleep here on the couch in the living room. Hope that's alright. And there's the shower. I left a towel in there for you."

"Oh perfect, I'll definitely be needing that," I sighed, relieved to wash away the grime of the day.

"Oh," he exclaimed, "and here's your box! Came in yesterday." He grabbed the box and gave it to me.

"Oh right! Thanks so much," I grinned, trying to hide the panic in my throat. *What do I tell him? Do I open it? Do I casually tell the truth as a joke and hope he laughs about it too and doesn't think I'm crazy? What if he kicks me out? Do I lie? What would I even say it was if I did lie?*

"So it's from your mom? You said it was something you forgot you needed for your trip?" Isaac questioned, and I was sure he knew somehow and was just trying to get me to confess.

"Yeah," I said nonchalantly. "She is super worried about me, and when she found out I forgot my flashlight, she wanted to send me my dad's that works even in pouring rain or something. I told her I could just buy a new one, but she swore that I needed this one. She likes to feel helpful," I emphasized, "and this was a way of letting her do that I guess."

Good save. I took a deep breath, hoping I was out of the danger of exposure. *It is technically a flashlight. So even if he asks to see it there is a chance that I could open it and show him without him realizing that it is actually a stun gun disguised as a flashlight.*

"Oh, gotcha," Isaac trailed off, seemingly uninterested. "So, what will you do tomorrow?" *Oh, thank God he changed the subject.* "Are you staying around here, or will you leave? Just asking because I go to work pretty early, and I don't have a spare key, so once you leave and lock the door, you'll be out for the day until I get back from work."

"No worries," I assured him. "As far as tomorrow goes, I've heard Austin is a cool town, so I thought about driving there for the day. It's not far from here right?"

"Nah, about an hour and a half or so without traffic," Isaac guessed. "I've only been once but it has a good food scene and interesting people for sure."

"Exactly what I need," I joked.

"Well if you're just going to Austin and you don't have a place to stay tomorrow night, I don't care if you come back and stay here again if you want to just make a day trip out of it," Isaac offered.

"Oh I didn't think about that," I admitted. "Is it okay if I play it by ear? I'll probably take all of my stuff with me in case I want to stay out in Austin somewhere, but I can let you know what I decide tomorrow."

"Yeah that works with me," Isaac replied. "Just let me know when you know. I'm easy." He paused. "Well I'm going to head to bed 'cause I gotta get up early, but make yourself at home, and there's some granola bars in the pantry if you want one in the morning for breakfast."

"Oh sweet, thank you! And thanks so much again for letting me crash."

"No problem. Happy to give you one less night sleeping in your trunk. I couldn't do it," Isaac laughed.

"It's not that bad actually! I slept great last night," I assured him. "Sleep well."

"Goodnight." Isaac closed his bedroom door, and I stared at the shipping box.

There is no way I am opening that thing in here. I'll open it tomorrow, in my car, when I am certain no one is looking. I tucked the shipping box safely behind my bag and laid down to sleep, wondering what tomorrow would bring.

{5}

SYNCHRONICITY OR NOT

I WOKE UP THE MORNING OF JULY 7TH IN ISAAC'S APART-
ment. My body was tight and sore from my hike and dumbbell
bruises. Isaac had already left the apartment to go to work, and
though he offered a granola bar, I felt bad taking from what turned out
to be the only box of food in his entire pantry. I went out to my car to
eat breakfast, grab a change of clothes, and open my weapon box.

I had parked right on the street downtown, and it was 9:00 on a
Tuesday morning, so traffic passed frequently as I sat, or some might
say crouched, in my trunk to reach my food box. I dug past cans of
black beans, tuna, and my giant tub of GORP (good ol' raisins and
peanuts) to find a chocolate chip protein bar. Protein bars were more
expensive than my granola per serving, so I only brought enough to
provide an alternate breakfast when I was tired of granola. Seeing as it
was only day two and I already cracked into the stash, I figured they
might not last as long as I hoped. As I took my first bite, I felt the pang
of muscle soreness in my jaw. I rubbed my cheek.

Jeez did I get punched in my sleep? At first I didn't know what it
could have been from, but then I remembered opening my first bag
of chocolate granola yesterday. I used a "high protein toasted quinoa"
granola recipe from one of those froufrou websites, and I must have

missed the step that made the raw quinoa edible. That stuff was so hard I felt like I was grinding pebbles with my teeth. I realized my jaw muscles were sore from the previous day's excessive grinding.

I expected to have to get my legs in shape to fit in with the out-doorsy hiker crew, but I did not know I would also have to train my jaw muscles to put up with the crunchy and chewy road-and-trail-life diet.

Maybe this is why people who spend a lot of time outside and love nature get nicknamed 'granola.' This stuff is no joke—perhaps it is a stereotype for a reason. Knowing I still had about thirty servings of that quinoa granola left to eat, I had plenty of jaw workouts ahead of me to whip my muscles into "granola" shape.

Okay, now to figure out this stun gun box. I grabbed the small pocket knife I had packed in my hiking backpack and started to cut through the tape. I opened the box to find an unimpressive flashlight laying in the box with a USB charging cable.

Dang, this thing does look super casual. And it's not a taser. Definitely a stun gun. But maybe I'll keep calling it a taser for fun. I took it out of the box. It was in its carrying case, which was just a little sleeve with a flap that velcroed over the top of the flashlight head to keep it in place. I carefully pulled off the top flap, holding the case the same way one might hold a newborn infant for the first time—gently, awkwardly, scared to drop it or set it off.

I looked around to make sure no one was looking, as one setting off a stun gun at 9:00 a.m. might have been suspicious. I didn't see anyone, but I was just sitting on the bumper of my trunk. I figured sitting in a normal place for a human to be in their car, like the driver's seat, might be stealthier and draw less attention. I walked around to the front seat, still holding the taser awkwardly.

Once I was inside with the door closed, I took a closer look. There really were no obvious signs that it was anything but a flashlight.

It probably would have been a good idea to ask mom how to work this thing when I was on the phone with her, but it's probably pretty self-explanatory, right? I turned it over in my hands.

There was one normal-looking flashlight switch on one side, where you slide the button up with your thumb to turn it on, and there was a small round button that protruded on the opposite side. It looked like you pressed that one down, and I assumed that was what initiated the electricity. I decided to try what looked like the flashlight switch first, but as far as I knew it could be tricky and actually be the taser button. I held it out away from me again. I took a deep breath.

One, two, three. I pushed up on the switch.

Okay. I took a deep breath. *That one is the flashlight.* The beam shined up to my ceiling, letting off a blue tinted, bright light. Another deep breath. *Now, the taser button.*

I held it out away from me again, and I could feel my heart pounding. I had never held one of these things before, and I really didn't know how powerful it would be, if it would make any noise, or if I would feel it doing anything while it was sending out electricity to the end surface of the flashlight.

One, two, three. I pressed the button.

Nothing happened. My heart was still pounding.

Hmm. Maybe I have to charge it first? I turned the stun gun back over in my hands carefully, looking for any other hidden buttons or switches. *Oh. Of course. The safety.* I didn't think about the fact that a handheld weapon probably has a safety switch on it. The stun gun's safety switch was on the butt of the flashlight, tucked inside a plastic rim so it wasn't as noticeable. The safety was in the on position, which was preventing anything from happening when I pressed the button.

I switched the safety to the off position, with the flashlight end sticking out away from me so that there wasn't any chance of me shocking myself like my mom did. I slid my hand into position, with my thumb over the button to engage the shock, extending my arm out away from me again. I felt like I was Harry Potter about to cast a spell. I took another deep breath.

I can't believe I'm doing this. One, two, three.

"*HOLY SHIT!*" I screamed loudly before I could even realize what happened. I did not shock myself electrically, but I was definitely shocked in that I was not expecting the stun gun to be so loud and violent. My heart rate had sky-rocketed. In the enclosed space of the car, it literally sounded like there were fire-crackers going off in my ears. I was so startled by the noise that I let go of the button almost right away, and I wasn't able to pay much attention to how it actually worked. I wondered if I could actually feel the electricity pulsing as it went off.

Now that I knew what to expect, I pointed the flashlight end away from me again, watching the end this time so I could see if the shock was visible.

This thing is no joke. I braced myself. I held the button down again for a brief moment, watching the end. As I held the button down I could see an electrical spark being sent out from one side of the metal plate on the flashlight end, emitting a visible bluish charge with every rapid succession of "POP POP POP POP POP."

My mother is crazy! A salesperson showed her how this thing worked and she actually WANTED to send it to her daughter? Oh my goodness. I'm so glad I didn't show Isaac. He would have thought I was a psychopath. And mom said she shocked herself with it?! I can't believe that. This thing looks lethal!

I shook my head. I love my mother, but in this moment I thought she was actually insane. However, I didn't automatically throw it in a trash bin, so maybe she was not the only insane one.

I made sure I turned the safety switch back on, and just to double-check I pressed the stun gun button again. Nothing. The safety was working, so I didn't have to fear accidentally shocking myself, for now.

I figured if I was going to drive across the country alone with a newly acquired taser in my car, I might as well keep it somewhere where it could potentially be made useful if necessary. I carefully tucked it back in its carrying case and hung it in the organizer behind my seat where I could reach it, though I wasn't expecting to need to. I set out on this trip to find a new side of myself. Emily Dobberstein carrying a stun-gun-flashlight was definitely a new side, and I couldn't tell yet whether that side felt more empowered or more anxiety-ridden with the taser opposed to without.

After running up to grab my last couple things from Isaac's apartment, I drove to find a place to grab a cup of coffee before heading to Austin.

"I swear, the Ethiopian pour-over is the best thing we have in-house right now. It has notes of jasmine and bergamot, like all of the best parts about a floral cup of tea but with the richness and depth that comes with an amazing cup of coffee," the barista emphasized, seeming like he was trying to impress me. He held a certain flirty kind of eye contact with me that I wasn't ready to hold. "I might even give you a traveler's discount." He raised his eyebrows.

"How do you know I'm traveling? You have secret eyes on the town or something?" I tried to ask playfully.

"This town isn't very big, and I haven't seen you before, and I don't think I would forget it if I had." He flashed his too-perfect smile. "So did I convince you?"

"About what?" I asked, confused.

"The coffee, silly," he joked.

"Oh. Right. Uh. Sure. Yeah. Why not," I stammered.

"Sweet! Comin' right up. I'll bring it over to you."

I gave him a quick thanks and turned to find a table. I don't know why I was so flustered. I didn't even like floral coffee, but the barista's forwardness made me feel awkward, and I wanted to end it quickly. It was roasting outside, so to stay cool I took a seat inside at a high-top in the corner to write and try to dissipate the fog of blended emotions floating around inside of me.

"Here you go," the barista startled me from a daze. "I took fifty cents off your order. Just pay when you leave." I said thanks, and he winked before turning away.

I still felt the lingering tension after my attempt at flirting back felt so unnatural and forced, like I was shaking dust off of something I hadn't picked up in years. The tension was concentrated in my shoulders, a heaviness that came uninvited and out of nowhere. It felt like I was cheating on an idea in my head. I didn't know how to identify it then, but I think what I was feeling was shame. Even though it had been over two months since I last saw or talked to Cam, I still had not managed to break the blind loyalty I'd subconsciously pledged to our relationship. Flirting with the barista somehow felt more like cheating, even though I was now free and single. I felt myself acting as if it was still my responsibility to protect a relationship that would never be reality again.

However, I had noticed other men again in the past weeks in brief moments, but it was almost in an equally extreme, unhealthy way. I would catch myself walking into a room and immediately scanning every man in the room, as if I was searching for the ideal. I wanted to see that one guy, if it wasn't Cam, who was supposed to come rescue me and make all of my dreams come true and wash away all of my pain.

The Christian culture I experienced often put extreme pressure on marriage. Marriage was presented as the ultimatum of adulthood, as if once you get married, all of your problems are solved and life gets easy, so long as you "saved yourself" for marriage, in other words, you remained pure by not having premarital sex. I watched it in myself, and I watched it in other girls I knew within Christian contexts. It showed up in how we talked about dating, in the paralysis we felt by the pressure to know if a guy was "the one" before we even started dating him. It was apparent in how we talked about guys in general, as if they held some secret answer to life that we didn't have within ourselves. It was obvious in our conversations about our dream husbands with our strict checklists and requirements. And secretly, under the surface, one could find hints of it in how we would quietly envy any woman we knew who had found a good, *Godly* man who was wooing her in the captivating way we had always been told about.

Relationships quickly become toxic when you lay all your unmet expectations at the feet of the marriage idol. I saw myself and other Christian women ripped out of the present into some supposed romanticized future, living there, longing for the day that our husbands would come along and scoop us up out of everything about our lives that was hard and dissolve all of our doubts and insecurities, as if we were powerless to do that on our own. We believed that our lives would not be fully meaningful until we found the perfect guy and got married to him, as if singleness meant something was wrong with us, as if we would never be totally fulfilled until we were married, as if marriage was the thing that would finally make us whole.

Marriage was my number one goal, and I diverted all of my happiness and joy to someone else in pursuit of it. I gave Cam power over my joy, and once he was gone I found myself already projecting that expectation that I would be rescued on to every new guy that I saw or met.

I was still enacting this story when I walked into the shop. I scanned every seat as if somehow I would just make eye contact with someone and know they were the one who was going to make me whole again. This time, I noticed myself searching for it in the barista's blue eyes. And the next day it would probably be someone different. A stranger sitting in a park. *Are you the one?* The guy pumping his gas next to me. *Are you the one?* The person hiking on the trail in front of me. *Are you my husband?*

"You like the pour-over?" The barista called loudly from the counter. There were only a few other people in the shop, and they didn't seem to notice or mind.

"Yep!" I held up my mug like a toast, smiled, and forced down another sip of coffee while he watched, pretending to enjoy it without making a facial expression that said otherwise. The barista nodded his approval and went back to work. I grabbed my journal from my bag and set it on the high-top. The sun shone through the window and warmed my arm as I wrote.

07/07/15, Day 5 -

I find myself walking into this coffee shop looking for someone to save me. Is this a defense mechanism in response to the break-up? Am I just trying to find someone to fill this void I feel? Or is this the manifestation of me being sucked into the lie that many young people in Christian culture are nurtured to believe, that marriage is this amazing thing that will fix all of your problems and wash all of your pain away? That if I just meet "the one," I'll be all set for happiness and success? That as a woman, I need a man to rescue me?

I think it is a little bit of both. I catch myself thinking things like "Hey, I'm on this once-in-a-lifetime life-changing trip. Meeting my new soulmate somewhere along the way just makes the most sense, right?"

But when I pursue affirmation from love or marriage as an expectation to fill this lack I feel in myself, it will only continue to rob me of joy. I want to learn that other people will never make me whole. I have to start with learning how to fill the void by loving myself. I must turn my attention to the stillness inside of me, and let that guide me. I must let the lack be my teacher, not the thing I search to fill with a drug-like something or someone, like I did for so many years with Cam. I have to let the lack point the way.

No one is going to do the work for me. No one is going to start my process of healing for me. Healing is hard and slow, and it is up to me to open myself up to the possibility of it and stop trying to find a quick fix to fill the hole, stop the bleeding, and numb the pain.

I continued to write and reflect on the first few days of the trip, thinking about what it might look like to start to heal from all of the mess I didn't know what to do with. In the past, when I sought healing, I would just pray for it, and have faith that God would make it happen. I didn't ever do much to pursue healing on my own. But I no longer knew if God was real, or if God was real, if God had anything to do with my healing, or if my healing was up to me. When I thought about praying, I mainly just had questions.

Is there something I am supposed to do here to help myself start to work through all of this? Is there something I'm supposed to be paying attention to? Is it possible to be led, by something outside of us, or even by something inside of us? Does God actually speak to us, or is Divinity something that is more a space to embody than a personal relationship? Who is my teacher? Who is my healer? Where is the gift? What about right now? What am I supposed to learn about myself today? Where is healing today?

May I be present to the stillness, to the whispers that guide me, regardless of who they belong to.

After reorienting my intentions, I closed my journal and looked around the shop. I felt myself longing to connect to someone today, to have a companion, even if it was just for a conversation or a short interaction.

I felt weird praying for a companion directly because I didn't really believe that it would do anything. Often when I prayed, "Atheist Em" showed up on the scene. She was what I called the part of me which resisted any concept of God, analyzed and combatted my experience and always had a rebuttal to whatever I tried to pray, rendering my attempt useless. Throughout my deconstruction of my faith, my attempt at prayer sounded something like, "God, give me peace—" *(but how can he give you peace if he's not conscious?)* "God, lead me—" *(but is God sovereign? Does God intervene at all? Is God a master puppeteer just moving all of us around? Do you have any say at all?)* "God, let me hear your voice—" *(feeling and hearing "God" is just a psychological rush of dopamine. Your experience isn't even real. It's all made up in your head.)* "God, heal me—" *(Why would a loving father heal you and not the starving child giving her dinner to her dying mother?)* "God—" *(Stop saying God. God is nothing but a cultural creation and a means of political control.)* And then I would get so frustrated that I would give up.

As I finished my cup of coffee, despite Atheist Em, I tried to pray or send an intention out into the Universe that somehow a companion would find me that day, in some way. In my head I thought I might find another young adult traveling alone or an old woman in a restaurant with a good story to tell, but what I found was nothing of the sort.

I walked out of the coffee shop, planning on getting in my car and quickly heading to Austin. My gaze was toward the ground as I walked down the creaky wooden steps, but when I got to ground level, I didn't see the ground. I saw paws—little black ones which I quickly realized belonged to a panting, perky, black dog that sat one step below me. I looked up, and she just stared at me. Her medium-length fur was covered in brown Texas dust as if she had been outside for days. I noticed she was wearing a faded pink collar with no name tag, so I went back inside to ask if she belonged to anyone, but I was met with blank stares and a couple nods of no. As I walked back outside and met her expectant eyes, the internal debate began.

Well what do I do now? Should I take her? Should I leave her? Should I try to call the animal shelter? Should I give her to someone else to deal with? I couldn't decide.

"Come on," I sighed. I snapped my fingers a few times, and immediately the dog happily trotted behind me as I walked over to my Jeep. She was panting rapidly, so I poured some water into a random cup I found in my trunk and gave it to her. She basically vacuum sucked the water out of the cup in seconds and begged for more, which wasn't surprising considering the 93-degree blaze of a morning that was only getting hotter by the minute. I squatted down to inspect her.

She looks thin, but her ribs aren't showing, so she hasn't been a stray for too long. If she has, she has been finding enough food somewhere to keep meat on her bones.

I gave her the remainder of my bland pumpkin-chia granola bars, another froufrou recipe website attempt gone bad. I had forced myself to eat as many as I could for snacks on the road, and though I didn't want to eat another bite of one, I couldn't bring myself to throw them away. Now I was glad that I hadn't. The dog swallowed them whole and slurped up every water refill I gave her until my bottle was empty.

I sat on the curb of the parking lot for ten minutes, battling the voices in my head that were arguing their cases of whether to take her or leave her. She plopped down beside me and sat patiently, wagging her tail, as if she was just waiting on permission to hop in and join the ride. I finally gave in. I still didn't know what I was going to do with her, but I felt silly sitting there for so long in the heat making no progress on an action plan.

"Alright. Come on," I called.

I opened my trunk and snapped my fingers again. The dog jumped right up and immediately curled up on my blanket like she had done it a hundred times before.

What are you doing, Em? I shook my head as I shut the trunk, walked around, and got in. I started the car, and when I looked back to make sure my new friend was still behaving, I saw she was already fast asleep, and I swear she was smiling.

Poor thing. She's exhausted. I sighed. *Am I seriously about to take a random dog with me to a city that I have never even been to before? I don't even have a leash! And what if she has rabies and attacks me? What if she pees or poops or pukes in my car? Oh God. She's in my bed. What if she has fleas? Or lice? Can dogs even get lice? I'm an idiot. Well, if she does, I guess it's too late to prevent an infestation now. But gross! What have I done? What if she belongs to some little girl who has been crying herself to sleep because old Maggie ran away again and then I lose her and the little girl is scarred for life from the trauma of losing her childhood best friend which would be all my fault?*

The list of negative possibilities went on as I drove down the road. I got nervous and overwhelmed and doubted my decision, so I pulled over in a random parking lot on the side of the road to try to sort through my thoughts and emotions. I looked up the shelter in Waco, but even though it was only three miles away and would have taken less than ten minutes to drive there and drop the dog off, upon seeing that it was in the opposite direction of Austin, for some reason I interpreted that as a sign that the dog was coming with me.

I'll just figure it out once we get there.

I turned on my instrumental playlist and settled into the straight-shot drive down Highway 35, laughing to myself because yes, I just stole someone's dog, and no, I had no clue what I was going to do with her, if she would even listen to me, or if she secretly had rabies and was "asleep" only to make me vulnerable so that she could attack my jugular from behind the seat. But it was fine. I wasn't worried about it. I couldn't help but feel as if she was sent to me.

"Cheers to the journey," I muttered aloud, trying to be hopeful, and the dog's ears perked up. "Maybe that should be your name." I looked back at her through the rearview mirror. "Journey." I smiled. "Cheers to you, Journey, my new companion."

What could have been an hour and a half car ride of anxiety and yelping and whining and pacing and puking ended up to be quite peaceful. Journey slept the entire way to Austin. Out cold. Didn't move an inch.

I don't know how people navigated spontaneous travel before technology and smartphones because with my lack of traveling experience or knowledge of how to plan for a trip like this, I fully relied on the internet to tell me what my options were to see and do in the places I found myself along the way. Having done about ten minutes of research on my phone about Austin before I left Isaac's that morning, I knew there were some pretty cool swimming holes in the area. Being submerged in some sort of body of water sounded awesome considering the fact that the air was currently so hot and humid I had begun to forget what it was like to exist in a state that wasn't sweat-covered, even inside of my car with air conditioning.

After finding out the world-famous Hamilton Pool was closed due to high levels of bacteria in the water after a recent flood, I tried Barton Springs, but I couldn't go there because it didn't allow dogs. Next I found Hippie Hollow, but it was a nudist swimming hole, and considering it was early on a Tuesday morning, I figured the demographic would only be creepy retired men and horny pre-teens on summer break, so I ditched that idea.

I ended up choosing Hipster Hollow, which I guessed to be a sister-hole to Hippie Hollow, kind of like how hipsters are one step below hippies, just a little less intense and exciting and exposed. The map on the website showed trails which led to the swimming hole, and nothing on the website said anything about the banning of canines, so I routed there.

We arrived at a public recreation park, and I discreetly changed into my swimsuit in my car. By the time I was done, Journey had woken up and looked at me with those expectant eyes again, wagging her tail as if asking, *"What are we going to do now, human?"*

I felt the odd pang of love that humans somehow can have for another species, which always had been so interesting to me. It was also slightly off-putting because she was so damn cute, and I didn't need attachment to a random dog that I was going to have to say goodbye to sometime within the next forty-eight hours.

Next on the itinerary was figuring out how in the world I was going to make a leash for her. I had no idea if she would listen to me or come when I called her, so in order to keep my anxiety at bay and her from running away, I needed a leash. I had a spool of some scratchy, old, blue rope that my dad threw in my car as one of those "in case you find yourself in some extreme unknown situation" things. I wished my rope knowledge was expert level where I could tie the most complicated knots with my eyes closed, but that was not the case. I figured I could at least make it into a basic leash if I tried.

To attach the rope to her collar, I followed an old saying I heard once: "If you can't tie knots, tie a lot." I went with a quadruple double-knot and hoped that it would hold. I held tightly to the other end and let Journey out of the car, and I quickly realized that she was going to be a tugger when she almost pulled my shoulder out of socket.

"Ouch!" I pulled her back over to me. I decided I should make a loop on the end of the rope to make it easier to hold, which ended up being just another embarrassingly messy quadruple double-knot that I fashioned the best I could as Journey pulled and thrashed.

"C'mon Journey," I called with apprehension as she excitedly led the way to the trail into the woods. I was still laughing to myself, with the question that seemed to be defining my experience more and more ringing in my ear: *Em, what the hell are you doing?*

We got about fifteen feet from the car before Journey got the shits. This awful green, slimy liquid flowed out of her and landed in a puddle on the grass. My stomach sank thinking about how close it was to seeping out in the bed I was going to sleep in for the next two weeks, and I was thankful that she was able to hold it until she was out of my car.

Yikes. What a nightmare that would have been.

"I guess your tummy couldn't take all that chia seed fiber in those gross bars I gave you," I said as I patted her head. Though she just excreted the most disgusting shit I have ever seen come out of a dog's body, she wasn't acting like she felt bad, so I coaxed her toward the trail.

After walking through muggy woods for a while, the trail opened up to a nice, rocky beach area on the Colorado River. The water was calm and crystal clear, and its surface reflected the deep summer blue of the cloudless sky above. There was a group of people settled into a calm part of the river toward the opposite bank. Talking with them could have been an opportunity for intimate connection with fun new friends, but I didn't feel like being social per usual, so I walked Journey down the opposite bank of the river. I was anxious about letting her off leash, but I wanted to try it anyway for the sake of saving my hand of more scratches. Thankfully, she didn't automatically sprint in the opposite direction.

She seemed like she had never been in the water before because she was doing that weird domestic animal thing where they walk over-dramatically and pick up and contort each leg like they're trying to walk through a foot of honey. After a couple minutes though, her canine instinct kicked in, and she started running and splashing around, snorting and trying to eat the water. I was inspired by her, and though I was worried about looking dumb running around in a river, I eventually trotted into the water with Journey.

Journey pounced about in an area that was only about a foot deep, and it was easy to run and splash with her without falling since I was wearing my Chacos and couldn't feel the sharpness of the river rocks. The chill of the water against my scorched skin instantly gave me a pleasure high. We ran back and forth splashing, and suddenly a sound I didn't recognize erupted out of me. I was belly laughing, and I hadn't genuinely laughed in months.

I think some of the most beautiful moments in life are the times when we forget ourselves and simply exist, fully in the present moment. I wasn't thinking about how silly I might have looked. I wasn't feeling self-conscious about what the people across the river might have been thinking about the crazy girl sprinting through the river with a dog. It didn't matter. It was just joy, the pure kind that bubbles up from somewhere deep within you and overflows in so much laughter you can't catch your breath.

I laid down in the shallow water, submerging my ears to where the water made a rim around the outer parts of my eyes and mouth. As I listened to the muffled hum of the underwater world of the river rushing over me and around me, I couldn't help but feel the need to say thank you. I didn't know to whom or to what, but it was the closest to the desire to worship I had felt in months, to let out a praise to the Universe for having sun and dogs and rivers that make you feel like you have the freedom to simply be. I made an intention at the beginning of the day to pay attention to what might be my teacher and to seek the subtle gifts. This moment, playing at this random swimming hole in the middle of Texas with a random dog I picked up on the street, this was teaching me something. This felt like one of those gifts. I looked up to the few clouds floating in the blue sky above me. I closed my eyes and breathed deeply.

Thank you.

I looked up and saw that Journey had ventured further down the river, closer to where it hooked around to the left where I couldn't see. I did my best attempt at a whistle and called her back. She came immediately, sloshing and dripping all over my backpack that I had retrieved and placed on the ground next to me.

"Good girl!" I exclaimed as I reattached her leash and gave her head a good pat. I saw that another person and dog were walking down the bank toward us, and I didn't know how Journey would react.

"Is your dog friendly?" a brunette who looked to be in her twenties called out to me.

"Yeah, she is!" I called back, not having any idea how Journey would interact with another dog, especially this massive, muscular English bulldog mix trotting over to her. I braced myself for the possibility of breaking up a dog fight.

The English bulldog came over. They did the normal butt-sniff introduction, and then before I knew it they were both chasing each other playfully in the water, and Journey tugged back and forth hard on the leash.

Whew, crisis averted. I took her back off-leash.

The woman's name was Ava, and she had just moved to Austin for a new nursing job. She told me that she recently learned her dog, Marker, loved the water, so she had started coming here to get some of his energy out.

"Why Marker?" I asked.

Ava laughed. "Because when he was a puppy he peed on literally everything, and the only way to not strangle him was to find something endearing about it, so we gave him the name Marker since he put his mark on everything."

"Clever," I chuckled. "I hope he grew out of that?" I asked.

"Yes, thankfully!" she laughed. "He's over a year now, so I think he's done with it." She paused for a moment, and we both watched the dogs splashing about. "Hey, you wanna see something crazy?" she inquired, raising her eyebrows.

"Um, yeah, sure. Why not?" I didn't know what to expect.

Ava grabbed a river rock a little larger than a baseball and got Marker's attention. She showed it to me. "Remember this one has this little orange stripe in it. See?"

"Okay." Now I was more interested.

Marker saw the rock and started hopping up and down, wagging his tail and barking, as if Ava held a juicy treat. Ava chucked the rock out into the river, and Marker bounded after it into water that was up to his neck, dove down underneath the water, came out of the water beaming with the rock in his mouth, sloshed his way back to Ava, and dropped a rock, a little larger than a baseball with an orange stripe through it, at Ava's feet.

Ava raised her eyebrows. "Pretty cool, huh?" She leaned down to pat Marker's head. "I just learned he could do this last week."

"Oh my gosh! No way!" I couldn't believe it. "That is crazy! I've seen dogs play fetch with a lot of things—balls, socks, sticks, frisbees— but playing fetch with heavy river rocks is definitely a first for me. I bet Marker is a professional at bobbing for apples!" We both laughed.

For the next ten minutes, I watched as Ava repeated this sequence. She found a rock, showed it to Marker, and threw it into the river. Marker would find it and bring it back to her, and not just any random rock out of the river, but always the same rock she threw in. If Marker didn't come up with it after bobbing down the first try, he would go down again and again until he came up with success. Then he would happily trot back over to Ava and plop it at her feet as if he was asking, "Look mom, aren't you proud of me?"

I sat back and watched while talking back and forth with Ava, who didn't have many suggestions for me since she was also getting to know Austin. I had never been very good at making friends quickly with other women, and here I still didn't know how to connect or what to ask about, so I mainly just directed my attention to the dogs and gave affirming cues while Ava chimed in occasionally. At one point I realized that she never asked anything about how long I had Journey or even what Journey's name was, and I desperately hoped she wouldn't so I wouldn't have to explain that I had abducted her from the streets of Waco that morning.

During the first couple of minutes watching Marker fetch the rocks, Journey would try to poke fun and play with him every time he came back to shore. Eventually, I got to see the full process of learned behavior take place as Journey slowly started to poke her snout under the water. The first few times she would raise it quickly, shake her head, and snort because she got water up her nose, but after some practice at holding her breath, soon she taught herself to dive to the bottom as well, imitating Marker.

I figured why not try and see if she could actually fetch a rock like Marker. To my surprise, when I picked up a rock and threw it a couple feet out into the river, Journey took a couple bounds through the water, plunged her head under, and came up sneezing and smiling with triumph as she pranced over and dropped the prized rock at my feet.

I felt like a proud parent who had just taught their four-year-old how to ride their bike.

"Good job, girl!" I patted her back and sides as she ran up to me wagging her tail and splashing me with water. My soul felt warm with the bliss of simplicity and sunshine.

Though I was having the most lighthearted fun I had experienced in a long time, my hunger pains were getting to a level that could no longer be ignored. It seemed as if hunger might be the driving force that would keep me in check during the day, because besides food and sleep, I didn't have any other time structure built into my days.

I said my goodbyes and best wishes to Ava and Marker. I reattached Journey's dysfunctional leash and walked her back to my car. Not only had I not thought through the dynamic of letting an unidentified dog lay down in my bed, but I then realized I had not thought through the dynamic of letting a soaking wet, sandy unidentified dog lay down in my bed. Journey did the classic dog wiggle a few times to shake it out, but her coat was still drenched with water, and I had only one solitary towel, which was supposed to be my one bath towel for the remainder of my month on the road.

It will have to do, I guess. I looked at the pathetic size of the towel when I laid it out on my bed pad. *She probably isn't even going to stay on it, but I guess there's no other option. At least she kind of had a bath in the river, and she isn't as dusty now, and if she has bugs, maybe at least a few jumped off in the water.*

It was even hotter than when we arrived, which I didn't think was possible. I was drenched in sweat yet again, something I was coming to accept would be my most frequent physical state throughout this trip. I changed out of my bathing suit into my blue dress. It was the only thing remotely normal-people-like, and knowing that Austin was supposed to have more of a hipster vibe than Nashville, I didn't feel as self-conscious rocking my river hair.

After walking around downtown for the afternoon and grabbing dinner from one of Austin's famous food trucks, I ended the day at a small park with some walking trails and a playground. I fed Journey the last of the chia bars for dinner and walked her on the longest walk ever afterwards because I was scared that she was going to have those nasty green squirts again. She never went to the bathroom after she scarfed them down, so I had a heart to heart with her.

"You know Journey, you're a pretty kick ass dog, but I'm going to like you a whole lot less if you shit in my car. And if you actually have an owner back in Waco, it would be in your benefit to be able to ride back in this car. So no squirts in the car, okay?" Journey looked up at me with tired but hopeful eyes that somehow reminded me of my own humanity. I smiled and gave her a good scratch.

While I sat on a bench near the playground to people-watch, Journey took a nap in the grass next to me. Two young boys ran up and asked if they could pet Journey, but as they tried to rouse her up from her nap to play, she wouldn't budge. At first I laughed and told them how tired she must have been from running around all day, but then I noticed a shaved spot with fresh stitches on her stomach that I somehow had not noticed until then. I bent down to look at her sutures and was punched in the gut with anxiety as every terrible explanation flooded my mind.

Oh no. What if she's not tired but actually sick and dying? What if she's already dead? I looked down and saw her stomach rise. Okay. Not dead. But what if she had surgery and some weird bacteria got into her stitches from the river and now they are eating her from the inside-out and it's all my fault? What if she was bleeding internally because her surgery failed? What if it was to remove a cancerous tumor but the cancer was too far that she was going to die so her owner let her run away because they couldn't afford any more surgeries? My mind continued to race with the endless tragic possibilities.

The boys' giggles brought me back to reality. Journey thumped her tail on the ground as the boys scratched her ears, and I tried to believe that she was just extremely tired from being a stray (for who knows how long) and walking all day in the heat.

"Well boys, you wanna give her one more good pat? I think we're going to head out so we can get this pup home."

"Bye Journey!" They giggled as they ran back over to their mom.

Shit. My stomach dropped. *I never texted Isaac to tell him about Journey.* When I decided to take Journey that morning, I made the decision that I would come back to Waco that night to sleep so that

I could take her to a shelter in the morning. *It is going to seem so inconsiderate to just text him last minute and be like, 'Hey I'm bringing a random stray dog back to your apartment complex that doesn't allow pets, hope that's okay!'*

I didn't have any other option, so I sent Isaac the most apologetic and informative text I could think of to explain the situation, assuring him that I felt like I was supposed to help Journey, that she was a good dog, and that I would take her to the shelter first thing in the morning. He said we could talk about it when I got there, but as long as she didn't pee or tear up anything, he was fine with it.

I coaxed Journey along, and I was grateful that she was so tired that she finally quit tugging because the skin on my hand was so raw from being rubbed by the leash all day that it was almost bleeding.

When we arrived back in Waco around 10:00 p.m., Isaac came out of his bedroom to say goodnight. Though his eyes looked concerned, Isaac reinforced that he was okay with Journey being there, so long as she stayed contained. I tied Journey's leash to the front door handle with the same quadruple double knot.

I told Isaac goodnight and thanked him for the fifth time for letting me bring Journey inside of his apartment. I promised him that she would not poop or pee or puke or any other repulsive word that starts with a "p," though I had no clue if she would or not. I hadn't seen any other green slime that day, but there was no way to know for sure. I felt bad, and I hoped it didn't seem like I was taking advantage of his offer to let me stay.

I brushed my teeth in the kitchen, standing there looking at Journey, and she stared back at me. I smiled, and through my toothbrush and foam filled mouth, I mumbled, "You sure you wanna stay in Waco?"

She wagged her tail but began to whine again as I turned my back to her. I gave her a quick glare and went to pee, and when I came back to lie down on the couch, Journey's whine became a squeal, and she thrashed away from the door handle.

"Shhhh! Cut it out!" I whispered harshly, but she kept making a ruckus. Worried that she would wake Isaac and exhausted from the day's excursions, I had very little patience to try to appease whatever her animal brain wanted at that moment, and falling asleep to her squirming and whining would be impossible.

I took her off the leash, glared into her eyes, and whispered, "If you shit on this carpet, I will murder you." She responded to her freedom by happily trotting over to the couch and curling up in a ball on the floor right below where my head lay. Journey fell asleep, snoring shortly afterward.

I guess that's all she wanted. "Looks like you formed some attachments today too, little pup," I whispered. I took a deep breath and patted her head before I curled up underneath my own blanket.

My thoughts were sporadic as I tried to fall asleep, but eventually I remembered the version of a prayer or intention I offered up that morning. I'd asked for a companion, and within minutes of praying, I was given the exact companion I needed, in the form of a little black, dusty street dog who reminded me what it was like to laugh and be silly just for the sake of it, something I had lost in the heaviness of those past months. However, although it felt sweet and special, I mostly felt confused.

Could that have been God, or was it just coincidence? How does prayer work? Is this just an example of synchronicity? Or the law of attraction? Is it possible that I prayed for a companion, some conscious God heard me, and then decided to send Journey to me? It seems irrational to believe that God could be so conscious that out of all of the constant noise and chatter of billions of people praying all over the world, God somehow heard my measly little petty prayer for a companion, and then consciously chose to answer it in the form of a stray dog. But if that is true, why would God answer my prayer but sit back and do nothing about the millions of people suffering from disease and hunger and oppression and war? Or is this just an example of confirmation bias, that I happened to have prayed for a companion and there was also a dog outside, and the dog's reaction to a visual stimulus of a human walking outside made it walk up to me, and I took that as God answering prayer when it very much could have been a coincidence? What if they aren't connected at all?

It was hard to view it as anything but confirmation bias, which was one of my biggest confusions and frustrations with the way I saw many Christians treat prayer. Someone prays to God for something, and two outcomes are possible. In the first, whatever they prayed for happens, and in that case there is confirmation that God answered their prayer. In the second, whatever they prayed for does not happen, and they attribute the unanswered prayer to it being confirmation that it is just "the Lord's will." Either way their belief in God is not challenged, because no matter what the outcome of the prayer, God is still in the clear, because God either answers the prayer, or it's just not in God's will. God is attributed benevolent consciousness in each scenario.

With either outcome that day, if I were to interpret it through Christianity—either I found a companion, and my prayer was answered, or I did not find one and therefore it was God's will for me to be alone that day. But I wasn't confident in Christianity. I wasn't sure God wanted anything for my life or could ever want anything for my life, because the idea that there was a conscious energy higher than myself felt like such an abstract, inconceivable idea which I could no longer see ever making sense in my life again.

But also at the end of the day, I wonder if the explanation of my prayer and Journey doesn't matter so much? Synchronicity or not, confirmation bias or not, answered prayer or not, maybe what matters is the fact that it happened, which I cannot deny. Regardless of the explanation, it is what I needed, and that is a real and true experience I can speak to, no matter the language I use to explain the "why." Maybe that's part of the point, not trying to prove so much, not trying to always get the language "right," but just opening myself up to what is going on around me, opening myself up to the possibility that we can ask for healers. Maybe we can ask for teachers and for help in seeking the gift that the day might bring, and a lot of the time we don't find what we're looking for, but sometimes we do, and those moments are a gift to be celebrated.

My time with Journey today feels like it brought the tiniest bit of healing and light and joy into my spirit, and though so much of my being still resists the idea, maybe I could call that source 'God,' the reverence that hums within me, the Source from which all things flow, that which cannot be named.

Still not quite knowing to whom or what to say thank you, I radiated my gratitude out into the Universe, hoping that some higher source of love, connection, and peace was radiating itself back into me.

{6}

DANCING IN THE SAME WIND

I OPENED MY EYES, AND I FOUND MYSELF STUMBLING, wrapped in darkness, trapped in those terrible hallways, breathing air that carried a sense of familiarity but was still heavy with panic. After so many nights here I knew the walls of the maze that surrounded me were built by bricks of emotions and thoughts I no longer understood, and they were haunted by ghosts of feelings I lost the capacity to feel. I had been trying to figure out how to navigate this maze for weeks and weeks, but I still had not learned the way to freedom. My heart raced as my eyes adjusted to the minimal light and fog, shining just enough to reveal the next ten yards of the hallway in front of me. I crouched and prepared myself for the impact of the first dark cloud that would consume me at any second, filled with the whispers that tormented me.

I sensed the black, tendril-like fingers of the cloud behind me closing in on my throat. I thought maybe I would just submit and let it kill me quickly this time to avoid the terror of the chase, but just before the tips of the cloud's sprawling fingers reached the surface of my skin, I bolted.

The race of horror I had run so many times in my dreams began yet again. I sprinted down the first hallway in front of me, and I ran blindly, barely able to see through the dim fog. I darted down one hallway after another, taking turn after turn, frantic with panic, hoping I would eventually escape the murky, dark cloud, which swarmed violently like a tornado at my heels, threatening to suck me in at any moment. At every turn I made, whatever matter the cloud contained beyond its dark exterior would clash with a bang against the wall, causing an explosion of bricks and dust and fear. I never looked back to see if I could catch a glimpse of what was inside. All I could focus on was getting away. There wasn't any pain yet. Only adrenaline. I sprinted on, trying to find a way out.

I glanced over my shoulder only to see it getting closer and closer. My heart pulsed in my throat, gagging me with my own fear. I knew that if I stopped running, the cloud would consume and suffocate me. Every time I tried to open my mouth to scream, no sound would escape my lips, filling me further with anxiety. I ran harder.

My body trembled, for I knew that the unfortunate characteristic of this maze was that only one path led the way to freedom, and in all of my nights in this place I had not found it. My lungs were burning, yet I kept going.

All other paths led to a dead end, and it was the dead end that scared me. If I could run in the maze of my mind forever, even if I didn't reach the exit to freedom, I would still be safe, for I would be moving somewhere, anywhere, that was not here. But I knew if I reached a dead end, I would have to turn around and retrace my steps, which meant I would have to face the cloud. The only way to escape would be to go back through the monster of emotion that chased me and breathe its suffocating air into my lungs as I pushed through it, which was the part that terrified me the most.

Sometimes I would reach a dead end and be able to hold my breath long enough to escape the cloud and start down another path before I had to inhale. However, eventually no matter what path I took, the hallway became too long and narrow, closing in on my shoulders more and more until I could not move further without turning sideways and shuffling forward with my back against the wall. With each shuffle step I took, the wall across the hallway came closer and closer to my face, until I eventually could go no further. The hallway became more like a crack, and I was lodged between its two walls.

Stuck with no room to move further in the way I was going, I held my breath and tried to turn and go the other way, running back through the cloud, but the cloud now filled the hallway so extensively that I could not hold my breath long enough to escape it. I was forced to breathe inside of it. It was that final moment that always paralyzed me, where I had no other option but to succumb to its overbearing presence. Its black tendrils wrapped around my arms and legs, binding me in a cocoon from which I could not escape, and I had to lay trapped in the pain that crippled me.

As I choked in the darkness, scenes were shown to me that I did not want to see, and thick shots of emotions filled my veins with dread, for I did not want to feel.

I saw flashes of bodies, his against hers, in the moment where all of the years of loving, loyalty, investment, waiting, sacrificing and submitting were betrayed.

"Charlotte and I had sex last night." Cam's voice shot like an arrow through the silence, sounding even more harsh in the nightmare than it did when I heard it in real life. I saw a vision of myself back in that dark field behind his house as I tried to walk away from him, but my legs failed me, and I watched myself collapse to my knees in the dirt.

"WHY?" my question bellowed through the dark cloud of my memory. I could do nothing but relive that terrible moment, helpless to escape it. I watched myself slam my fist into the cold, hard ground as I tried to drag myself to my feet.

"I'm not sorry," Cam's voice echoed, over and over again, increasing in volume.

I'm not sorry.

I'm not sorry.

I'm not sorry.

I was now tied to the ceiling above Cam's bed with tape over my mouth. Cam and Charlotte came into the light, as they always did, without any knowledge I was there, and I was forced to watch the only man I had ever let inside of my world slowly make love to a woman about whom he knew little beyond her name.

"STOP! GOD PLEASE FUCKING MAKE IT STOP!" I wailed.

From the depths of the cloud came a chilling snicker. *"God? God can't help you. God isn't even real. It's all a lie. You're all alone. Everything is meaningless. Just give up. Just give up. Just give up."* The voice coaxed me on and on, and I wanted to. Giving up sounded better than living another second in this state. I tried to shut my eyes, but still the visions repeated over and over again on the screens of my eyelids. My chest felt like it had been broken open and emptied of everything that once held it together. My head pounded with the realization that comes when you feel like you have lost everything and have nowhere to go. My ears were ringing from the piercing lies. I could barely breathe as I searched for some feeling of not being completely alone, but there was no one. Cam was gone. And God was gone too. I was abandoned in the cloud. I wept and choked until the pain became too much to bear, and then I woke up.

I gasped as my eyes shot open. My body shook, and my muscles were tense from the same brutal nightmare I had woken up from so many mornings that it had become normal. Journey lifted her head inquisitively, and I took deep breaths as my reality in Isaac's living room washed back over me.

The nightmare never changed. It had played in my sleep almost every night since the last night I saw Cam. I had barely noticed the break from it during the first few nights of my trip until its return that night at Isaac's. I guessed with the excitement of the beginning of the trip and feeling joy for the first time in months, I had been distracted, but today I was reminded that the source of the nightmare remained deep inside of me. My subconscious still wrestled with the shadows of my trauma.

My eyes were void of tears, but I desperately wished they weren't. I could only feel the tip of the emotional iceberg. I no longer had the gear to help me explore the part of myself under the water's surface without the risk of drowning or freezing to death. I grabbed my journal from the coffee table.

07/08/15, Day 6 -

The nightmare returned, and it leaves me feeling like my grief will always consume me, and I will never exist separate from it or outside of it. My grief feels massive, overwhelming, inaccessible, unnavigable, impenetrable.

But maybe that's just how it is in the beginning, when healing feels impossible, too great of a task. Maybe that's why it just has to happen to us. We can't wish it upon ourselves. We can't rush it. We can't speed it up, or slow it down. Healing is given to us, one slow moment at a time, each moment allowing us to breathe and feel a little deeper than we could the day before. I know that moment sprinting through the river with Journey yesterday was one of those slow moments, and I want to believe that it somehow dissipated a tiny portion of my grief. But I wonder if every ounce of healing I find will still be met with torture while I sleep? Will this nightmare ever leave me? How do I dissipate the cloud without suffocating to death? How do I find the courage to face it?

I sighed as I pushed my post-nightmare thoughts aside. I rolled over and saw the sun peeking out over the building across the street. Journey looked to be snoozing again, but when I reached down to rub her side, she looked up at me through drowsy eyes and thumped her tail once on the floor.

"Good morning to you too," I cooed, feeling a stab of sadness when I remembered that I would have to say goodbye to her in a few hours. I decided that I would take her to the local animal hospital to see if they had a dog of her description in their recent abdominal surgery records. I had no clue if they could do that, but taking her there felt better than taking her to the shelter. After I dropped her off, I would drive toward New Mexico.

From my quick assessment of the floor and furniture in Isaac's apartment, nothing major seemed to have been destroyed by dog teeth or excrement. Hoping to keep it that way, I put on my shoes, untied my quadruple double-knot from Isaac's front door handle, led Journey out, locked the door, and walked outside. Journey was still slime-free.

I felt the sadness of our parting biting at my heels. I pulled up the address of the animal hospital, drove three short miles, and walked in the front door of Northside Animal Hospital with Journey. I was painfully reminded how sore and raw the skin on my hand was when

Journey tugged the fraying plastic rope over my skin like sandpaper in attempt to say hello to a tiny, white, pampered poodle across the waiting room.

"Ouch!" I choked quietly. "Stop it!" I dragged her away and walked to the front desk window.

"Hi," I peeped to the uninterested lady at the front desk and paused briefly, remembering that I had not planned out at all how to explain the story of the events that led me to this moment. "Um, I found this dog near Common Grounds coffee shop yesterday," gesturing to Journey, who was still tugging toward the poodle. "She has a collar with no tag, but she has a scar on her stomach that seems to have been from a recent surgery. I was wondering if there was any way that you could search your records for an abdominal surgery performed here on a dog that fits her description?"

The lady looked at me with a raised eyebrow. "Well, that was nice of you to bring her here. We unfortunately can't look her up in the system just by the scar, but we do have a device that will be able to detect a tracking chip in her neck if her owners happened to place one in her. Want me to check her for you?"

"Oh. Sure, I didn't think about that. Thanks so much." I smiled as I handed the leash to her. She noticeably judged my quadruple double knot rope leash, but without mentioning it, she led Journey through the door. I was left alone in the lobby with the poodle and its owner who was nose-deep in some magazine, not acknowledging my existence.

I turned when I heard a door open and saw the lady already back with Journey.

"We found a chip!" she exclaimed. "We called her owner. He's local. He'll be here in fifteen minutes!"

"Fifteen minutes? Oh. Wow! That's, great," I chirped, trying to sound excited, though part of me still wanted to escape with Journey and continue driving west with her hanging her head out of my passenger window, her slobber creating abstract splatter-paint art all down the side of my car. I grabbed Journey's leash and led her over to a seat.

I'm excited for her, aren't I? I mean, she gets to be reunited with her owner, and I know I can't keep her... I had considered it though, taking her. I had come up with all sorts of extreme scenarios to make it make sense. Tying her leash to my backpack as I hiked into the Grand Canyon, making her a bed on top of all of our backpacks in our trunk, sharing my food with her at night, running through more rivers with her as we crossed the whole country together, but I had to remind myself that it would just be too much and too complicated. Plus, the fact that she had an owner changed everything. I could pretend like I was doing her a service by keeping her yesterday because I didn't know for sure if she had a home, but if I took her today it would be conscious stealing.

So there I sat, Journey panting next to me, my hand resting on her back, nervously awaiting our goodbye.

I wish that I could say that the reunion was dramatic and filled with tears and exclamatory 'thank you's' and hugging and a young girl with a pink bow in her hair named Sally running in and wrapping her arms around Journey's neck, crying because her doggy had finally been rescued, but we all know cheesy movie endings don't often happen in real life.

Journey's owner was a pudgy, burly man with dark, curly hair and round glasses. He shuffled inside the side door wearing a stained white undershirt and sweatpants. His eyes were groggy, as if he literally rolled out of bed to drive there. He didn't even seem excited when he saw Journey.

"Damn dog dug under the fence again," he mumbled as he took the leash from my hand. "Come on Roxie."

Roxie? Seriously? This is the most kind, rad, fun, adventurous, amazing dog companion in the world, and her name is Roxie?? It felt like she was being robbed of all of her grace. Roxie felt like a lie, a stage name, a fake personality that Journey was forced to live inside, and I hated it for her.

I tried to smile and jokingly mentioned taking Journey on an adventure yesterday, but the owner seemed uninterested in anything but finding the fastest route back to his bed. He mumbled a quick thanks and raised his hand as he walked toward the door. Journey's ears were back as she shuffled behind him. Suddenly, they were out the door, and Journey was gone. The man didn't even give me back my rope.

I tried to find comfort as I walked to my car by telling myself that I did the best thing I could do for her, but I could not help feeling as if I just led her back into the abusive relationship from which she was trying to escape. Her owner probably didn't actually abuse her in a literal sense, but I bet that man did not run through rivers with her and take her on trips. Her potential seemed abused to me, as if she was not getting the quality of life that she deserved. She was such a great dog.

Looking back now, I think that maybe I felt so strongly about this because Journey seemed a lot like me in an odd way—escaping a negative circumstance over and over again, knowing she would find more life outside of the fence only to somehow end up back inside its grips, waiting for another chance to be free. Journey's cage was physical. She was trapped inside the barriers of a literal wooden fence, where her entire world existed in a single backyard that was made for her. She could escape whenever she had enough time to dig a hole underneath the fence, when the ground was soft enough to penetrate, and her owner wasn't home to stop her.

My fence had been more of an emotional barrier than a physical one. I didn't have to dig my way out of my relationship with Cam or out of my toxic form of Christianity. The fence door was never locked. I was always free to leave, but I believed I had to save my failed relationship, and I had to save my faith. I didn't realize that staying in the fence was only fighting for my own emotional death. The only way I would leave the barriers of the fence was if the fence was blown up, and I couldnt do anything to save it.

I began to realize that maybe freedom is not always found by walking through a wide-open door because there are situations where we might not have the strength or courage to make ourselves do it. In those moments, when we refuse to leave, something is sent our way to shatter the fences, and we are forced into the scary freedom we have been resisting.

To those who grew up in a secular context or with a more progressive form of religion, Cam having sex with a random woman, even though it was less than twelve hours after we had decided to end our long history together, might seem like it was not as big of a deal as I made it. It may seem like it was "just sex," or "just shitty." You might be thinking, "It sucks, but you were technically broken up, right?"

True, but in my evangelical Christian brain, steeped in a culture which valued "purity," I believed that having sex was the most intimate and sacred act in which you could engage with another person. I believed that Cam had all of the answers and that my value was based on what he thought about me. Cam choosing to have sex with a woman he barely knew, right after we broke up, and then telling me about it the next day, intentionally saying he wasn't sorry, was the most intense way that he could have hurt me psychologically and emotionally at that point in my life.

It sent the message that even though Cam knew me better than anyone in the world, and even though I did everything I could to appease him, it was not enough to gain love, that something was inherently wrong with me, that it was my fault. I was not enough, and there was nothing special about me to make anyone want to do the hard work of loving me. With my understanding of sex at this point in my life, which mostly came from what I was told by my religion, Cam having sex with someone else so soon felt like he had intentionally rendered everything about our four-and-a-half-year relationship meaningless. With my identity wrapped up entirely in our relationship, it felt like he had personally attacked and squandered my very soul, rendering me meaningless and worthless as a person as well.

Now, years later, I know that Cam doing something so hurtful would have been the only way for me to leave him for good. I would have continued to sacrifice my happiness, my desires, my needs, for the sake of helping him, of holding on to the idealized picture of what we could be. After that night though, hearing he had no remorse, I could no longer find an excuse for him. It was the moment that shattered the fence, and part of me shattered with it.

I still felt like a walking shell of a person, like I was missing the parts of myself that made me, me. Trauma and depression strip parts of us away, and sometimes it seems like those parts will be lost forever. Through searching constantly and finding nothing, I came to realize the parts of myself that felt lost would have to be given to me, that it was not about going back and finding something or someone that used to be me. I had to find a new identity by walking and moving forward, by paying attention to what moved me, what inspired me, what made my heart come alive. I knew that if I was going to build a foundation out of my own self, I had to find a way to stand without breaking. That still felt like too much some days. Finding some sort of power beyond myself felt necessary, but the path to discovering it was not clear. I wanted to be grounded in something, I just didn't know what.

Santa Rosa is a tiny town nestled in the heart of the New Mexico desert right off the renowned Route 66. I came upon Santa Rosa during my research about swimming holes in the southwest, which is odd because I never would have expected there to be a crystal-clear swimming hole in the middle of the desert where rain and significant water adventure attractions are scarce. However, upon further research, it turned out that the random little swimming hole was actually a world-famous spring called the Blue Hole.

The Blue Hole attracts thousands of scuba divers every year with its perfect diving conditions in an area of the country where scuba diving is obviously not a common pastime. Its crystal clear water makes up one of the seven lakes connected by an underground system of water tunnels that run underneath the desert floor. The Blue Hole stays at a constant sixty-one degrees Fahrenheit in all seasons. It runs roughly eighty feet deep to the bottom and down to two hundred feet in the caverns that continue through a small hole on the spring floor, making it a perfect spot for scuba certifications and casual dives for more experienced scuba divers who live in the middle of the U.S. where clear waters to dive in are few and far between. Visibility is consistently at 100 feet because the water is constantly being replaced by the spring system.

I had never been to New Mexico before, but I had plenty of time to use at my leisure, and driving to an arbitrary town of five square miles in the middle of the desert just to jump in a clear pool of water seemed like enough of an excuse to go to me.

I felt extra alone after leaving Journey, and my drive across Texas did not give me much distraction to help. The drive was the kind of straight where there are barely curves in the road, the kind of straight where it literally looks like someone drew the road on the map with a ruler. It was the kind of straight where the only deviation in the alignment of your tires happens when you swerve as you semi-fall asleep at the wheel due to the lack of trees, buildings, birds, color, and other visual stimuli. Compared to the exciting, lush, ever-changing mountains at the beginning of my trip, the barren nothingness of Texas seemed so empty. It was almost as if Texas was a mirror in front of me, and its reflection embodied how I felt, giving me no relief from the reminder that I was alone on the road again. The excitement of solitude was starting to wear off, for the more time I spent alone, the more everything inside of me was rising up. I had some inner knowing that once whatever it was reached the surface, I would not be able to hold it back.

I would get to a stop sign or stoplight to turn only five times the rest of the day. I had already driven two hours on Highway 6 North, but the seven-hour stretch of I-20 and 84 West ahead of me was daunting. Today would be my longest day of driving yet, a total of 556 miles, and since I didn't leave the animal hospital until almost noon, I wouldn't get to Santa Rosa until way after dark. I stopped for a coffee and welcomed the extra caffeine running through my veins. I would need it for the seven hours left of this emotionally and physically challenging day.

What in the world?

I was somewhere past Abilene when I first saw them. I had been on the road for almost four hours, and I came over a hill to be faced with a horizon dotted with little white objects, and after a few minutes I realized that the objects were moving.

Oh! Windmills! I realized what they were once I could finally see the details of their propellers moving sleepily in the open air in contrast to the still background. I had never seen more than a few windmills in one field, but here there were hundreds, if not thousands of them, scattered across the landscape. Some faced east, some west, some north, some south, so that no matter which way the wind was blowing, the amount of wind power that could be harvested would be maximized at any given moment.

My eyes were locked on their revolving limbs as if I was in a trance. Something about how they were all rotating at different speeds and angles, catching the wind in every direction that it would come sounded like a metaphor to me, and I took time to ponder it.

What if this is how God works? Why is there such a necessity to be streamlined into one macro-colonialist religion where we have to have everyone on the same "side?" What if a difference in belief or approach to God does not mean that one person is inherently wrong and the other is right? Could we all be right? I know that there are forms of Christianity and other religions that have used and continue to use the name of God to justify terrible things, so I can't say that just because someone claims something is God or good or just means that it is, but when you no longer believe that everyone in the world must be converted to a specific form of Christianity like I used to, the idea that I could be talking about the same Divine energy in other traditions does not seem as insane to me.

What if God is more like the wind that always flows through the air, even when we cannot see it? What if all of the different saints, gurus, religions, and prophets of the world are like windmills spread out across a field, all facing different directions, so that when the Spirit of God flows by, they might be able to catch its wind and speak of the form of God they experience from that angle? The wind from the East might feel and sound a little different than the West, but what if it is all the same wind? What if it is all God? What if it is the same Source? What if we all grow from the same Ground? What if it is all Divine, but we get so caught up in differences of language and culture that we miss out on the fact that we are all windmills dancing in the same wind? Or like the old Chinese proverb I keep quoting throughout my deconstruction, what if we really are all fingers pointing to the same moon?

Throughout my deconstruction I couldn't get over the fact that it seemed like so many Christians in the West were missing the point when they made their religion so legalistic, strict, and small. When I was in church, I saw more people checking off boxes than doing the hard work of figuring out how to actually live more like Jesus. It often made me feel like overturning tables, like Jesus did in the temple. In the Christianity I was handed, it seemed to communicate a message that goes something like, "Everyone must look the same and worship the same and act the same, and God only comes in this certain form at this certain time and anything that moves you that is not this exact thing is not God, and anything that is not God you should fear and distance yourself from, so that you are not taken into Satan's grips and lost forever." There was only one direction the windmills could face, and any wind that came from another direction was pretended to not be real.

Maybe instead of making the approach to God a heavily supervised and regimented military sequence full of strict boundaries, it might be better to orient ourselves like a field of windmills on a fluid axis, ready to move to catch the wind of the Spirit from whatever angle it might come. What if the windmills catching the wind from a different direction are not in competition or opposition to us, but what if they actually can give us the gift of seeing the wind when we can't feel it moving us from the direction we face anymore?

In my experience, I have been rigidly facing West for a long time, and I have doubted if the wind was still there to move me and give me energy. What if there is something from other religions, prophets, and gurus that can point me back to the moon and remind me of a side of God that I have lost sight of, or help paint a new picture of God? What if the wind has been blowing this whole time, but I was so set on it coming from a certain direction, that I couldn't feel the fact that it was always there?

I didn't have answers, but I could feel the importance of the questions, and I knew I had to keep asking them. I knew I had to keep my arms open in expectation of the wind to come, possibly from a direction I never expected.

At some point on the drive I was lost in my mind, thinking about anything and everything to keep me awake. I thought for a while about how Texas highway exit infrastructure made no sense to me. Later I wondered where rural Texans ate because there weren't any restaurant signs along the highway. Eventually I found myself regretting the fact that I inhaled all four giant peanut butter cookies I bought from a gas station when I got sleepy about thirty minutes before. Somewhere in the middle of noticing my stomach ache, I was jolted back to awareness further by the vibration of my phone.

I picked it up to see that it was Ethan, my brother.

Odd. He never calls me just to casually chat.

"Hello?" I asked, not knowing what to expect.

"Hey dude," Ethan's casual tone echoed back to me. "Soooooooooo question."

"Go."

"If I bought a plane ticket to California, would you pick me up?" he asked.

"WHAT?!" I was not expecting that. "Are you serious?"

"Yeah I'm looking at plane tickets right now. I'm about to buy one to San Diego, but I wanted to make sure you would pick me up first."

"Umm," I paused. A million things were running through my mind. "Yeah. Yes!" I yelled, smiling. "Of Course! Are you sure you're not joking?"

Ethan laughed. "Nope, I'm serious. I was thinking about it after I got back from Young Life camp in Colorado and I was like, well I could work a job I don't really care about for the rest of the summer or I could see if I could join in on the adventure. California obviously won."

"Dude. Yeah, please come. I would love it if you joined. I am planning on being in San Diego by July 10th, in two days, so you could maybe try to fly in the next morning on July 11th? I didn't really have set plans anyway. I'm sure we can find something to do in California for those four or so days before Will and Sydney arrive."

"Cool. Sounds good to me," Ethan agreed.

"The only logistical thing I can think of that wouldn't be ideal is that we only have three permits for backpacking the Grand Canyon. I had to apply for them months ago, and according to what I've read the rangers are pretty strict about checking them at campsites, so you would probably have to chill by yourself and sleep in the car or something those two nights. But beyond that, if you join our other plans, it should be totally fine. Cramming all four of our packs in the trunk will be interesting, but we will make it work."

"Yeah I'm fine with doing whatever by myself during the Grand Canyon," he said.

"Great! I think it would be fun to have some time to explore alone anyway," I pointed out.

"Cool. Well, I'm gonna do it."

"Do it! I can ask Will and Sydney to make sure, but I'm sure they'll be okay with it. I'll text them when I hang up with you and let you know when I have confirmation. I just want to give them a say since that half is their trip too, you know?"

"Yeah for sure. Just let me know."

"Will do."

"Cool."

"Cool."

"I can't believe this is happening!" I squealed.

"Ha yeah it's going to be pretty epic."

"Okay I'll talk to you soon. If they are good for you to come, I might call you once it gets closer to the 11th to talk about flight details."

"Alrighty. Bye Em. Love ya."

"Love you too, E."

I hung up the phone, in excitement and disbelief. I anxiously did that talk-text thing, where you can talk into your phone and somehow it knows what you are saying and translates it to a text, asking Will and Sydney if they would be fine with Ethan joining in.

I was surprised by how quickly they responded because they were notorious for not being the fastest repliers, but within a few minutes I had an excited confirmation from both of them, which finalized the fact that Ethan was going to complete our quad of adventurers.

I texted Ethan. "Coast is clear. Buy away!"

My phone vibrated shortly after. "Done. Flying into San Diego at 10:00 a.m. on July 11th. See you then."

I spoke-texted again, trying to be safe, though the road was still so straight and empty that I probably could have safely texted with my hand. "Yay I can't wait! I'll call you as time gets nearer. So glad you're coming. Don't know what we're going to get into, but I have a feeling it is going to be pretty incredible." I threw my phone back onto the seat next to me.

Well that changes things. All of that happened so fast. Ethan is coming to California! Wait. Ethan is coming to California? Oh no. Ethan is coming to California. I felt a slight sense of dread once my excitement halted with the sudden realization that I had no idea what it would be like traveling with him.

It has been so long since we've been in the same place for more than a few hours, and now we're going to be together twenty-four hours a day for two and a half weeks. What will the dynamic of our interactions be like? Will we get along? Will we have enough to talk about? Does Ethan even know how to backpack? Does Ethan even have a backpack? How are we going to manage both of us sleeping in the car? Will he still like me? Will I scare him if I'm not happy and fun all the time? Did mom and dad tell him about me not really believing in God anymore? If not, will he be upset if he finds out? My thoughts raced with apprehension and the guilt of feeling how distant I had been from him the past two years. Ethan and I grew up with very little space between us, in age, in hobbies, in interests, but that had not been the case since I left home.

Though I originally thought about working on an organic farm on the coast for a couple days in California and had wanted to be by myself for longer, somehow my attachment to that plan completely changed once Ethan called me. I had this weird familiar feeling in my gut that let me know this was the right thing, that it would be good somehow, that Ethan was supposed to come. Even though I was nervous and had no idea if it would be fun or easy or terrible or hard, I was excited. Ethan was coming to California.

I settled into a period of silence, watching the horizon as it was refilled with windmills over and over again. I turned on Manglehorn, an eerie, futuristic instrumental album by Explosions in the Sky, and the combination of listening to that and seeing nothing but windmills for miles and miles and being the only car on the road made me feel like I had been transported. The unfamiliar and undeveloped landscape around me made it feel as if I had gone backwards or forward in time all at once, yet somehow I still existed in the present, as if my existence transcended the construct of time. It was as if all relativity had vanished because suddenly everything was all the same. I continued on, alone, in my small little Jeep, guided across this vast landscape by the same stick-straight highways that had led me now almost six hours across Texas.

The few trees that dotted eastern Texas had shrunk to shrubs and bushes now that I was on the other side of the state, and the lush greens had faded to desert yellows and browns. I laughed to myself at the thought that the only types of vegetation that rose above three feet in this area were windmills and power lines.

My picture of America as I knew it was ever stretching and growing, and I could feel my sense of self growing with it. Since I'd been raised in the Bible Belt and hadn't traveled much outside of the southeast corner of the states, I'd thought that all of America must be like the South. That was the only face of America I'd seen. Sure, I knew that there must be some differences between the regions, but I hadn't fully understood that my picture of America had been painted with a limited color palette until now, as I slowly made my way across the entire country, mile by mile. I was realizing that America was so much more vast and diverse than I could have ever imagined.

At first I felt robbed, like I hadn't been given the full story, like I'd been given an old and out-dated picture of what my country was when there was this whole other America out here. But then I realized that I was also partly at fault, for I'd allowed my contempt for the conservative nature and close-mindedness I often experienced in Southern culture to turn into contempt for the entire country as a whole. All of my incorrect assumptions left me uninterested in finding out what America was for myself for a long time. I felt like I needed to apologize for being so stuck-up and judgemental, for the America I was experiencing did not match up with the constricting, limited, monotonous place I'd made it out to be in my head.

I'd never felt proud to be an American before. In fact, before I left on my trip, I'd spent time daydreaming of what it would be like to just move and make a new life in another country so I wouldn't have to be attached to the United States anymore. But I knew that leaving wasn't the answer. My problems I was trying to avoid would follow me, and the things I believed to be wrong about America wouldn't dissolve just because I went to another country and pretended America didn't exist.

But what did it mean to commit to staying in this country when I still had so much to learn about it and so many biases to break down? I knew through and through what it meant to be a part of the South, at least I thought I did, but what did it mean to be a part of the United States as a whole? If I hadn't understood America to make an accurate judgement about it before leaving on my trip, would I be able to when I returned?

I was only half-way across. There were still so many states before me. So many people, so many cultures, traditions, and foods, and it was all America. America wasn't just Georgia. It wasn't just the South. It was a giant canvas with only a tiny corner of it filled in, and I had been viewing the whole thing as if it was just the tiny corner. When I got back to the South, would I feel differently about my home, about where I come from? Would I appreciate it more? Would I resent it for handing me a biased view of a country which was only becoming more captivating and interesting and beautiful with each new day on the road? Where would my sense of place be when I got back? Who would I be when I got back?

All of the sudden rain drops started splattering across my windshield out of nowhere. It came down harder and harder until even with my windshield wipers going at the highest speed I could barely see.

What is it with this storm? I'm in the desert! I thought it rarely rained here? I had slowed from 70 miles per hour to 55 miles per hour, and I noticed that I was still flying past people driving no more than 30 miles per hour in the right lane. *That's weird. I know it's raining but it's not that bad. It rains in Boone all the time, and we never drive this slow, even on curvy mountain roads. Maybe the stereotype about Texans not being able to drive in the rain is actually true, that it rains so little here it gives people anxiety to the point of driving 30 miles per hour in the right lane.*

It was only long after my trip that I found out there is actually a justifiable reason for their timidity and caution, when a friend who grew up in Texas informed me of an extremely important detail about Texas roads. So much oil builds up on the highways during the extended periods of no rain that when it finally does rain, the roads get covered with a thin, slippery film of oil, which can make your car spin out easily.

So it turns out all of the other drivers I flew past were actually just trying to assure they retained their lives. Meanwhile I zoomed on through the downpour at 55 miles per hour confidently and ignorantly past all of the slowpokes, shaking my head, thinking, "Suckers!" as I left them in the dust. All the while they were all probably shaking their fists and cursing back at me for being a crazy person asking to end up upside down in a ditch.

Thankfully I survived my apparent death wish unscathed. The storm stopped around 6:30, and I needed food. I'd also been playing way too closely with the chance of ending stranded and having to walk to a gas station in the downpour, so I needed to find somewhere to fill up as well.

Muleshoe ended up being the town of choice, mainly because of the name. I don't think you can get more middle-of-nowhere-in-Texas than Muleshoe. I pulled into a gas station, filled up my tank, and parked off to the side so I could fix my dinner.

I dug my camping can opener out of my food box and wrestled a stubborn can of black beans for a couple minutes. I finally got it open and drained the liquid from the can into the gas station trash can, and then I dumped the beans into the one dinner bowl I brought. I'd packed a spice storage contraption that held six spices separated in one canister, so I was able to add some cumin, garlic powder, salt, and pepper, along with a small can of salsa, to spice up the beans. They could have used some red onion, cilantro, lime juice, hot sauce and some tortilla chips, but for a trunk dinner at a gas station in Muleshoe, Texas when you've done nothing but drive in a straight line for over six hours, it wasn't too bad.

I snuck my dirty dishes into the gas station bathroom to wash them, which was probably not allowed. I forgot dish soap, so a rough rinse of my bowl and spoon had to do. I followed my black beans with a course of GORP, and finished with an apple I bought in the gas station on my way out, hoping the cashier wouldn't question my wet, freshly cleaned dinner bowl sticking out of my bag.

As I crossed into New Mexico, the sky seemed giant, otherworldly, more vast than I had ever seen it, and the land was so flat that it looked like the world was flipped, and I was driving upside down on one giant ceiling of a sandy building that went on forever.

I kept thinking about how beautiful the stars would be in this massive sky with no light pollution to get in the way. I was tempted to just park my car right there on the side of the highway, lay in the grass as the sun set, and stay the night, but something in me didn't feel confident about pulling off there, and I was too restless to get to Santa Rosa to stop.

I watched the sunset as one of the most majestic, never-ending skies I had ever seen transformed before me. To my left, a thunderstorm hung so low it seemed like I could almost reach out and touch it with the tips of my fingers. It moved like a giant animal, slowly grazing over the fields next to me, its dark gray abdomen supported by small columns of rain falling quietly down to the crop rows below.

As it moved past me going the other direction, a golden sky blazed afire toward the horizon. A streak of beaming light emanated from just above the ground. The rays of its source expanded across the blue sky, touching the wisps of cotton candy clouds to my right. The smell of wet earth filled my car, and the sound of the fresh shower from the outskirts of the passing thunderstorm gently pitter-pattered on my windshield.

A freight train was now crawling by on my left, like a caterpillar in the sand, moving in the direction of the thunderstorm I was now past. I looked back toward the horizon to watch the sun slowly show itself in full force. The bright ball of fire dropped below the cloak of clouds that previously shrouded it, revealing itself with a luminosity that made my eyes burn. I had the sensation of my stomach dropping, a bodily reaction to sudden raw beauty which always had amazed me.

In a flash the dark, gloomy, overcast world I had been driving through for hours was filled with piercing light, and the land around me now looked completely different. There was not another car in sight. It felt as if the sky was painted for me. It told me of my own soul, and I knew that somehow we were both part of the same story.

It was dark within the hour, and somehow even though I felt like I had spent five years on the road that day, I was still an hour outside of Santa Rosa. It sounded like rain had started falling again. There were little drops collecting on my windshield which quickly became hard to see through. However, when I turned my wipers on, a thick, sticky film spread across my windshield, so dense that I couldn't see through it at all. I immediately pulled over to the side of the road using my side windows because I couldn't see anything straight ahead through the muck, and the fact that there were no streetlights or other cars headlights for miles didn't help my inhibited visibility.

When I got out to inspect the situation, I realized the pelting sound I heard wasn't rain drops but the rhythmic death of hundreds of bugs with extremely sticky insides. I tried to spray some of my wiper fluid and let my windshield wipers do the work, but the slime didn't go away at all. I realized I would have to wipe it by hand, but I wasn't prepared for wiping bug guts off of my windows. I had my bath towel, which was already dirty from Journey, and adding bug guts to the thing I was supposed to dry my naked body with did not seem like an appealing idea. I didn't have any other towel or cloth though, so I dug through my glove compartment hoping to find another option. I thankfully found some wadded up used napkins from who knows when.

I only had about eight ounces of water left in my water bottle, so I poured a tiny bit on one of the napkins and began scrubbing away at the explosion of guts. I made sure to use the water sparingly because my only other scrubbing liquid options were saliva or urine, which did not seem like they would help the situation.

If there is one way to look like a damsel in distress that could be snatched by the passerby creeper, it's standing on your tire to scrub your windshield with a paper napkin at 10:30 p.m. on a pitch-black night on the side of a highway in the middle of nowhere. The only signs of civilization were little lights twinkling far away on the horizon. One pickup truck drove by, but it was after I was already back in my seat with the door closed, so they didn't show any signs of stopping.

I was able to clear a large enough spot at my line of vision to be able to keep driving safely, but I didn't have enough water to clear my whole windshield. I couldn't turn my wipers back on because they would just smear the guts around and cover the cleared spots again, so I just drove really slowly and squinted to see through the tiny slits of gut-free windshield.

I thought Muleshoe was something, but I think wherever I am now is the most in-the-middle-of-nowhere I have ever been. It was darker than I had ever seen. I was alert, tense, and on edge to make it to Santa Rosa. I didn't easily get freaked out during this period of my life, but I started to get even more uneasy as I watched my cell service drop slowly down from full bars to three, to two, to one, to none, back to one again, back to none. *What if I break down? What if I get a flat tire? What if someone sketchy stops to help me and something bad happens, and I can't call for help because I don't have phone service?* I felt as if I was betraying my own dignity, but I actually grabbed the stun gun out from behind the seat and sat it in the cup holder next to me.

Darkness reaches a whole new level when there are no other head-lights, no light pollution from nearby cities, no street lamps, no signs of any other people around. The sky was still full of clouds, so there wasn't even light from the moon or stars. Just complete darkness, except for my headlights. I knew this was just the Earth's natural state without human inventions, but being used to the glow of comfort from LED lights everywhere, it was hard to sit in the eeriness of it all.

Eventually I convinced myself that I was not in imminent danger and decided to just focus all of my attention through the gut-free spac-es to the edge of where my headlights reached. The consistency of the gentle rolling hills of the New Mexico Desert were comforting.

Up, down, up, down. Breathe.

The sparkles of light on the horizon grew in size, and finally, I saw a small, rickety, green road sign with an arrow pointing down the road for a truck stop. You know you have been in the desert for too long when you pull into a grungy truck stop at 11:00 p.m. and all senses of safety and comfort flood toward you instead of away from you.

This was one of the larger truck stops with showers and other fa-cilities for truck drivers on the road for a long time. I probably could have gotten away with sleeping in the parking area, but the parking lot was mostly empty, and the few people I passed gave me looks I could not decipher, so I figured I would drive a half mile further into "town" to see what my sleeping options were there.

It turned out that there was a Holiday Inn, a more well-known establishment than I was expecting in this tiny town of 2,700 people. Santa Rosa was basically just a 'T' intersection of a few "highways" that were more like backcountry roads which met up with the famed Route 66. No matter the logic, after so much unfamiliarity, seeing a recognizable name like Holiday Inn made it seem like a safer parking lot than anywhere else. There were at least a dozen cars in the parking lot, so I just parked and hoped there wasn't a security guard that would have noticed when no one ever got out of my car.

After being on the road for almost nine and a half hours, and af-ter feeling so triggered and heavy that morning after the nightmare, I was completely exhausted and could barely think of much past being unconscious as quickly as possible. I ditched the idea of trying to dis-creetly brush my teeth. I went about the awkward climb into the back of my car. I reached around to the front seat cup holder, grabbed my stun gun, and sat it in the back-seat cup holder.

This Blue Hole better be worth it. I was out within seconds of my head hitting the pillow.

{7}

PAINTED BLACK

I SHUT MY EYES TIGHTLY AFTER OPENING THEM TO THE blinding sunlight that filled my car the next morning. Waking up with the sun was new for me. It felt violating to my body that still craved sleep, but I couldn't help but feel grateful for the contrast to the on and off rain the day before. My jaw muscles still felt like they were recovering from a long bout of crossfit, so my unforgiving quinoa granola wasn't going to cut it today, and my relentless hankering for something savory would not go away. I climbed to the front seat, still wearing the same tie-dye shirt I wore the day before. I looked in the rearview mirror to see my bed-head curls sneaking out of their previously neat braid, and I tucked the straggler strands back in where I could.

I routed to the Route 66 Restaurant for breakfast. I figured splurging on a local chorizo breakfast burrito on Route 66 was a requirement for a road trip across America. I received questioning looks from all of the restaurant patrons who seemed to be the kind of locals that start every morning at one of the only restaurants in town. I stuck out like a sore thumb in my tie-dye shirt. There was no question that I wasn't from there.

As I inhaled the most scrumptious and greasy meal I'd had since Nashville, I looked along I-40 West on my map to see where I should drive next. I wanted to avoid any major metropolis, so I looked past Alburquerque and into Arizona. I remembered someone telling me once that Flagstaff was a must in any Arizona road trip, and since it was six and a half hours away, I figured reaching it by dark was doable. Maybe I would even stop at Petrified Forest National Park on the way to stretch my legs. I'd never heard of it, but why not?

The Blue Hole was only a few miles from the restaurant. Within ten minutes I reached a faded billboard that said "Blue Hole" in all caps, underlined by an arrow that I assumed to have been red at some point but was now closer to a crackly pink. It seemed like everything was faded here, worn by time and heat and lack of rain. As far as I could see the landscape was some variant of faded yellow or brown. I wondered how people survived here with so much heat and so little green.

The crackly pink arrow led me into a dusty gravel parking lot, and my tires stirred up brown dust that seeped through my cracked windows. It was only 10:30 am, and it was already close to 100 degrees, which felt like a personal attack against my terribly low heat tolerance.

The SCUBA certification office bathroom hadn't opened yet, so I parked and changed into my swimsuit in my car, successfully avoiding flashing my boobs and butt cheeks to any onlookers. I walked down to the water, and my stomach dropped a little when I peeked over the edge. I could see straight down, all the way to the small black silhouettes of early morning divers swimming far below. There was another group of divers bobbing on the water's surface, preparing to go down to meet those distant figures, and then suddenly they were gone, and bubbles rose to take their place.

Maybe this is how people can stand to live in this barren furnace of a town.

I looked to my right where sandy, rocky steps led up to some boulders which you could jump off of into the hole, and I cringed when I saw "61 degrees" in bold letters in the middle of the informational board next to the stairs. I had no idea what 61-degree water would feel like when one's body was completely submerged in it without a wetsuit. I was torn between testing the water before I jumped or just going for it, but I ended up walking over to the stairs opposite the jumping rocks to dip my toes in to get a quick feel for how insane I was. It was a mistake.

I shouldn't have felt the water. I should have just dealt with the cold once I was in it because now, instead of only being filled with excitement and adrenaline, there was also a significant amount of dread in the mix. I learned from cliff jumping into the Verzasca River in Switzerland that I don't love being in water below sixty-five degrees. No, to be more specific, I actually hated being in water below sixty-five degrees. My body almost went into shock when I hit the water in Switzerland. My reptile brain kicked in before I could consciously decide what I should do. All my brain was thinking was, *"OUT OUT OUT!"* I swam faster than I ever thought I could until I was panting face-down on the shore. I hoped that this would not be the same experience, since there was an audience, above and below water.

I took off my tank top to reveal my pale abdomen, fully aware this was the first time I had been in a bathing suit that summer and fully aware of my newly acquired love-handles and thighs that had a little more thunder in their step than they did a year ago. It was hard to ignore the pangs of insecurity I felt with every sucked-in step as I walked past two tanned and toned guys who just arrived wearing lifeguard shirts.

I hated myself, and I hated myself for hating myself, but it was a cycle I couldn't just snap out of. I could not rid my mind of the body shaming that poured into it. I longed to get out of this cycle. I tried to shake it off as I walked past the lifeguards.

At least I'll have someone to save me if I go into shock or forget how to swim. I approached the steps leading up to the jumping rocks. *Okay. This is going to be fun. Right? And if not, at least it will be a good story.*

I tried to coax myself out of my timidity as I climbed the stairs. The air was extremely hot and muggy now, and knowing that I only had to swim about ten yards to get back to warmth was somewhat comforting, but anxiety spiked my heart rate.

Em. You drove to the literal middle of nowhere in New Mexico to do nothing but jump in this one damn body of water. You will hate yourself if you leave without doing it. You have to. There's no exception. You have to.

I knew I had to, but that didn't help my heart rate slow down. I made my way to the top of the boulders that hung about fifteen feet above the water. I looked down, took a deep breath, and mentally prepared to jump in.

"Yew want us to take yer pit-cher before yew git in?" I heard a voice call behind me.

I turned around to see two women in their fifties, one smiling at me from the shade of her straw hat and the other with wrinkles of age and many laughs extending from the rim of her sunglasses.

"We saw yer camruh sittin' on the bee-yench and figgur'd we'd owffer!" yelled Sunglasses.

"Oh, um," I paused, as I was a little caught off guard. "You know what, yeah, why not?" I blurted out.

I hadn't been taking pictures often during my first days on the road, mostly because I was driving a lot, but also because I had intentionally put a pause on social media. I had become totally addicted and needed to detox from Instagram. It's amazing how apparent your actual desire to take a photo becomes when photos are only for your personal pleasure and viewing instead of a tool to get fake affirmation in the form of a "like" on social media.

I realized a few months before that I often took photos, not because I cared to have the photo for myself, but so that I could post pictures on social media to seek out that quick hit of dopamine that comes with every notification of a new like or new comment. I knew that I needed to take a break until a healthier intention could be brought into my picture taking. I found that I was living my life through a camera lens, trying to capture and hold every image as if I owned it, and its job was to serve me. I realized that I never truly experienced the raw and natural present because I was always trying to manipulate it with camera angles and filters that made it look more beautiful or more perfect or happier or more whatever-would-get-the-most-likes.

But Straw Hat and Sunglasses offered. I wasn't doing it only so that I could post the photo somewhere, so I guessed I didn't have to feel too guilty about it. I handed them my orange camera.

Straw Hat said she would try her best to get me in mid-air, but she "wutn't so great at this pho-taw-graphy stuff." I tried to assure her that there was no pressure to capture the perfect moment and that any picture would be greatly appreciated.

I walked up to the edge and swallowed hard as I inhaled and exhaled a long, deep breath.

"Want us to count?" Sunglasses called from behind me.

"Yeah go ahead!" I called back. I felt the pressure of accountability. My heart pounded.

Here we go.

"One! Two! Three!"

I flailed and braced for impact. My first mistake in entering the water was forgetting to point my toes because the first thing I felt was the slap of my flat feet against the water's surface, sending pins and needles up my legs. My second mistake was forgetting to blow out my nose as I entered, for not only was the water as shockingly frigid as I expected it to be, but it was extra shocking when it shot so far up my nose I was sure my sinuses had been turned inside-out.

My third and most miserable mistake was one I can't exactly pinpoint, but either something I did or something I didn't do caused my bathing suit bottoms to shoot straight down to my ankles, like all the way down, where my shins met the top of my feet. Thankfully my first mistake in forgetting to point my feet was helpful here, for if my feet were not at a ninety-degree angle to my leg, my bottoms might have slipped all the way off, floating down to the spectators fifty feet below, leaving me totally butt-ass naked in the clearest water I've ever seen.

Somehow, despite the chaos of my breath being taken from me, the shock of cold water shooting up next to my brain, and suddenly being submerged in an ice-bath, I retained enough reflex capacity for my hands to immediately reach down and grab my bottoms just in time. Unfortunately, if any of the divers happened to look up to find the source of the crashing sound above them, I'm sure the sight from their point of view was not a pretty one as I desperately sprawled and scrambled to shimmy my bathing suit bottoms back up to my waist before I swam up to the surface to meet the eyes of those watching from above.

My dignity was not totally saved. I only half-succeeded in getting my bottoms back in place, for once I surfaced and immediately started to make my bee-line freestyle swim toward the concrete stairs, my bottoms drifted halfway down my butt and hung there, exposing my pale crack and cheeks to whoever was looking down on them. I probably would have been more mortified if I had more time to think about it, but at the moment the only thought in my brain was, *"OUT, OUT, OUT!"*

I was panting once I reached the stairs, but I tried to force a smile through my chattering jaw and the embarrassment that comes when you have been unintentionally exposed in public, specifically public that consists of attractive, young lifeguards whom you would have liked to impress. I turned around to see Straw Hat and Sunglasses waving at me from the rock.

"I got it!" Straw Hat yelled down as she extended a thumbs up. I hoped she meant the jump and not my pale butt cheeks highlighted by sunshine and blue water.

I power-walked toward my towel with arms crossed over my chest to hide my very awake nipples, not wanting another body part to be unintentionally put on show for everyone. The sun was high overhead now, and I could already feel its hundred-degree heat quickening the thaw of my chilled skin. With my towel finally wrapped tightly around me, I walked behind the lifeguards so I would not have to make eye contact with them, and I made my way back up the stairs to retrieve my camera.

"Turned out great!" yammered Straw Hat as she showed me the photos. Somehow she was able to get the sequence of my jump in three pictures—one as I left the rock, one in mid-air, and one as I hit the water, before the revealing of the rump, thankfully.

"Wow, not so great at this photography stuff? You're basically a professional!" I joked. "Thank you so much! These are awesome!"

"No problem!" Sunglasses replied happily. "Yer a lot braver than us. We just wanted to stop and take a look before we kep' goin.' We never thought of jumpin' in 'til we saw yew wawk up. Glad we got to help!"

I talked with them for a while and found out their true identities. Straw Hat was Karen from Oklahoma City and Sunglasses was Tanya from some small town in Texas. They were life-long friends on a road trip together to go visit Karen's daughter and newborn granddaughter in southwestern Arizona. After thanking them and wishing them safe travels, I walked back to my car.

The stale, suffocating heat engulfed me as I entered the driver's side, and I quickly turned on the A/C for some relief. Though I still felt a slight pang of embarrassment from potentially scarring the poor divers with my spread-eagle attempt to save my bathing suit bottoms, my jump into the Blue Hole was exhilarating and refreshing, and I was glad that I made the decision to drive to the literal middle of nowhere just to jump in a little pool nestled in hundreds of acres of desert.

I pulled up directions to Flagstaff.

Four hundred and thirty-five. Oh no.

Four hundred thirty-five was the number of miles I would drive without turning according to the GPS instructions from the Blue Hole to Flagstaff, Arizona. When I was planning my day earlier I didn't even think about the fact that I would drive on I-40 the entire day.

This is going to be a long day. Hopefully I can stay awake.

I pulled out of the parking lot, and drove the only direction that existed in my world then—west.

With the monotonous landscape, there wasn't much thought stimulation, so my mind was fairly quiet throughout the drive to the Petrified Forest National Park. There were small plateau-like hills to my left, but they were too far off to see much of their detail. Besides that, sandy soil and small shrubs made up the most consistent geography. Occasionally I would see some outcroppings of red rock from the highway, but I was driving by so quickly that it was hard to fully absorb it.

The silence was only interrupted when an occasional exit sign appeared on the horizon and I would try to guess what fast food restaurant would be on the sign. Fast food had been the only source of thematic cultural connection I noticed as I drove across the country. The high frequency of fast food restaurants, even out in scantily populated areas of rural New Mexico spurred thoughts not only about the strength of America's addiction to fast food, but also America's addiction to immediacy.

We want immediate food from a drive thru, immediate care from a doctor's office, immediate answers from the internet, immediate entertainment from a television, immediate connection through social media because we no longer know how to sit in unknowing, to rest in moments of silence, or to give up our control over our circumstances. We reign over our precious time like kings, only to wage war on those who do not fulfill our need in the exact moment that it comes about.

We order food at a restaurant and treat our waiters poorly when the food takes longer than we would like it to. We walk into a doctor's office and write a bad review if they don't take us back the second our appointment time comes. We curse the truck in front of us that is driving ten miles per hour under the speed limit, and our entire day is ruined over the fact that we do not get to be in control of our speed, instead of sitting back, enjoying the drive, and getting there whenever we get there.

The moment we become bored, we need immediate entertainment or connection, which we seek from supercomputers in our pockets, and heaven forbid that we don't have LTE service and have to wait a few extra minutes for the page to load because we only have 3G, where we sit there bouncing our knees waiting, frustrated and impatient.

Immediacy is a scary addiction, and I think it often bleeds into how people approach spirituality and religion. I've seen many people in the Church, including myself, approach concepts like God and existential meaning expecting to receive a fast, clear-cut, well-defined answer to unknowing. If those immediate answers to combat our doubts and questions don't come right away, we don't know what to do with ourselves. Most of us are not handed the emotional tools to navigate a lack of answers. Not having answers is uncomfortable, and we aren't taught what to do with our discomfort, except push it down or numb it with other things.

Humans, with their fancy prefrontal cortex that allows them to plan for the future, don't always know how to sit in the realm of discomfort and unknowing with open hands. It seems like a mass of people flock to systems of religious structure that provide them with the most immediate answers to the hard questions, where the work is already done for them, where they submit to the ease of a spoon-fed faith and latch on to answers with strict legalism and stubbornness because they adopt the whole system as the one right way without ever having analyzed it for themselves or considering the fact that it could be fallible. I know I did.

I feel like this blind approach is what often leads masses of people, in the States especially, to throw themselves into submission to elders or theologians or politicians who have already set up a whole perception of the world for them. Who is in, who is out, who has truth, who doesn't, who *belongs to us, and who belongs to them. This is then accepted as ultimate truth because immediate answers are more attractive than the difficulty of going on one's own journey. Letting an institution give them the answers is more comfortable and easier than doing the hard work of critiquing and questioning the institutions they let rule their lives.*

That is what my faith has been my whole life—a spoon-fed meal of ideas, laws, and answers that I adopted as my own because I thought that's just what you did. I never considered that there was another way to eat, another way to discover, to taste, to feel. I eventually realized my stomach had only been connected to a feeding tube my whole life, and I didn't really know what it was that was supposedly being fed into my body. I'd never taken the time to ask what it was made of, what it actually meant to me. Then, once I began deconstructing my faith, it was as if that feeding tube had been cut off, and I didn't know where to get sustenance anymore. I observe myself now tempted to seek some sort of immediate fix to my starvation, some sort of framework that will help things make sense right away. But the last thing I want to do is replace one addiction to fundamentalism to an equal and opposite addiction to fundamentalism.

I was startled out of my contemplation by the sight of three horses without bridles galloping in the grass along the highway. They looked so wild and free. I knew I had been like them before, but I had to reach far back in my memory to when I was a child, running through the yard without worrying if my hair was brushed or how dirty my mud-splattered shirt was. I could find vague moments in my adolescence, when I was able to break through the social pressures of middle school and remember that who I was had nothing to do with what other people thought about me. The moments got fewer and farther between once I looked into my highschool and college years. I'd crumbled under the unrealistic expectations placed on me by my community. I'd been made heavy by a person to whom I gave too much power over my joy. Now that he was gone, I wondered when I would run like those horses again, with my hair blowing in the wind, my legs moving as fast as my body will let them, my knees and ankles strong, my head high and confident, afraid of nothing. No bridle to bind me, no reins to restrain me. Just wild, natural, free, strong, confident, and beautiful.

Once I got close to Petrified Forest National Park, I could see a pod of dark grey clouds lurking in the distance. As I reached the entrance, those clouds decided they'd waited long enough and started to leak big, slow tears from their heavy eyes.

Since it was raining, I decided that I would just drive around in the park until it either stopped raining or I got bored. I drove along a winding road that formed the spine of a ridge. All of the ridges in the area were striped with multi-colored layers of rock that were stark even through the rain. There was an overwhelming hint of red rock everywhere, but hues of oranges and whites and even purples were smeared throughout the reddish sea, telling of thousands of years of time and space and weather and changing mineral deposits that had led to this very moment. I was suddenly in the renowned painted desert that I had always heard about, and it felt surreal.

I am 1500 miles away from home, alone, in the middle of the desert, in the pouring rain. I felt surprised at myself. Today was day seven. It had only been a week since I left Boone, but I felt like I had been away for years, and I started to recognize parts of a woman I was only beginning to get to know. There was a voice that had re-joined the chatter in my head, one I recognized but hadn't heard speak up in a long time. It was gentle, grounded, and sure. I knew it belonged to me, and I could tell it existed independently of Cam, independently of Christianity, independently of all of the people I had been for the sake of fulfilling expectations placed on me by others. I wanted to know that voice again, to claim it, to speak it, to shout it, to embody and embrace this voice of a woman who was nothing but me. I couldn't always hear it, but I trusted that it was there and felt empowered to know that my voice was returning to me. I vowed with everything in me to never let it be silenced again.

As the storm continued to roll in, the tourists started to roll out of the park. Pairs of headlights shone through the thick shower as dozens of cars passed me going in the opposite direction toward the park's exit. Though I could barely see anything around me, for some reason I felt like I should go deeper into the park. I figured the rain couldn't last too long. After all, this was the desert.

Sure enough, after about ten minutes of driving, the rain slowed to a trickle, and shortly after that the sun started to peer through the clouds again. I felt oddly connected with this place, as if I was coming home, even though I had never stepped foot in a desert before Santa Rosa. Besides the beauty of the colored rock layers melting into each other, the desert was probably the least welcoming or comforting landscape I had ever seen. It looked harsh, barren, unforgiving, and unapologetic, but something about it made me want to draw closer. I saw a sign for a pull-off ahead, and I decided to get out and walk around since the rain had halted.

I stretched my arms high above my head, my palms doing a handstand against the cloudy sky. The stiffness of being in the car for four and a half hours was apparent in my knees and back. I began walking away from the parking area, into the sand and scrawny brush that was still damp after the rain but drying quickly in the heat that had returned full-force.

I saw the trunks then. Segments of petrified tree trunks, fossilized roughly 225 million years ago according to the sign at the beginning of the park, were scattered throughout the sand on all sides of me. I walked over to a petrified log laying long across the ground. Its width rose three and a half feet up to my stomach. I ran my hand along the polished surface, over the hardened and crystallized quartz now filling many of its rings. The bark of the log was burly, covered in browns and reds and oranges, matching the wrinkled plateau-looking rocks that dotted the far-off ridges, but the inside was totally different. At the exposed cross-section was a rainbow of fire. Red melted into orange, blurred into yellow, and blended into white. Some spots were glossy and reflected the light of the sun starting to peek through the clouds again, and the matte areas around them provided contrast to highlight the shine even more.

I walked further out, away from the log. My feet crunched across the pebbles and sand, sounding like sonic booms in the desert's vacuum of silence. I stopped walking and took a moment to observe the silence that enveloped me, the silence of being completely and utterly alone in the wilderness. No cars, no birds, no wind, no leaves rustling. Just me. And air. And sand. And 225-million-year-old trees. And wild, open space as far as I could see. My heart pounded hard in my chest.

I looked out across dunes and rocks and shrubby things that looked like sea anemones across an eccentric ocean floor. I felt as if

I had been transported to a new planet. The air had a new thickness about it, and the ground a new solidarity. I felt unified with this odd land, as if I was an extension of it, as if we somehow spoke the same language.

Is this because we are the same? Because my interior looks much like this—dry and brittle and cracked and barren?

I felt something deep in my being lurch and give way. I closed my eyes and allowed myself to sink to that depth, directing all of my attention internally.

Inhale.
Exhale.
Breath.
Stillness.
Silence.
Darkness.
Down, down, down.

All of the sudden, I was facing the cloud from my nightmare.
I did not look away.
I do not want to be afraid of you.
Why are you here, and what have you been trying to tell me?
Why am I trapped in this desert inside of me? Why can't I find my way out? Why are there seasons of spiritual deserts, of dryness, of darkness, of death? Why can't I find life?

(*The moments that followed are beyond human language, but to continue the story, I must attempt to bridge the gap between language and my experience. The words 'God' and 'The Divine' are used without pronouns because what I experienced did not have a gender.*)

What followed those questions in my meditative state is hard to recount. I was filled with a sensation of pulsing energy that radiated throughout my entire body. My arms and legs tingled with warmth. My body became heavy, somewhere between submission and ecstatic bliss, and I was overcome with reverence for and connection with something beyond and higher than myself.

In this state, words that I was not coming up with on my own started to flood my mind from a source that seemed to be outside of me, beyond me, disconnected from any form of thought I had ever experienced. Since I did not have my journal and pen with me, in the midst of this experience I pulled out my phone, opened my notepad app, and clicked the voice-to-text feature on the keyboard (where you speak and the phone's database translates your words from audio input to text output). Words flowed out of me, effortlessly and eloquently, in perfectly-crafted sentences without any intention seeming to come from my rational brain's control.

For those of you questioning a "speaking in tongues" episode, it wasn't like that. The words were in English, but it didn't seem like there were even synapses firing in my own brain that would have translated into the words that came out of me. It was as if something, some energy I cannot explain, literally took control over my mind and body. The words seemed weighty and significant, but I could not consciously process them until they stopped coming and I could read them back to myself.

Just as suddenly as the words came, the words reached an end. I was wrapped in silence again.

What. The. Fuck. Just. Happened? My eyes were wide, frantic.

Feeling something between terrified and mesmerized, I began to read the essay now contained in my notes app. I didn't know what to expect.

Well here we go.

"There is something beautiful about our spiritual deserts, for when we are put in deserts, it is nothing but a blank canvas for God to paint it how God sees fit. Sometimes God paints it with gorgeous rainbows whose colors emit radiant joy and happiness and light-heartedness, and those are the most beautiful seasons where we can run and venture with God without being afraid, where we trust God fully without doubt and let our hand form a bond so tight with God's that we let it lead us wherever it pleases. But sometimes that certain orientation of colors doesn't work anymore, for it is no longer life-giving to us or God has something that would be more beautiful in mind. In order for God to have the ability to

paint that new picture, God must first paint our deserts black—a black so dark and thick that no colors from our previous painting can get through, for they would only taint the beauty of the new creation God has in mind next.

A blank slate, a fresh start, a new, pure canvas to work with.

However, once we see God make the first move to dip the paintbrush into the black paint and make contact with the canvas to which we are too attached to leave behind, we beg and plead, "No, no, don't take it away, for this is what's best for me, I know it!" and we steal the paintbrush from God and say, "I will do this on my own account. Let me do it by myself. Let me paint over the areas I want black and let me keep the areas I want from before in their original color, for I know what is best for me—I am in control."

But little do we know this leaves us more disillusioned and lost than we would have been if we would have just let God paint everything black in the first place, for by trying to do it on our own, we leave ourselves in this limbo of desperately trying to preserve and hold on to things from before yet trying to make something beautiful out of what stirrings we see in the newness that God is calling us into, and it's no use. In this state we are stuck because what we had before is already ruined, yet it is not ruined enough to force us to leave it behind and try to make something new again.

Sometimes, we have to let the Divine paint everything black, a black so dark that we almost think we are dead, for as much fear and insecurity and helplessness linger in the depths of that darkness, there is also a transcending peace that resides there—where we know nothing, where we are sure of nothing, where purpose and meaning are nowhere to be found, where we have absolutely nothing to hold on to, where we desperately plead for vision. There is serenity in coming to the place where you can say you literally know nothing in this world and have to start back at the very beginning in order to create some sort of root system to hold you in place again while the storms and winds rage around you. And since you have let yourself feel and see what resides in the darkest part of your soul, you know that you cannot go *any deeper. You cannot go to a place of more despair. You have hit rock bottom, and it is here where you are humbled, where you are refined and made new again, where you are reborn and built up from the miry clay into a new being, a new and better and higher version of yourself, a higher version of humanity—A Spirit that has learned a little more about itself and that has become a little more like the Divine Universe which created it, which is a beautiful thing.*

Not all have the courage to allow their canvas to be painted completely black, but you must find the strength to go there. Push down into the depths of your soul, into the deepest parts of your heart and mind, into the ugliest parts of your pain, and do not shame yourself or criticize yourself for what you discover there, but embrace it.

Let it hurt when it needs to hurt.
Let it feel good when it needs to feel good.
Cry.
Laugh.
Shout.
Whisper.
Praise.
Curse.
Rejoice.
Lament.
Let yourself feel fully the emotions you find at the deep dark, for it is only then that you will enter into a new state of freedom that you have never seen or tasted.

We were created to live this life in its most raw state, fully in the present moment, where we have the courage and boldness to live entirely in and by the Spirit, where we live by breathing It in, only to breathe It out again."

I read the passage slowly and intently, trying to soak in the words, feeling overwhelmed and intimidated because what had just happened was so incredibly unexplainable. Tears spilled down my cheeks, but not because I was able to take the words to heart. My defense mechanisms were triggered and prevented me from feeling the impact of the experience, even though I desperately wanted to know it was God. There was no doubt what had just happened was mystical. I could not bridge the gap between my experience and language. I wanted to believe the message was what I needed to hear, but I had so many walls up against the idea of God that I couldn't get past them to actually seek what the message that just came out of my mouth could mean for me.

The more I tried to open myself up to let the words sink in, the more angry and closed off I became. I didn't understand it, but I could not deny the fact that what just happened really happened. I had the essay typed out on my phone to prove it, but I could barely make out the words through Atheist Em's defensive shouting. She came out with guns firing, over-analyzing my experience already, screaming in response, *"I DON'T EVEN BELIEVE IN YOU!!"* I tried to stay calm.

All of my repressed and unnamed anger and resentment toward God and the Church was boiling up all at once, and I didn't know what to do with it. I wanted to scream, but my voice was suddenly nowhere to be found.

The sun was gone and raindrops fell again, merging with the streams of tears on my cheeks. I didn't know what to do besides go back to my car and move on, because what else are you supposed to do when you suddenly have a mystical experience in the middle of the desert that you don't know what to do with?

I walked back to my car, which remained solitary in the car park, and got in to leave. I drove back the way I came, my thoughts spiraling in windy switchback curves to match the road. I was not relieved. I was not at peace. I was not filled with love.

I was filled with rage.

Now? You show up now? Not then? Not when I was face down on my bedroom floor crying out to feel you again in the midst of thought cycles that took control of my mind and shut me off from all of my emotions? Not when I was pouring through books and podcasts and Bibles searching for answers to my questions? Not when I could have gotten away from Cam the first time? Or the second time? If you're real, and if you're conscious, you just stood by and watched while I got betrayed in the worst way possible at that point? You didn't show up when I had panic attack after panic attack, alone, trying to catch my breath, praying that all of this would somehow just be able to stop, even if that meant the potential of ending my life? I am so tired of all of this! I have been aching for meaning for months, and I have been so scared and alone. Why would you show up now of all times when you never showed up when I needed you?

What the hell do I do with this? I don't know if I believe in God anymore yet my body was just taken over by that specific feeling I have felt radiating from my chest out to my fingertips, similar to my past experiences of God. What do I do with the fact that this presence somehow still showed up, all the way out here, in the middle of the desert, when I don't fully believe God could exist?

All of my conflicting emotions continued to come out in tears. I didn't feel connected, inspired, or healed. I did not feel comfort, relief, or taken care of. I felt angry, resentful, and terribly confused.

I became so overwhelmed that I started to work myself into a panic attack. My throat got tight and my breathing rate increased, but the harder I tried to breathe, the less air I felt like I was inhaling, propelling me further into anxiety and fear. I was triggered, and I was re-experiencing all of my trauma in my body. My heart rate escalated, and my breath got even shorter, making my chest feel even tighter. All sense of safety had fled from me. I wanted to curl up in a ball and hide. The last thing I needed in this moment was to have an extreme panic attack in the middle of the desert, alone.

The only way I knew how to cut off a panic attack from the past was to repress whatever I was feeling, grow numb, or look away. I had learned how to flip a switch on my emotions, so I just shut them off. I stopped thinking about what just happened—the voice-to-text essay, the anger, the unanswered questions. I did not have the emotional capacity to process them at that moment.

I thought I was ready to sit with the darkness, but not like this. And if that was somehow God, God would have to wait.

I drove the last forty-five minutes into Flagstaff completely numb. I reached the exit to Flagstaff just before the sun fell behind the layered mountain ridges in the distance. I vaguely remember the mountain silhouettes standing strong against the sunset sky as I drove up, but the drive was mostly a blur. I shook the lingering thoughts about earlier away again. I wanted a distraction.

I had no idea what I would do once I got out of my car in Flagstaff. I was still in the same tie dye t-shirt I'd been wearing for a couple days now. I felt gross and decided that I wanted to change into something else before I got out and walked around. I pulled into a gas station before I got to the heart of downtown so I could use the bathroom and change. Out came the blue dress.

I confronted my new look in the bathroom mirror, and my greasy hair, dusty skin, and puffy post-crying eyes did not exactly compliment my attire.

Well, this is just the best I can do today.

My stomach reminded me that I had not had dinner, so I dug yet another can of tuna out of my food bin and started to open it like I was disabling a time bomb, holding it as far away from my body as possible, afraid of spilling tuna juice all down my dress and having to carry the stench with me the rest of the evening.

Downtown Flagstaff met me with a glimmer of small-town mountain hospitality in its eyes that made it seem like a Western, higher-elevation version of Boone. I drove around the grid of buildings, restaurants, shops, and bars that covered an area about a half-mile wide, and the sign for the Grand Canyon International Hostel caught my eye.

Maybe that would be a good place to find someone that knows a little more about this town, and maybe I could find someone with a laptop charger I could use. I parked in an underground parking garage and started walking toward the hostel.

The creaky hinge of the front door directed all eyes in the main lobby toward me as I walked inside. One pair of eyes immediately caught my attention. They belonged to an attractive, tall, curly haired blonde sitting at the front desk, looking to be somewhere in his twenties.

Oh perfect, a distraction.

"Hi," I called with my sweetest smile as I walked up to the front desk.

"Hello there. Are you checking in?" he asked, matching my smile.

"Oh no, I'm not staying here. I'm just passing through," I started. "I saw your sign and came to ask if you had any suggestions of where I should hang out tonight. I was thinking about trying to catch some live music somewhere. Do you know any places that would have a band playing?"

"Hmm. Live music," he trailed off. "I don't know any places for sure, but you could check out Hops on Birch. It's a casual bar that sometimes has bands playing in the evenings. Besides that, I don't really know."

"Got it. Thanks, anything helps. I didn't exactly come prepared with a detailed itinerary," I mentioned, hoping he would ask more questions.

"Oh, where are you passing through from?" He stopped me before I turned away.

"Um, kinda far from here," I replied, chuckling. "I drove here from North Carolina."

"Wow. Drove all the way from North Carolina just to come to the glorious Grand Canyon International Hostel?" he asked, spreading his arms dramatically and raising a flirty brow.

"Yeah I just needed some adventure, you know? Just threw a dart at a map, and Grand Canyon International Hostel in Flagstaff it was. Got in my car right then and there, drove through the night and here I am." We both laughed. "No," I continued, "I'm actually on my way out to California. I left about a week ago, slowly making my way West. I heard Flagstaff was cool, and it worked out to stop through."

"Sweet, that's pretty bold," he replied. "Are you going to go to the Grand Canyon before you move on? You know we're only like an hour and a half south of it."

"Not now. I'm going with friends in a couple weeks once we start heading back east. Our permits are for July 22nd through the 24th. I'm picking them up in San Diego on the 16th, and then we're going to backpack in Yosemite for a couple days before backpacking into the canyon."

"Man, that sounds like a blast. I've always wanted to go to Yosemite," he confessed. "Hike half dome for me, okay?"

"We'll see if that happens. We don't have permits because we didn't plan very much, so we're going to play it by ear. But if we make it on half dome, I will carve your name into a tree on the way up, which I'm realizing I still don't know." I smiled and raised my eyebrows expectantly.

"Jake." He stuck out his hand.

"Nice to meet you Jake. I'm Emily," I said, grabbing his hand and shaking it firmly and gently at the same time. I looked away shyly, not able to hold his penetrative, blue-eyed gaze because it seemed to be saying something I couldn't quite decipher.

"Well Emily, if you don't find something to get into tonight, you're welcome to come back and hang out here. We'd love to have you," he paused. "A lot of people hang out in this common room, and I'll be here until eleven."

"I will keep that in mind. I'll see you later maybe," I extended as I walked toward the door, smiling again as I turned and shut the creaky door behind me. Jake from Flagstaff made me feel giddy, and I didn't know what to do about it.

The sun had fallen behind the mountains now, and the last bit of light was hanging in the air before nightfall. Flagstaff sat at 7,000 feet in elevation, over 2,000 feet higher from beginning my day in Santa Rosa, and the temperature reflected the climb. The mountain air had dropped to a chilly sixty-five degrees, which was refreshing after my scorching time in the desert.

I walked in the direction toward the bar that Jake told me about, and I crossed over Route 66 on the way there.

Wow, Route 66 followed me all the way out here from Santa Rosa this morning. Jeez. Today has been so long. First the restaurant, then the blue hole, then Petrified Forest. The confusion from earlier threatened to well up, but I pushed it back down because I still wasn't ready to find somewhere to put it.

As I approached the door to the bar, I could hear the quick melodies of a banjo floating through the air. Bluegrass was exactly what I was looking for.

I pulled out my ID as I approached a typical hard-ass-looking bouncer. He took my ID between two fingers and flipped it toward himself.

"Twenty-one and over only," he remarked indifferently.

"Wait, really? I just want to come in and listen to music," I pleaded.

"Sorry. Law in Arizona is that anyone under 21 has to be accompanied by their parents to go into a bar."

"Um, parents?" I questioned doubtfully.

"Yeah, anyone under age has to be accompanied by their parents to be able to enter a bar. Or your spouse, but I assume you're a little young for that." He raised his eyebrows.

"Wow. Okay. Interesting." I paused. "Well, do you know anywhere else I could innocently listen to live music within walking distance?" It was hard to hide my annoyance.

"Nah, I don't know much. I just started working here. Sorry, ma'am."

I turned around after blurting my thanks. I quickly researched the law regarding underage attendance in bars in Arizona, and sure enough, only persons twenty-one and older are allowed in, unless you are accompanied by a parent, legal guardian, or spouse of legal drinking age. It seemed ridiculous to me.

It was 8:30 p.m. on a Thursday night. My entertainment options just went from two to one. I walked back in the direction of the hostel.

As I reached for the doorknob, I felt my nerves flutter at the thought of seeing Jake again. Flirting with him felt foreign, but earlier it came more easily than I expected. I took a deep breath, anxious in anticipation of where this would go.

The door did that terrible creaking again, which made my subtle entrance way less cool and poised.

"You again," he noticed with the same captivating smile.

"Me again." I smirked. "Turns out you Arizonians don't trust that someone under twenty-one years old can go into a bar alone to listen to music without leaving illegally plastered. So here I am."

"Oh bummer. How old are you?" Jake asked.

"Twenty. But I feel about seventy-two on the inside. You?"

"I feel that," he replied, laughing. "I'm twenty-four."

Not too old to sleep with. I was caught off guard by how quickly that possibility came up in my mind, not ever having considered going home with a stranger before. The adolescent message I received about one-night stands was that *"only whores slept with strangers,"* but I auto-matically felt attracted to him, I questioned why going home with him would ever be a bad thing.

I shook it off and asked him if he happened to have a Mac laptop charger or if I could ask around to see if someone else had one. He didn't, so I made my way down the female hall. I tried to peek into rooms without giving off the air of a total creeper. Diverse faces stared back at me, and most of them said no to the charger. Eventually toward the end of the hall, a rugged, curly-haired girl said yes. She dug through her bag and grabbed a charger out of a bundle of sprawling wires. She said she would come out in a little bit to get it back from me, and I offered up my thanks and promised I wouldn't go walking away with it.

I hung out in the lobby as I looked up the best way to get to Temecula from Flagstaff. The next day, July 10th, would be day eight on the road, and my last day driving completely solo.

I mean if there's any night to sleep with a stranger, tonight is the night. I was still shocked by my forward thoughts, but as Jake and I talked further, they only got stronger.

I talked for a while with Magpie, a woman in her mid-twenties who also worked at the hostel and Cassie, another woman in her late twenties who was talking about how she had been to forty-five countries already. We shared travel stories, and they gave me some suggestions of where I should go next. Jake wasn't super engaged in the conversation at that point because people kept coming up to the desk needing his help, but he made an effort to chime in when he could, continuing to make the kind of eye contact that made my heart race.

Around 10:00 the girls went to bed, leaving Jake and I alone.

"So, mysterious girl who sleeps out of her car most nights," Jake began, "where are you parking your car tonight?"

"Good question. I hadn't really decided actually..." I trailed off. "I'm currently parked in the parking garage downtown but can't stay there overnight, so the only idea I had was to find some back mountain road around here to park for the night. Do you know any?"

"Well, I don't know any good back roads, but I was going to say that if you need a place to crash that is not your car, I have a futon in my living room that is open, and you're more than welcome to stay there," he offered.

I couldn't deny to myself that I was secretly hoping the whole time he would offer that. I tried my best to play it cool and hide the butterflies swarming my stomach.

"Wait, are you sure? I mean," I gathered my thoughts, "my car is great, but I'm definitely not attached to sleeping in it, and a shower would be really great."

"I have one of those too, and you're welcome to use it for free," he paused and smiled. "On one condition."

"Uh-oh. And what might that be?" I asked playfully. I had no idea what to expect.

"You give me a ride home. I rode my board here, and though I enjoy it, it is kind of a trek on that thing, especially in the dark." He gestured to his longboard resting against the cabinet behind the desk. *As if he wasn't already attractive.* "Plus, that way I can just show you the way to my place. What do you say?" He raised his eyebrows.

"Oh. Yeah. Of course!" I exclaimed, relieved that he did not openly proposition me right off the bat. "Well, if you're sure you're fine with it, I'd be down to hang and stay at your place," I remarked coolly. Even though I'd never just "gone home" with a guy before, I had no overwhelmingly negative gut feelings about it.

After finishing his closing duties, Jake grabbed his longboard, and we made our way to the parking deck through the lamp-lit streets. Jake told me how he was working at the hostel just for the summer between graduate school sessions, and how he recently got back from a scholarship in Australia playing rugby, but I was mostly paying attention to the panic running through my head.

I mean, people do this all the time right? We've talked on and off for a couple hours, and he seems kind, and funny, and thoughtful, and adventurous, and definitely attractive. Is there some sort of clarification that is supposed to happen verbally up front about how this night is going to go? Am I supposed to say up front what I'm okay with and what I'm not okay with? Am I really doing this? Is this a good idea? He did mention his futon in his living room so maybe he's not even interested, but I don't know his expectations with inviting a woman to stay over at his place. Is this just him offering a couch? Or is there more going on here?

Oh no. What if he grabs my hand while we're walking? What would I do? Maybe I'll just cross my arms over my chest and pretend like I'm cold. I crossed my arms. But then what if he thinks I'm cold and then puts his arm around me to warm me up? What then? Ugh. I don't know. I'll leave them down I guess. I put them back down.

I hoped that if a conversation needed to be had, it would be obvious when the time came, so as we finished the walk to my car, I tried to enjoy the simplicity of walking down a new city street with a guy I just met and felt attracted to.

We climbed a flight of stairs and entered Jake's apartment through a side door that opened into a small living room.

"Welcome to the humble abode of apartment 263," Jake said in a courteous manner.

"'Tis lovely," I replied jokingly.

"My room is through there." Jake gestured towards a closed door across the living room. "And my roommate's room is upstairs. The futon is there." He pointed to some unwelcoming cushions on a metal frame, but it was more of a bed than my trunk. "Though the only thing," Jake continued, "is that Blake, my roommate, is out drinking tonight, and there is a chance he will barge in not so quietly in a few hours. So if that's not something you want to be around for," he paused, "you're also welcome to sleep up in my room."

My heart raced again, but I played it cool.

Well I don't really want to be laying here when a random drunken stranger comes home to find me unconscious and vulnerable on his couch. "Yeah, I think maybe your room might be best," I agreed. I trusted Jake more than I trusted whoever his roommate might be.

He showed me to his room, which was filled with only a few items. A queen-sized mattress on the floor, a guitar, a bookshelf, a small dresser, some rugby gear, a few ultimate frisbees, and a couple abstract art pieces. Upon seeing his minimalism and noticing everything in his room that I was interested in, I felt even more attracted to him.

"Ultimate frisbee, huh?" I asked. "Do you play much?"

"Oh yeah, we have a pretty significant club league here. I play every week. Do you?"

"Actually, yeah I do," I replied. "And I'm pretty good," I raised my eyebrows and giggled.

"No way, you?" he asked jokingly. "Nah I'm just kidding. I bet you could crush at some ultimate. If you wanna stay a couple more days, you could play with us on Saturday."

"Wow, wanting to keep me around already?" I bantered. He blushed. "I wish. It's been a good while since I've had a good ultimate game, but I have to be in California by tomorrow. I made plans to stay with some friends, and my brother is actually flying into San Diego Saturday morning."

"Whoa! What? Did you say that earlier? That's awesome!" he exclaimed.

"Oh yeah I guess I just mentioned the part about my friends coming with me to the Grand Canyon," I started. I told him the rest of the story about how Ethan decided to come last minute. Conversation trailed on to psychology, which Jake studied in college, and he had some interesting things to tell me about some study on rats he did the previous spring. I scanned through his bookshelf while he talked, only becoming more impressed with the Wendell Berry poetry compilations and Jungian psychology books.

Conversation came to a lull. I felt the tension, and I knew he felt it too, but not knowing where we should go next I asked if I could take a shower, both because I was gross but also so I could buy some time.

I closed the bathroom door and turned on the shower. My thoughts started spiraling again. Elegant finger-picked melodies trickled under the door from Jake's guitar. *Jeez he just keeps getting more attractive.*

I had a lot to think through, so my shower was by no means rushed.

Is this the moment where I just say screw it all? Where I abandon everything I ever believed about sexuality and purity and saving sex for marriage and have sex with Jake from Flagstaff? I'm super attracted to him, and his body from what I can tell thus far is strong and chiseled, making it harder to not think about. It could be nice.

What does virginity and saving sex for marriage even do anyway? Does repressing one's sexuality until marriage help people or hurt people? Because I've only seen it bring about intense body shame, insecurity, and unrealistic expectations for what sex is supposed to be, as well as all of the abuse that comes out of repressed sexuality.

Has purity culture contributed anything positive to my life? It sure as hell hasn't set me up for the safety, joy, and provision it promised. My friends who have had premarital sex seem way less messed up than I feel right now. Purity culture seems like it has only set me up for more pain. I checked all the boxes, I saved myself. I refused to have sex when there were hundreds of opportunities to do so with Cam. I remained pure and retained my virginity to give it away to my husband when I got married, only to have it all blown up in my face when Cam betrayed me.

If I didn't believe so strongly in saving virginity for marriage, maybe things with Cam would have been different, or if they weren't different, maybe having a more liberal view of sexuality, where purity is not the only healthy option, would have at least made Cam losing his virginity to a stranger so soon less hurtful to me.

Jake seems like a great guy; would losing my virginity to him be so bad? Maybe having sex would help me understand why Cam did what he did and said it wasn't a big deal…

What is the moral thing to do in this situation? How does one navigate morality when one's moral compass has been stripped away or rendered untrustworthy? Before, my actions were navigated by a list of 'do's and 'don'ts,' most of which was handed to me by the Church. But now I don't know what from the Church should be trusted. I have no idea what I should or shouldn't do.

Part of me thinks it would be totally okay to have sex with Jake, yet another equal part of me is screaming that it is a terrible decision, and not only a terrible decision, but a wrong decision, and I no longer have a clear sense of knowing which side is me. How can I feel two completely opposite ways so intensely at the same time, yet they both are coming from inside of me? Which one do I trust?

Maybe this confused state is not the best context in which to lose one's virginity. I probably shouldn't have sex with Jake if I can't even reach a point where I feel any consistently certain way about it. The last thing I want to do is have sex with a stranger without thinking about the implications. Cam did that to me already, and I didn't want to reenact my trauma by doing it again to myself. Don't I have more dignity than that? Does sex even have anything to do with my dignity?

I had no answers, and no one to ask for help from, no friends to call, no safe mentors I trusted to ask for advice. I had been finished washing for at least five minutes now, and I was just standing underneath the warm water, waiting for the courage to get out.

I dried off and got dressed. I brushed my teeth, and I was still searching for a final answer of what I would do when I left the bathroom. I don't think I made my decision until I opened the door.

I walked out of the bathroom. Jake looked up and smiled but continued plucking away softly on the guitar. I took a seat next to him on the bed.

"So I saw that you have Daniel Quinn's Ishmael on your bookshelf. Have you read it?"

"Have I read it? About ten times," he replied. "Have you?"

"Maybe not ten times, but definitely more than once. I saw it earlier, and it reminded me that I should be a little more open about why I'm on this trip."

His casual expression took on one of genuine concern. "Yeah, sure, what's up?"

"*Ishmael* is the book that my ex-boyfriend introduced me to when we were sixteen, and it was the first book that opened my eyes to the fact that I did not really know how the world worked, that there was more than one way to interpret reality, that the way we do life, especially in the West in our addiction to growth and excess and control and manipulation of the earth, might not be sustainable and might actually be harmful and unethical," I started. "It really changed my life."

"Yeah, it had a similar effect on me too, something I think is important for everyone to consider, that there is more than one way to exist," Jake agreed. "So what does *Ishmael* have to do with your trip?"

"Well *Ishmael* itself doesn't have so much to do with my trip directly, but I do associate that book with my ex-boyfriend, who is one of the reasons I am on this trip. Long story short, I'm fresh out of a pretty toxic multi-year relationship, and I'm not exactly in a place where I want to," I paused, "Um," I swallowed, and then I rattled the rest quickly, "*do* anything. Tonight, I mean. With you. I haven't had sex before, well, like, not *sex* sex, because I was raised super conservative Christian and though I'm not really there anymore I don't really know how I feel about this because I don't do this often. Actually, I've never gone home with a guy before. I don't know what you were hoping for tonight, but I thought it was important for you to know that I'm in a really weird place, and I don't know what I'm feeling. It's really soon to be with someone else." I took a breath and braced myself for Jake's reply.

Contrary to my expectations that he would think I was a lunatic, Jake's response was caring.

"Emily, thank you so much for being open and telling me that, and I'm sorry that things ended badly." He paused. "I didn't know how to say this at first, but now that you opened the conversation up, you should also know that I don't really do this either. I've actually never asked a girl to come home with me from the hostel before. I just thought you were really interesting and super beautiful when we were talking at the hostel," he blushed as he said this which I thought was sweet, "and I wanted to spend more time with you, so I went out on a limb when I asked you to stay. I honestly wasn't expecting you to say yes, and this whole time I've been trying to figure out the best way to let you know that I don't have any expectations about how tonight's going to go. I don't need anything from you. But I would like to hold you, if you would be okay with that." He held his gentle eye contact with an equally gentle smile.

I felt like I had been reduced to a puddle on the floor, but I mopped myself up enough to choke out, "I would be okay with that."

Jake set down his guitar and crawled up to the bed from his spot on the floor. He grabbed my hand and led me to lay down next to him. He wrapped his arms around me, and the warmth of his skin against mine already made my heart race faster. I hadn't been hugged like this in months. He pulled me closer to his chest, and I nestled my face up close to him, my breath collecting warm and humid in the small passageway of air between my mouth and the smooth skin of his neck. His curly locks brushed the top of my ear, and though it tickled I did not move my head. I savored everything about his touch, and I could feel it melting away the anxiety I had about how this night might go. I was sure that he could hear my heart pounding.

Before Jake got up to turn the light off, he grabbed my face with one hand and looked into my eyes. I was completely caught off guard, but I didn't resist it.

"Can I kiss you, mysterious and beautiful Emily?" he whispered.

I laughed and closed my eyes, fighting to find an answer. I met his gaze again. "I'm sorry." I shook my head. "I just don't feel ready to do that right now. You're amazing, and I'm extremely attracted to you, believe me. I just don't feel confident about doing anything tonight, even though I know you are not expecting anything more than a kiss when you say that."

He shook his head in agreement. "Oh, of course not. And that's totally fine. I mean, if that is how you feel, I can't argue with it," he assured, "even though I *reallllllly* want to kiss you right now." He grinned.

"Thank you for understanding, Jake. I'm really glad you asked me to stay."

"I'm really glad that for some reason you said yes."

Jake got up and walked across the room to turn the lamp off. When he came back to bed he pulled me close again, spooning my body from behind. His tight stomach radiated heat as it curved along my spine, and his warm bicep rested over my side. I laid in the tension, trying to trust that I had made the right decision for tonight. He leaned over and kissed my cheek.

"Goodnight Emily," he whispered.

"Goodnight Jake," I replied as I snuggled closer to him.

With Jake's warm breath on my neck, I reflected on the day in incredulity.

This is officially the weirdest, most unexpected, most confusing day I've ever had. I don't know how to make sense of the contrast from what happened in the national park earlier to what is happening now, but I think that task is too much for my brain until at least tomorrow. I did want a distraction after my panic attack earlier, and Jake surely has been a distraction. All I know for sure right now is that I'm sleeping with Jake from Flagstaff, and somehow, I'm feeling okay with it.

I think sometimes we just need to be held. Maybe it is possible for it to be nothing more than that. Maybe it doesn't have to be a sign that we are selfish or using someone, so long as there is open communication and intentions on both sides are clear. Maybe our need to be held is just a sign that we are human. It's unfortunate that people who hold too tightly to strict legalism of do's and don'ts in every scenario are often robbed of the fulfilment of this need, halted by the shame that is placed on physical human contact outside of marriage.

Jake and I sleeping together was not sexual because we chose for it to not be sexual. Just because I was lying in bed with a handsome, intellectual, muscular, thoughtful, gentle guy with his shirt off, whom I was extremely attracted to, did not mean that our animal brains were going to take over. I was totally in control of my body, unlike what I had been told my whole life would happen if I put myself in a *vulnerable* situation where temptation is too strong or where there were many *stumbling blocks*, like a situation so crazy as sleeping in the same bed as a person of the opposite sex.

I would like to believe that sometimes people are sent to us for a brief moment to make us feel slightly less alone in the world. They are the exact gift that we need at that very moment, and maybe our only response is to say thank you.

{8}

IMPULSE

AFTER A SECOND OF DISORIENTATION ONCE I OPENED my eyes, I remembered that the golden forest in front of my face was the back of Jake's head. *Wow Em. Yep. You just slept in a stranger's bed. With him in it.*

I considered sneaking out without any goodbye, but I figured that after how sweet Jake was to me, I at least owed the guy a thank you and a farewell.

I reached over the side of the bed to grab my journal out of my bag, trying to make as little movement as possible so I wouldn't wake Jake. My thoughts were still on a hamster wheel. The internal debate that started in the shower the night before had not remotely settled. I began writing.

07/10/15, Day 8 -

I slept with Jake. We didn't do anything last night because I couldn't decide how I felt about it. Even though part of me would be fine with at least making out with him, I don't know how to know if it is okay or not, if it would be triggering, or if I would only think about Cam. Now that Cam is out of the picture, and I don't line up with my old concept of sexuality through purity culture, what is my sexual ethic? Does it change now? Am I still bought in to saving my virginity for marriage? How do I know what is right?

Part of me woke up happily soaking in Jake's warmth radiating next to me, looking forward to the tension, knowing that I would probably give in and enjoy kissing him for a while, but another part of me woke up in panic, fearing that I had done something terribly wrong, wondering if shame and blaming myself and repentance is the appropriate response. Which one is me?

Someone that wasn't raised in fundamentalist, evangelical Christianity might think that me sleeping with Jake is not a big deal, but the only message I have ever been sent for twenty years has been that physical interactions with the opposite sex are super taboo. Sleeping with a guy you just met is unheard of, unless you want to carry a word like slut or whore attached to your name forever. But would I be a slut if I just made out with him? Most of me thinks that is ridiculous, but in the world I am coming from, casual hookups do not get praise or affirmation. Casual hookups are dirty. Casual hookups are sin. Casual hookups are damned to hell.

Life gets really confusing when you have a law that you believe in and abide by fully, and then suddenly you realize that law might not exist and that following it might actually cause more pain than breaking it. Is my hesitance to being with Jake only remnants of the shame culture around sexuality in the Church, or is there actually a moral dilemma here? Is there a universal sexual ethic, or is it relative? Obviously there are important moral distinctions regarding consent and rape, but in consensual sexual encounters, what is okay? If sexuality is relative, how is it possible to set any boundaries?

The Christianity I know has affected the way that I view my body and how I view what other people do with their bodies, and it is hard filtering it to find what is true and healthy. When you are raised via fear-based thinking that the only acceptable relationship pre-marriage is one that is heterosexual, fully-committed, pure, and sexless, the possibility of engaging in any relationship outside of those strict boundaries is overwhelmingly intimidating and scary.

I remember the preacher at my church in high school standing at the pulpit during a 'Love, Sex, and Dating' sermon series, and he literally preached, word for word, that "having pre-marital sex will harm you and your partner more deeply than any other sin." I know this because I have these words written, underlined and highlighted, in my journal from that year. Who wouldn't be terrified, at fourteen going into high school, to ever let a guy's penis come near her?

I always heard growing up, even from my parents, that if you have sex before marriage, it would negatively affect your marriage forever, and your marriage would never be as healthy as it could have been if you saved your virginity. Until now, I always believed that having sex with someone would leave me with a soul tie, where a literal part of my soul would be attached to that person forever. I didn't want myself scattered about, used up, or left behind with different guys, as I heard would happen from analogies presented in church. I wanted to be able to share my whole self with my husband one day.

For years, the idea that I would not be able to connect fully to my partner because I gave some of it away to random guys along the way was terrifying. Even though I believed that Cam would be my husband, in the chance that he wasn't, having sex with him and supposedly ruining my chances of having this "perfect" marriage the Church kept telling me about was not a risk I wanted to take.

These thoughts were reinforced by the only people I spent time with—my one circle of Christian friends, pastors, and family influences in my life. I heard them say judgmental things when they found out someone had sex with their boyfriend or heaven forbid, got pregnant outside of marriage. I heard them call people sluts and whores, but it was mostly girls that got shamed, not guys, which seems even more messed up to me. I sat with and watched friends of mine weep during prayer sessions held because they had lost their purity, praying that it would be redeemed in some way *as if they were broken and less-than because they had sex. I saw so many Christians disassociate themselves from those who were not on the pure and right path.*

I've had Christian leaders scare me coming from a hormonal standpoint, claiming that when you have vaginal sex with a partner, the oxytocin released in a vaginal sex orgasm is different, that it binds your brain to the person you are with forever. But I have also heard that an orgasm is an orgasm, and that the same oxytocin is released regardless of whether the means to the orgasm was via hand (yours or someone else's), mouth, penis, or any other way. Which is it? And what about the thousands of women who save themselves for marriage but don't orgasm the first time they have vaginal sex? Or the second? Or the third? Or maybe ever? Are they still less "virgin" than people who have had dozens of orgasms non-vaginally?

The Church scares young people into purity. It doesn't educate them into purity. It leaves us all scared, confused, and asking a million questions internally that we can't ask externally. It causes us to repress our sexuality, believe our bodies are bad, and heap shame upon ourselves. The only resource we have to find answers is the internet, which is the last place we should be sent to get answers about sexuality.

I never questioned any of it until I was forced to be face to face with the fact that just because I checked all the boxes does not mean that my boxes are right or that my boxes will save me from pain. Looking back at my experience, having purity culture slammed down my throat from a place of fear, it didn't leave me with much besides judgement, shame, confusion, repression, and questions, so many questions, and I think it's time to leave everything else behind except my questions.

I don't know what I think, but I do know that I was not set up with a healthy understanding of sexuality, and I know that it sucks that there was not a safe, judgement-free space for me or anyone else to ask these questions growing up in the Church. I know that it is an important conversation that I want to dive into without fear or shame, but from my experience I'm probably not going to find a healthy conversation about sexuality inside the

Church. I feel overwhelmed with all of the things that I used to
believe in and know I must leave behind, but I don't feel like I
have any place to process—

I picked my pen up mid-sentence when I felt the warmth of Jake's
hand meet the small of my back and continue slowly, up my spine, all
the way up to my neck. My skin ached to be touched. It is amazing
how you don't know how much you have missed and craved physical
touch until you are presented with it again. I turned around and said
good morning with a smile, still not quite knowing how I wanted this
morning to go. I told him I wanted to finish journaling, so I tried to
continue writing while he proceeded to rub my back.

He pulled my hair back softly behind my ear and whispered gently
into it, coaxing me to put my pen down and just lay with him. He cud-
dled up next to my side, and it felt so comforting to feel the curvature
of another warm body fitting into mine again. As his hand continued
its course along the curves of my back and shoulders, the debate was
continuous in my head, a constant battle between the "I" that wanted
to give in and kiss him and the "I" that thought it would be wrong to
kiss him, that I would be betraying something.

After the last months with Cam leaving me feeling powerless and
undesired, Jake's coaxing made me feel powerful, like I had control
over him, and denying him while hearing that I was still desirable gave
me some sort of sick confidence that I am not proud of. After minutes
of deliberation and distraction from his soft palm stroking my back, I
couldn't take it anymore.

Oh what the hell.

I rolled over, and I kissed Jake from Flagstaff, for a long time. I had
only kissed one person in the past five years, and though Jake's lips felt
foreign, they were gentle and inviting. I enjoyed the playfulness of it,
and though I did feel present and in my body as things got more heated, I was aware of the fact that it was void of emotional connection.
It's different, kissing a stranger, but the last thing I felt was that it was
wrong or shameful.

Jake rolled on top of me, with one of his hands on the back of
my neck and the other starting to slide up my shirt, nearing my
breast.

"Is this okay?" he whispered as his hand slid higher.

"Ummm," I paused, placing my hand on his, debating if I should just let go and give in to the pleasure of the moment. "I don't think so. I'm really enjoying this, believe me, but kissing is the maximum that I'm okay with today. If that's not okay with you we can stop." I felt like I needed to apologize.

"Stop? Are you joking? I would kiss you for years, Emily. I still stand by what I told you last night. I don't expect anything from you. I don't want you to feel pressured to do more than you're okay with. Kissing is more than okay," he assured.

I shook my head and smiled. "Jake from Flagstaff, those eyes sure make it hard for a girl to say no to you," I whispered and giggled, as I pulled his face down to kiss him.

Though my time in bed with Jake was sweet, caring, and pleasurable, I did notice a subliminal tone of grief. I was reminded of all of the mornings spent waking up and being held by Cam like this before things got bad, and I knew it would never happen again.

Will I always think about Cam every time I'm with another guy? Will I always carry this ache with me, or will it eventually pass away?

I tried to let go of my reservations, my questions, and my judgement of my experience. It was taking me out of the present moment. I chose to accept my decision to kiss Jake without criticism, shame, or the need to make excuses. I relished how glorious it felt to be held and kissed, for I had to say goodbye soon.

Not having any experience in the "one night stand" lifestyle, I was not quite sure how one proceeds to say goodbye to a stranger they just met and slept with all within a twenty-four hour period, especially since I knew that I would probably never see him again.

"Thank you so much for letting me stay with you," I said as Jake walked me down to my car, "and for being so sweet to me. I hope hostel life continues to bring connection and excitement to you."

"Of course." He pulled me in for a hug. "I'm really glad I met you, Emily. It was refreshing to spend time with someone who understands." He pulled away. "And I'm serious. You cannot leave this area without going to Sedona!"

"Jake, it's already eleven o'clock! The drive is at least seven hours without stops. I have to go straight to Temecula!"

"You're already going to be late, so why not be an hour or two later? I promise, it's nothing like you have ever seen, and it's barely out of your way as you go down the mountain. Plus, when else are you going to have time to just casually stop by one of the coolest rock formations in the country?" He looked at me in a you-know-I'm-right kind of way.

"Ugh," I sighed. "You're right. Maybe I will. We'll see."

"Okay. Get outta here. Good luck on the rest of your trip. You're a really amazing person, Emily. I hope you find what you're looking for out there. Take care of yourself. Keep searching for truth."

I could sense that we both were under the assumption that our connection ended here and that we wouldn't continue communicating, so I didn't feel the need to clarify that.

"Thanks for everything." I kissed him once more and got in my car.

Soon I was driving south on I-17, feeling unprepared for the long day of driving ahead. I wound my way through steep curves down the mountain. Ponderosa pines stood over a hundred feet tall on the hills around me. I noticed the beginning of the West coast feel I'd always heard about. The pines made me antsy to spend the next couple weeks in the woods.

I didn't realize how quickly the exit for Sedona would come. It came and went so fast that I couldn't decide quickly enough whether I was going to stop or keep going. I got off at the next exit that came a few miles further down the mountain to stop for a second and think.

Jake is right. When else am I going to be able to just casually stop by Sedona?

I let Megan know that unexpected plans came up, I was going to get to Temecula later than planned, and they shouldn't wait up for me.

I got back on the highway, going in the direction from which I had come, riding on an impulse, my eyes peeled for the exit to Sedona.

I had never heard of Sedona before Jake told me about its famous bright red sandstone, so I had zero ideas of what I was about to drive into. It wasn't long before I saw giant heaps of that sandstone jutting out of the ground, rising in all sorts of oddly-shaped formations that looked like they were on fire in the sunlight. Even from a couple miles out, I knew Jake was right. You don't just skip out on an opportunity to drive through Sedona.

I routed to the trailhead of Bell Rock, a suggestion from Jake. It was an easily accessible trailhead right off the road to a giant, you guessed it, bell-shaped rock. Despite feeling glad that I turned around, I was still feeling nervous about making it to Temecula at a reasonable hour, so I wanted to make it quick.

It was already noon and beyond sweltering outside. I had a line of sweat on my upper lip within minutes of turning off my car. I threw my running shoes on anyway, hoping that I could go for a short jog without getting too dehydrated.

I took a quick look at the trail map to try to get some sort of idea of how far it was to the actual rock formation, but it wasn't very helpful. I took off, hoping the faster pace of jogging opposed to walking would at least let me see more of the trail in the same amount of time.

The trail was fairly flat for a while. The packed orange-brown sand reflected the sun's light into my tired eyes. A couple minutes into winding my way through short, shrubby terrain, a bullet of fear shot through me.

Oh no. I'm in rattlesnake country now. I wonder if I'll see one. I've heard they're everywhere out here. I've never seen one in the wild before. Might be kinda cool to see one while I'm out West since they're not as common back home. From far away of course. Jeez, I hope I don't come across one laying across the trail. I think I would shit my pants. Would I wait for it to pass? Would I have to bail and turn around? What would I do if I got bit? Do I know snake bite first aid? Suck the venom out? Cut it open? No, I don't think that's right. What am I doing out here all alone? I barely have cell service. I didn't tell anyone that I was coming here. I don't have my ID on me. I'm such an idiot.

It never fails to amaze me how the slightest feeling of fear often opens up a door for self-deprecation to come in and completely suck me out of my entire experience. I tried to shake it and keep going, not without anxiety when I saw a stick up ahead or heard a rustling in the shrubs beside me as I ran by, for I could not muster up another explanation other than that every rustle was a rattler just waiting to pounce.

I arrived at the beginning of the ascent of the actual rock forma-tion free of deadly snake bites. It really did look like a bell, with all sorts of crazy vertical sandstone spires jutting out of the top. I looked for signs for the ascent trail, but there was no longer one clear direction up. There was just a sign with "Bell Rock" in cracked, faded red paint and an equally faded arrow that pointed in the direction of the rock, which looked more like a mountain to me. I looked at my watch. 12:30.

Well, when in Sedona...

I found out that Bell Rock is mostly just ridges of sandstone that rise up level after level, but not all of them are safely walkable, and even if they are, not all of them lead higher, which can make for a confus-ing scramble. Despite the hike supposedly being a pretty popular spot, there weren't many other people around. I could just barely see the small silhouette of a person toward the top, and I figured I would keep scrambling my way up in that direction as best as I could.

As I scrambled, got stuck, turned around, retraced my steps, and tried a different way, I ended up on a steep zig zag of various boulders and ridges of sandstone. I had to incorporate my hands in order to stabilize myself, making it more like rock climbing than hiking. I was covered in sweat but invigorated. I climbed up almost completely alone in yet another incredible desert landscape completely different than what I saw in the Petrified Forest National Park yesterday.

My body paused as my mind was transported back to what had happened yesterday afternoon—the feeling of being taken over by an energy that was not myself, the wanting to believe that it was God, the anger and confusion in knowing that I didn't have any other explana-tion besides that it was. Jake had been an easy distraction that allowed me to shove all of it down and not deal with it. Now that I was alone again, I felt the experience tugging at me, beckoning me back, calling me to pay attention to it.

What do I do with it? Was it even real? Was it just a hallucination? Was it just a weird rush of neurotransmitters? Atheist Em's voice was like a record player caught on a deep scratch, skipping and skipping, not able to push through the thing which halted its normal func-tion. Atheist Em knew how to be an apathetic skeptic, but Atheist Em didn't know what to do with an experience that could not be rationally explained or analyzed, where she was not in full control.

Atheist Em remained in skeptical analysis as I continued to climb higher and higher.

I did not realize how far I had gone up until following what I thought was a side trail around a corner of a sandstone wall on my right ended at a cliff that dropped straight down at least a hundred meters. My heart dropped to my waist as I halted and peeked over and out into the valley. I hadn't turned around once to see the view behind me as I climbed because I was so focused on my internal chatter. My body was just performing robotically, and I had not been fully present in it.

Below me stood waves of various dark green shrubby things and bushes woven between ridges of sandstone, rising up until the treeline ended. Everything above that was plateau-looking, exposed red sandstone, which from where I was standing looked like it wrapped Sedona in a wide, arc-shaped hug. The sandstone hills, or rocks, or mountains depending on one's requirements of classification, rose up in the same slanted, stacked levels as Bell Rock, stepping up into different shaped peaks. Some were flat, some rounded, some column-like. The sky was scattered with clouds, its blueness seeming extra striking contrasted to the fiery landscape below and around me. There was the slightest breeze in the air that made the sweat-drenched hairs on the back of my neck stand at attention. My heart rate was still pumping strong as I caught my breath. My lungs expanded with air and released it in the programmed rhythm they have always known. I sensed something in the air whisper, *"Just be here."*

Being here meant that not only did I have to be present with where my body was, but it also meant being here with my internal self. Pressing into what was going on inside of me felt scary.

I slowly crouched down and scooted my way onto a rock that jutted out to the edge of the cliff. I sat with my legs dangling in the open air. I thought back to yesterday. I pulled out my phone. I hadn't read the words in my note since right after the experience. I thought that maybe at this moment, up on Bell Rock, away from people, and at a calmer internal place, it might start to sink in without as much resistance. I opened my notes app. I clicked on the first one. I read it again.

"There is something beautiful about our Spiritual deserts, for when we are put in deserts, it is nothing but a blank canvas for God to paint it how God sees fit. Sometimes God paints it with gorgeous rainbows whose colors emit radiant joy and happiness and lightheartedness, and those are the most beautiful seasons where we can run and venture with God without being afraid, where we trust God fully without doubt and let our hand form a bond so tight with God's that we let it lead us wherever it needs to take us. But sometimes that certain orientation of colors doesn't work anymore, for it is no longer life-giving to us or God has something that would be more beautiful in mind, but in order for God to have the ability to paint that new picture, God must first paint our deserts black—a black so dark and thick that no colors from our previous painting can get through, for they would only taint the beauty of the new creation God has in mind next."

I paused and thought for a moment. *The canvas of my life was once rainbow-colored and joyful and light, when Cam and I were healthy and everything about Christianity made sense. With the way things ended with Cam and my relationship with Christianity shattering, I spiraled into darkness. My canvas was painted the deepest and thickest black paint I could imagine. But if there is a new creation, where is it?*

"A blank slate, a fresh start, a new, pure canvas to work with.

"However, once we see God make the first move to dip the paintbrush into the black paint and make contact with the canvas to which we are too attached to leave behind, we beg and plead, "No, no, don't take it away, for this is what's best for me, I know it!" and we steal the paintbrush from God and say, "I will do this on my own account. Let me do it by myself. Let me paint over the areas I want black and let me keep the areas I want from before in their original color, for I know what is best for me—I am in control.

"But little do we know, this leaves us more disillusioned and lost than we would have been if we would have just let God paint everything black in the first place, for by trying to do it on our own, we leave ourselves in this limbo of desperately trying to pre-

serve and hold on to things from before yet trying to make something beautiful out of what stirrings we see in the newness that God is calling us into, and it's no use. In this state we are stuck because what we had before is already ruined, yet it is not ruined enough to force us to leave it behind and try to make something new again."

I had felt the nudge forward into something deeper and wider and more open, but I'd been resisting the new thing because I'd been too scared to let go of the old. I knew that I wasn't growing. Growing any more meant letting some things die, and I wasn't ready to grieve the death. I clutched to control. Cam and my constructs of faith had formed my entire identity. I was scared if I let go of them there would be nothing left of me. *But here I am on this giant rock, baking in the Arizona heat, without Cam and without my old concept of God, yet my heart is still beating with a passion for something beyond the limits of the old thing. I'll never be able to resurrect the old back into its original shape, form, and function, and maybe holding on to the old things that are already void of life is what is keeping me from fully discovering and experiencing the deeper and richer life being offered to me.*

"Sometimes, we have to let the Divine paint everything black, a black so dark that we almost think we are dead, for as much fear and insecurity and helplessness linger in the depths of that darkness, there is also a transcending peace that resides there— where we know nothing, where we are sure of nothing, where purpose and meaning are nowhere to be found, where we have absolutely nothing to hold on to, where we desperately plead for vision. There is serenity in coming to the place where you can say you literally know nothing in this world and have to start back at the very beginning in order to create some sort of root system to hold you in place again while the storms and winds rage around you. And since you have let yourself feel and see what resides in the darkest part of your soul, you know that you cannot go any deeper. You cannot go to a place of more despair. You have hit rock bottom, and it is here where you are humbled, where you are refined and made new again, where you are reborn and built

up from the miry clay into a new being, a new and better and higher version of yourself, a higher version of humanity—A Spirit that has learned a little more about itself and that has become a little more like the Divine Universe which created it, which is a beautiful thing."

I've been scared to let myself feel the pain, doubts, fears, and insecurities in the deepest parts of me. If I just let myself experience my rock bottom and see that I can survive it, maybe there will be some sort of meaning and life on the other side. I want to believe this. I recognize my unknowing, and I think I'm supposed to start there—in the tension of ambiguity. I want to create a root system again. I want to believe that there can be rebirth and resurrection. I want to believe I can be whole and healed Emily. I can see a vague vision of her in my mind, full and thriving, but I can't see her clearly enough yet to know the way forward. I don't know how to find her.

"Not all have the courage to allow their canvas to be painted completely black, but you must find the strength to go there. Push down into the depths of your soul, into the deepest parts of your heart and mind, into the ugliest parts of pain, and do not shame yourself or criticize yourself for what you discover there, but embrace it."

Do not shame or criticize myself. Just observe it and embrace it.

"Let it hurt when it needs to hurt."

But that's so hard and scary.

"Let it feel good when it needs to feel good."

I'm afraid to feel happy again.

*"Cry.
Laugh.
Shout.
Whisper.*

Praise.
Curse.
Rejoice.
Lament.

"Let yourself feel fully the emotions you find at the deep dark, for it is only then that you will enter into a new state of freedom that you have never seen or tasted.

"We were created to live this life in its most raw state, fully in the present moment, where we have the courage and boldness to live entirely in and by the Spirit, where we live by breathing It in, only to breathe It out again."

I filled my lungs with a large breath and slowly let it out. The essay wasn't as scary as I remembered, and taking time to soak it in from a better internal place left me hopeful and expectant. I looked back out across the valley, over the shrubs, over the dust, over the dryness. I still didn't know how to trust that I could step off the cliff of my pain and go all the way to the bottom of it without dying, but I knew that it was time to jump.

I wanted to give in to my canvas being painted with something new, but before I could do that, I knew I needed to grieve what had been painted black. I wanted to find the new state of freedom past the deep dark. I wanted to believe there was something more, whether it be some conscious God or whether it was simply the Divinity I carried within me. I wasn't ready to reconstruct yet, but I felt hope in the possibility of reconstructing. I hoped one day my spiritual house would stand again, and maybe that new, beautiful canvas would be the piece of art hanging on the front door.

In my hopelessness, I could have never found the words that came to me in the petrified forest on my own. I was taken somewhere. I was given a higher and wider perspective, and a deeper filter. I didn't know any other word large enough or wide enough or vast enough to name what that experience was besides "God," the word humans have used for thousands of years to point at that which cannot be named. It felt like God, the source from which all things flow, the ground of being, the reverence that hums within us. God was suddenly outside of the pretentious excess, outside of the constructs, outside of the legalism, outside of the lies, outside of the manipulation, outside of the need for rigid religious labels, outside of the need for one unchanging, ultimate truth, and a world of endless possibilities unfurled inside of me.

I felt giddy with excitement and anticipation for the coming days. Though I didn't have language for it, it felt like I could see a little clearer. The first week on the road I felt like I was running away from everything I didn't want to look at, but now I realized that I needed to run toward it. I was still scared, but I didn't feel paralyzed by my fear anymore.

I looked out across the red Sedona landscape once more. I got up to leave, and I almost ran down the entirety of Bell Rock. There were places that were super sketchy, and one slip or wrong move would have promised major injury or even death, but I was so invigorated that I didn't care. I was ready. It was time to seek. It was time to look my trauma in the eyes and ask it how it was my teacher. It was time to hold the face of my pain and ask it to guide me home.

California met me with purple, hazy mountains silhouetted against a simple and sweet cotton candy sunset. I noticed this odd sensation while I was driving. It was something I might have felt before but hadn't felt in a long time, so it was hard to put my finger on. I felt as if even though there was still so much to process and figure out, and even though I had no idea what I was going to do with my life after this trip, I was not supposed to be anywhere else in the world than right there—in my little car abode, welcomed by purple mountains and a land I had never been to before.

For the few hours since leaving Sedona and driving through Phoenix, my thoughts had completely settled into a constant state of just being. There was nothing to be done, there was nothing that I needed to wrestle into making sense, there were no burning questions, there were no thought cycles taking me out of the present moment. I had everything I needed, and I had this overwhelming sense that everything was going to be okay. I didn't know it then, but looking back now, I think what I felt was peace.

I pulled into the Taylors' driveway in Temecula at 10:30. I was ravenous since my tuna and granola lunch after Bell Rock was long gone and I had only snacked on GORP on the drive. I needed dinner.

"Dobby!" I heard a man yell my high school softball nickname loudly through the dark as if it was not 10:30 p.m. in a residential, family neighborhood.

It was Jeff Taylor, Megan's dad, who had walked out of the garage to meet me, followed by Robin, his wife, and Megan, my friend from high school. I hadn't seen them or talked to them since they moved to California when Megan graduated.

"Ahhh!" I squealed quietly, trying not to wake the neighbors. "It's so good to see you!" I gave everyone hugs. "I'm so sorry I got here so late! I ended up making some last minute plans that had me leaving Sedona later than expected."

"Late? Whatchu talkin' about girl, it's Friday night and time to par-tay!" Jeff exclaimed while doing a small celebratory dance. We all laughed.

"Oh yeah, I guess it is Friday. I haven't had much of a concept of time since I left," I noted.

"Come on in. We saved you some dinner," Robin said as we turned around to walk inside. "I'll heat it up for you while you bring your stuff in."

"I see your dad's still a jokester," I whispered to Megan as we walked inside.

"Ohhhhh yeah," she giggled, raising her eyebrows and nodding her head. "Not much has changed with us, but jeez, tell me about you! I can't believe you drove all the way out here by yourself! I can't wait to hear about how it has been so far."

"Yeah I'll have to tell you all about it once we get inside and I get some food in my body. I can barely think straight right now," I confessed, laughing.

"Yeah girl, let's get you some grub," Megan agreed.

Grub was all I wanted.

We spent the evening telling stories and catching up, and it was only when Megan asked me when I was heading out tomorrow that I remembered that I had totally forgotten to let them know that Ethan bought a plane ticket and was arriving tomorrow morning.

"Oh my gosh, I forgot to tell you guys," I began quickly. Everyone looked at me expectantly. "So you know how I originally said I was going to explore Cali solo? Well, my brother actually called me a couple days ago and said he was buying a plane ticket to San Diego, and he's flying in tomorrow morning and I have to go pick him up."

"What?!" Megan shrieked.

"No way!" Jeff yelled.

"That is so fun!" agreed Robin.

"Yep, Ethan is coming tomorrow! I'm so sorry. I had every intention of letting you know the day he decided to buy a ticket, but somehow it slipped my mind! Obviously a little last minute, but is it okay if he stays here with me tomorrow night too so we can figure out what we are doing the next couple days?" I asked.

"Of course!" Robin replied right away. "We would love to see him and hang out with you a little more before you head on."

"When does he fly in?" Megan asked. "Because my friend Bonnie is also flying into the San Diego Airport tomorrow."

"Oh really? Hold on, let me check." I pulled up Ethan's flight information in our text message thread. "He arrives at 10:00 a.m. on Frontier flight F9552."

"Wait. I think my friend arrives around then." Megan paused and began scrolling through her phone. "Ha! That's hilarious. They're on the same flight! Frontier flight F9552!"

"Well that's convenient," I laughed, and everyone giggled.

"Yeah, more than convenient," replied Megan. "That makes things super easy. I can drive, and once we pick them up, we could walk around San Diego or go to La Jolla or something!"

"Perfect. That sounds way less complicated than I was expecting tomorrow to go." I felt relieved. "Hey Robin, thank you so much for saving some dinner for me. It was delicious!"

"Of course! Feel free to have more!" she offered.

"Oh no, I'm stuffed. And exhausted. I think I might head upstairs and induce myself into a food coma for the next eight hours." Everyone laughed. "Does anyone see my camera? I need to plug it into my laptop so I can back up all of my photos."

Everyone looked around for a moment. "Oh, here it is! Fell between the cushions." Robin handed it to me.

"Yeah, back those suckers up. You would hate to lose them! If you didn't have a photo of Journey I might have not believed that you were a dognapper," Jeff winked.

"Might take it up as a new pastime," I joked back. Robin handed over my camera. "Thanks. Well, goodnight everyone. See you in the morning!" I climbed the stairs to the guest bedroom.

"I'm going to make pancakes around eight o'clock!" Jeff shouted up the stairs while I was brushing my teeth.

"Wow, you're really spoiling me! Sounds great!" I called with a mouth full of toothpaste foam.

I had a mystical experience in the middle of the desert yesterday, I made out with Jake from Flagstaff all morning today, now I'm suddenly with family friends from high school when I was a completely different person, and Ethan comes tomorrow. Any confidence that I could even remotely predict how this trip is going to go from here is officially gone.

{9}

A GEORGIAN'S GUIDE TO GETTING THE HELL OUT OF GEORGIA

GROWING UP, HIS BEDROOM WAS ALWAYS RIGHT NEXT TO mine. He was born only two years after me, allowing us to be playmates as soon as he joined the family. He was my baby doll before he could walk, my dance partner to songs about elephants and lions when he was a toddler, and my Lego and fort building partner a couple years later. He grew into my frogger competitor, then my wrestling partner, then my backyard baseball partner, then my basketball rebounder, and then eventually, my basketball opponent. He was the Luke to my Leia for most of our childhood.

Ethan and I shared many passions, but basketball was the one that connected us the most. We both played on our school teams during the winter and on travel teams during the summer. When we weren't playing on teams we were playing each other or shooting together in the driveway. I beat him until size and strength played to his advantage. Our roles reversed, and then I was the one being beaten, and badly. In our later high school years there were multiple times our pictures showed up next to each other in local newspaper articles about our performance in the games that week. Those were always moments where we really felt as if we were part of the same tribe.

However, once basketball season ended the spring semester of my senior year, and I had free time outside of sports for the first time in my life, I spent any moment I could with Cam. Since I was gone most of the time, Ethan and I slowly began to lose our sense of closeness. After a summer of growing apart, I moved four and a half hours away to Boone for school and only came home for holidays. Once Cam and I became really toxic, and I became unstable mentally and emotionally, I completely disengaged from my entire family. I didn't know what to say to Ethan anymore because I was scared my depression would be too weird or hard for him. I had always tried to be the strong older sister through the years of our parents' constant fighting and the tension of not knowing whether or not they would divorce. I didn't know how to step down from that role. I was scared to show him that I actually felt like I was dying inside.

I felt as if I had abandoned him. I took college as a way out in order to suppress my parent's relationship toxicity, but Ethan had still been in it alone for the past two years. I had never asked him how he was doing. I felt like I had not been the sister he needed, and for that I felt shame.

As Megan drove us to the airport, my nerves were buzzing.

What will it be like being back together after so much distance? How do I even prepare for that? Has he noticed that I'm different now? Should I ask him about mom and dad? Will it be something he would even want to talk about? Will we get along? I feel so out of touch with him. I don't even know what questions to ask. I feel unprepared, and I'm scared that things won't be what he expected when he decided to come. But he was the one who had the idea to come, so something in him wants to be here.

Ethan arrived in California sporting classic Ethan attire which falls somewhere between prep and hipster. He was rocking a white v-neck t-shirt, slim fit khaki pants rolled up at the ankles, and white high-top vans. He looked more like Heath Ledger than ever with his curly, dirty-blonde locks framing his face and hanging almost to his shoulders.

"Hey Em," he gave me a nod as he walked out from the gates. I instantly noticed how deep his voice sounded, and how he looked much more adult-like than he used to. Most of his awkward, lanky high schooler features were gone, which I guessed made sense. He was eighteen now.

"I can't believe you're here!" I cheered as I raised my arms to hug his six-foot frame.

"Yeah it's pretty crazy that this actually worked out," he offered back, in his too-cool way.

"Wait, is that all you have?" I gestured to his small backpack which looked like one might take on a casual stroll through the park.

"Yeah, I decided to just bring a carry on instead of checking a bag. I have my hiking boots, my chacos, a couple shirts, a couple shorts, a pair of pants, socks, underwear, my hammock for camping, and a blanket. What else do I need besides that?"

"A blanket? Is that it there, tucked in the outside of your bag? That thing is as thin as a tapestry!" I laughed. "You know we are about to sleep outside for the next two and a half weeks, and unless you sleep like a furnace, this sheet might not keep you warm when it gets down to the forties and possibly the thirties in some of the higher altitude places! You didn't bring a sleeping bag?"

"Uhh, yeah I didn't really think about that. I packed pretty quick," he said and shrugged his shoulders nonchalantly. "I'll be fine." His voice was deeper with maturity than the last time I heard him speak in person, which was months ago.

Though I was concerned, I was not the least bit surprised. It only made sense that Ethan would randomly buy a ticket to California, show up entirely and utterly unprepared, and feel no concern about it in the slightest. He had always been that way, and at some point in the previous eighteen years, that personality trait became endearing to me.

"Oh, hey Megan," Ethan said as Megan walked up with a girl who looked about my age.

"Hey Ethan! Long time no see! Welcome to California!" Megan gave him a hug. "This is my friend Bonnie. I don't know if Emily told you but we found out you both were actually on the same flight, which made picking you up super easy for us!"

"Whoa no way! Did you have a layover in Denver?" Ethan asked Bonnie.

"Yep, flew in from Seattle!" Bonnie confirmed.

"Sweet," Ethan replied. "Nice to meet you. So, are we ready to go? I'm starving!"

"And the starving bear lives!" I joked and nudged his shoulder. I often called Ethan "the bear" because most of the time you could bet that he was either starving and needed food immediately, or he was taking a nap. Only sometimes did he fill his time with other things.

As we walked to the car, I noticed that most of my anxiety from earlier had dissipated. There was still a chance that things could get tense, or that we wouldn't get along, or that our travel dynamics wouldn't mesh, but now that he was there, I was mostly just excited that he decided to come. Ethan was in California. I had no idea what to expect, but only time would tell.

After we grabbed a quick lunch, we routed to La Jolla, a famous seaside community north of San Diego with gorgeous coves and cliffs along the beaches.

"I think Bonnie and I are going to walk around in some shops for a while," said Megan when we found a place to park along the main street by the beach. "What are you wanting to do today?"

"Oh, I'm definitely getting in that water," Ethan decided.

"Did you happen to squeeze a bathing suit into that tiny bag?" I asked.

Ethan rolled his eyes. "Yes, I did, thank you very much. And I know exactly where it is." He snatched it out of his bag. "See? Efficiency. I know what I'm doing."

"Yeah I think we'll probably walk along the beach for a while," I agreed. "Maybe we can meet back at the car in an hour?"

"Sounds great. See you later!" Megan waved.

Ethan and I walked down the beach to explore. I had heard of La Jolla before, but I didn't know it was close to San Diego. We walked down some stone steps to a small cove, and scattered about in the deep blue water were blob-like sections of bright turquoise, where the water was clear as glass.

Ethan ran through the rocky sand into the water, and he ran out just as quickly.

"Dang that water is freezing!" He yelled as he ran back up to me.

"Not like Panama City in the gulf, huh?" I asked. "You're covered in chill bumps!"

"Go feel it!" he urged.

I walked down to dip my toes in the water. As a frigid wave climbed the beach and washed up to my ankles, I gasped slightly, but I stood still as the cold wave washed back out to sea. I looked out to the horizon.

Hello Pacific Coast, nice to meet you. It felt odd having finally arrived there after eight of the fullest and longest days I had ever had. It seemed like an entire year had been crammed into one week, and there were still weeks ahead of me that I expected would be just as full. Was I ready to give in to the potential to be changed that much?

Ethan was skipping small rocks on the smooth cove surface, something he had always been better at than me, and I looked around at the dozens of people dotting the shore around us. I thought about the difference between my journey to the Pacific Coast and the journeys of most of the other people there that day. Some walked there perhaps, some probably drove less than ten miles from their house, some maybe drove a few hours from a different part of the state, some possibly flew from their hometown directly into San Diego, but I had driven. Across the entire country. By myself. I wondered what the actual hour and mile count was to this moment.

I felt shocked that I had spent eight days driving alone with my thoughts without having a total mental breakdown and landing myself in a psychiatric ward. Though I had intense moments so far, the darkness inside of me wasn't consuming me like I thought it would. I was so scared when I left Boone. I feared that the solitude would make me feel worse, that it would be too much to bear all of this alone, but I already felt lighter. My pain stung a little less than it did a week ago. I felt like I had been broken open, like a tilled garden broken open after a long winter, ready to receive the seeds that would be planted at the arrival of spring. I was ready to grow something, and for the first time in a long time it seemed there were some nutrients in the soil. Maybe something beautiful could grow up from the dark and out into the light.

"Em!" Ethan yelled to get my attention. "Let's climb across this cliff to get to the beach area over there!" He pointed to another section of sand about fifty yards down the coast, but between where we stood and the next cove was a long section of rocky cliffs that we would have to traverse. It looked safe enough, and there was a group of folks who had climbed up and across to sit on one of the flatter ledges between us and the beach. If they could do it, we probably could too.

"Okay let me grab my stuff!" I called back. I snatched my backpack from the sand and trotted over to where the cliff started to rise.

Ethan and I started to climb, and soon we were standing on a three-foot-wide ledge that dropped thirty feet down, straight to the ocean. The sandy shore had sunk down to deeper, darker water, where powerful waves were crashing hard against the boulders that backed up to the cliff, exploding in salty mist. My stomach dropped as I looked. I wasn't scared of heights, but I also did not like the idea of falling.

"Let's climb to the next ledge!" Ethan shouted above the roar of the waves. "I think that one will get us all the way across to where we can climb back down to the sand up there!" I could barely hear him.

I nodded my head and followed. Ethan confidently scampered up first. I waited for him to get up before I started my climb, fearing that if he slipped we would both go tumbling over the cliff. Once he was up, I took my backpack off because it was awkward to climb with, and I hoisted it up to the next ledge. Before I could process what was happening, my camera bounced in slow motion off the upper cliff where I tossed my bag, slipped through my sprawled fingers, fell past my kicking feet that tried to stop it mid-bounce, and tumbled down the thirty feet of rock below me. I watched, frozen, as its orange glimmer was swallowed by the next swell.

"Damnit!" I screamed once it was out of sight, and I sat down on a rock on the ledge to breathe and collect my thoughts, trying not to react in anger.

Ethan walked back over once he realized it was my camera. "How did that happen?"

"I totally forgot that I hadn't secured my camera from when I took a photo earlier. I had only rested it in the water bottle pocket on the side, so when I tossed my bag up, out it fell," I trailed off. I was trying to be kind to myself, but the judgmental voices inside my head tried to tell me how much of a forgetful idiot I was.

"That's super frustrating. I'm sorry Em," Ethan attempted to console me.

We both sat in silence for a couple minutes. I stared at the rocks below where my camera had hit, and my heart pounded at the thought of what could have happened if I tried to reach out over the cliff to try to catch it. I could have easily lost my balance and tumbled over the ledge with it. Even though I was upset at the inconvenience of losing my camera, I was glad that I wasn't broken on the rocks as well.

I interrupted the silence with an attempt to help myself make light of the situation. "Well, maybe that was just the Universe's expensive way of telling me that I needed to live this day a little more in the moment instead of worrying about taking pictures." I immediately became self-conscious that I said Universe instead of God and wondered if Ethan noticed or cared.

"Yeah," Ethan chuckled, thankfully not acknowledging the Universe part, "I was scared you were going to reach out after it! That could have ended really badly."

"I'm glad it was just the camera and not one of us. The first thing I thought about was that I'm so thankful that I remembered to upload all of my photos last night! If I hadn't backed them up, I would have lost all of my photos from my trip so far, and I would have been way more upset right now."

"That would have sucked," Ethan agreed. "It's just a camera. It can be replaced. Let's get off this thing and go lay on the beach."

We finished the climb over unscathed, and I reminded myself to do my best to keep God from coming up between us. Ethan seemed so innocent and happy. He was fresh out of high school, and he had just spent a week at a Christian YoungLife camp in Colorado where he told me he had one of the best weeks of his life. What was I going to say to him? *"Hey that's great and all, but I don't believe that your experience was real?"* Who am I to judge if his experience was real or not, or anyone else's for that matter? I have had multiple experiences (my church called them God encounters) in the past, and I fully believed they were real then. And they changed me. Just because I might believe differently now, does that make those experiences less real and true? And what about the mystical experience that just happened in the desert? That was real. Even though I don't know what to call it or how to explain it, it was real.

I have seen the way Ethan's Christian faith has impacted him and the way it has informed the ways that he carries himself, all of them ways in which I respect. But in the midst of it I don't know how to credit an institution whose policies and practices I'm not in full support of anymore without feeling extreme cognitive dissonance. How do I reconcile all of the positives which I have seen Christianity bring about in people's lives, and even in my life, with all of the toxicity and abuse and hurtful things I have realized it can perpetuate as well?

Just because I've deconstructed my beliefs, it doesn't mean that I want or need to drag Ethan into my questions and doubts with me when he seems to be thriving. It is not my place to force my beliefs or opinions about the Church upon him. Hell, I barely even have language for where I'm at right now. I already feel like I messed up my relationship with mom and dad, and I don't know if any of my friendships will ever be the same. I can't bear to add Ethan to the list of folks I have to grieve. Maybe God just won't come up.

"I meant to ask you last night, how many miles have you driven so far?" Jeff asked as we sat down to the table to eat pizza back at the Taylors' house.

"Good question. I was actually wondering about that today. Do you mind if I add it up really quick? Don't want to be rude having my phone out at the table," I said slightly sarcastically, knowing that they wouldn't care.

"Oh no, of course. We're all curious!" Robin emphasized.

I grabbed a piece of paper and pulled up my GPS on my phone. I broke the miles and hours on the road down by day, and conversation trailed to other things in the meantime.

"Alright I have it!" I interrupted Ethan telling Jeff and Robin about the seals we saw at La Jolla. "These are all rough estimates, especially the driving times, but they're as accurate as I can guess. From Boone to Franklin to Little Rock to Waco to Austin back to Waco to Santa Rosa to Flagstaff to here to the coast of San Diego today is roughly 2,900 miles and forty-six hours on the road."

Everyone was shocked, including myself. I knew the number would be high, but I hadn't realized I had literally spent almost two entire days driving over the past nine days, more if you also count the hours that I slept in my car.

"Dang girl! You already have some remarkable stories, and I bet you'll have even more in a couple weeks!" Robin said.

"I'm impressed that you didn't give up! I get so sleepy when I drive that I don't think I would be able to make it," Bonnie laughed.

"You know what I think you should do?" Jeff interjected. "I think you should write a book about your travels, and you should name it, *A Georgian's Guide to Getting the Hell out of Georgia.*"

Everyone erupted in laughter.

"No, I'm serious! No one from Georgia, I mean, no one that I know, has ever done anything like this, and so many people from the South don't travel a lot or don't know how to travel. But I think everyone should travel! It changes you and teaches you things about yourself that you wouldn't learn otherwise, and people need help believing it can be accessible to them! I think it could be a money maker, just saying," Jeff shrugged.

"Hmm, I don't know. I've never thought about writing a book before," I began, "and I still feel like a novice traveler, but maybe the next couple weeks will help me feel more prepared to talk about traveling. I feel like I'm eternally trying to catch up to the present. So much has happened already!"

"Speaking of the next couple weeks, where are we going to go tomorrow?" Ethan asked. "Have you done any research, or are we just wingin' it?"

"So far I've mainly been just wingin' it," I admitted, "but I would like to sit down and look at a map after dinner to decide where we could go. We can't go too far since we need to be back here on the 16th to get Will and Sydney. I turned to the Taylors. "Do you have any suggestions of places we should go this week? Maybe along the coast?"

We spent the rest of the evening researching how we could fill the next four full days before we would drive back to San Diego to pick up Will and Sydney. Los Angeles was out of the picture because it was too giant and overwhelming, and I didn't want to deal with the traffic. It didn't make sense to drive too far north because we would be driving back up to Yosemite with Will and Sydney in a few days. The Taylors suggested that we drive up the valley as far as we could without having to rush and get on Highway 1, the Pacific Coast Highway, the road that runs roughly 660 miles down the California coastline.

The Pacific Coast Highway is apparently internationally famous, but since I had never been to California, and I did no research before arriving, I was oblivious of its existence.

"Yeah you gotta' get at least up to Big Sur, if not further up to Monterey," Jeff encouraged. "Robin and I drove that section a couple years ago, and it is one of the prettiest drives we've ever been on."

"There's lots of hikes along the PCH too," Megan added. "As well as a million beaches you can explore."

"Well E, road trip down the Pacific Coast Highway?" I asked.

"Road trip down the PCH it is," Ethan agreed and gave me a high five.

"Alright youngins, we're going to bed," Jeff said. "It's about a seven hours' drive to Monterey, so you might want to go to bed too."

"Right. I guess we have another long day tomorrow," I nodded. "You're driving first," I looked at Ethan in that older sibling you-better-do-what-I-say way.

Ethan rolled his eyes. "We'll see. Goodnight. I'll see you in the morning. What time are we getting up?" he asked.

"Eight o'clock sharp."

Ethan grunted. "That's so early!"

"We have to get on the road! The adventure begins! Get psyched, bro, it's gonna be rad," I exaggerated in my best California surfer accent and poked him playfully in the stomach.

"You're so weird," Ethan quickly brushed my arm away, unable to keep a straight face.

I smiled. "You know you love me. Remember, eight o'clock!" I called behind me as I climbed the stairs.

"Yeah, yeah," grumbled the bear. "Eight o'clock."

{10}

PLAY

BEFORE WE LEFT THE TAYLORS' HOUSE, ETHAN AND I AT-
tempted to see what it would be like to sleep in the trunk
together. I moved my closet box and the tents to the back
left corner of the trunk to make room for Ethan to lay next to me.
I laid down where I had been sleeping, squeezed as far as I could
against the gear to my right, and asked Ethan to come lay down
to my left. He crawled in next to me, laid down, scrunched up his
broad shoulders, and awkwardly bent his long, lanky legs over the
tents at the bottom.

"Mmm, so comfy…" Ethan muttered sarcastically as he turned
and looked at me. His face was two inches from mine and contorted
into an expression that looked like someone was suffocating him.

I tried to keep a straight face but lost it and laughed hard, and
Ethan, as well as the Taylors and Bonnie, who were watching us, joined
in. Laying directly on top of each other would have been more comfortable.

"You guys look like a pack of sardines in there!" Jeff bellowed, still
laughing.

"I mean, it could maybe work, right?" I tried to sound hopeful.
"I wasn't expecting to sleep in my car with anyone else because I knew

once I was with Will and Sydney we would be camping, but we'll make it work."

"Um, no. I'm sleeping in the front," Ethan stated definitively as he exited with as little smoothness as when he crawled in.

"Well, if your trunk sleeping arrangements don't work out, there are a few campgrounds along the PCH as a last resort," Megan suggested.

"We'll keep that in mind." I smirked as I awkwardly got out of the car.

"Well, should we take a group photo before you guys leave?" Robin asked.

"I can take it," offered Bonnie.

"We'll have to take it on my phone since my camera is no longer. May it rest in peace," I joked and handed Bonnie my phone.

We lined up in front of the house, and Bonnie snapped a shot of us with the Taylors. We all exchanged hugs and said our goodbyes.

I stepped back from hugging Megan and looked at Jeff and Robin with a smile. "Thank you so much again. Our time with you was really a gift." I waved as I opened the door to the passenger's seat. Ethan started the car, and we set off toward Monterey.

We had been driving for about five hours, and a while after passing through Bakersfield, we started passing hand-painted signs advertising ridiculously cheap produce. Then, we saw one that we couldn't ignore.

"Did that sign really just say ten avocados for a dollar?" Ethan asked.

"I think so, and the next one said ten grapefruits for a dollar too," I added. "But there's no way that's real, right? Avocados are normally at least a dollar fifty for one at home!"

Ethan shrugged. "Wanna stop? I think the sign said it's the next exit."

"Yeah, why not? Hopefully they're not serial killers luring millennials with cheap avocados." We both laughed.

We turned off at the next exit, and sure enough, we saw a van with its trunk open, and a sign that said "ten for one dollar" in giant letters.

The wrinkled farmer sitting next to the van assured us that the price was correct.

"How many should we get?" I asked Ethan.

"Go big or go home," he said with a grin.

"We'll take ten of each please," I said. Ethan handed the farmer two dollars and received ten bulging grapefruits and ten perfectly ripe avocados in return.

"I really thought it was a scam," Ethan shook his head as he dumped the avocados into the food box in the back.

"Yeah, I hope we can eat all of them." I followed by dumping the grapefruits next to the avocados. I stepped back and took in the sight of our treasure. "I feel like we just won the lottery. I've never been able to afford ten avocados at once. Are we sure we don't need another ten?" I asked excitedly like a kid in a candy store.

Ethan laughed. "I think we can do ten, but twenty might be a little excessive. I'm feeling a giant batch of guacamole for dinner tonight though!"

"Mmm, good idea," I agreed. "Want a grapefruit now with lunch?"

"Yeah, I'm hungry. But you've gotta open it," Ethan handed one to me.

"Why me?"

"Because I suck at it! I always get juice everywhere, and then it's so torn to pieces by the end that I don't even want to eat it. It's hard, okay?" he whined.

I rolled my eyes. "Okay give it here," I cooed like I was talking to a baby, and Ethan nudged my arm.

"Stop it," he chuckled.

I peeled the grapefruit without massacring it, and we slurped and chewed, sitting on my back bumper, looking out at the dry valley with perfectly ripe grapefruit juice dribbling down our chins.

"Think we can make it to that Redwoods park Jeff told us about? What was it called again?" Ethan asked as he stuffed another grapefruit slice in his mouth.

"Oh right. Henry Cowell Redwoods State Park near Santa Cruz. Let me check," I paused and checked directions. "It's three and a half hours from here, so we'd get there around five or five thirty depending on traffic and stops."

"That's doable, I think. We could grab the rest of the stuff we need for guacamole somewhere on the way in, make it at the park for dinner, and then walk around for a while?"

"Sounds great. What else do you want for lunch? I have tuna, or granola, or beans, or nuts. Running a little low. Maybe we could restock the food supply later too."

"Well, all of that sounds gross. But I guess I'll take nuts and granola. I can't do tuna without mayonnaise and relish like mom makes it."

"One of the many sacrifices one must make in life on the road."

"Yeah, yeah, but I'm going to need something else besides this stuff. This is not going to do," he scoffed.

"Such a diva." I rolled my eyes.

"And proud of it." Ethan grinned.

I was expecting Ethan to be more talkative on the drive, but he was happy to listen to music the whole time, which helped my introvert battery retain some of its charge. One of my roommates had given me some mixed CDs for my trip, and Ethan and I listened to them on repeat, specifically the song "Sweet Disposition" by Temper Trap. I'd never heard it before, but it quickly became our road trip theme song.

After getting off I-5 at Los Banos, we took the Pacheco Pass Highway west up into the hills to cross over to the coast. We met up with the Pacific Coast Highway for the first time at Watsonville, and I felt antsy to experience the views that the coming days would hold. After stocking up on groceries and the rest of our guacamole ingredients, we routed to the Henry Cowell Redwoods.

The trees in the park were staggering. It was as if we were suddenly seeing trees from a squirrel's perspective. Something about standing in the presence of gentle redwood giants standing confidently in shadow and light was holy. Unfortunately we only had time for a quick walk since we were running out of daylight, so after thirty minutes of exploring, we scarfed down a batch of heavenly guacamole like we hadn't eaten in a week, and then we continued on to Monterey.

As we entered the Monterey city limits, the sky abruptly transitioned from some light hues of pink at the start of sunset to a piercing, flamboyant pink, and deep, radiant purples.

"Look at the sky! It's gorgeous! Let's stop soon!" I squealed.

"I see signs for a beach up there." Ethan pointed out. He read the sign aloud as we drove up. "Del Monte Beach parking. Sound good?"

"Perfect."

We walked down the short boardwalk to an expanse of sand that led down to the smooth ocean surface lapping at the shore.

The sand reflected the same intense pink as the horizon. Soon the pink became more concentrated into a neon-like haze which hovered just above the sealine as far as I could see in both directions, seeming both a million miles away and so close that I could touch it. A cloud of seagulls soared in front of us and above us, their white underbellies dyed pink in the light. They were silent as they swayed back and forth in the wind, and I wondered if the sunset had taken their breath away, too.

"Hey Em," Ethan whispered. "See that group of like a thousand seagulls over there?" He pointed to the large group of birds. I hadn't noticed them settle while I was looking out toward the horizon. I already knew what he was going to say, but I asked anyway.

"Yeah, what about them?"

"Want to run through them with me?" he asked expectantly, as if there could only be one answer.

Part of me felt like it was another "too-silly-to-do" request. I wanted to tell him only little kids run through groups of birds to disturb them for no reason. Besides, we'd risk being pummeled with bird poop from all angles. Another part of me gently whispered that I should surrender the story that I was too sad to have fun.

I took a deep breath. "Got your GoPro?" I asked. I dropped my journal and pen out of my hand into the sand.

"Yep." Ethan's smile grew.

"Turn it on."

"You ready?" he asked.

We whispered in unison. "One, two, three!"

We both sprinted as fast as we could through the sand toward the birds, and soon the whole flock erupted in dancing chaos around us, squawking and screeching. It is one thing to scare a few birds at a park, but hundreds of seagulls surrounding you on all sides is a completely different experience.

I was belly laughing before we even reached the birds, and once we were in the heart of the swarm, I looked at Ethan and could see through the feathers that he was out of breath, too. We laughed so hard tears filled our eyes. I took in the pink world that enveloped us. The sky, the water, the birds, the sand, and even our faces reflected the same hue. I forgot all about my hesitation, and I was nowhere but standing in that exact moment, fully present to the incredulity of what it is like to be encompassed in a cloud of birds at sunset, on the coast of California, with someone who shared my blood.

There was something Divine about it all. I ran through the sand with my hands in the air, and it felt like an embodied act of worship, of celebration, and contentment. I'd given myself permission to experience genuine joy again.

Running next to Ethan, it didn't matter if we believed the same things, or if he knew all the details about why I was on this trip. All that mattered was that we were there—running, spinning, and laughing, together. I had been questioning why Ethan was supposed to come on this trip, and in that moment I saw the first glimpse of an answer. I realized that Ethan might be there to help loosen my stubborn grip on sadness, and to gently remind me that even as an adult, I still had permission to play.

At some point, I'd allowed the permission to play to be taken away from me. It might have been the way Cam sent subtle messages about what was acceptable behavior, but it also might have just been my reaction to trauma. At some point I made the decision that even on easy days, I had to be serious all the time. I felt like I had to be in a constant state of internal reflection. I could only be playful when I felt safe, and since I no longer felt safe internally, I couldn't feel safe externally either, so I stopped playing. I had become so identified with my depression that it became my baseline, and it had become so comfortable that I was scared to leave it and take the risk of stepping into what it might be like to be happy again.

Ethan reminded me that maybe that silly part of my personality hadn't been eradicated. Maybe it had just needed the perfect moment of running through a horde of seagulls to be coaxed back out. The door it had been hiding behind had been opened, and joy rushed in.

After finding that the Best Western parking lot was too small for us to go unnoticed, we tried the Hilton Garden Inn down the street. That parking lot was on a hill, and in the same way that you would slide to one side of your tent if you pitched it on a hill, we would have slid to one side of the car if we parked it on a hill, which was a no-go. We eventually ended up at Embassy Suites, which had a giant, flat parking lot with a decent amount of cars to tuck ourselves next to. The street lights were the only unfortunate thing about it—they were so bright it seemed like daytime.

"I'm just going to sleep in the front," Ethan decided. "That way we both can stretch out without being on top of each other."

"Are you sure? I don't feel like sleeping up there will be very comfortable." I felt bad for not having a better option.

"Nah, it will be fine. It will be just like sleeping in a recliner. But I do need something to go over my eyes. This one light is shining through the front right in my face."

"Here." I gave him my head wrap, a multi-use band of fabric used as a scarf, breathing mask, or headband. "Wrap this around your head to cover your eyes."

Ethan didn't seem impressed as he took it, but once he put it on his head, he smiled like he was posing for a picture and gave me a thumbs up.

I laughed. "I cannot take you seriously with that thing on. Maybe you'll have really fun dreams about playing pin the tail on the donkey." We both laughed. "Goodnight. Hope you get some sleep. Wake up whenever we wake up?" I asked.

"Yeah, I guess so. I don't imagine we'll sleep much past sunrise," he said. "Goodnight."

"Glad you're here, E," I finished as I settled into my trunk bed.

"Me too."

In less than five minutes Ethan's breathing transitioned to long, deep, repetitive sighs, signaling that he had fallen asleep.

Right. The bear can sleep anywhere. I rolled over, and I followed him into hibernation.

{11}

MUD AND STARDUST

S PIKY PINE TREES SHADOWED THE ROAD AS WE DROVE INTO the heart of Point Lobos State Reserve. It had only been about thirty minutes since we'd left our parking spot in Monterey, but I already felt relieved to be heading back into the wilderness. As we wound our way deeper into the forest, I was grateful that the logistical planning that consumed the past couple of days was complete, and now it was time to just explore again. Time already seemed to slow down. I was excited that there wasn't much we had to worry about the next few days besides eating, walking, driving on one road in one direction, and finding somewhere to sleep.

We stopped at the first trailhead we came to in the park. We walked for a while along the perimeter of Whaler's Cove, up a straggly trail over a cliff, and down to a smaller cove called Bluefish Cove. The water, though it was deep, looked like it was clear and calm. Heaps of dark seaweed bobbed on the surface in continent-like clumps.

"I continue to be fascinated by how quickly the terrain changes out here," I mentioned as we walked back to the car to drive further into the park. "Between the dry desert valley yesterday, the redwoods last night, and this coastal cove tucked away in a forest of pines, I feel like we visited three different countries in the last twenty-four hours."

"Totally," Ethan agreed. "These beaches are so much different than the beaches on the east coast. Let's try to get closer to those big rocks down there next to the water."

We found a trail that led to the furthest point of the small peninsula. Since the tide was out, we climbed down to some flat, exposed rocks next to the water's surface.

I hadn't thought about Cam all day, which was rare, but as I stood there watching the waves crash against the rocks my grief came back and punched me in the gut. Despite everything that had happened, I ached to be with him. I had never been addicted to a drug, but I had been addicted to Cam. The detox had begun, and my withdrawal symptoms were intense.

I told Ethan I was going to sit and journal for a while, and he left me to walk further along the rocks to explore the tide pools.

07/13/15, Day 11 -

I sit here next to the crashing waves, in complete beauty, physically free to go wherever I want, but I still feel so weighed down by the absence of Cam. Ethan is here, and I don't know how to tell him that I'm not okay. I don't know how to make him understand how I can be laughing and genuinely lighthearted one moment and just as quickly switch to somber and sad. I miss Cam, and I want to tell myself that it is normal, but I cannot help but feel shame.

It makes me question all of the times I could have left before things got bad, wondering if there was something I could have done to save myself from all of this. How do we forgive ourselves when we stay too long?

I heard Ethan walk up behind me, and I closed my journal.
"You ready to leave?" he asked.
"Yeah, I think so." I attempted to smile. I walked back to the car in silence, but Ethan didn't seem to mind. "I don't mind driving for a bit," I offered.
"Okay." Ethan threw me the keys.
I put in the trip soundtrack, the same mixed CD we had already listened to five times through. "Sweet Disposition" rose in tempo and

coaxed me out of my heaviness. Soon the windows were down, our hair was flying in the wind, the music was blasting, and I remembered how to feel alive.

We continued along the highway which was like a thread that intricately stitched the mountains and the sea together, joining their two worlds in stark contrast. We spent the rest of the day hiking in the rolling, dry, treeless mountains of Garrapata State Park and stopping at various beaches in Andrew Molera State Park. I was still having a hard time forgiving myself for staying with Cam too long, but the beauty of the sheer cliffs and powerful turquoise waves helped soften me.

After having guac round two for dinner, we ended the day by hammocking next to the babbling Big Sur River in Pfeiffer Big Sur State Park. It was helpful to have space to recharge for a couple hours without feeling like I had to be in constant conversation with Ethan. We tried to see if there was camping available there, but all of the sites were full, so once the sun started to go down, we packed up our hammocks so we could drive and find a place to park the car and sleep.

When we walked up to the car, I caught a glimpse of myself in the reflection of my car window. I was sweaty and salty from our hiking earlier, and my curls were chaotically crawling out of my French braid. I smirked because even though I looked like I had been electrocuted, something about letting go of the need to be put together was comforting.

"Should we find a place to watch the sunset?" I asked as I joined Ethan in the car.

"Sounds good to me. Maybe back at that lighthouse," Ethan suggested.

We tried to drive out to the Point Sur Lighthouse which sat atop a rock that was over three hundred feet tall at the end of a long point of land, but the gate to the gravel driveway was closed. We parked the car off to the side of the gate since it was still beautiful looking out toward the rock that seemed to jut straight out of the sea.

The temperature had dropped into the high fifties, so I pulled on sweat pants and grabbed my flannel once I got out of the car. The sun hung behind thick clouds, and the sky was filled with a less impressive array of colors than the night before with the seagulls, but I was still drawn to the dark greys and blues. There was a slight breeze in the air, and I pulled my flannel tighter around me as I watched the tall grasses dancing in the dim light.

I broke the silence. "There's something really nice about making a point to pay attention to the sun. When it rises, when it sets, taking time to watch it appear or disappear. I think it's so easy in normal life, whatever normal life means, to get so caught up in our pursuit of success, whatever success means. When we're trapped in the rise and grind of the machine, we forget that we are tiny bodies made of mud and stardust, inhabiting this giant, amazing rock hurling through a vacuum at thousands of miles per hour around an enormous ball of fire that emits rays so powerful they can burn our skin, yet are vital in making the plants grow which our lives depend on. And while we are so caught up in our tiny human world, the earth and all of the other planets and stars and moons and suns just keep doing their thing, over and over again, day after day, year after year, forever."

I realized I was ranting, and I looked over to Ethan to see if he was interested in what I was saying, or if I should keep my thoughts to myself. He nodded his head and seemed to be listening, so I continued.

"And we just forget about it. We get sung to sleep by the mainstream society lullaby which coaxes us into forgetting that the world is a magnificently magical place, bursting with life and beauty. We get so busy making the machine of the economy run, that the sun sets, and we don't even notice. We get crammed inside corporate offices lit by electricity so we can stay awake longer so we can be more productive and do more. We fill cities with so much fake light that you walk outside at midnight and barely notice that the world is completely dark. The sun rises and sets, and it's glorious, yet we don't pay attention. It's just light. It's just dark. It's just day. It's just night. We have forgotten how to let our imaginations be captivated by the things we take for granted."

"Yeah," Ethan nodded, "I felt that while I was out at camp in Colorado. It got so dark there at night. When I saw the stars I realized that I forget about the sky a lot at home because there's so much going on. The sky doesn't seem like the most important thing to pay attention to."

"I definitely forget too." I admitted. "I think we all forget, but so far on this trip I've been reminded of the importance of paying attention. Back in Boone, I never slowed down enough to pay attention to the little things—the beads of dew on the grass every morning, the melodies of birdsong, or that specific stillness you find on top of a mountain that you can't find anywhere else in everyday life.

"I'm beginning to see that the constant busyness we wrap ourselves in keeps us from an important cyclical rhythm that grounds us in reality. That rhythm helps us know when it's time to work and when it's time to rest. Without it, once you get on the hamster wheel, you never know when it's okay to take a break, and then suddenly you're eighty and realize you worked your whole life away. This trip has helped me start to slow down and remember the fact that we exist is a miracle when it's so easy to forget what a gift it is to be alive. Most of the time there are a million things that matter more to me than what the sky is doing. But right now, there is nowhere else to be but here, being present to the fact that being a human with consciousness on a planet in space is spectacular. And I think that's pretty beautiful." I paused. "Does any of that make sense?" I looked at Ethan, who was staring out toward the horizon, the corners of his mouth slightly turned upward.

"Yeah, I know what you're saying. I think it's important, too. I mean, I think this is where God meets us. He gives us these things to make us happy and to point our eyes back to him."

The sudden Christian language made me cringe, and even though my contemplation led me to thinking about Divinity, I still couldn't handle being face-to-face with my prior understanding of God. I knew what Ethan was trying to say, but something in my brain still felt broken. I had this fear that I was about to be found out, like I needed to hide to keep myself safe.

"I mean," Ethan continued, "I haven't been gone for as long as you have, and at home I was sleeping in until ten or eleven every day, but I can imagine that being up with the sun and being outside to watch the sunset every night is way different. I'm excited to watch more. Can we try to watch the sunset as many nights as we can for the rest of the trip?"

I was brought out of my fear and back to reality. I smiled. "Yes. I would love that."

"I was just thinking before you started talking that it's pretty mind-boggling that you could get in a boat right there and start paddling, and you would eventually get to Asia. It's different looking at a two-dimensional map. You think, 'Oh yeah it's just a straight shot over.' But the earth is a sphere, and my brain hurts trying to think about how one can ride in a boat on a seemingly flat ocean for that long and never be able to see the curve of the planet. I get what you're saying about not ever slowing down enough to think about stuff like this. The simple stuff really blows your mind when you take time to think through it." He shook his head. "Amazing."

"Right? We live in a society that does its best to strip us of our wonder, because wonder inspires people. Wonder connects people to their creativity. It urges people to question the way things are, and inspired, creative people who question the way things are, well, they're dangerous to the machine. Our economic structure needs workers that keep their heads down and don't ask questions. We are told that wonder is for children, and taking time to sit in awe, to be inquisitive, to feel amazement at simple things is something you leave behind when you enter adulthood, but I think that's bullshit." *Shit, I just cussed in front of my little brother.* "Sorry for cussing. But it is."

Ethan laughed. "Don't apologize. I'm not six anymore."

"I think I used to live from that place of wonder, but lately I've just been keeping my head down and pursuing the life that I thought everyone is supposed to live. I've been so distracted that I've forgotten to pay attention, to wonder. I want wonder back in my life."

Ethan gave an affirming "mmm" and nodded his head, but he didn't say anything else. I didn't push further because I couldn't tell if the conversation was getting to be too much for him. I didn't know where I could go from there without conversation getting too close to Cam or God.

Once the sky darkened so much that we could only see the rough outline of the lighthouse, we left to find a place to park for the night. There were not as many pull-offs from the road as I was expecting, and no matter where we parked it was going to be conspicuous. We ended up having to backtrack to the area around Andrew Molera State Park, and we found a small gravel pull-off from the highway right at the top of the hill next to the campground entrance.

"This is so obvious!" I did not feel confident about our parking choice. "I hope no ranger from that campground down there comes knocking on our window in a couple hours."

"I think we'll be fine." Ethan did not seem to care, which made me feel slightly better.

We brushed our teeth next to the car in total darkness, in fear that having any of the lights on in the car would blow our cover. We spit in the woods and swished and cleaned our toothbrushes with our water bottles. I had begun to love the simplicity of the hygiene routine on the road, and I noticed I had been much kinder to myself when I didn't have so many opportunities to look in a mirror and find everything wrong with what I saw. We quietly snuggled into our resting spots, and I laughed at how awkward Ethan's long, cramped body looked in the front seat.

"I don't know how you think that's comfortable, but I'm glad it's working for you," I whispered to him. "Goodnight."

I was sleeping soundly, dreaming about something random, and then an unsettling, insistent noise pushed its way into my dream, increasing in volume.

What is that? I focused my attention on the relentless sound, but I couldn't make sense of it in my dream state. The terrible blaring kept getting louder and louder, and then I realized the sound was real.

My eyes shot open and I sat up so fast that I'm certain I got air. I was disoriented. Everything felt like it moved in slow-motion. I was sure an eighteen-wheeler was going to pummel us at any second, and I braced myself. When I looked out of the back of the car, everything around us was dark. There were no other car lights, yet the piercing honk was unchanging. Then I recognized it a few seconds later.

Wait. That sound is coming from my car.

I spun around quickly to see Ethan completely sprawled out across the front seat. His legs were stretched up and across to the driver's side, and his left heel was pressed hard against the steering wheel, directly over the horn. Somehow, despite the fact that it had been almost ten seconds of a non-stop, full-blast, blaring, car horn, he was still completely and entirely dead asleep.

"ETHAN!" I screamed and knocked his foot away from the steering wheel, finally giving my ears, and everyone else's ears in the valley, a break.

"What? Huh?" He blinked his eyes open. He was disoriented from the jolt, but as soon as he saw my face he looked scared. "What's wrong?" he squeaked.

"Dude! Your foot decided to plant itself on the freaking steering wheel, and the horn has been blaring for the past ten seconds. You slept through the whole thing! How is that even possible? Were you dead?"

"Ha! Seriously? No way," he mumbled sleepily and closed his eyes again. "I definitely didn't hear it."

"Then we need to get your ears checked. I was dead asleep, and it scared the shit out of me! I thought we were about to die!"

Ethan laughed. "Well, we didn't. Can I go back to sleep now?" He leaned back in the seat and turned his head away from me.

"The campground is definitely awake now, so hopefully no one comes to check to see if we just got in a wreck, or we're going to have to move." I looked down to the flickering lights through the trees below and knew a camp warden was going to come any moment.

"Don't worry about it, just go back to sleep." Ethan moaned as he adjusted his pillow. "And pass me my blanket. I'm cold."

"I'm pretty chilly too," I tossed him his tapestry blanket. "Probably good to test that thing out before we hike up into the Sierras. It's going to be at least fifteen degrees colder than it is here."

I grabbed the thermometer keychain out of the seat organizer pocket.

Fifty-two degrees. This is not a night for a tank top anymore. To warm up, I grabbed my wool pants and sweatshirt. Soon I was back asleep, and we both slept through the night with no more episodes of terrifying horns.

{12}

EASY AS PIE

I HAD BEEN UP FOR THIRTY MINUTES OR SO THE NEXT morning, and my extremely consistent body clock did not care that Ethan was still asleep. If we were in the middle of the woods it wouldn't have been a big deal. I could have easily exited the car, gone behind a tree, dug a hole, and went about my business, but we were no more than ten yards off the side of the highway. The tree line behind the car dropped down a slope so steep that I could not have balanced well enough to do the job neatly. Even though it was only a little after seven, cars were already flying past us in both directions, so trying to poop in any private manner was impossible. But I had to go. Bad.

I tried to squeeze myself together because I didn't want to wake Ethan, but once the possibility of things coming out of their own accord became more likely, I decided to climb around to the front seat and start the car.

"What are you doing?" Ethan winced when the sunlight reached his sleepy eyes.

"Um. I have to... poop. And I don't think I can wait much longer. I'm going to drive back to Pfeiffer Big Sur State Park to find that bathroom we saw yesterday."

Ethan chuckled. "Gotcha. Well I'm going to go back to sleep."

"I don't care what you do," I said. "I just need a toilet pronto."

After twenty minutes of clenching, I pulled into the campground area and pretended I didn't see the sign on the bathroom door that read, "Toilets for campers ONLY." I ran in, just in time. On my drive out to California, it was more acceptable to use gas stations and the occasional fast food restaurant to relieve myself, but out here with few facilities around for the average passerby, finding appropriate places to use the restroom was an additional hurdle to navigate.

"What do you want for breakfast?" I called to the front seat once I got back to the car, waking Ethan again. I snagged a serving of chocolate granola for myself, and Ethan opted for the other, since he is of the rare kind that does not like chocolate in any form.

After breakfast and lounging around for a while longer, Ethan also took advantage of us being near a flushing toilet. After he was finished, we drove to park at the trailhead for a hike to Pfeiffer Falls and get a view of the Big Sur Valley.

We hiked in silence most of the morning, which I was grateful for. We were back in a forest full of gargantuan redwoods. I spent the morning thinking about Cam, trying to give the memories space to be named so that they could flow out of me, taking their pain with them.

We reached the valley overlook, and the lighthouse from the previous night stood in a skinny line on the coast. Ethan whipped out his phone.

"Whoa, there's service up here!" He immediately started checking all of his miscellaneous notifications and messages. It had been easy for me to stay detached from my phone when it was just me, but when Ethan wanted to be constantly connected and checking his phone when he could, it was hard to ignore. Thankfully, I left my phone in the car.

"What are you doing? We are literally on top of a secluded mountain with one of the best beach views I've ever seen, and you're really getting on social media right now?"

"I told Matt I would call him!" Matt was Ethan's best friend back home.

"Could you not just be here right now and live in the moment?" I was annoyed. "You could just call Matt when we get back to San Diego, but you do you." I walked away before it turned into an argument.

I sat on a bench away from Ethan so I couldn't hear him talking.

After a few moments of muffled conversation, Ethan ended his phone call and shouted over to me. "Hey Em, I was thinking while we were hiking up…remember Trace Miller, the guy who played on my travel basketball team last year?"

"Yeah. Why?"

"I'm pretty sure his family moved back to L.A. a couple months ago, and I thought I could try to get in touch with them. Maybe I'll ask if we could stop by and see them. And possibly stay there. I mean, only if that would be okay with you."

"Oh. Umm," I paused. *That was not what I was expecting. Part of me wants to protect my original intent to keep our trip as rugged as possible. I really like sleeping in the car, it's way more interesting. Would it be awkward staying with them? I don't know them well. Could be nice to shower though.* "Well, I like the idea of staying on the road like we have been, but I guess if somehow they say yes, I could be okay with sleeping there. Do you have his mom's number? What's her name again?"

"Trish Miller. Yeah, I checked when I pulled out my phone. I have it. I'm going to call her."

"Isn't it weird to randomly call and ask to stay there? We'll reach L.A. tomorrow night, which is about as last minute as you can get when you haven't spoken to someone in over a year."

"Em, literally the worst thing that can happen is that she says no, and we do the same thing we have done for the past two days." Ethan had always been much more comfortable asking for unrealistic things than me, which is probably why he was so good at milking the youngest child factor with my parents.

"I guess you're right. Why not add another unexpected change of plans to this trip?"

So, from a secluded lookout over the Pacific Ocean, after barely touching our phones since we left the Taylors' house, Ethan called Mrs. Miller.

"Here. I'll put it on speaker phone." He held his phone in his palm. It rang a few times, long and low.

"Hello?" Mrs. Miller's voice came surprisingly clear through the speaker.

"Hey Mrs. Miller. It's Ethan Dobberstein."

"Ethan? Oh my goodness! Hi sweetie! How are you? What's going on?" It was obvious that she was caught off guard.

"I'm good! So, this is super random and very last minute, but my sister is on a road trip out West, and I flew to California a couple days ago to meet up with her. We're currently driving down Highway 1 back to San Diego, and we're going to be passing through L.A. I remembered y'all moved back out here a couple months ago. Any chance you are going to be around and we could stop by? Tomorrow?"

"Oh tomorrow! Wow! Seriously?" She sounded excited now. "That's awesome!" I thought she was about to give us a hard no, but she retained her cheer. "It would be such a treat to be able to see you both! Please come by if you have time! We live in a quieter neighborhood on the outskirts of L.A. called Long Beach. Trace unfortunately is at camp this week, so he won't be home, but I will be here, and I'd be happy to cook dinner! Where are you staying?"

"That sounds great! Dinner would be awesome!" He looked at me with questioning eyes and raised eyebrows as if to simultaneously ask if I was okay with the conversation that was happening right now and to say 'I told you so.' I shrugged my shoulders and nodded my head, signaling that I was in. "We have actually just been sleeping out of Emily's car along the way, so we were planning on doing that again tomorrow, but I was wondering if we could actually stay with you tomorrow night too?"

My entire body felt tense. I felt like a self-conscious parent that just observed their kid obliterate some sort of social norm that they have been trying to teach them for years. I couldn't believe that we were asking her so straightforwardly and last minute. I hoped she didn't feel pressured.

Trish didn't seem to care about his forwardness. She replied with eagerness. "Yes, oh my goodness, please stay at our house! I can't imagine what your parents are thinking right now. Both kids on the road all alone? They will get a hoot out of you guys staying with us. I'll make dinner, and you can relax and get clean. I assume you haven't been showering?"

"Ha, no," Ethan answered. "Showers are not a thing for us currently."

"Well, come on over and rest and enjoy some air conditioning! I bet you've been hot! You think you'll be here around dinner time?"

"Uhh, I'm not sure actually. We don't know where we're sleeping tonight. Hold on a sec." He held the phone away from his mouth. "Em, what was that town you talked about stopping near tonight?"

"San Luis Obispo," I reported.

Ethan began talking again. "We will most likely be near San Luis Obispo, so we won't have a super long drive to get to you tomorrow. We might be there closer to lunchtime, if that's alright. If not we can hang out somewhere else until we can come."

"Oh yeah, San Luis Obispo is only about three hours from us. Come whenever you want! I'll be here all day."

"Okay great! Thanks Mrs. Miller! We really appreciate it."

"Of course! I'm so glad you called. I'm excited to see you both! Tell Emily I said hi!"

"Will do. I'll let you know when we have an ETA, but service out here is pretty spotty so I don't know when that will be. See you tomorrow! Thanks again!"

They both said goodbye, and Ethan hung up the phone.

"See, easy as pie," his voice fluttered in an intentionally dramatic Southern accent.

"Oh my gosh you just asked her straight up? I was dying inside!"

"You gotta ask for what you want in this world, or you'll never get it." He smiled.

I rolled my eyes, but I was grateful for the offer. Staying in L.A. was never something I wanted to do, but a free place to stay with a flushing toilet and hot water was hard to say no to.

That night, as the sun started to fall toward the horizon, we stopped at Pismo Beach. As we walked out onto the pier, the waves gently lapped the wooden posts below us. Marijuana smoke filled the air. I automatically thought of Cam.

"Have you ever smoked?" Ethan asked as we walked toward the end of the pier.

"No, I haven't. I'm not totally opposed to trying it one day, but I have a pretty negative association with weed because of Cam. He smoked almost constantly, and I felt like I could never trust him, because I didn't know if what he said was him or if it was the weed."

Ethan shook his head and sighed heavily. "I'm so pissed at him. I hope y'all are done forever. Please don't ever go back. I'm sorry that things sucked so bad."

"Nothing in me wants to, but it doesn't make it any easier. We spent so much time together, and now it feels like a part of me died. It's still weird that I might not ever see him again."

"Yeah I'm sure it's super weird. And hard. It will take time, Em. You just have to be patient through the suck and keep reminding yourself what you are worth."

I gave a half smile and thanked him, though I didn't know how to explain to him that I couldn't just flip a switch and turn my self-worth back on because I had tried with little success. Regardless, I was grateful that we had at least named something about Cam so it would no longer feel unmentionable.

"Does this place remind you of the pier in Panama City?" Ethan interrupted the silence when we were almost back to the beach. "With all the people and shops and restaurants?"

"Yeah it does, actually. I was thinking the same thing. We went there for so many years, which was fun in its own way, but think of how much we could have seen if we would have gone somewhere new every year. Being out here has made me think about taking a family camping trip out West, with mom and dad maybe."

"Yeah that would be cool." He didn't have anything else to say, and I was caught up in an internal debate of whether or not I should take this as an opportunity to ask about how things have been at home.

Should I ask him about mom and dad? If they're still fighting a lot? How he is dealing with it? If it makes him nervous? If he thinks they'll finally get a divorce? If he's ready to move out? If he's mad at me for checking out once I left? If he thinks he'll go far away for college?

We walked around the bright streets in the cold to kill time until it got dark enough to sleep, and I couldn't bring myself to open my mouth and jump over the hurdle of my own shame. Shame of not being there for him when things were hard, of being a bad sister, of not providing stability when our parents couldn't. Shame does that to us. Shame acts as a giant roadblock that prevents us from moving forward into healing and growth. Shame forces us to sit stagnantly. I didn't know how to begin to say that I was sorry.

"I have to poop," Ethan proclaimed. The juxtaposition of his comment and what I was thinking was comical to me. "I think I'm going to go into that diner over there and sneak to the bathroom."

"Yeah, sure. Maybe I will too, and then we can go back to the car and get it ready to go to sleep. But you have to lead the way, and if they yell at us, you're doing the talking."

Ethan rolled his eyes. "As long as you look like you know what you're doing and walk confidently, normally no one asks questions."

"Do you want your toothbrush? If we make it to the bathroom we'll have an opportunity to brush them at a normal sink."

"Yeah, thanks." Ethan shoved his toothbrush and his toothpaste in his pocket, and I tucked mine in my day pack.

We walked in the front door and were met by a smiley hostess.

"We're just stopping by to say hey to some friends in the back," Ethan smiled confidently, and I smiled too, trying to play it cool.

"Yeah sure, go ahead," the hostess nodded her head back toward the dining room, where the bathrooms were.

I laughed as soon as we were out of earshot.

"How are you so good at this?"

"Told ya. Confidence is key." He smiled and disappeared into the bathroom.

"That hostess was probably swooning over your Heath Ledger curls so much that you could have asked for her wallet and she would have handed it right over." I joked as we walked back to the car. "I feel like your hair is even curlier than when you got here." I reached up and ruffled his hair.

"Yeah, it actually looks way better when I don't shower," Ethan agreed confidently. "Something about sweat and salt keeps it like this. I'm thinking about not using shampoo anymore altogether."

I shrugged. "I support that. If there's any time to fully embrace being a dirty hippie, it's now."

"Where are we sleeping tonight?" He changed the subject.

"I thought here possibly, but I saw a sign at the front of the parking lot that said no overnight parking, and I don't want to risk it. I figured we could just find another hotel."

"Sounds good," Ethan agreed.

We drove to a Hampton Inn that sat above most of the rest of the city. We parked the car facing a rock wall that would prevent anyone from being able to see in the front windshield, since that was the easiest place for someone to catch Ethan sleeping in the passenger's seat. I settled into the trunk. It was cold again, so I changed into my pants and sweatshirt, gave Ethan his sheet, sank into my sleeping bag, and fell fast asleep.

{13}

BURNED

AFTER A DUSTY, SWEATY, ANTICLIMACTIC HIKE TO A dried-up waterfall in Malibu the next day, we decided to find a beach to hang out at until we could meet up with the Millers. Santa Monica was the first beach we came to, having no idea how popular it was.

We parked at the Santa Monica Pier and stepped out into a level of beach life I did not know existed. I had never seen anything like it. To our right was a circus of restaurants, fair rides, and a ferris wheel. There were tourists and string bikinis, drink stands and light up toys. To our left was a massive outside adult jungle gym. People were scattered about doing pull-ups, push-ups, yoga, squats, sit-ups, rope climbs, ring hangs, you name it, all on the beach, covered in sand and sweat. I couldn't help but immediately notice all of the shiny biceps and triceps and six packs, on both men and women, but I tried not to stare too long. I dug my bathing suit out of my clothes box. Ethan and I took turns changing in the car.

"How long should we pay for parking?" I asked as I lathered my shoulders with sunscreen.

"I don't know. Trish texted me a little while ago and said that she forgot they had dinner plans tonight. We're going to meet them after, so we have a lot of time to kill. We might as well do the maximum two hours."

"Jeez. Ten bucks for two hours!" I was shocked when the machine spit out our ticket. "I don't understand how people afford to live here. Four dollars a gallon for gas? Five dollars an hour for parking? California is not set up for broke college kids." Ethan laughed.

"Let's go check out the workout area. Some of those dudes were doing some impressive tricks on the rings." Ethan pointed to our left.

"Yeah, sounds good." We made sandwiches for lunch and packed a beach bag to take with us.

We walked up to the workout area, and it seemed to be available for anyone to use for free. There was a small area with kid-sized things to the right of the main one, and children were climbing around, showing off and competing. Not much was different on the adult side.

"I would be in the best shape ever if I had access to this for free," I noted.

"Yeah. Being able to work out and jump in the ocean afterwards? Sounds like the perfect combination to me," Ethan said. He walked over to the ropes, and I followed.

"I feel like Californians are a whole new level of healthy. Literally everyone here has a six-pack." I tried to not feel self-conscious.

"Wanna climb these ropes with me?" Ethan asked as he started up one.

"Wow, I haven't done this since elementary school," I said as I tugged on the one next to him, trying to work up the courage to try. I climbed up more easily than I expected. I guessed I had retained more of my upper body strength than I realized, but it could have been adrenaline—I didn't want to make a fool out of myself in front of a whole crowd of the most in-shape people I had ever seen. The second time I climbed up, it didn't go so well. I supported myself with my feet to slow my descent, but I slipped down the rope too fast. I felt the sharp bite of rope burn on my left foot. I tried to play it cool, so I didn't pay much attention to it right away.

Ethan was already walking toward the ocean when I got down, so I grabbed our bag and followed him out into the sand. I walked for a couple seconds, and then I finally became aware of the searing pain coming from the medial side of my left foot. I looked down, and my stomach dropped when I saw a gaping hole in my foot that was now filled with bloody sand. The pain got more intense.

Oh no. This isn't just a small rope burn. When I slipped, the friction burned off multiple layers of my skin. I must not have felt it at first because of the adrenaline. I put weight on it. *Ouch.* I tried to limp on it, and the sand just dug deeper into the inch-and-a-half-wide circular wound.

Maybe the saltwater will be good for it. I hobbled down to the water's edge, shifting my weight by walking on my toes on my left foot and supporting my weight with my right leg.

"What's wrong with you?" Ethan asked when I got to the water.

I braced myself for the approaching wave and winced when the saltwater created an explosion in the nerves of my foot. "That," I pointed down to my foot. The raw, bleeding skin looked even brighter now that the sand was out of it.

"Oh yuck! How did that happen?"

"Rope burn. Bad. The second time I came down," I uttered through the pain. I gritted my teeth and held my foot under the water again.

"That sucks! Do you have something to wrap it with in the car?"

"Yeah, but I'm not going to go up there yet. I'll probably just hang out on my towel for a bit if you want to swim."

"Okay. Now get out of here with that. Don't want your blood to attract Jaws. I'm not trying to die today." Ethan dove into the next wave, and I limped to my towel.

I looked down at the bloody wound and let out a sigh of disappointment. *Damnit. This is the last thing I wanted to happen. It is going to suck to have to hike on it for the next two and a half weeks.*

I limped to the car to catch up with Ethan, who had gone back to change, not without completely filling the burn with sand again. I rinsed it with my water bottle once I reached the car, and then I did the hard job of pouring hydrogen peroxide on it to disinfect it. It stung so badly my eyes crossed. I covered the wound in antibiotic ointment and wrapped it loosely, hoping the gauze wouldn't stick itself to more skin that I would have to rip off later.

I offered to drive, and even though the GPS said it was only thirty minutes to the Millers' neighborhood, it took us an hour and a half.

We met the infamous monster of L.A. traffic shortly after leaving Santa Monica. Since Ethan passed out almost immediately when we got in the car, I only had myself to keep me company.

We arrived to the Long Beach neighborhood around 6:30 p.m., but the Millers were still an hour and a half from being done with dinner. We killed time by stopping in a local park a couple blocks from the beach. There was a play being performed in the park's small amphitheater titled "Shakespeare by the Sea." It looked like it was free and open to the public, so we decided to walk over and watch it for a while. The bear was starving and swore he could not wait another second for dinner, so we brought armfuls of cooking materials over to a picnic table at the back of the amphitheater. My left foot had not stopped constantly burning, and every step I took the sting was more than apparent.

"How does this thing work?" Ethan asked, holding up the Pocket Rocket, our tiny backpacking cook stove which for some reason we had not used yet. I'm sure we could have planned more warm, cooked dinners on our days on the PCH, but since I was also new at using it, we had opted for easy meals we didn't have to heat or cook until then.

"Wow, you're really going to use that thing right here, in the middle of the park with all of these classy people around?"

"Well yeah, I told you I wanted my Ramen tonight. I've been waiting for three days now!" He opened up the small, twenty-cent square package of dried noodles.

"People are going judge us hardcore for cooking Ramen noodles in the middle of a park during a fancy play, but you do you. Screw on the IsoPro fuel cartridge to the bottom, turn this knob on the side which lets out the gas, and then light it with the lighter. Then you can turn the knob to adjust how powerful you want the flame to be. And obviously boil the water first."

"I'm not that dumb," Ethan made a face while he poured water from his water bottle into a small pot.

I scarfed down a decadent peanut butter, banana, raisin, cinnamon, and honey sandwich while his water boiled.

"I'm going to walk a couple blocks to the beach to watch the sunset. Wanna meet me in a little bit? Make sure you rinse the pot out before you stick it back in the car please."

"Yeah, will do." Ethan had his feet casually propped up on the bench while he blew on a fork full of steaming Ramen. His dusty pants and white t-shirt, which had been his main napkin the past couple days, stood out in the middle of a crowd of Polos, button down long-sleeve shirts, dresses, and high heels.

"We've been pretty good about this whole watching the sunset every night thing," I heard Ethan call out as he walked up from behind me and sat down in the sand.

"Oh, hey. Did you get kicked out for being a dirty hippie eating Ramen in the middle of a nice park?" We both laughed.

After hanging out on the beach for a while, Ethan got a text from Trish saying they were on the way back from dinner. We walked back to the car, and after a terrifying episode of Ethan running a red light at a busy intersection while trying to defog my windshield, we finally reached the Millers' gated neighborhood alive and safe.

The road wound up and around a fairly large hill that overlooked the city. Since I knew that a ritzy neighborhood in L.A. was not cheap, I figured the houses we passed were close to a million dollars a piece, if not higher. It was only when we started to pass giant three-story houses with manicured lawns and three car garages that I processed the fact that we were about to spend the night in what would probably be the nicest house we had ever stayed in. The fancy pillars, arches, columns, flowers, and dainty lights that met us when we pulled into the Millers' driveway confirmed that.

"Holy shit." It escaped my mouth before I could think.

Ethan smirked. "And now you see why I wanted to stay here so badly."

"I knew they definitely weren't poor, but I was not expecting this."

We knocked on the giant front door and Trish opened it excitedly.

"Hey guys! Come in!" She brought us both in for hugs. "Sorry we couldn't wait on you for dinner. I forgot that we had told friends we would go out with them tonight, but I did have leftovers in the fridge from last night that I heated up for you. You okay with pork chops?"

Though we technically already ate dinner, a second dinner was a 100% yes when we walked in the door and smelled real food after going three days on peanut butter sandwiches. We crammed our faces with pork chops, stuffing, green beans, and fruit, but I did notice that I wasn't able to eat as much as I expected. I guessed my stomach had shrunk from eating way less than normal on the road.

"Do you want to shower?" Trish asked when we had finished our catching up at dinner.

"Yes!" Ethan and I yelled out at the same time.

I did not know a shower could feel so glorious. Even after dipping in the ocean at Santa Monica I felt like I had ten layers of grime on me, and the water running off my body was still brown. My foot stung terribly in the warm water, and I clenched my teeth as I scrubbed the wound, making sure that all of the sand was out of it before I bandaged it again before bed.

I couldn't quite catch up to reality. Even though it had only been three days on the road, coming into a nice house with a home-cooked meal and a hot shower felt so foreign. I felt the contrast even more when we sat down in the living room with Maddy, Trace's sister, who was watching the ESPY awards. I didn't even know what the ESPY awards were but going from days of a spartan existence on the road to being pushed into the lap of luxury was a bit of a shock.

It was hard to bridge the gap between spending most of my time in the natural world to watching rich, sports celebrities on TV decked out in expensive suits, dresses, and diamonds. I felt like Katniss Everdeen from *The Hunger Games,* ripped from her tiny, rural town and suddenly placed in the Capitol, overwhelmed with the drastic difference of lifestyle and feeling like an outsider. I was grateful for a place to sleep, but I felt tense. I didn't know what life would look like after this trip, but I knew I was done pursuing the kind of life where wealth, money, status, celebrities, and fancy clothes was celebrated. This trip was showing me a new way to live, where material possessions and status didn't matter, and I wanted to push further into it.

{14}

THEN THERE WERE FOUR

"TELL ME ABOUT SYDNEY AND WILL. YOU SAID YOU don't know them very well?" Ethan asked while we were in standstill traffic the next afternoon. We had spent the morning relaxing and recharging when we heard that Sydney and Will's flight was delayed a few hours.

"Well, I've been around them for the past two years because they were both in the same church and college campus ministry as me. We have a lot of the same friends, but I didn't really talk to them until about a month ago when Sydney found out I was going on the trip and asked to come too."

"So, she just asked you straight up and you said yes even though you've never hung out much before? What if she's crazy?"

I laughed. "I don't think she's crazy. She's pretty quiet and doesn't talk much, and she seems pretty easy-going. Will is similar. Extremely introverted. Keeps to himself for the most part. He's done a lot of camping and traveling before this and has actually been to a few spots we'll be going. He'll be helpful when we backpack."

I didn't mention to Ethan that I'd thought about my distance from them already. I didn't trust many people during this time of my life, especially new people. Since Sydney and Will didn't really know me personally while I was a worship leader, I hoped we could start a friendship from scratch. I wanted them to know present-day me instead of who I was before I started deconstructing. The idea of making new friends was terrifying though, and I didn't know if or when I would feel safe enough to be open and honest with them.

"Wasn't Will a worship leader at your church too?" Ethan asked.

"Yeah. And he's the son of one of the main leaders of the church. But he's not anymore. I mean, not a worship leader anymore. He's still a son. That sounds weird. Whatever, you know what I mean." We both laughed.

I knew that Will had quit leading worship and that he didn't come to church as much anymore. I heard through a line of church gossip that it had been a big deal in his family and in the community because Will had sung and played music for the church since he was a teenager, but I didn't know the full story. I didn't know him well enough yet to ask for more details, but I had this weird gut feeling that we might be in a similar place. I wondered if I would ever find the guts to bring it up in conversation.

"How old are they? What do they look like?" Ethan reminded me that I was in the middle of a real conversation.

"Sydney is twenty-five, about my height with long, curly, auburn hair. I think she studied art in college, and she likes to hike. I don't know much else about her. Will is twenty-four, maybe 5'11" or so, with wavy, dirty blonde hair. He's quite thin, but super athletic. He's also a videographer, so he'll be shooting a lot of footage while we're in the national parks."

I had a lot of respect for Will, and I was more nervous about him coming than Sydney. He might as well have been a Christian celebrity in our small town. Everyone swooned over him, especially women. He was an extremely talented singer. He loved science and psychology. He made really beautiful photos. He was an intellectual *and* avid outdoorsman. I couldn't deny that I had swooned over him a couple times myself. I did feel the slightest attraction to him, which made me nervous because he had many of the same qualities as Cam, and I was uncertain of how that would affect me. Would I be self-conscious around him? Would I be distracted by him being there? Would he feel attracted to me and make things complicated? I already felt vulnerable around guys, and I didn't want to fall for Will out of a rebound after Cam, but I worried that in spending two weeks on the road with him, I would.

"Well hopefully it will be fine with all of us being crammed in this car. We're obviously not all going to sleep in here, right?" Ethan looked concerned.

"Of course not. We would hate each other by the end," I chuckled. "Tonight after we pick them up from the airport we'll actually drive north of San Diego to stay with someone in Sydney's family—an uncle or cousin that she doesn't know well but who said we could stay with them. Then, it's camping every night from there on out."

"Oh sweet, another bed!"

"Well, no guarantees about a bed. I don't know how big their house is, and they have kids, but at least we're guaranteed another roof and a toilet." I still felt guilty about staying in so many houses on my supposed grand living-out-of-my-car adventure. Staying in houses felt like I was cheating on the rugged trip I had told people I was taking. I feared that people would think I was disingenuous. I didn't want to be seen as a poser.

"And where are we going tomorrow?"

"I think the plan is to drive straight to Yosemite," I replied. "I don't know anything about campsites or hikes besides the famous Half Dome." I laughed remembering how little planning we had done for the second half of the trip. "We only have a rough outline, and I haven't talked to Sydney and Will at all since I left, besides asking them if they were okay with you coming. The only thing we are guaranteed is our backpacking trip into the Grand Canyon July 20th through the 22nd, which is when you will have to figure something else out since we don't have a permit for you. Besides that, we're going to have to be really flexible because I don't think we're guaranteed a campsite in Yosemite. If we don't get one, I don't know what we'll do. We probably should have reserved something, but I guess it's too late now." I shrugged my shoulders.

"Well, adventure here we come?" I could tell he was trying to hope for the best. I was too.

Will and Sydney walked from baggage claim seeming much more prepared than Ethan when he arrived in California. They both carried large backpacking bags, and they were both wearing their hiking boots instead of stark white vans. Sydney's auburn hair was neatly braided down her back, and Will's dirty-blonde locks peeked out of his Patagonia ball cap. We exchanged hellos and hugs, and I introduced them to Ethan.

"Are you hungry?" I asked as we exited the airport.

"Starving," Will replied. "Have you had In-and-Out Burger yet?"

"Nope. What's that?" Ethan asked.

"I haven't, but a juicy burger sounds glorious," I admitted.

"It's a fast food chain that's only out West," explained Sydney. "We would go to it growing up when we came out to visit my mom's brother, and it's an experience everyone has to do at least once. After a long day of traveling, it sounds perfect."

"Sounds great to me. The car is that way." I pointed to the parking garage across the way.

"What happened to your foot?" asked Sydney once she noticed I was limping.

"She tried to be too cool to impress the body builders at the beach," Ethan called over his shoulder.

"No," I emphasized my annoyance. "I climbed a rope on the beach at the Santa Monica pier yesterday, and I slipped a little bit getting off of it. It's a pretty bad rope burn. I rubbed a good bit of skin off, but I'm hoping that it will heal before we have to do too much hiking."

"I'm so sorry! That sounds awful! You think you'll be okay to hike in Yosemite still?" she asked.

"Oh, I'm hiking no matter what. It just might hurt like hell and make me go a little slower, but I'll catch up eventually. I'm going to leave the bandage off most of the day today to help it air out and start to scab over. Right now, it's just really wet and oozy."

"Yikes," Sydney scrunched her nose.

"Sorry, I know it's kind of gross," I laughed. I opened the trunk. "Oh, right. The bags. Ethan, can you help me move everything to the back?" I felt embarrassed that I'd forgotten to rearrange all of our things in order to fit two more humans and their stuff into the car. Their bags barely fit, but with enough shoving and car Tetris, we were eventually able to shut the trunk.

"We'll probably need to figure out a better system tomorrow before we hit the road," I noted. "Sorry it's so disorganized."

"No worries!" assured Will. "Let's go crush some cheap burgers."

After we had devoured some animal-style In-and-Out burgers and started to feel like full humans again, Will got the group's attention.

"So I already told Sydney this, but I have a significant update that I haven't told you yet because texting about it would have been too complicated. Keith and Heather are in Yosemite right now, and they wondered if they should reserve a campsite for us. I told them I would have to talk to you first."

"Who are Keith and Heather?" Ethan quickly asked.

"They go to our church. Their family is really close with Will's family, so we hang out with them a lot." answered Sydney. "After hearing from them that most of the campgrounds in Yosemite are fully booked, we figured it might be nice for us to have a place lined up at least for our first night in the park."

Will nodded. "What do you think?"

My stomach sank. Keith and Heather were the supervisors of the leadership team at the church. I hadn't spoken to them since I'd left the worship team. The few times I went to church after I quit, I'd avoided them. They were quite literally the last people I expected to be with on my trip. Keith and Heather individually did not cause harm or spiritual trauma to me directly, but they still thought I was the same person I was when I was on the worship team, which worried me. Hanging out with leaders from my most recent church community for a couple days straight was not the most ideal way to detach from the trauma I was trying to heal from. However, I knew we needed all the help we could get since we didn't have any reservations in Yosemite.

"Wow! Um." I swallowed. "Sure! We can try to meet up with them." I couldn't tell if what came out of my mouth was true, or if it was the last thing that I wanted. I didn't want to disrupt the group dynamic right off the bat, so saying yes seemed like the only option.

"Cool," Will smiled, seeming relieved. "I told them we would let them know our ETA when we have one. I asked if they would send the location of the campsite they get for tomorrow night. They said service was spotty in the park, so it might be a little complicated finding them, but we can play it by ear."

"This whole trip sounds like it is going to be playing it by ear," Ethan uttered nonchalantly, and everyone laughed.

"Are we ready to head on?" I asked. "It's already 8:00, and the sun is setting, so we better go outside so we can keep our pact."

"What pact?" asked Sydney.

"We decided to watch the sunset every night if possible," answered Ethan, "which probably won't be that hard if we're spending all of our time outside for the next couple weeks."

"Oh gotcha, I can be down for that pact." She smiled and shut the car door.

We played the mixed CD for Will and Sydney as we rode to Sydney's uncle's house north of San Diego. It was obvious that everyone was tired, for no one forced conversation. Will and Sydney also changed the introvert to extrovert ratio from 1:1 to 3:1, which helped. I felt a little less fearful of how the next two weeks were going to go. I was hopeful. Maybe we could be friends.

{15}

IN THE DARK

O UR STAY WITH SYDNEY'S UNCLE WAS SHORT, SINCE we arrived just to sleep and left right after breakfast, but we were grateful for a place to sleep and a sunny driveway to park in while we reorganized the car. We spent some time figuring out what fit where best, where the heavy stuff should go, where the bulky stuff should go, what needed to be easily accessible, and what could be buried underneath everything else. Our only option for the food box was to leave it in the middle seat in the back. We thought it could turn out badly if the people in the back got hungry and ate too many snack rations, but the box could be helpful by providing a smell barrier between the two people in the back once we were all on day four or ten with no shower.

Before hitting the road, we bought groceries and reorganized our food so that Ethan and I shared one food box and Sydney and Will shared the other to keep everything straight. I had most of what I needed for breakfast and snacks, but I had grabbed some more tuna and beans for backpacking in Yosemite. Now, after many more years of backpacking experience under my belt, I know that relying on heavy, canned beans as one's main source of backpacking food is not energy efficient. I didn't know how to plan lightweight dinners then, which would add difficulty for me later, but we all have to be beginners at first.

I was antsy to get to Yosemite, but Will and Sydney wanted to hook over to the Pacific Coast Highway and drive north on it for a while so they could see the coast, which would add a couple hours to our already eight-hour drive to Yosemite. I wasn't thrilled to see the coast again, but I had to remind myself again that the trip was no longer just about me.

"When you fight, fight for love." The lyrics of a song by John Lucas flowed out of the speakers gently and peacefully four hours into our drive. We didn't think about the fact that it was a Friday, which meant the already-bad L.A. traffic would be even worse than normal. We were standing still on the highway, and any forward movement we were able to achieve seemed to be in inches instead of miles.

Though John Lucas's lyrics were lighthearted and had been some of my favorites in previous years, listening to that line repeated over and over again that day did nothing but remind me how sad I was. I felt angst about the idea of love, and I wasn't sure why I would ever want to fight for it again when it had led me into so much pain. Even though I was surrounded by three people now, I somehow still felt crippled by loneliness. My mood continued to drop, and I sat quietly and pretended like everything was fine as my thoughts spiraled in the back seat. Will had offered to drive, and Ethan sat across from me with the food boxes crammed between us. I tried to play it cool as I pulled out my journal to scrawl out some thoughts in hopes of stopping them before I worked myself up to crying while being surrounded by people I didn't know how to be honest with.

07/17/15, Day 15 -

And the overwhelming, chaotic chatter returns to take over my mind once again. My defenses fall short at the fall of the first tear that makes its way down a turned cheek that tries to hide it. I shut my eyelids in attempt to make my tears turn around and go back in the direction from which they came, back to their pushed-down homes as simple thoughts inside my head. That works for a little while, but the stares of the ocean cliffs looking back at me through the car window do not hesitate to remind me that I am not telling the truth, that repressing the shadows inside of my mind only gives them all the more power. But even if I tried, telling the truth amidst these people I barely know would possibly be met with blank stares and questioning eyes... It would only leave me feeling more isolated. Less seen, and more alone. Will it be like this forever?

Having people around you means nothing if you can't be your full self with them, if they can't see you, either because they don't understand or because you don't let them, like I'm doing now...I know that feeling seen and known and loved requires me to be open and meet people in the middle, but I'm so scared of being hurt.

Though I feel frustrated with myself and wish I was further along, I want to grant myself permission to be in process. Healing is a journey that makes no sense when each day is looked at separately and individually, so therefore each day must be taken with a grain of salt in knowing that though the salt burns your open wound, it plays a crucial role in the completion of your process, where you finally see light in the deepest, darkest caves of your hurt and pain, not at the beginning, but at the end when suddenly the heaviness and pain are no more, and you see the reason and significance behind every second of every good and bad day that led you to that point of freedom, where you understand why a little more clearly, where your heart has been made a little more whole.

Will parked the car and turned off the engine. I didn't even realize that we had made it to the coast. I became aware of a vague nausea in my stomach. It was probably car sickness from writing and looking down for so long, so I was grateful for an opportunity to walk around.

I took some deep breaths as we walked around on the cliffs of a private neighborhood off the highway. I didn't have the physical or emotional energy to explore, so I just sat down and waited for everyone else.

"I checked my phone," Will began as he and Sydney walked back from looking at the tide pools, "and Keith sent a text with the name of the campground they are at tonight. We won't have service once we get to Yosemite, and it's a pretty large campground, so we might have to just walk in and see if we can find them."

"Do we have to hike in?" Ethan asked.

"I don't think it's a backpacking campsite, but we might have to walk a couple hundred yards or so. We'll have to see when we get there. Keith said that they were heading back to the campsite now, where they don't have service, so I can't exactly ask them any more questions about it."

"Back to that whole go with the flow thing I guess," Ethan shrugged.

"Aren't we going to get there pretty late?" I looked at my watch. "It's almost six now, which would put us there no earlier than eleven."

"Yeah. It's going to be a long night," said Sydney.

"Yep. We'll enter in the dark," Will replied. "I'm honestly pretty stoked about it. We're not going to see much going in, which means we're just going to wake up in the middle of the park. It's going to be staggering."

"Whoa, I didn't think about that!" Ethan said.

"I have little idea of what to expect. I've seen maybe one photo of Yosemite, and I don't really remember it. I'm excited!" I smiled. "Should we make dinner?" I asked as I reached in the car for the food boxes.

We ate our banana and peanut butter wraps while looking out over the ocean, and after we routed to get gas, we turned inland on Highway 41-North which took us four hours up and across to the other side of the state.

We finally got to the first entrance of Yosemite around 11:00 p.m., and it was so late that there was no ranger at the gate. We couldn't rest yet, for we still had forty miles of a long, winding, mountain road to reach the area of the park where Heather and Keith were hopefully still camping. We could only hope that we would be able to find them as we drove through the blackness.

I began wondering again what the dynamic would be like. *Will I be on edge around Keith? Will spending time with him trigger the same feelings of isolation I felt at church? I said nothing to him besides that I needed to quit the worship team because I didn't have energy, and I haven't been back to church since Easter. Has he noticed? What if church comes up? Will he ask why I haven't been there? I just don't want to be on edge the whole time, waiting to be found out.*

We had ten miles left until the supposed campsite area, and for some reason I hadn't thought about rolling down the window until that moment. My expectations for a twinkling star-lit sky were completely blown out of the water.

I gasped. "The stars! Guys, look! We have to stop!"

Ethan parked the car. When we got out and looked up, we all were silent. There was nothing else to say.

I cannot explain why being in the presence of majesty can bring about a bodily reaction, but looking up and seeing more stars than I had ever seen before moved something inside of me to the point that tears were rolling down my cheeks, and I could not stop smiling. While part of me wished that we could have come into Yosemite during the day, I was glad that we were entering in the dark. Something about not being able to see the whole picture made me that much more present to the mystery of the moment.

When we reached the campsite parking lot, we could see the looming mountains around us silhouetted faintly against moonlight, but we had no idea of the full magnificence that stood in the shadows. We didn't know where to begin to look for Heather and Keith because there were several entry trails to the larger camping area in the woods. We were exhausted, and I could tell that everyone was on edge. We'd been on the road for twelve hours, and it was approaching midnight.

"Sooooo, what now?" Ethan broke the silence.

Will grabbed his headlamp. "I'll be right back." He ran down the access trail near where we parked.

"What? You're just going to go run around in the woods until you find them?" Sydney called after him.

"Yeah, what else are we supposed to do?" Will's light on his headlamp was the only thing we could see. It bobbed off into the woods, and then it disappeared.

We waited in the dark next to my car. The stars peered down through the alpine canopy above us. Ten minutes passed, and then the bobbing light reappeared in the darkness, growing in intensity until it reached us.

"I found them, somehow," Will panted with a relieved look on his face. "I think we should only take the bare minimum with us tonight. Does everyone have a hammock?"

We all nodded yes, waiting for further command.

"Okay, for simplicity's sake let's sleep in our hammocks tonight, and we'll figure out tent stuff tomorrow."

"I'm so tired I can barely think straight," mumbled Sydney. "Let's go."

We fumbled through our various bags and boxes to get our hammocks and sleeping bags, accidentally blinding each other with our headlamps when we forgot and looked directly into another person's face. We awkwardly apologized and slid past each other to get to different parts of the car. It wasn't too chilly because we were still in the valley, so I just grabbed pants and a jacket instead of putting on my base layers. We ditched any hygiene routines and stumbled along a rooty trail for five minutes or so until it opened up into a wide clearing in the middle of the forest. Tents of all colors were scattered like giant drops of splatter paint against the pine straw, and something about suddenly being surrounded by dozens of strangers sleeping in the woods made me giddy. Will walked us over to a blue tent along the edge, and Keith poked his head out.

It was disorienting arriving in the middle of the wilderness on the other side of the country and meeting up with someone from home, but I was grateful to see him.

"Hey Keith!" I whispered as we approached. "Thanks so much for doing this for us."

"Aw, it's no big deal!" he whispered back. "We're just so happy y'all made it safely! We were praying fervently that you would find us and that everything would work out, and look, the Lord is faithful!" I was already cringing. Keith got out and hugged Will, following with Sydney and I. "Hey Ethan! I'm Keith." Keith extended his hand, and Ethan shook it. "Glad you're here! We'll talk more tomorrow," Keith whispered.

"Hey, thanks, me too. Excited to sleep!" Ethan rasped and clutched his armful of gear tighter across his chest.

Keith pointed across the space to a cluster of sugar pine trees. "Over there is where you should set up. Sleep well, and we'll see you in the morning!"

I zigzagged my way through the field of tents and knobby roots, trying not to trip and smother a sleeping stranger in their tent. I didn't know what we would have done without Keith and Heather finding a campsite ahead of us. We would have been stranded in the middle of Yosemite with no idea where we could sleep, at midnight, with no cell service to research anything. I fell asleep swaying slightly in my green and gray hammock, snuggled up in my sleeping bag, excited and anxious to wake up in the morning and meet Yosemite in full light.

{16}

MILDRED

WHAT IS WRONG WITH THE SKY? WHEN I OPENED MY
eyes, sleepiness prevented my brain from coming up
with an explanation of why the sky was gray. I followed
the gray up between the trunks of the evergreens, through the bristled
branches, only to realize that the gray continued going up and up and
did not end from my viewpoint in my hammock. *Oh my gosh. That's a
mountain. And I can't even see the top.*

I tried to muster the courage to get out of my sleeping bag and face
the frigid air so I could get a better look, but when I tried to pull my
left leg out, I felt a painful tug on my foot. *Oh no. My burn. I forgot to
wrap it last night, and it's stuck to my sleeping bag.* I tried to shimmy my
sleeping bag down past my waist so I could get a better look. I wanted
to avoid pulling off as much skin as possible. I separated my foot slowly, but not without reopening a few small spots that were now bleeding
through the new, transparent layer of skin that had started to grow.
Ugh. This thing is going to take forever to heal.

I carefully stepped out of my hammock with my good foot, and
then I eased my left foot into my Chaco. The unfortunate thing about
my Chacos in this situation was that they had straps that zigzagged all
across my foot in many angles, which made it even harder to get my

shoe on without dragging a strap over my fragile wound. Thankfully, once the shoe was all the way on, the burn rested in a gap between the straps, so it didn't constantly rub. Only the outer rim of the circular burn was low enough that I would walk on it when I stepped. The angle of my foot when I slid down the rope at least kept me from burning the sole of my foot, which would have been much harder to navigate. I limped through the woods to find a view of the mountain peaks which towered just out of sight. It seemed like no one else was out of their hammock, so I walked alone, and a grin continued to spread across my face as the anticipation grew. *I can't believe I'm in the heart of Yosemite.*

I reached an opening free of trees, and a wide, gravel trail wound to my left. I stepped out on it and was met by the most gigantic mountain I had ever seen. I didn't know the name of it, and I didn't need to. It was just there, immense and intimidating, a hunk of earth hanging where there should be sky. I was startled out of my captivation by the sound of a stick breaking in the woods to my left. I quickly turned my head to see Will coming from the opposite direction. *Good, not a bear.* I didn't know he was awake. We didn't say anything to each other, because there was nothing to say. He just laughed and threw his arms up in the air, gesturing toward the mountain as if to say, "Can you believe where we are right now?!"

It was hard to take in, but I already knew I was in the presence of something sacred.

I walked back to the campsite to find that the rest of the group was now awake and sitting around a fire next to Heather and Keith's tent.

"Hi Heather!" I smiled and waved. She had been sleeping the previous night when we arrived.

"Hey Emily! It's so good to see you!" Heather tucked her shoulder-length brown hair behind her ear before taking another bite of oatmeal. "It's been a while. Did you sleep well?"

"Yeah, I did actually! It's pretty chilly this morning though!"

"It does get pretty cold at night here, but it warms up a good bit during the day. Want some oatmeal?" asked Heather.

"Oh yeah, that would be great. Thanks." Heather handed me a bowl of oatmeal with raisins and honey. "I'm excited to get on a trail today," I said after swallowing my first sticky bite.

"Yeah, these mountains are incredible," Keith gushed.

I looked back up to the sky and took another bite. Even though the conversation was casual, I could feel tightness in my chest. I felt on edge, like I needed to keep my defenses close in case a question was asked that I didn't know how to answer. Conversation topics could go anywhere with Heather and Keith, but I knew that they frequently talked about God and Christianity, and specifically a version of God I didn't believe in anymore. I worried that a triggering question or statement could happen at any moment, and the fact that I couldn't control where conversation would go over the next couple of days was unsettling.

"We were thinking about hiking to Nevada Falls today," Keith mentioned as I sat down on a rock next to Sydney to finish eating. "Three point four miles up, I think. It's one of the most popular trails in the park, and today is supposed to be beautiful."

"That sounds great to me," I shrugged. "I'm sure you heard that we have very little plans, so any information or suggestions are welcomed! Are y'all okay with that?" I faced Sydney, Ethan, and Will, who all nodded their heads in agreement.

"Keith, you were saying you went to the ranger station early this morning, right? To ask about permits for backpacking?" Will asked. "What did they say?"

"Oh yeah! So, the way it works is that you can day-hike without a permit, except for Half Dome, but you have to book those ones months in advance, so we won't be doing that. You do need a permit for any overnight backpacking and any campground in the frontcountry, where we are now. It's okay that you don't have reservations because they keep forty percent of the permits open for first come, first served, which is what Heather and I have been doing. It just requires getting up early and waiting in line. There are loads of people here this week, and most of the main backpacking permits are all booked up."

"Bummer. Well, ideally we want to backpack at least one night." Will replied.

"I figured, and I didn't ask you this morning because y'all were still sleeping, but I woke up with the sun and figured I would go ahead and go to the ranger station, and I got us backpacking permits for Snow Creek."

"Oh, cool! I've never heard of it," Will said.

"Is it hard?" Ethan asked.

"I don't think so," answered Keith. "I found out about Snow Creek from Tim, who we met yesterday. Tim is this awesome guy that is really spiritual and loves nature and the earth. He says he doesn't label himself, but I swear he loves the Lord." *Why does Tim have to call it "The Lord" in order for his experience of Divinity in nature to be valid?* I felt frustrated as Keith continued. "He has lived out of his camper with his dog for the past fifteen years and has done a lot of hiking in Yosemite. He said he hiked to Snow Creek a couple years ago, and it's his favorite spot in the whole park, even better than Half Dome. He said that few people know about it because everyone just tries to hike Half Dome or Cathedral Lakes or Cloud's Rest, so it's free of tourists and you have an amazing view of the valley all to yourself most of the time."

"The less people the better in my opinion," Sydney uttered.

I laughed. "Yeah. Me too."

"The only thing," Keith's tone changed, "is Mildred." He and Heather both smirked.

"Who's Mildred?" Ethan raised his eyebrows.

"Mildred is a bear that lives up near Snow Creek, and apparently she is pretty smart, and really active, which is one of the reasons this trail is less popular. You have to have a bear canister everywhere in Yosemite to hide the scent of food or hygiene products that could attract bears, but Mildred has figured out that the bear canisters mean food. And, she is known to sometimes roll them to the edge of the cliff next to the campsite and push them off."

"Wait, seriously?" Sydney asked. We all were chuckling nervously.

"Why does she roll them off the cliff?" Ethan asked. "That would suck pretty bad if all of our food just got pushed off and fell hundreds of feet down. We would have nothing to eat!"

"I guess in her bear brain she knows that if she pushes the canister off the cliff it might break open on the rocks," Will observed. "But maybe her bear brain is limited to know that she can't safely get down to it to actually be able to enjoy whatever is inside."

"Yeah, exactly," Keith agreed. "The rangers said it is totally safe, and they gave us some suggestions about how to protect our food or scare her off if she pays us a visit."

I don't know how it can be totally safe when a giant black bear often hangs out in your campsite, and the last thing I want to learn is how to scare off a bear. I felt anxiety creeping up my spine to my neck.

"I mean, when in Yosemite, I guess?" I tried to sound confident.

Will laughed. "Yeah, I'm still down."

"I would honestly be fine with any campsite," Sydney added. "I just want to hike and have a place to sleep."

"I'm good with it. As long as Mildred doesn't steal my food. I will fight her," Ethan muttered.

"The bear face-off. Could be pretty entertaining," I joked. We all laughed.

"Cool. Then it's settled," Keith decided. "We'll day hike and explore the valley a little bit, and then we'll caravan over to the Snow Creek trailhead. We can hike up from the valley, or we can hike down from Tioga Road. The Tioga Road way is a little longer, but it's more gradual. It's about an hour's drive from the valley."

It felt comforting to have a plan and a place to sleep. I just hoped that it wouldn't involve waking up to Mildred towering over my hammock in the middle of the night.

After we packed up camp, we drove across the valley to the trailhead for the waterfalls. The access trail was a madhouse. The reputation for Yosemite being Disney World in July turned out to be accurate. There were so many people walking that it felt more like waiting in line, which made it hard to be present, but once we got past the hordes of people I was able to sink into a place of pure awe.

The hike to Nevada Falls was much more difficult than I expected it to be. The Mist Trail gained over two thousand feet in elevation over the six and a half mile loop to Nevada Falls and Vernal Falls. It was like being on a stair stepper for three and a half hours, which in normal life would have felt like torture, but the view was a distraction, both from how fast my heart was beating and the pain pulsing from my burn.

We sprawled ourselves out on the warm, granite boulders next to Nevada falls for a while, soaking in the sun as a steady, gentle mist blew down on us. I looked around me at the diverse demographic of hikers and thought about our crowded walk to the trailhead when we started the hike. I was annoyed at first by the people filling the sidewalk and shoving like it was a race to get to the trailhead, but as I walked I started to pay attention to all of the different people we passed. Most people I walked by looked me in the eyes and smiled, most even saying hello. Once I pushed through my frustration about it being crowded, I felt love for the people we passed. No matter whether people were Indian, Japanese, Australian, Mexican, Chinese, Canadian, American, German, African American, French, or any other nationality, the borders between us seemed a little less tall. I saw myself in them. I saw them in me. Our pasts, presents, and futures, our emotions, families, and flaws, our passions, insecurities, and wisdoms all converging in shared humanness.

I can't stop thinking about what a good gift it is to be human. We are all so different, yet we are also somehow one. I want my life to grow from that foundation. Everyone belongs. Everyone is greeted with a smile. Everyone is welcomed.

I think the oceans we often believe separate us are actually just really wide, ankle-deep lakes, and they only become oceans when we believe them to be uncrossable. I want to live a life where there are no oceans of separation, and I don't find that in the Church. I want to be in more environments where I am able to look into the eyes of a stranger and connect simply because of our humanness, where we build authentic relationship before we ever need to bring up what we believe. Because everyone belongs, and the first place we belong is together. But what does that look like in practice?

Even though it was only about three miles as the crow flies to the trailhead for Snow Creek, Big Old Flat Road and Tioga Road, the only roads that would take us there, ran in a wide, forty-mile loop up around what seemed like an entire mountain range. Shortly after leaving the valley, the road tilted upwards, and it only became steeper as we continued. We found out that the gas station at the intersection of Big Old Flat Road and Tioga Road was the last gas station available, so we made sure to fill up. We had to fork out $4.20 a gallon, more than I had ever paid for gas in my life, but we did not want to risk running out of gas up there, knowing Tioga Road would only take us higher into remote wilderness.

On the drive from the valley to Porcupine Creek, we climbed from 4,000 feet in elevation to 8,100 feet in elevation. The constant popping and acclimatizing that came with climbing over 4,000 feet in a matter of an hour was a lot for our ears to handle. From Porcupine Creek, we would begin our 1,700 feet of descent into the Snow Creek backpacking campsite.

I had never backpacked to a campsite before. I didn't exactly know what I needed to bring, but I felt embarrassed to admit that aloud. Ethan was done packing in minutes, but that was because he barely brought anything with him in the first place, and everyone else looked like they knew what they were doing. Instead of asking to make sure I wasn't bringing too much, I just brought everything that I thought might be helpful. What I did not know then, is that you should never justify bringing random things on a backpacking trip just for a rare case scenario, because soon your pack is forty-five pounds even though you are only camping for one night. I heaved my pack up onto my back and followed the others to the trailhead.

The rapid change in elevation brought on an earache, and combined with my aching shoulders and my throbbing foot, it was hard to be present. The trail was downhill almost the whole time, but it still left me wincing and exhausted. Pain shot through my foot with every step, but eventually, once my brain got used to my nerves constantly firing, it became a dull feeling in the background.

Around 6:30, the dense forest opened up to a small clearing of pine straw that looked to be the tent space, and then the forest abruptly ended. From there, smooth granite extended out about twenty yards to a steep cliff that dropped hundreds of feet down. Half Dome stood tall and round in the distance, and I was shocked by how much of the park we could suddenly see. We immediately threw our bags down and hurried over to the cliff to get a better look.

"I'm feeling pretty grateful for Tim right now," I whispered when Sydney and I stopped and stood a couple yards from the cliff's edge.

"Right? I would have never known about this." She took a deep breath and stretched her arms up over her head. "I'm so glad we're done walking for the day. My back is killing me."

"Same! I felt like a baby walking down," I admitted. "Hiking with a pack is totally different. I can tell my body isn't used to it.

Hopefully going back up that tomorrow isn't going to be too terrible."

"I'm going to go find a spot to set up my hammock," Ethan said. "Wanna come?"

We all walked over to a cluster of pines that surrounded a small fire pit containing a few charred wood fragments that looked like they had been burned within the last forty-eight hours. We hung our hammocks in a large semi-circle, and Heather and Keith set up their tent in the middle, near the fire pit. We each brought out our various lightweight, compact cooking contraptions. I was thankful Ethan and I had used mine at least once so we didn't look like total noobs. Ethan boiled water to make Ramen again, and after he was done, I heated up my can of beans and instant rice.

After dinner, we rinsed our pots and pans in Snow Creek, and we soaked in our sweet solitude in silence as we watched the blue sky start to transition to purples and pinks. Thunderstorm clouds hung foreboding in the distance. *I hope those are moving away from us.* I already had chills, and the night would only get colder. The idea of adding rain on top of that fact made me shiver more.

I walked out and sat on a flat boulder near the edge of the cliff. Shortly after, Ethan sat down next to me. We looked out over Half Dome in silence for a while.

"I think this might be the most beautiful mountain view I've ever seen," Ethan began. "I figured it would be cool, but not this cool."

"Yeah," I nodded. "This barely even looks real to me. I'm having a hard time processing it."

"How are you holding up?" He asked after a moment of silence. "I mean, with the whole Cam thing. You've been pretty quiet the past couple days."

I'm surprised he noticed. I paused briefly before I replied. "It's been hard honestly. I think about it pretty constantly, which makes it difficult to be fully present. I often feel weighed down by a heaviness I can't always find words for, and I don't really know what to say when I feel like that. I don't want to fake that I'm okay all the time."

"You don't have to pretend, Em."

I teared up. "I know. It's just hard to know what to do with all of the emotions inside of me sometimes."

I timidly leaned my head to my left until it stopped on Ethan's right shoulder. Even though it was a small gesture, it felt like I had just leaped across a chasm of vulnerability. It felt like I was being honest about the fact that I had a lot to bear. It felt okay to need people, even if that just meant resting my head on my brother's shoulder when I couldn't hold my head up anymore.

We sat and watched the stars emerge between the clouds, little lamps turned on in faraway galaxies one by one. Once the sky was blanketed with beams of light and we were too cold to sit anymore, we walked back over to the campsite. We carried our water bottles over to the creek and took turns using Keith's water filter. When I left Boone, I didn't even think about what to do for water filtration while we were backpacking, so I was grateful to be traveling with people that actually knew what they were doing. Keith had this little stick that we swirled around in our water bottles, and something about the level of ultra-violet light it emitted killed off any unwanted bacteria and made the creek water safe to drink. It felt like we were doing voodoo magic, but as I gulped down half a liter and refilled my bottle to filter it again, I hoped the magic worked because I was not trying to puke all night with Mildred lurking about.

"The ranger gave me a tip about what to do to increase the likelihood that Mildred won't get away with stealing our bear canisters," Keith informed us as he started gathering everyone's pots and pans. "I need everyone to gather your food, toothpaste, deodorant, and anything else with a scent and put it in these bear canisters. When you're done, grab every large metal object that you have, and bring them over here." He walked over to a large fallen tree that stretched across the edge of the campsite.

We did as Keith asked and brought our various pots, pans, and metal mugs over to where he was standing.

"The ranger said that we should cover our bear canisters with anything that would make noise if it was moved or clawed at." Keith shoved both bear canisters up underneath the massive log and covered the fronts and sides of them with all of our metal cooking equipment. "The hope is that if Mildred tries to paw at this pile to get to the food, we'll hear her beating on the metal pans, and we'll be able to scare her off."

"Oh good," Sydney emphasized sarcastically. "I feel way better."

I laughed. "I'm hoping that we won't hear any metal pots clanging at all tonight, but if a bear comes, I'm going to leave it to you to do the scaring, okay Keith?"

"Aw, it's no big deal y'all! We have bears like these at home in Boone!"

"That doesn't make me feel much better," I admitted, "but at least now our food hopefully won't be thrown off a cliff."

We brushed our teeth in a clearing far away from where we slept in case our toothpaste spit would smell good to Mildred. It was totally dark now, and somehow an additional layer of stars had added themselves to the dense clusters of light above us. The storm that threatened to approach earlier seemed like it was going to stay away. Half Dome's shadow floated in mid air, watching over the valley that settled into sleep.

Though the rain never came, the temperature continued to drop. I shivered for a while, tossing and turning in my hammock. My sleeping bag seemed to have reached its temperature limit, so I wondered how Ethan was doing with nothing but his small sheet. My anxiety about Mildred lingered still, but it wasn't like I could sleep anywhere else, so I accepted that I would just have to find a way to get over it.

{17}

THE TREES WE CLING TO

THE ENTIRE NIGHT WAS MISERABLE. I COULD NEVER GET comfortable, and I tossed and turned in my hammock constantly. I was exhausted from hiking all day and desperately craved sleep, but I was so cold that my body felt like it was in survival mode. I couldn't relax until the sun began to rise and thaw me.

I didn't hear anyone else moving yet, so I assumed they were still asleep. I tried to remind myself to be present to the fact that I was waking up in the secluded heart of the High Sierras. Even if I barely slept, being there was still a gift.

The morning was quiet besides the occasional chirping bird. However, after a while, I heard what I thought sounded like a muffled snort under my hammock, as if an animal had quickly breathed out of its nostrils. My heart did a nose dive to the pit of my stomach.

Oh my God. It's Mildred. I know it. The smell of the gaping hole in my foot has lured her in, and this will be my final doom. She is going to attack at any moment. She'll start with my foot and move up slowly. The more I listened, the more I swore I could hear rhythmic inhales and exhales that could only be coming from a terrifying, food-canister-chucking black bear. My heart pounded so hard I was sure that its echo would reach Sydney behind me and wake her.

After what seemed like hours of suffering in the torturous ignorance of not knowing what Emily-killing monster was licking its chops beneath me, I finally mustered up enough courage to peek over the edge. I braced myself to meet Mildred's dark bear eyes.

I peeked out over the rim of my hammock, bracing myself for death, but there was nothing under me but pine straw. My anxiety dissipated, and embarrassment took its place.

Jeez, chill out Em. It was probably just one of the guys breathing heavy or something. I tried to coax myself into relaxing. It's amazing what false realities fear will muster up in our minds.

Now that my head was above the rim of my hammock, I saw that the storm clouds from yesterday had passed, and visibility had cleared significantly. Nothing but blue sky remained. Half Dome stood starkly accentuated against the bright sky. Since Mildred was nowhere in sight, I pulled my legs out of my sleeping bag so I could go to the bathroom. My foot wasn't stuck to my sleeping bag this time since it was wrapped safely in a bandage under my sock.

After a couple minutes of looking out over the valley, I walked back to assess the status of my companions. I looked toward Ethan's hammock, and I couldn't keep laughter from erupting out of me. All I could see were Ethan's giant clown feet hanging over the rim, fully laced up in his boots, thick with every pair of socks he brought with him. His legs were swollen, made of sweat pants stacked on top of khakis. I could see the corner of his feeble sheet hanging over the side, and knowing that he only had a light fleece jacket and a hat, I was sure that he slept even less than I did. He looked pitiful, but at least he appeared to be alive and breathing.

He cracked open his left eye. "What?" he muttered, smirking.

"Nice boots," I whispered across to him, laughing again.

"Shut up. It was so freaking cold last night. I didn't know what else to do besides put everything on! I literally didn't sleep at all. I'm so tired." He pulled his sheet over his head.

"Same here. I got up around two and put more clothes on. I didn't fall asleep until the sun started to warm up the air. It's going to be real fun hiking back up on no sleep."

"I didn't sleep either," Sydney chimed in from her hammock once she realized we were awake. "Did you, Will?"

"Nope," we heard a muffled voice coming from Will's hammock which was wrapped tightly in a cocoon fashion around his body. "Let's just nap here all day."

Keith unzipped his and Heather's tent and began putting his boots on. "We only have the permit for one day, and there will be more people coming down tonight I'm sure. We probably shouldn't stay too much longer because we'll have to wait in line to find a camping permit for tonight too."

Heather climbed out after him. "Did anyone hear Mildred last night?" she asked.

"No, but I had plenty of anxiety about the potential of hearing her," I admitted, and we all laughed.

"Looks like both of our bear canisters are still there. Should we make some breakfast?" Keith walked over to disassemble our mound of metal.

We boiled water and made six bowls of oatmeal. I took mine over to the cliff edge to soak up the view one last time. I was excited about continuing our exploration of the incredible landscape of Yosemite, but I was dreading our seventeen-hundred-foot ascent back up to the car. While hiking down with my pack was semi-hard on my foot, knees, and back, hiking uphill would be a different story. My dumbbell hike in Little Rock didn't prepare me very well.

I heaved my pack back up from the ground and squeezed my arms awkwardly to get them under the straps without dropping the pack, wincing when the heavy weight returned to rest on my sore shoulders. My pack felt awkward. My body wasn't used to it, and I hadn't figured how to work with the dozens of straps, buckles, and velcros on my backpack that were more confusing than helpful. I also had no idea how to pack a backpack appropriately, so my weight distribution was totally off.

But Will is carrying all of his videography gear, which makes his pack way heavier than mine, and he's still trucking up the mountain like it's no problem. I need to stop whining. I continued climbing, even though the heavy pack pulling on my shoulders made my posture look more like a dog on a leash being yanked back. I could barely stand up straight.

After an hour of climbing, another storm rolled in. Once we arrived at the split in the trail, rain drizzled steadily, and a light fog had settled in the forest. Turning right led back to the car, but turning left led to North Dome, which was apparently another amazing viewpoint of the valley according to Keith. We knew nothing about it, but according to the map it was only a couple miles on a relatively flat trail. Heather and Keith weren't feeling the extra trek, so they decided to head back to the car to try to get a camping permit for the night, but the rest of us figured, why not?

"Maybe we should leave our packs in the woods since we'll come back this way to get to the car," I shamelessly suggested as we all quickly dug through our packs to find our rain covers. I didn't want to have to wear my pack any more than was absolutely necessary.

"I'm fine with it, as long as we find a place that's not obvious and is mostly out of the rain. I don't want my gear to get wet." Will looked up at the sky anxiously.

We found a spot under a secluded rock about fifteen yards into the woods, decided to risk our stuff getting soaked, and stuffed our packs under the rock overhang. We covered them as best we could with our hammock rain flies and headed down the trail hoping we would not regret our decision to go to North Dome.

The feeling of taking a heavy pack off after a long morning of hiking up a steep hill is quite like walking on the moon: you weigh much less than normal, and each step is separated by a moment of floating over the ground before you come back down again. The sweat on my back now exposed to the wind sent a chill down my spine, but I was elated to have my shoulders free from constriction. I stuffed my journal and pen in the inside of my rain jacket, cinched the hood tighter around my face, and floated forward into the foggy rain.

The mixture of rain and pine made the air muggy and sweet. The air was chilly, but Will was the one in front, and I was learning that his pace was almost superhuman. Since the rest of us tried our best to trot along with him, we had no trouble keeping warm.

I worried the view might be concealed by the storm, but right when we got to the North Dome rock face where the trail opened up, the sky opened up with it. The sudden sunshine glimmering off the wet granite made the view that much more extravagant. Since lightning still flashed in the distance, we decided that walking all the way to the end on completely exposed rock, when we were the tallest objects around was not the wisest idea, lest we be electrocuted. We were content with walking down a little bit and scattering ourselves about the rocks to sit and reflect.

Our mouths could not find words in this place, and we did not force them to do so. I sat on my granite blanket in silence, gratefulness welling up in my heart and reverence humming deep in my bones. I looked out across the valley. I could see smoke rising from a few places far in the distance, and I wondered if it was remnants from the wildfires we heard had recently wreaked havoc in the forests around Yosemite. I thought about how sad it was that so much of the land had been consumed by death, but these thoughts were interrupted by a memory from a day when I was hiking in the Linville Gorge in North Carolina a few months back, when I overheard a park ranger discussing wildfires with the group he was leading.

The ranger spoke of how wildfires are imperative for a certain species of tree to be able to survive, thrive, and reproduce. To avoid a detailed account of the microbiology involved, his general explanation was that the outer covering of a certain tree's seeds is so thick and tough that it takes the intense heat of a raging wildfire to be able to penetrate the covering so that the seed can germinate, sprout, and have the opportunity to grow into a new tree. Without wildfires, certain species of trees would not exist.

I wiggled my journal out of my rain jacket pocket.

07/19/15, Day 17 -

I am reminded of trees that need wildfires in order to produce new life, and I believe this microscopic process points to a deeper existential truth. I wonder if sometimes the trees we find ourselves clinging to in our lives, whether for comfort, a sense of safety, or the need to feel in control, eventually need to be demolished by a wildfire in order for new growth to begin. When this happens, the wildfire at first seems to wreck any hope we have left in the world. It destroys our expectations of what we thought the tree would be for us in the future. It might make us lose hope in anything good in the world. It might make us reject the idea of love. It might make God seem like God doesn't exist, or if God does exist, that God doesn't matter. It might make us question everything we've ever known, and we might see no place in which to put our faith and trust.

But what we cannot see is that the tree was always supposed to die. The heat of the wildfire that destroyed it is the only force strong enough to penetrate the hard coverings of the seeds that fell down from the old tree long ago, waiting underneath the soil to be cracked open so they may bring new life.

We forget that sometimes new growth is only possible through intense heat and pressure. We forget that sometimes new meaning is only found through our hard outer coverings being broken open. We forget that sometimes new trees can only grow when we let go of the old trees we cling to.

"We should probably start heading back," Will's voice came from behind me. "We have to meet back up with Keith and Heather and set up camp." I turned around to face Will and Sydney. I noticed they were sitting really close to each other, so close that it caught me off guard, and once I turned around Sydney subtly began to scoot over a bit. I hadn't paid much attention to their interactions so far, but for a split second I wondered if something was going on between them.

"Okay, I'm ready to go." I closed my journal. "E, you ready?"

Ethan opened his eyes from his snooze and squinted looking toward us into the sunlight. "I guess."

"Wait. Did we talk about a meeting place with them?" Sydney asked as we started walking back through the woods.

"They said they would just be hanging out at one of the parking areas or something," Will replied. "I guess I didn't think about needing to establish something more specific since we won't have phone service…" he trailed off.

"Um, yeah! And it's not like this park is small!" Sydney seemed agitated. "There are like a million parking areas." She sighed. "It's too late now. Let's just keep moving."

We found our bags decently dry. As I hoisted my pack up, I tried to psych myself up for the final part of the climb and attempted to ignore my throbbing foot and aching back. I was close to being out of gas and on the verge of sliding into a grumpy mood, so I spoke very little as we hiked. Will led the way, and he and Ethan kept the same speedy pace all the way. Sydney and I eventually fell behind them, unable to keep up with them. I wasn't insecure about being slow because I knew I wasn't going to enjoy it anymore if I forced myself to go faster than my body was ready for. I walked behind Sydney, and again I wondered about her and Will.

Does the fact that they were sitting so close together at North Dome mean anything? Or am I just reading into things too much? I don't know them that well yet, but they don't seem like the kind of people who would want to share close body space with anyone unless they actively chose to do so. Sydney has been one of Will's main models in all of his videography projects, so I know they have spent a lot of time together. They are both cool and attractive, so it would make sense if they were into each other. I don't really want to compete with Sydney for Will's attention, so maybe assuming that Will and Sydney are attracted to each other could be the boundary I need, and I think I feel relieved about that.

"Jeez, finally!" Ethan dramatically called out once Sydney and I crested the last hill and arrived at the parking lot. "We've been waiting for twenty minutes!"

"Um, not all of us are mountain goats like you and Will." Sydney rolled her eyes.

"Can I have the keys?" Will asked.

"Whoops. I gave them to Mildred. And it's Ethan's job to go retrieve them," I made a funny face at Ethan while I dug my keys out of my top zipper pocket. We hadn't had lunch yet, so we all scarfed down various snacks and chugged all the water we had left. Our bags were quickly stuffed in the trunk in a disheveled fashion, and we headed off on a blind hunt for Heather and Keith.

After driving back and forth within a five-mile radius in either direction from the trailhead for thirty minutes, we all were on edge. It was approaching four o'clock, and we were antsy to set up at a campsite so we could relax and eat dinner. We needed to walk around for a while to let off some of the steam of our frustration because we were tired of looking for them, so Will turned into a random picnic area full of cars. Once we pulled to the very back of the lot, there sat Heather and Keith, making tea.

"You've got to be kidding me." Will shook his head as we pulled up.

"Well, at least we found them," Sydney tried to lighten the mood. "We just know now that we need to make sure we talk about specific plans any time we separate so this doesn't happen again."

"Good thing we found you guys!" Will's voice held frustration. "We had no idea where you would be."

"I'm so glad!" Keith got up to give him a hug. "We figured it made the most sense to just stay put so that we both weren't driving all over the place and constantly missing each other. We realized we messed up not making a plan before we split up, but we prayed that you would find us, and look, the Lord is faithful again! And guess what. We even found a campsite, and we can stay there for the next two nights. Look at God!"

I resisted his words. The last thing I believed about prayer was that God was involved in minimal things like giving people a front row parking spot at the grocery store or helping someone win a contest or saving a campsite for those who do no planning, but I was grateful that Heather and Keith reserved a campsite for us, regardless of whether God was involved or not.

"Thanks a lot for doing that. You guys have really saved us as far as plans go," I emphasized. "We might have all been sleeping in my car if it weren't for you being here!"

Heather smiled. "We're so happy it all worked out."

It started sprinkling again, so Will, Sydney, Ethan and I all piled in my Jeep and followed Heather and Keith to the next campsite. We brought our tents out for the first time and set them up in the rain. Sydney and I pitched my orange and gray four-person car camping tent, which was utterly excessive in size for two people. Will set up his backpacking tent, and Ethan swore he wasn't sleeping outside again after not sleeping all night at Snow Creek, so he chose to sleep in the car.

We fixed a quick pasta dinner and prepared ourselves for a cold night of sleep yet again. There was word around the park that there might be a hurricane coming in within the next twenty-four hours, so we considered the option of ditching our last day in Yosemite and heading to the Grand Canyon early. We still went to bed hopeful that we would not have to leave this dreamland quite yet. I actually fell asleep well before sunrise this time, for the lower elevation temperatures were more forgiving, and there were no Mildreds to fear.

{18}

BECAUSE I AM

ORTUNATELY, WE DID NOT WAKE UP TO 60 MPH WIND gusts and pouring rain. Instead we woke up to a gentle breeze and a partly cloudy sky. Sydney was still sleeping, so I did my best to crawl out of the tent without waking her or spilling the puddle of rainwater that had collected on top of the tent. I saw Keith, Heather, and Will sitting by the fire when I stood up.

"Some hurricane this is," I mumbled sarcastically as I sat down to warm my hands and prep water for breakfast. "Do you think it would be too ambitious to try to hike today? Have you heard anything from the rangers about the weather?"

"Rain isn't supposed to come until possibly this afternoon," Keith answered. "The three of us have been talking, and I say we take our chances and go for it. There's a trail that's not too far from here that leads up to Cloud's Rest."

"That's the one trail that my friend said we absolutely have to do," emphasized Will.

"Sounds good to me," a voice called from inside my tent. I guessed I did wake Sydney up after all.

"Well, I guess the only option when you wake up and realize you have a clear day in Yosemite that you weren't expecting is to hike all day, right? Ethan will be fine with anything; we just have to wake him up or he'll sleep til noon." I walked over and beat on the tent, dodging the water droplets that ricocheted off. "Time to get up little bear," I cooed.

"I'm up, I'm up," he grumbled. "Cut it out."

The hike to Cloud's Rest started with a decently flat, lazy trail that curved through the woods and over rocks, but then it suddenly rose straight up with a very steep three miles that tested my patience. I didn't talk much again and just focused on putting one foot in front of the other. I could tell that my legs were fatigued from Snow Creek.

We arrived at a fork in the trail, where one direction led up a daunting, brutally steep trail to Cloud's Rest, and the other led along a gentle trail to the Sunrise Lakes—a trio of lakes, bound together in a sisterhood of clear, cool waters and pristine, calm, quiet views.

"What do you guys want to do? Should we try to make it to Cloud's rest?" Will looked at us with excitement in his eyes.

"I'm down!" Ethan replied quickly.

"Keith, you've done this before and know generally what to expect. Do you think it's reasonable?" Will asked.

"It's doable for sure," Keith started, "but we would have to really push it to make it up in time before the afternoon storms arrive. The entire last part is above the treeline on exposed rock, and we don't want to mess with any lightning up there."

"I could be persuaded," Sydney said, though her facial expression and body language communicated, *I'm feeling the opposite of what my mouth is saying.* I was starting to pick up that she was likely to go along with whatever the most people wanted to do, even if she didn't necessarily want to.

I had a feeling that I should speak up. I could tell that Sydney didn't want to go, and even though hiking Cloud's Rest sounded awesome to my brain, my foot was signaling that it needed a break.

"What if the ladies take the calm walk to the lakes and you guys go ahead and tackle Cloud's Rest? My foot is screaming, and I don't want to push it too hard since we'll have to hike into the Grand Canyon two mornings from now."

The guys shrugged their shoulders and nodded their heads. I looked at Sydney and Heather for approval.

"I'm fine with that." Sydney looked relieved.

"Yeah, I'm pretty tired, too," agreed Heather. She looked at Keith. "Just be safe up there please. Don't push it if there's lightning." Her voice was stern.

"We won't. Boys," Keith looked at Will and Ethan like a drill sergeant, "I'm not kidding when I say we have to hike this thing fast." Will and Ethan nodded with serious faces. "Will, do you want to lead?"

Will turned and took off down the trail. Ethan and Keith followed behind him.

"Wait!" Sydney called. "Where are we meeting?"

"Back at the campsite! Thanks for remembering!" called Keith.

Sydney turned back to face Heather and I. "I just want to make sure that we don't have a miscommunication like yesterday and end up driving around forever. Also, thank you for suggesting this, Emily. I did not want to hike up anymore, and they still have like six miles or something."

"Yeah, no thank you," I agreed. "Especially when Will is leading the way. That dude hikes faster than anyone I've ever known!"

"He's always been like that." Sydney grinned with a flash of endearment that looked slightly more than platonic.

Sydney, Heather, and I arrived at an alpine lake as smooth as glass. We were at the highest point we had been in the park, around 9,200 feet, but the sun was out in full force which took the bite out of the air. We all took our shirts off and laid out on the warm granite slabs. I worked my boots off and slowly peeled off my socks to help my foot air out. The bandage had disconnected from my foot, and the burn oozed red when I peeled the bandage away.

"How is it doing?" Sydney asked.

"Well, I don't think it's infected or getting worse, but it doesn't exactly look like it's getting better."

"Probably because you've had to walk on it constantly," noted Sydney. "I'm impressed that you've been able to hike as much as you have with that thing. It looks really painful."

"I think there's a small ring of new skin along the outskirts of the hole. I want it to scab over, but like you said, I'm afraid it will stay open with how much I have to walk on it. It might just have to heal from the outside in."

"I hope it heals soon. I wish there was something I could do to help!"

"No worries. It's okay. There's nothing I can do but try my best not to think about it constantly and try to enjoy walking. Thankfully it's easy to be distracted here, and I'm sure there will be things to distract me in the Grand Canyon too. I can't believe we'll be hiking down it in less than forty-eight hours."

"Yeah, I'm a little nervous about that hike," Sydney chuckled nervously. "It's like three times the elevation change of what we did yesterday. Hopefully I don't pass out." She stretched back out on the rock.

"As long as we don't get dehydrated and we take it slow, we should be fine." I laid back as well. As I felt the sun warm the exposed skin on my stomach, I became particularly aware of how much more space my body took up compared to Sydney's. She seemed to have a perfect body. Slender arms, flat stomach, thin, toned legs. I felt like an ogre laying next to her, and the body shame cycle returned.

Of course, Will would choose Sydney. She's beautiful, thoughtful, kind, and adventurous, and she has a perfect body. Way better than mine. I'm so flabby now. I'm so out of shape. Why are my legs so big? Why are my shoulders so broad and bulky? I sighed. *I'm doing it again. Comparison kills.* I tried to repeat the mantra to convince myself that I was worthy of love, and that comparing myself to Sydney was adding unnecessary negativity to my day, but the negativity continued. I tried my best to ignore it and attempted to snooze, hoping that after my nap I would feel a little less self-conscious.

Once Sydney, Heather, and I finally arrived back down to flat ground, we passed time by collecting firewood for that night. I happened to have to go to the bathroom at the exact right time, for when we packed up our wood and drove back to the portable toilet at the trailhead, Will, Keith, and Ethan came trotting happily down the last part of the trail.

Keith immediately praised God aloud for continuing to "hold us in his hand" and providing perfect timing for us to meet back up. I internally begged to differ but smiled and nodded like I agreed. Will couldn't stop gushing about how spectacular the view was from the top. I felt a pang of jealousy, but I knew that opting out was the right decision. Ethan bragged about how much climbing they had done and how quickly they had done it. To give him credit, they did climb almost two thousand feet, which was impressive, but I couldn't help but take it as an intimidating reminder that I would hike twice that out of the Grand Canyon in a couple days. It also would be thirty or forty degrees hotter, and I would be carrying a pack that was probably too heavy for me, but I tried to push those details out of my mind.

We headed back toward our campsite, hoping that it would survive the torrential downpour that began on our way back. We stopped by a little restock store on the side of the road since going back to just sit in the rain wasn't very appealing. I was tempted to buy every junk food item and five over-priced freeze dried camping meals, but I decided to say no and settle with my boring beans and rice again. I hadn't checked my bank account in a while, but I assumed there still was not much wiggle room.

We arrived at our tents to find them sopping wet but standing strong. The rain didn't last long, so once it ended, we made dinner and began mentally preparing for what we would need to pack for the Grand Canyon the next day.

After spending all day feeling like I was fighting myself, I knew I needed to journal before I went to sleep. Once Sydney and I brushed our teeth and climbed into the tent, I asked if it was okay if I turned my headlamp on for a while. I turned it on the dullest setting and grabbed my pen.

07/20/15, Day 18 -

I feel like I've been wrapped in insecurity all day. I also have Sydney here, which creates a constant open door to compare my body to hers, as if somehow my deviation from what she looks like is an accurate measure of my beauty. I know that her beauty is not a way to measure my beauty, but how do I stop the toxic cycle of comparison?

I know that when I compare my body to that of another woman, I propel the chain of female objectification by objectifying both her body and objectifying mine, supporting the message that we are only defined by our bodies, which I consciously don't believe. Is this the story I want to tell? No, but how do I retrain myself to look into a woman's eyes instead of looking for all of the things that she is, and I am not?

May I claim the beauty I do not have to suck or squeeze or compare or change myself into. May I claim the beauty I embody, simply because I exist, because I have life, because I am.

{19}

IN THE GRAY

As Sydney and I began packing up our soggy tent, I felt a little bummed. Even though this was our fourth day waking up in Yosemite, I was only just beginning to take in its immensity. We said our farewells to Heather and Keith and thanked them multiple times again for helping us out so much with permits. Spending three days with them wasn't as triggering as I expected it to be, but I felt like I was walking on eggshells the whole time, waiting for them to ask me directly about worship team. That never happened, but Keith did talk constantly about God—what God was doing, what God was going to do, what God was saying to him, what God had to say about each of us.

I didn't know what to do with people like Keith anymore. From the outside looking in, his practices and beliefs in his evangelical, charismatic Christian framework really worked for him, and he believed in it with his whole being. He had held a mentor role in my life while I was a leader in the campus ministry, and I felt saddened by the possibility that I might not be able to connect openly with him again, that I might not ever speak the same God language as him again, that we might never address the elephant in the room: why Emily left church. Despite my internal tension, I gave Keith and Heather both a big hug when we'd finished packing, and I told them I would see them back in Boone.

Now that we had some practice packing, unpacking, and packing again over the past five days of being together, Ethan, Will, Sydney, and I each knew what our role was in the packing process. I organized the middle of the car, balancing both food boxes on top of each other between the two back seats. Ethan handled all of the gear on the left side of the trunk, stuffing the sleeping bags in last next to the window. Will tackled all of our backpacks on the right side of the trunk, carefully aligning them so that they would not roll out of the car when we opened the trunk. Sydney controlled the giant pile of stuff that needed to fit in the car and handed each of us whatever random item made sense to go in the car next. Though it looked chaotic, we had formed a system that worked for us. We started to feel like a team.

We exited the park on the opposite side from where we entered. After about thirty minutes of driving uphill and more ear popping, we drove through Tioga Pass at 9,943 feet in elevation, which is the highest drivable mountain pass in the entirety of the Sierra Nevada Mountains. We had no idea Tioga Lake even existed, so when the road took a long curve down and around and suddenly opened up to a lake so clear and calm that it reflected a perfectly smooth, upside-down mirror image of the mountains surrounding it, we were mesmerized. Will pulled the car over without question, and we got out to marvel at the perfectly reflected panorama.

I walked out to the furthest point on a small peninsula that jutted out into the lake, and I felt like the upside-down mirror image was relatable. Throughout my deconstruction, I existed in that double image, with two opposite parts of me reflected often in the same moment. The angry nihilist lived in darkness and shadow, while the mystic in me existed in light and clarity, summoning me to hold on to a thread of hope that there could be meaning in a spiritual story greater than myself.

Some days I was filled with nothing but cynicism and pessimism, where I looked upon the world and saw hateful, greedy, meaningless chaos, a sea of animals fighting for the crown that would give them ultimate rule over the rest of reality. On these days, I often could find no solid purpose for living, no reason to believe in any higher power, no confidence that unconditional love could exist.

Yet I could not deny that I had days both before and after I started deconstructing my faith, and even moments so far on the trip, where I clearly felt something I could not attribute to anything but that sense of Divine connection. In these moments it was as if my being and all life around me was a constant manifestation of what we try to point to with the word "God." I felt connected to all of the life that had come before me and would come after me, and my spirit transcended space and time.

In this moment, standing there at the edge of Tioga Lake, looking out at the mountains reflected upside down on the lake's surface, I tried to hold both sides of myself in loving tension. I held the contrast in my open hands and was somehow still separate from it, looking at it from a place I cannot quite describe, but a place that somehow seemed like a deeper self—one that witnessed my beliefs, emotions, and doubts.

For the first time I felt like I could take a step back and exist comfortably in the gray space in-between the black and white. The gray space was a place institutions and dualistic systems swore was dangerous and should be feared. For most of my life I had feared it, but I wasn't scared standing there in the gray. I didn't feel like I had to judge myself for the contradiction, and for the first time, I didn't feel like I had to choose between skeptic or mystic. I was somehow both and neither. Something about it brought peace. Something about it pointed to the possibility that ambiguity might not be as scary as I thought, and it might actually be the very place the wisdom, truth, and life I sought would be found.

Maybe that is where our true selves lie, in that gray in-between place where we can hold the entirety of ourselves tenderly with love and without judgment. Maybe, it is in that place where the truest light of life shines its face on us, and we are made new.

After a fairly boring driving day through some of the most barren landscapes I had ever seen, we pulled into the Grand Canyon KOA at 11:15 p.m. It was the only campground we could find within an hour of the park that wasn't booked solid. It wasn't ideal because if we wanted to be on the trail by sunrise at 6:00 a.m., we would have to take the shuttle to the trailhead at 5:30. That meant waking up at

4:00, packing up camp in the dark, and being on the road toward the Grand Canyon by 4:30. We needed a longer night of sleep, but this was our only option, and we had to find a way to roll with it.

The campground was right off the road and packed with giant RV's, which felt obnoxious after primitive camping in Yosemite for the past four nights, but it would have to do. It took even longer to get to sleep because when we went to pick up our registration packet, it wasn't left in the folder by the office door like the manager told me on the phone, so we had to walk around the campsite in the dark hunting down a camp warden to tell us where our site was. We already were irritable and exhausted from what ended up being ten and a half hours of driving with traffic, not including stops. Arriving at our assigned, unattractive, small slab of concrete and gravel, which was only about twenty-five feet from RVs on either side of us, did not help the morale.

"I'm sleeping in the car," Ethan groaned loudly once we pulled up to our less-than-comfortable-looking rest area.

"Shh!" I whispered harshly. "You're going to wake everyone up!"

"Good! Maybe they'll leave and we'll have more space!" he huffed. I could tell he was grumpy and ready for bed.

We tried to set up camp as quietly as possible, but we made a racket when we had to move the giant picnic table off of the concrete slab so we would have room to sleep. The table was too heavy to lift, so Will, Sydney, and I just had to drag the table over the concrete until we could get it out of the way. We hoped our neighbors wouldn't come out and yell at us for making a ruckus at what was now midnight.

We were too exhausted to set up our tents, so we laid out our sleeping pads and bags and planned to sleep right there, out in the open. It felt silly that we were paying so much money to sleep for only six hours at a campsite we wouldn't even see in daylight, but it was nice to have a real bathroom to freshen up in. Unfortunately, even though the bathroom had a shower and we were on day five of no showers, there was no energy or time, so we went to bed with the same greasy hair and salty bodies. It was kind of gross when I thought about it, but I was getting to the point where I barely even noticed how grungy I was.

Around 1:30 a.m., I woke myself up when I started to roll over in my sleep. When I opened my eyes I immediately woke to full consciousness and totally forgot that there would be any reason to go back to sleep. I had always heard of people saying that on really clear nights you can see extremely dense parts of the Milky Way's spiral shining in the sky. I never understood what they were talking about until then.

A misty streak of dense, cloudy light spread out across the expansive blackness above me, as if it had been wiped across the sky with a giant paintbrush. It illuminated the sky in various intensities, but it was almost like the light emanated from a space behind a spider web of dark strings woven throughout it, and I wondered what caused that. I saw stars more accentuated than I had ever seen, and the concentrated band of light and stars and sparkles and milk-like haze radiated majestically in the gargantuan sky. I looked to my right and saw that Sydney's eyes were open too. She laughed when she looked at me and saw that my jaw still had not closed.

"This is the most unbelievable sky I've ever seen," she squeaked and giggled. "My brain doesn't know what to do with it."

"I've never seen the Milky Way like this before," I whispered back, "and I had no idea it was this impressive! I didn't know the sky could look so detailed without a telescope! This even beats the sky that first night driving into Yosemite!"

As I laid there looking up at the stars, I reflected back on our time in Yosemite.

The past three days have been some of the most serene, healing days I have had in my life. Yosemite was good for my heart and soul, but I still feel tension, like I need to let something out or push through something, but I don't know how to access it. Maybe I need more time alone to find out what it is. There won't be many people in the huge hole in the ground we'll walk into tomorrow, so hopefully I can find space to process. I still feel intimidated by the Grand Canyon. It will be the most significant physical effort I have ever completed, if I make it out.

I don't know how long I laid there, contemplating and enchanted, but I made sure to take back my thoughts earlier about this campsite being the worst.

{20}

THE DESCENT

W E INSTANTLY FORGOT HOW TIRED WE WERE WHEN
we first saw it. We approached the rim of the Grand
Canyon on the shuttle ride, and we all had our faces
pushed up against the windows on the left side of the bus. It was
impossible to fully process the gargantuan chasm spread out before
us. We looked out and down into the cascading ridges, and a thousand levels and colors of rock rose and fell in a masterpiece of reds,
whites, oranges, and browns. A combination of blunt and jagged
peaks rose randomly with no rhyme or reason at various levels. With
the deepest point of the canyon being 6,000 feet below the rim, over
a mile down, we could probably see less than half of the canyon from
where we sat. It already seemed to go on forever, and the fact that
what was before us was only a portion of the canyon was hard to
wrap our minds around.

We were the only people on the 6:00 a.m. shuttle with large backpacks, so either everyone else backpacking down to the Bright Angel
Campground that day had followed the trail guide and started their
hike before sunrise, or we were ahead of the crowd. Since the sun was
already lighting up the sky, I figured we were probably the stragglers
bringing up the rear.

"Which trailhead are you hiking down, and where should I pick you up?" Ethan asked as we got close.

I grabbed my trail map from the top of my backpack. "We're hiking down the South Kaibab Trail, which is a terribly steep trail that descends 4,780 feet in seven miles. Then, across the river to Bright Angel Campground tonight," I followed our route with my pointer finger along the dotted trail lines, "back across the river tomorrow morning, along the River Trail, and up the Bright Angel Trail halfway up the canyon to Indian Gardens Campground. Sleep there tomorrow night, hike up the rest of the Bright Angel Trail on," I paused, "what day will that be?"

"Today is Wednesday. So, Friday morning, the 24th," Ethan answered.

"Right. Friday morning." I nodded and continued. "I don't know how long it will take us to get up that day, so maybe we can plan to meet at eleven o'clock or so? If we leave at sunrise I don't imagine it taking more time than that, unless my foot gives me problems, but I'm hoping it will be fine."

"Just rub some dirt in it, right?" Ethan joked.

"I don't know if that's exactly what they tell you in wilderness first aid," I laughed. "Are you still going to hike down with us a little ways?"

"Well duh. Maybe for an hour or so."

"Hey Will and Sydney!" I called out to get their attention once Ethan and I got off the shuttle, and we ran over to them. "Let's make sure to fill up our water bottles before we go down. I read that the trail is completely exposed with no shade the whole time, and there's no water access until the campground. Temps will most likely get up above one hundred at some point today."

"Good point. Want me to fill everyone's up?" Will offered.

"I was thinking, I guess there's no use in checking to see if we forgot something now since it's too late to go back," I said as he handed me my filled water bottle.

He chuckled. "Hopefully we didn't forget anything too important. The elements here are pretty relentless." He looked up to the blaring sun above us.

"Have you ever done anything this intense?" I asked Sydney as we walked over to the ridgeline to get our packs ready.

"Definitely not. I probably would have been too intimidated to do it if it weren't for you and Will. Thanks for carrying the tent. Let me know if it gets too heavy and we can rearrange packs."

"No worries. Thanks for carrying some of my food to counter it!"

Since we figured there probably would not be trees at the bottom for hammock camping, Sydney and I decided to bring the tent to camp. However, it was not a lightweight three-pound backpacking tent which one probably should carry when one backpacks one of the most challenging trails in the country. I was an outdoors novice, so I didn't know any better, and my palace four-person car camping tent weighed in at ten and a half pounds. One of the articles I read said that you are only supposed to carry ten to fifteen percent of your body weight. The tent alone already put me at half of what I was technically supposed to carry, and my two days of food (also not lightweight since I chose canned beans and tuna for my meals), half gallon of water, clothes, first aid equipment, flashlight, Chacos, journal, and miscellaneous other things I probably did not need took up way more than the other half of the recommended pack weight. At first my pack was much heavier than Sydney's with the whole tent and all of my stuff, so she took some of my things to balance the weight more equally.

"How much does your pack weigh now?" I walked over to pick up Sydney's pack before she put it on. It felt just as heavy as mine did. I shrugged my shoulders. "I think they're pretty equal."

"Will, how much does yours weigh? You have your whole tent and all of your camera gear, right?" Sydney called over to him.

He laughed. "Come feel."

Will's pack was bulging at the seams. Sydney and I went over to test it, and we could barely pick up one of the straps with two hands. Ethan picked it up after us.

"Dude, this thing is going to break your back walking all the way down there!" Ethan exclaimed.

We all laughed. Will brushed it off. "I'll be fine. I need my gear to shoot footage, so it's the only option. I've carried it before." He didn't seem concerned.

"Yeah, but not all the way into and out of the freaking Grand Canyon!" Sydney looked at him with eyes that had a vague sense of flirtation.

She's into him, I know it.

"Oh hush," Will emphasized playfully. "Let's go, shall we?" Will hoisted his giant pack up on his shoulders with dramatic confidence. "See? Easy." He turned and walked to the South Kaibab trailhead. A wooden sign hung next to it with an arrow pointing in the only direction we would be going that day: down.

As we began our descent, I could barely take in the immensity of the landscape that only got more vast with each step. The dimensions and depths were hard to measure because there was no relativity, no way to compare one spire or cliff line to another. It was like looking into an endless abyss.

After the equivalent of walking down steep stairs for an hour, we reached Cedar Ridge a mile and a half down from the rim. There was a pit toilet there, so we all took advantage of being able to pee in privacy before we went further. The squatty shrubs along the trail weren't much to hide behind if you needed to relieve yourself.

"I think I'm going to head back up from here," Ethan said as he trotted back over to us after scrambling around various outcroppings of rock taking footage. Will, Sydney, and I were sitting in the red dirt, and the only thing on my mind was wondering why the hell we chose to hike into the Grand Canyon in the middle of the day at the end of July.

"That makes sense," I nodded. "I think this is the common turn-around for day hikes. We're going to miss you!" I got up to give him a sweaty hug.

"Good luck finding a place to sleep!" Sydney squinted looking up from the ground and waved.

Will gave Ethan a fist bump, and then Ethan extended his hand toward me.

"What?" I asked, confused.

"Um, keys?" His face looked like he might as well have said *'duh.'*

"Oh, right." I laughed and unclipped them from my pack and handed them over. "I guess you'll need these. We won't have cell service when we get back up to the rim, so there won't be any way for us to let you know if our ETA changes. Just be there at eleven and stay there until we find you."

"Yeah, yeah. I got it, I got it," Ethan urged.

"Okay. Have fun. See you in two days. I love you. Be safe. Don't climb up on some dangerous rock to get a cool shot and fall off a cliff please. That happens out here you know." I shot him a serious look.

He laughed. "I'll try not to. Love you too." He turned and threw up a peace sign over his shoulder. We watched him for a few moments until he disappeared around the corner of the ridge.

Though the views were astounding and the trail followed a scary but invigorating ridge that surpassed all of my expectations of how beautiful the canyon would be, the trail was not good for anyone's knees, especially mine. It was so steep that it was mostly like walking down steps the whole time, but the steps were much deeper than normal stairs, so we had to brace ourselves for every single step down we took, trying not to fall, slip, twist an ankle, or hyperextend a knee. The South Kaibab Trail is the trail the guided groups come up on pack mules, so there was also trampled, squishy red mud all along the way. The wet mud sometimes took up so much of the trail that we had no choice but to just tramp through four inches of it, leaving our boots caked up to our ankles.

My foot was burning from the constant impact of stepping down. I tried to step down with my right leg every step to take away some of the force on my left foot, but my right knee could only take so much. Eventually I had to switch. I could tell that my scab had rubbed away to my raw skin again, but there was no other option but to keep walking. We were half-way down from the rim. There was no turning around now. I always thought those fancy hiking sticks were for outdoorsy grandmas, but now I understood how they would be helpful. I wished I had something to lean on to take some of the force off my knees when I stepped down over and over again. I would have looked for a walking stick along the trail, but there were no trees, and therefore no sticks. The only thing that might have looked like a stick along the trail would have been a snake, and I definitely didn't want to reach for one of those.

Sweat was dripping off all points of my body—my nose, my chin, my elbows. It ran into my eyes, and the combination of sweat and sunscreen kept my eyes on fire almost the entire walk. My hair was soaking wet with sweat underneath my hat, which I was glad I brought even though I hated wearing hats. Red dust found its way into every crease. My legs shined orange in the sun from it. My face was streaked with it from using my dusty hands and forearms to wipe sweat away from my eyes.

The hike got to the point where it was not only physically exhausting but paying so much attention to every single step eventually became mentally exhausting as well. At one point, Sydney suddenly walked off to the side of the trail and threw her pack down on the ground. She walked over to a rock near the cliff with her hands on her hips, facing away from Will and I. I'd noticed she had started to slow down, and I could tell she was mentally done without her saying it. I didn't know her well enough to know if it would be helpful to say something encouraging or not, so in fear of saying the wrong thing and her potentially freaking out on me, I just kept my mouth shut. I didn't think Sydney was the freaking out externally type, but just in case.

Will and I took the opportunity to take our packs off too. We each stood separately, looking out across the unforgiving canyon, trying to muster up the perseverance to keep walking. I couldn't help but think that Cam would love being here.

I really wish I could just erase him from my memory so he stops popping up in every beautiful moment and tainting it with grief.

Even though being with people distracted me from thinking about him, I was still grieving, and I reminded myself to allow space for that.

"How is your giant pack now?" Sydney asked Will once she collected herself.

"I'm feeling it, but I just want to keep going because the sooner that we get down there the sooner we can take these things off for the day. You both good on water?" he asked.

"I have a liter left," I answered.

Sydney drank the rest of one of her bottles. "I have one liter left now as well."

"Okay, let's make sure we're downing water. It's only going to get hotter as we go down, and we don't want to mess with dehydration out here." Will looked at me. "What does your thermometer say?"

I unhooked the carabiner that attached my thermometer to my pack as I took another sip of water. "Ha," I choked. "Ninety-five."

We couldn't help but laugh. After evening temperatures in the forties in Yosemite, ninety-five felt like a furnace.

"Ugh. I can barely stand to be outside in ninety-five degree weather sitting in a swimming pool, much less hiking the Grand Canyon with a pack that feels like it's half my bodyweight!" Sydney exclaimed.

"It makes sense why it's so important to start this hike so early," said Will.

"It's probably going to be over a hundred degrees when we get down there." I shook my head. "I'm not necessarily looking forward to that part, but I am looking forward to sitting down. Maybe there will be water we can get in."

"Did you see the view of the Colorado river back there at Skeleton Point?" Will asked. "Pretty cool."

"Yeah, but it still looks like it's a million miles away," Sydney muttered, not hiding her lack of enthusiasm. "I mean, don't get me wrong. This is absolutely gorgeous," she spread her arms wide, "but it's hard to fully take it in when you're in pain."

"I think we only have about three miles left. The river is around four miles from Skeleton Point," I looked at my watch, "and we've been walking for a while since then."

"I'm going to take the rear this time. I'm going to be pretty slow." Sydney moved behind me, and we continued our long journey down.

When you are walking three miles on a flat road, you could probably get it done in less than an hour if you walk quickly. However, walking three miles straight down, in ninety-five degree weather, in the blazing sun, with no shade, carrying a heavy pack, with a hole in your foot, and with knees that ache with each step takes much longer. It feels more like crawling. I eventually reached the point where I couldn't think about anything but bracing myself for the next step. I wanted to continue to be intentional about taking in the grandeur around me, but it got to the point where I barely noticed anymore. I just wanted to be at the campsite.

Suddenly we turned a corner and saw the Colorado River, milky orange and much larger now, only a hundred feet down over the cliff we stood on. The water rushed violently through rapids in chalky, muddy orange-brown swirls. We hobbled down the last steep part of the South Kaibab Trail and came to the foot of the Black Suspension Bridge, also known as the Kaibab Suspension Bridge. The five-foot-wide steel bridge extended 440 feet across the Colorado River which churned 60 feet below the floor of the bridge. The powerful roar of the river was unsettling after walking in the silent air of the upper parts of the canyon for so long, but I mostly felt relieved to finally be there. It was the first stretch of flat trail since we had left the rim.

"Flat road! We made it!" I yelled over my shoulder to Will and Sydney, who were now both behind me.

"Jeez, I thought we would never get here!" Sydney yelled back. She leaned over and put her hands on her knees.

"Careful, don't lose your balance. I don't have the energy to save you if you fall off the bridge into that river," Will joked as he looked over the rail of the bridge. Sydney and I laughed.

Will let out a triumphant hoot that echoed over the rushing brown water underneath us. The descent was finally over.

Once we crossed the river it was like we had been transported to another universe. We were met by an unexpected oasis at Bright Angel Campground. There was now just as much green around us as there was brown and orange. I could hear birds chirping. There were trees, real trees, not the tiny shrubs that we had seen on the way down, and trees meant shade. As we got closer, Bright Angel Creek trickled clear and peaceful to our right, running along the entire ridge where the campsites were located.

We chose the first open campsite next to the creek for no reason but that it required the least additional walking and carrying our packs. It didn't have much shade, but it had a picnic table and enough space for two tents. All I could think about once we got to the campsite was one, I needed food. Fast. Two, my clothes needed to come off, now. Three, I needed to be submerged in that water as soon as possible.

"I'm getting in that creek pronto," Will muttered through his mouth full of granola bar. He immediately took his shirt off, paralleling my thoughts exactly.

"Me too," Sydney said as she threw her pack down in the dust. "Emily, what's the temperature now? It feels way hotter than it was higher up on the trail," she panted.

I set my pack down against the picnic table and squatted down to look at the thermometer, acutely aware of the pain that radiated from my bent knees. "Oh you know, just a balmy one hundred and four degrees. No big deal. Prime temperature, really," I replied sarcastically.

Will laughed. "That's ridiculous. I haven't been in one hundred and four degree weather in years! Well, cheers to us for pushing through. We made it!"

I ignored the part in the backpacking brochure that said things like, "immediately put all food, toiletries, and plastic bags in the food storage cans" and "always keep your backpacks hung on the provided elevated hook with the zippers open to prevent animals chewing through your pack." I didn't have the energy to care. I unwrapped a Clif bar, grabbed a handful of nuts, and limped down to the river in my sports bra and underwear. I gave zero shits if that was socially acceptable or not. I scarfed down the food in seconds. I probably needed to eat much more than I did, but I was so hot that I could barely think about doing anything but cooling off.

The creek became our home for the day. There were ten campsites or so at the campground, and the stream above us and below us was dotted with people from the other sites as well. It was hard to want to do much else with it being so sweltering. There was no other way to sustainably keep cool through the hottest part of the day.

At one point, Sydney and Will had moved to some shade under one of the trees on the bank, leaving me alone in the river. I looked up as high as I could, and I thought about all of the people at the rim who would never know what it was like to hike all the way down here, and I felt sorry for them. Looking at the Grand Canyon from the rim was one thing, but physically being taken over every ridge and spine and crevasse on the way down was much different. There was an oasis here that they would never see, the gentle, humble heart of the Grand Canyon that they would never know.

The more I think about it, hiking into the depths of the canyon today feels like an appropriate spiritual analogy. Many people plant themselves on the rim of their beliefs, and they refuse to move an inch. Some spend their lives in fear of anything that challenges what they can see from the rim, and they feel like they have to defend themselves and preserve their viewpoint at all costs.

In my experience, I have seen many Christians do this with their beliefs about God. They limit God to what can be seen from one viewpoint in the canyon of reality, even though God fills the entire canyon and is not bound by any rim, path, or viewpoint. They act as if their perch is the only place from which one can receive an "accurate" image of God, and they think seeking an image of God from any other viewpoint is not only wrong, but damnable.

Many Christians won't go deeper because going into the depths of the canyon might expose hard questions with no answers, might expose hypocrisy in themselves, or might allow the Devil to grab hold of them if they open their mind too much, which I was told growing up. They might tell those who try to go to the bottom of the canyon that they are wrong, but I think it is because they are scared to see what lies at the bottom of the canyon themselves. It might mean changing something or waking up to something new, whether that be at the bottom of their own personal experience, trauma, or darkness, or whether that be at the core of their religious, spiritual, political, or other institutional beliefs.

Staying at the rim is one way to live a spiritual life, and life might be easier there and more comfortable there, telling yourself that what you can see of the canyon from where you stand is all there is. I know what that is like just as well as anyone. I lived at the rim almost my entire life, and I know how difficult it is to leave it. But I wonder if leaving the rim is not only important, but a necessary part of the spiritual experience. I wonder if we all eventually must realize that the canyon God fills is much more expansive and complex and multifaceted than what the canyon seems like from a single viewpoint along the rim.

Maybe I've been looking at my deconstruction from the wrong perspective. Maybe choosing to go on this journey is choosing to open myself up to the possibility that my viewpoint was limited. Maybe God is much more dynamic than I used to think. Maybe I cannot live a fully integrated, conscious life without exploring the entirety of the canyon, where everything belongs. Maybe leaving the rim and pushing as far as I can into the scary questions and doubt might lead to an oasis of life at the bottom that I cannot reach otherwise. Choosing to stay on the rim would be choosing to stay asleep, for when I started deconstructing, it felt like waking up for the first time.

I want to keep waking up.

God, there are so many things I don't know and don't understand. I barely have spiritual language that works for me anymore, but I want to rid myself of the fear of not knowing anymore. I want to have the courage to keep going. I want to know myself, and I want to know the Divine within me and within all people. I want to hold space for a spiritual life again. For stillness. For Spirit. For Life. For Love. I want to take part in the dance.

Deconstruction has been so incredibly lonely, and there have to be more people that are on this same hard descent into the unknown, away from the rim, where all of the people they love stayed behind. May I be led to them, may some sort of deeper community be formed eventually out of this experience. I want to believe that there is meaning in all of this. If there is more I need to explore in myself, may I be led there so I can start to hand all of this back over to the Universe to be cleaned and made new.

May this depression continue to seep out of me. Some days I don't know what else to do besides lift all of this up to the Universe and just say, "Here. Take it. I can't carry it anymore." Some days I am so heavy I feel like I can barely walk. I want to feel light again. I don't want to have to compensate by just making myself be strong enough to walk and carry all of this alone.

I know there is a part of me that is dying. I thought for so long that I had to save her, but I'm realizing now that maybe she needs to die. She, who required dualism, who required clear-cut answers, who required certainty, who required being right, who required knowing, who required a community that looked and acted and thought like her to exist and function comfortably. The grief of saying goodbye to that part of myself has and will continue to be painful, but I know that I can't take her with me to where I need to go next. I still need help recognizing what I need to let go of and what I need to hold onto. Show me the death that I must give into so I might continue to wake up and be reborn.

As I laid there in the river, with the water surrounding my face and washing over me and under me and around me, I was reminded of the word 'baptism.' Not a baptism that supposedly makes a person a Christian—I certainly wasn't being dunked underwater by a pastor after saying the sinner's prayer. This baptism didn't make me a part of an "in" group. This baptism in an oasis of water simply felt like the beginning of something new. I found myself praying:

Let this river be the water that makes me new. Let this be my baptism, here at the bottom of the canyon, in the middle of the hidden oasis found only by taking the less traveled path. I felt you, God, Divine, Spirit, whispering to me when I was seven, and I believed it was you then. I want to believe that it was you in the desert, and I want to believe that this is you speaking to me now, whether you are a being or whether you are love or whether you are simply the truest part of my consciousness.

May I hold on to the point of the descent even on the days when I am crippled by nihilism, doubt, and hopelessness. May I live those days trusting that I will find my way back to the Oasis, back to the Center, back to the Source. May I learn how to sit with the All, may I pry my hands open in the discomfort of ambiguity when I want to cling to certainty, and may I seek the ways that giving in to the descent might set me free.

I don't know how long I let the water rush over me, but in this meditative state I understood a little more clearly what the mystics say about the power and transcendence of rebirth.

"Is four thirty too early to eat dinner?" Sydney asked as she walked over to me in the shade where I had moved to nap.

I laughed. "I don't know if dinner too early exists in the backpacking world. I'm pretty starving too. It hit me about ten minutes ago. Maybe we should go back and actually set up camp, and then we could make dinner?"

"Cool. Will already headed back to the campsite to get a snack. He gets pretty grumpy if he doesn't eat soon after he gets hungry."

"Hanger is a real thing, especially when you hiked all day carrying a pack that weighs as much as a grown man in temperatures forty degrees higher than you're used to." We both laughed.

"Jeez, no wonder it feels so hot! See that sign?" She pointed at the campground information post. "There's a heat index thermometer hanging on it. It says one hundred and fourteen. We are insane!" She laughed and shook her head.

"Wow. One hundred and fourteen. That's a first. Insane is one way to put it. Maybe next time we should come when it's not the end of July."

As we walked into the campsite, Will called out, "Hey Emily, bad news. I think the squirrels found your pack."

"Oh no!" I walked over to find my bag of trail mix hanging out of a two inch hole that some animal had chewed through the top pocket of my pack. The plastic bag dangled with a hole chewed in it as well, and nuts scattered the ground. "Do you think any of it is salvageable?"

"I wouldn't mess with it. I saw a sign when we first entered the campsite to stay away from the squirrels because they might carry a fever or disease or something."

"Oh, yikes. Bummer. I guess this is why they have those bag hooks. Well, half of my snacks just became inedible. Less weight to carry though," I shrugged.

Sydney laughed. "I probably have almonds to spare. Plus I'll take anything for my pack to be lighter tomorrow."

"I think we're all in that boat. After dinner and breakfast we'll all be a pound or two lighter, as long as we poop tomorrow," Will spoke casually. We all laughed.

"Man, never thought about pooping to help shed weight," I chuckled, "but I guess you're right."

"Hey, every ounce counts in the backpacking world." He shrugged his shoulders.

"How are your bodies doing after the hike down?" I asked when I sat down at the picnic table and felt the fatigue in my quads.

"My legs aren't that bad now that we've been able to rest, but my knees are still aching," Sydney answered while massaging her calves. "I was so mad at you guys on the way down, though. You and Will were going so fast, and I was just in pain and wanted to chop my legs off."

Will and I laughed. "Yeah, the sensation in my legs was so intense that I couldn't feel anything else, so I just kept going," Will replied. "I'm sure it will be different tomorrow when we go up."

We ate our dinner at five o'clock. Even though I could have just gone to sleep right then, we decided to walk around for a bit to stretch our legs. I cleaned my foot with hydrogen peroxide after being in the river and wrapped it loosely so I could limp along. We meandered down a side trail to Phantom Ranch, where people can pay a high price to sleep in luxury at the bottom of the Grand Canyon. There were some fruit trees planted throughout the small trail around the ranch, and we found a couple ripe figs for dessert.

The intense heat of the day finally broke once the sun fell behind the ridge that towered over the campground, and the temperature dropped quickly. I finally stopped sweating around eight o'clock. I stood on top of the picnic table and did yoga for a while to stretch as best I could before more tightness settled in my muscles with sleep. Sydney joined for a while from the ground, but she didn't stay long before going to bed.

I ended my yoga session alone, breathing deeply while on my back, staring up at the moon shining overhead as darkness began to settle around me. It was a such a clear and quiet night. The only sound I could hear was the gentle trickle of the creek to my right. I thought about sleeping right there on the picnic table out in the open to see the stars come out, but I eventually decided to go in the tent to stay away from the diseased squirrels. Even though it was only 8:45 p.m., after not getting much sleep the night before and having such a physically and emotionaly challenging day, my eyes didn't stay open for long.

{21}

THE ROCKS WE LEAVE BEHIND

I HAD FALLEN ASLEEP ON TOP OF MY SLEEPING PAD IN SHORTS and my sports bra, but at some point during the night it got cold enough to make me shimmy into my sleeping bag, which I was not expecting after the 114 degree heat index. I was still getting used to the extremes of the desert. We woke up and poked our heads out of our tents to see that it was not only already mid-morning and in the 80's, but we were also the only ones left in the campground.

"Well, I guess everyone took the advice of every single informational source that exists and left before sunrise," I noted as we stood up outside of our tents, creaky and sore. "I didn't set an alarm because I wasn't expecting us to sleep for ten and a half hours!"

"I guess we were a little tired," Will said, chuckling.

"I bet people walked past our tent this morning and shook their heads at us being amateurs," added Sydney. "But after not sleeping and hiking in the heat my body needed to recover. My knees were killing me after all of the pounding yesterday. I hope hiking up will give them a break."

"Yeah, probably not as bad on our knees but death to our muscles maybe," I squeaked as I grabbed my right foot behind me to stretch, wincing as my tight quadricep refused to budge.

We went about our morning routine of brushing our teeth and hoping that we could go to the bathroom before we started hiking. The pit toilets at the campground were much more convenient than trying to find a secluded spot on the open trail. After we all successfully excreted a couple ounces, we sat down at the picnic table with our breakfasts and added a few more ounces back. Even though I would carry my breakfast in my stomach, something about not having to carry it on my shoulders was the slightest bit comforting. I looked to my right and soaked in my last moments in the presence of Bright Angel Creek's trickling serenity. I ached thinking about leaving it and re-entering the brutal heat and dust on the ascent to Indian Gardens, 4.7 miles and 1,320 feet above where we sat then.

I grabbed another handful of almonds and chugged a liter of water. I closed my eyes and wished for the water, protein, and fat to efficiently penetrate my cells with the nutrients they needed to carry me through.

Sydney and I robotically folded, rolled, and stuffed our dense tent into its stuff sack with ease and efficiency compared to the time it took to pack in the beginning of the trip. I doctored the wounds of my backpack by stuffing the squirrel-chewed hole with a shirt to prevent anything from falling out as I hiked, and I tried to clean and wrap my gooey, pink circle of raw skin on my foot as best as I could.

The first part of our hike up to Indian Gardens wasn't too bad. My heart rate was elevated, but it was manageable. There were embers in my thighs but no raging fire yet. However, after about thirty minutes, we came to a bend in the trail, and when I saw what stood before me, all of my confidence evaporated, and intimidation took its place. The infamous Devil's Corkscrew switchbacks loomed above us, zigzagging up a steep expanse of which we could not see the top from where we stood. Devil's Corkscrew shoots up 500 feet in elevation in just half a mile, and it seemed I crawled up it more than I walked. I was so lightheaded when I got to the top I worried I would pass out. Thankfully, after stopping for a break and chugging some water, I was able to keep my bearings, and I pressed on to catch up to Will and Sydney.

Once we conquered the Devil's Corkscrew, the rest of the hike to Indian Gardens was just hard, not unbearable or life-threatening as

I'd expected. The view looking up the trail was disheartening at times because there was no break in the incline, but being able to look back every once in a while and see the Grand Canyon reveal itself to us in reverse was enough of a reward to help us continue climbing.

My underwear was drenched in sweat. Instead of hanging at my waist, they now rested at a super awkward place right in the middle of my butt cheeks, and every few minutes I had to stuff one of my hands down my pants to retrieve them. I was learning that there was no way to backpack with poise and grace. However, I was hiking in the back of the group, so I didn't have to apologize to anyone but the potential rattlesnakes hiding under the rocks. I knew there were a ton of them in the Grand Canyon, so I was on edge slightly as we hiked. I would have liked to see one from afar. I kept my eyes peeled.

The heat felt even more suffocating now that we were hiking up steep inclines compared to walking downhill the day before, and it slowed our pace immensely. I had trouble keeping myself from over-heating, and heat exhaustion was not something I wanted to mess around with in the middle of desert canyon wilderness. I had to take a break every fifteen minutes, and though it was difficult, I tried to silence the voice in my head that said I wasn't strong or capable enough to keep going.

We finally arrived at Indian Gardens after about three hours of hiking. It was another sudden oasis surrounded by a cluster of trees with a small stream running next to it. We noticed the campground was empty when we got there, which meant we were able to call dibs on the one campsite with a bit of shade provided by a small tree to its right. Though we were drenched in sweat and exhausted, the tempera-ture was only ninety-three degrees which felt refreshing compared to the oven at the bottom of the canyon. Setting up camp felt like too big a task when all I wanted to do was cool off in the stream and take a nap, but I knew the sooner we set up the sooner we could rest, so I mustered up enough energy to help Sydney with the tent. Once our orange and brown portable home stood secured, we sat down in the red-orange dirt with Will, scarfed down lunches of tuna, granola bars, and nuts, and chugged water until we thought our stomachs were going to pop.

Our only option for passing time during the hottest part of the day was to find refuge by the water again. We walked down a small trail that opened up to a flat bank of the stream. The first thing I noticed was a giant boulder in the middle of the stream that was begging to be napped on. I decided to go back to the tent to grab my sleeping pad, and when I came back to the stream, I laid it out on the boulder so I could rest in a little more comfort. There was a slight breeze, and some sprinkles of mist from the waterfall to my left occasionally settled on my skin, sending tiny droplets of delight through my veins. I stretched out and closed my eyes, soaking it in.

I tried desperately to take a nap, but I couldn't get Cam out of my head. The more I tried to divert my thoughts from him, the faster the flashbacks, both good and bad, flooded my mind. I didn't miss him specifically, but I missed the idea of him.

Jeez. Letting go seems like one long process of one step forward, and two steps back. I had such a moving day yesterday, yet here we go again.

I felt so trapped and isolated in my pain, which was ironic since I was quite literally trying to take a nap on an isolated boulder in the middle of a river. I didn't know what to do with my grief. While a familiar fight against painful thoughts began, an unfamiliar presence of compassion and grace sat down next to me as I fought myself.

You don't have to do this, you know. You don't have to do this alone. You don't have to pretend like you're okay. I love you. You might not have control over how Cam treated you. You might not have control of how his psychological manipulation and his choice to have sex the night you broke up affected you emotionally. But you do have control over how you treat yourself. You don't have to be your own abuser and perpetuate a cycle that permits the abuse to continue even now that he is gone. You have the power to end the cycle within your own being, and that starts with first admitting that you're not okay.

I knew I needed to be with someone as I tried to sit with this, but the thought of having to verbally name that to Sydney or Will horrified me. We weren't even that close yet. I had only told them that Cam was really hurtful, which was the tip of the iceberg. I had told Syendy how things ended on our hike down to Snow Creek, but I didn't know how much Will knew. I didn't know how to bridge the gap, but the voice mixed with firmness, love, and kindness from somewhere within me continued.

Get up. And go over there.

I fought back. *Over to Sydney and Will? No way! Why? I don't want to interrupt their time alone. What if they're trying to have privacy, or what if they're trying to have a conversation that I don't need to be a part of? What if Will is asking Sydney to be his girlfriend at this exact moment? What if they feel awkward and don't know what to say when I tell them I need help?*

Though I resisted, I knew I couldn't take the torture of the movie scenes playing in my mind much longer. I could feel my heartbeat pounding in my throat.

The compassionate voice piped up again. *You matter to them, and they care about you. Your needs are important and valid, and there is no sense in robbing yourself of the gift of being seen by a friend. I know you are afraid of being misunderstood. I know you are afraid of being rejected. Those are valid feelings, but how long are you going to hold on to this, Em? Your fear is just trying to keep you safe. It is possible to thank it for trying to protect you, and gently tell it that it is welcome to voice its opinion, but it cannot rule your decisions. Why are you keeping yourself in isolation? Might you accept the possibility that people shouldn't have to bear feelings like this alone?*

Get up. And go over there.

I didn't want to get up. I quite honestly wanted to tell this voice to fuck off, that it was lying, that trusting people was too risky, but I didn't know what else to do. The walk through the stream over to Sydney and Will felt like it took years. They had their backs to me so they couldn't see me, and they couldn't hear me approach because my steps were muffled by the rush of the water.

Once I reached them, I couldn't even force a verbal hello. Sydney extended a soft smile, and I just sat down next to her in the dirt of the bank without saying anything. I stared at my feet as the clear water flowed over them, hoping that it would somehow wash my emotions away.

The inner voice coaxed me to be brave, and just as I did with Ethan at Snow Creek, I chose the courageous act of slowly tilting my head until it suddenly rested on Sydney's right shoulder. My entire body was tense and uncomfortable, but I didn't know what else to do. Sydney did not flinch. She didn't look at me, and she didn't say anything. I was terrified that she was going to be like 'what the hell are you doing,' and push me off in disgust, but a few seconds after I laid my head on her shoulder, her hand found mine in the small space between us. Tears started flowing steadily and silently down my cheeks.

I didn't have to say anything. She intuitively knew that all I needed in that moment was to just sit together. I chose to lean in instead of running away, and it was a hard but brave act of opening myself up to be seen. It was a whispered confession that said, *"I am not okay. I cannot do this alone. I need you."* It was a silent, pleading question, *"Will you sit with me in the silence where there are not words? Will you stand in solidarity with me in my pain, helping me validate the way I feel? Will you help redirect my eyes toward hope when I am blinded by despair?"*

With the simple touch of a hand, Sydney communicated a silent whisper in reply that let me know what I needed to hear and feel. *"I see you. I value you. I love you. I stand with you in the grief, in the space where there are no answers."* Her response was more profound than anything she could have ever said to me in that moment. I didn't need answers. I just needed someone to sit with me in my grief, and she did.

"I'm so angry," I choked through the silence as I lifted my head and wiped my cheeks. "I just feel so overwhelmed. I think about Cam constantly, even when I don't want to. Every time I close my eyes I see him, either in a good memory, or a hurtful one. He's gone, yet no matter how hard I try to let go, I still carry him with me. I just want to be able to go one fucking day without thinking about him, but I don't know how to make it stop."

Sydney looked at me with compassionate eyes. "But can you make the pain stop without paying attention to it first? What have you been thinking about?"

"It's just that I knew there would be all of the negative and painful parts of our relationship which I would have to grieve, but what I didn't realize until being on this trip is that I also have to grieve all of the good things about Cam and our time together, which is almost harder to let go of. I have to let go of the person Cam used to be. The Cam who constantly made me laugh, who challenged me to critique my thoughts and actions in a positive way, who helped me believe I was beautiful without makeup, who pushed me out of my comfort zone in all of the best ways, who slow danced with me in the kitchen, who convinced me that I was smart enough to push into philosophical books no one else my age seemed to be ready for and brave enough to challenge the supposed one right way to live…" I took a deep breath and exhaled slowly. "I loved all of those things about him, and I still do. It's easy to grieve the Cam who treated me like shit toward the end. It's easy to be pissed, let go of that person, and not want anything else to do with him. But I have to grieve all of the parts of Cam that I fell in love with, treating them almost as if they died. Holding on to them will do nothing but make healing and moving on that much more difficult."

"That does sound really hard. I'm sure the weight of it all is so much to carry." Sydney squeezed my hand. Will nodded his head, which was his first gesture that showed he was listening, but he kept his eyes focused on the page of his book and didn't say anything. It seemed he'd intuited that this was a conversation in which Sydney was better suited to support me. This was true, but I was grateful to know he was listening and that I could be open and honest around him without him obviously judging me or shaming me for feeling, as I had been accustomed to with Cam. It had been hard to get to know Will since Cam left me with a significant bias against guys, but something about Will choosing to sit with Sydney and I in that raw space when he could have easily left and avoided the conversation made me believe it was safe to trust him as a friend.

I hugged my knees to my chest. After a moment of silently watching the water trickle over my toes, I continued. "There's also all of these hopes and dreams that we had, plans we were making together, and my mind often gets overwhelmed with the what-ifs and the could-have-beens. I think I have to grieve those too." I shook my head. "When people talk about grief they make it seem like it is just what happens when someone dies, but there is so much more to grief. There is grieving the bad. There is grieving the good. And in this case, there is also grieving the life I thought I was going to have or could have had if things didn't happen the way they did—if Cam hadn't gone into the military, hadn't chosen his specific job, hadn't been turned into a robot who had to believe emotions were bad, had he not repressed his anger and taken it out on me… I have to let go of the dreams that could have come true, the adventures and experiences we could have shared. Even though those things were never reality beyond thoughts in my head, I still got attached to them, and detaching them is painful."

"Mmm," Sydney nodded her head. "I've never thought about it like that, but I can totally understand. And it's probably extra hard to give yourself space to name what you're feeling now when, from what you've told me, it seems like Cam kind of trained you to do the opposite."

"Exactly. I get trapped in toxic thought cycles when I try to resist days like this. My negative thoughts feel paralyzing, and I'm tempted to find anything that will help me run away from them. I know running away is not the answer though. I know now that grief cannot be pushed aside. The only way out of this cloud around my head is not around it or over it or under it but through it. I don't want to repress it. I know I have to feel my pain in order to heal from it. I have to name my negative thoughts and emotions, but doing that alone often seems like too much to bear. I was sitting over there by myself trying to fight the swarm of negativity in my head, and I didn't know what else to do besides come over here."

Sydney smiled. "I'm really glad you did. And regarding what you just said, I think that's why healing comes to us in small steps," she added. "We're never ready for the whole thing all at once. We have to open ourselves up to healing slowly, one day, one hour, one minute at a time. We can't rush it."

"Yeah, you're right." I nodded. "This might have to be a slow-moving process, but I have to learn how to be okay with that instead of judging myself for not being further along in healing or comparing my grief and healing to that of another's experience, wondering why I am not as far as they may be."

"Healing isn't a competition," she said gently. "It's not a race that can be won or lost, or a challenge to be conquered. You can't compare your process with someone else's, nor can you compare intensities of pain. Suffering is suffering, whether there is meaning in it or not, and it's important to validate your feelings."

"I just feel so silly, because in many ways, especially from the outside looking in, it's 'just a break-up.'" I used my first and middle fingers to emphasize the quotes. "I find myself comparing, thinking about everyone that has situations much worse than this. Yes there was some emotional abuse that I feel pretty messed up from, but he never hit me. I didn't get raped. There's no life-threatening medical diagnosis. No one died. I'm a privileged white girl. I've always had my basic needs met. I've experienced very little injustice in my life. It doesn't feel right to complain. It's so hard to convince myself that it's okay to feel what I'm feeling and that I'm not being overdramatic. But at the same time, I know there's so much more underneath the surface than just the fact that Cam and I broke up, and it's way more than Cam choosing to have sex with someone else so soon."

"But whose voice is it that is telling you that you're being overdramatic?" she asked.

I sighed. She was right. "Cam's."

"So, give your voice space to speak up, to tell you what you're feeling, and pay attention. Cam may have silenced your voice, but he's gone, and you don't have to be silenced anymore," she emphasized. The tears welled up in my eyes again. I wanted to believe her. "Letting Cam's voice stay in your head continues to give him power over your joy instead of claiming that power for yourself. Try to give yourself space to name the grief as it comes up without fearing what Cam might say about it if he were here." She paused for a few seconds. "Have you forgiven him?"

I sighed. "Some days I think that I have, but others I'm still so incredibly angry. Any attempt at extending forgiveness still feels like I don't fully believe it. I mean, he never said he was sorry. Actually, he explicitly emphasized multiple times that he was not sorry, which makes it ten times harder. Granting unconditional grace to someone so close to you who caused you pain with zero remorse feels almost impossible. If I'm honest, I think I've been waiting for an apology to be able to forgive him."

"Do you think he'll ever do that?"

"Honestly, unless some radical transformation happens in him, probably not. I think he would be too attached to his pride to admit that he did anything wrong or hurtful, especially when I was so often the one that was blamed for our conflicts."

"I totally get that it is hard to forgive him without an apology. You definitely deserve one," Sydney said sternly. "I was reading somewhere a couple months ago about grief rituals, how our society doesn't deal with grief well anymore because we so often just repress it in the West. People think it's bad to show emotion, or to cry or whatever.

But I think sometimes we need some sort of ceremony to mark changing events or circumstances in our lives. Maybe there's something you could do as a physical representation of letting go of Cam, some sort of forgiveness ceremony."

"Yeah, maybe. I definitely want to do whatever I can to help myself move on, even with the possibility that I will never hear the words 'I'm sorry' come out of Cam's mouth. I know that remaining in unforgiveness doesn't do anything but keep my joy in Cam's power. I'm sure as hell done with that." I smirked, trying to lighten the mood, and Sydney giggled softly.

"Hey, thanks for trusting me enough to be vulnerable and tell me how you were feeling," Sydney said as she made intentional eye contact with me, and I was on the verge of tears again. "I know you've been processing a lot, and I'm sure you need a lot of time to reflect alone, but just know that I'm here if you need me. I know we are still only getting to know each other, but this trip is really special, and I'm really thankful for you as a friend."

"Aw, Syd!" I didn't really do hugs at this point in my life, but I attempted to give her an awkward side hug and wondered if she felt as awkward as I did. "Thanks a lot for listening to me word vomit my feelings and not running away or thinking I'm a crazy person."

She laughed. "Of course. You're not crazy. You're just hurting. And that's okay. Should we go make some food? I think Will headed back to rest and get stuff ready for dinner."

"Oh," I looked over to where he was sitting, "I didn't even realize he had snuck away. Yeah, dinner is exactly what my body needs now."

As we walked through the stream to the other bank that led back to the campsite, something that Rob Bell said on one of his podcasts a couple months back surfaced in my mind. I thought about mentioning it to Sydney, but I still didn't know where she stood with Christianity. I was pretty sure she still went to church, and it was hard to tell how much it still meant to her. I was scared to mention an author who had been branded as a total heretic in the evangelical community when he published a book about the possibility of hell not existing a couple years back. I feared if she found out I listened to Rob Bell on a regular basis that she would no longer want to be friends with me.

On this podcast episode though, Rob Bell said something about grief that really stood out to me when I heard it, but until my conversation with Sydney it had been buried and forgotten in my mind. He'd said, "Any change is a form of loss, and loss must be grieved." I recited it over and over in my head as we walked back.

Any change is a form of loss, and loss must be grieved.

Almost every aspect of my life and every relationship close to me had changed in some way, if not externally then internally. So much change meant I had experienced many forms of loss, and therefore I had many things to grieve. Maybe it wouldn't happen quickly, and maybe that was okay.

After another meal of beans, granola bars, and tuna, we walked a mile and a half out to Plateau Point to watch the sunset. After about thirty minutes of walking on a relatively flat, dusty trail, we arrived at a smooth peninsula of rock which ended in sheer cliffs on all sides. I walked right up to the edge. I could see the murky Colorado River far below us now. There was no protective barrier, and the cliff dropped off so suddenly that when I looked over it I could feel the chance of my sudden death rising up from the depths beneath me.

I thought back to my hardest nights in the months before I'd left on my trip, when at times, in the deepest shadows of my pain, when the loneliness and hopelessness felt too much to bear, I'd pondered what it would be like to end my life. I never reached the point where I had a plan to kill myself, but the thought of it was enough to terrify me, especially coming from a Christian background where suicide was taboo, and mental health was claimed to be an issue of faith instead of hormones and neurotransmitters that don't give a shit about how much you pray or to which God you pray to, like I know now.

I would be lying if I said that in that moment, standing on the edge, I didn't think about how easy it would be to jump. I recognized the thought inside of myself, but instead of fearing the thought and trying to repress it like I had in the past, I welcomed it with compassion. I closed my eyes and reached back into those memories when I was curled in a ball in the dark, just trying to survive the night. I imagined sitting beside my previous self and whispering to her, *"I know you feel so unsafe, and I know that has been so scary to you. You are held and loved. You will not always feel this way. Everything is going to be okay."*

I opened my eyes and soaked in the view from the edge for one more moment. I was no longer there curled up in the dark. I was here, in the midst of pure beauty, my heart beating with a thirst for life I swore I would never let myself forget. This trip had reminded me that beyond a doubt, my life was worth living. Choosing to stay despite the pain was power. Choosing to face the darkness and expose it with the light of healing was resistance. Choosing to stand at the scary edges without going over them was the only way forward. I stepped back from the edge, my smile spreading ear to ear.

I walked away and took a seat on a small boulder about fifteen yards from the edge to take in the massive castles of rocks and spires around me. They almost looked like cathedrals rising up, which was fitting since the Grand Canyon had felt more like an authentic church experience than I ever had inside an established church building.

It was almost more impressive to be in the middle of the canyon opposed to the top or the bottom because we could look through thousands of layers and millions of years of rock both toward the rim towering above us and also toward the river rushing below us. Both the rim and the river looked to be a thousand miles away.

I sat there for some time by myself. For a while I didn't think about much beyond the immensity of the canyon and how the rock glowed like soft embers in the golden hour light, some of them emanating a gentle pink hue in the shadows. As I watched the sun begin to dive into the red ocean of rock around me, I remembered my conversation with Sydney earlier about grief. I thought that on this trip I would find something or someplace large enough to hold my grief, but even standing there looking out into the Grand Canyon which seemed as if it quite literally went on forever in every direction, my grief somehow still felt larger.

I remembered what Sydney had said about the need for rituals and ceremonies to help ourselves move through grief. It reminded me of something I experienced during a campus ministry retreat at the beach a couple years back. On the last night, we were instructed to find a shell or a rock in the sand and to sit with it for a while, thinking about something in our lives that we needed to let go of. We were supposed to pray for God to heal us from whatever the shell represented had done to hurt us, and once we felt like we were ready, we were to get up from our place in the sand and hurl the shell in the ocean as a physical way to let go of whatever we held onto that didn't serve us. Of course, then, it was much more structured with Christian language, but I wondered if I could do something similar now without using triggering language.

I stood up and walked closer to the cliff's edge again. I picked up a palm-sized stone that had broken off from one of the larger rocks along the ledge. I took a deep breath, and I thought about sitting by the steam earlier that day, feeling so controlled by the fact that I could not seem to leave Cam behind. I knew it was time to let go of the need for an apology in order to move forward. I knew it was time to make an attempt at forgiveness.

I thought of Cam, but not the Cam I experienced at the end—the harsh, angry, dark Cam. I thought of the Cam I saw in every good and happy memory, the truest Cam, the healthy Cam, the whole and integrated and inspired core of Cam, the loving and gentle Cam. With my eyes shut, I held him close in my mind. I imagined facing him and looking into his soft, kind, blue eyes. I clenched the rough rock tightly in my smooth palm. I took a deep breath.

Cam, I am so angry. At you. At the fact that it feels like the military turned you into a monster. At the fact that it seemed like you knew it, you let it happen, and you didn't care. At the fact that you internalized your anger and pain and projected it onto our relationship. At the fact that you decided you were in control of my emotions and my body. At the fact that I chose to believe you and numb myself to try to save something that was already dead.

I don't know why I let you berate me for feeling. I don't know why I let you be the one that had all of the answers. I don't know why I let you control me. I don't know why you chose to have sex for the first time the night we broke up. I don't know why you had to tell me about it. I don't know why you needed to emphasize that you weren't sorry. I let that rip me apart. It's haunted me. But, I'm not going to give you that power over me anymore. I don't need an apology from you in order to pursue healing and wholeness.

In the same way that I want to believe in my own healing and whole-ness, I want to believe in yours as well. I know that your life felt like it was crumbling beneath you then, too. I'm sure it was scary. I'm sure you felt so alone. I'm sure you felt overwhelmed with your trauma and didn't know how to deal with it. I hope with all that is in me that one day you have the courage to face yourself, your pain, and your anger, and that one day you find the truth you are looking for. May you find space in your life to seek freedom and healing and love. May you retain the dreamer I saw in you. May you retain your love for the world even in the midst of all of the darkness you could never understand.

This is my peace offering. My ceremony of forgiveness. And I'm not doing it for you. I'm doing it for myself. You don't get to control my happiness anymore. I might never hear you say that you're sorry, and that is a reality that I am choosing to accept, so that it will no longer be a roadblock in my path to healing. And though it hurts to part with you, I must let go, and I must replace your voice inside of my head with mine.

May this be a funeral. For who you used to be, for who we used to be, for who I used to be. Those people are gone now, and so is that couple, with all of their joy, heartbreak, trauma, fights, memories, hopes, and dreams. I have to grieve the good, and I have to grieve the bad. I must go where the light is, and that means that I must leave you behind.

"Em, are you ready to head back?" Sydney's voice startled me.

"Um, yeah, one sec!" I called back.

I held the rock close to my chest. *Thank you for being what I needed for a season, for helping wake me up to the fact that there is more than one way to be human in this world. But I don't need you anymore. I'm realizing I'm already free, and that maybe I've been free from you the whole time. I just need to believe it.*

I took a deep breath, and then I threw that rock out into the canyon as hard and as confidently as I could. I stood invigorated in the stillness and watched the rock fall. It was the only movement in my view besides the river churning far below untill the rock's form dissolved in the distance. I turned to walk away, grateful that every step I took was another step further from that weight I used to carry. I was lighter, a little more healed, and a little more whole.

As I left the cliff's edge and walked toward Will and Sydney, I wondered about Ethan. Had he watched the sunset from wherever he was?

Was he okay? Will finished packing up his camera gear, and we were about to put on our headlamps and walk back, but Will noted that the moon was so bright that we probably didn't even need them. The trail was completely illuminated, and we decided to walk the flat mile and a half back to the campsite by moonlight.

We watched the stars come out, one by one, dotting the sky with a stark brightness free of light pollution, a privilege I was still getting used to. I noticed tiny flashes of light up closer to the rim, which I assumed to be photographers who had set up for a night shoot. Looking up at the rim reminded me of the baptism moment in the stream at the bottom yesterday, and I wondered what life would be like when I emerged from the canyon of this trip and was back home, back in my old life where I used to live on the rim. I wasn't sure where I would go from here, but I had peace about it.

While we walked, the temperature continued to drop, and I was grateful for time to experience the Grand Canyon at night. After so much time in the blazing heat, I celebrated the darkness and the cooler air. It was like we had the opportunity to get to know a softer, gentler side of the Grand Canyon, out of the spotlight. I felt like after all of the revelation yesterday and today, I was walking through the dark a little softer and gentler, too.

We arrived at the campsite and brushed our teeth with the last bit of energy we had left. The sky seemed like it would not bring rain, so Sydney and I decided that we would leave the rainfly off so that there would be more airflow. We whispered goodnight to Will through the mesh in our tent, and after some time looking up at the sky, we all settled into the beginnings of sleep.

The fluttering of my eyes and thoughts started to slow as my brain accepted permission to rest, but the sudden sound of Will violently jolting up in his tent immediately called my mind back into a state of full consciousness. Both mine and Sydney's eyes shot open, and we looked at each other through the moonlight in confusion and concern.

Will's shaking voice pierced through the darkness bearing news that brought a chill to my bones. "Guys, there is a freaking. Huge. Rattlesnake. *In our campsite.*"

"What?" Sydney's shrill voice cut the darkness.

My stomach dropped. *No. No no no no.* Coming into this trip I'd wanted to see a rattlesnake in the wild for the first time. After zero sightings during our time in prime rattlesnake territory thus far I'd begun to intentionally look for them throughout the day—in the shade under rocks, in the brush next to the trail, in the sunny spots on the boulders we passed—but the last place I wanted to see one was from behind thin mesh fewer than two feet from where I was supposed to lay unconscious and vulnerable for the next eight hours.

However, sure enough, as I slowly raised myself up on my knees to look out through the mesh of the tent, my stomach dropped as the light of my headlamp illuminated the body of a four-foot long rattlesnake as thick as my calf. Its slit pitch-black pupils reflected the light from the sides of its pointed, triangle-shaped head, and it inched its way across the dirt, flicking its terrifying tongue every few seconds.

"*Oh. My. God,*" Sydney whispered. The mixture of intimidation, fear, and awe in her voice matched what I was feeling in my chest. The three of us held our breath as we watched the snake cross our entire campsite in silence. Those few seconds of waiting felt like years. I just knew it was going to coil up and strike us through the mesh at any moment. I let out a sigh of relief when the last rung of the snake's rattle disappeared into the darkness. I looked at Sydney, half smiling and half wincing as I shook my head in disbelief.

My voice broke the thick silence. "I can't stop thinking about the fact that if we had come back from Plateau Point five minutes later we would have stepped on that thing. It's darker here with the trees around us, and without headlamps we probably wouldn't have seen it." I felt the chill still fresh down my spine.

"Wait. You're so right. I can't imagine. I don't even want to think about it." Sydney shuddered. "Will, how did you know it was there?"

"I heard a noise really close to the other side of my tent," Will whispered across to us through the see-through mesh of his tent, "and at first I was wondering what sort of animal was walking through the brush. I thought it might be one of those squirrels, but then I realized the sound was too constant to be something that was taking individual steps. I was like, wait, that is something slithering. And then my brain alarm was like, snake!" He emphasized the words by throwing his hands up in the air and whispering a little louder. We all laughed.

"Yeah, we heard you jump up in your tent! I thought you had just flinched in a dream or something," Sydney whispered, still laughing.

"I wanted to see a rattlesnake, but Jesus, not like that!" I squealed.

"Well, I guess there's nothing else we can do but sleep. Be careful if you have to leave the tent to go to the bathroom during the night," Will warned.

"Oh, hell no," Sydney grunted. "I am not leaving this tent until the sun rises!"

I laughed. "Worst case scenario we can just pee in my water bottle."

"Gross!" she laughed.

"Sucks for you guys, all I need to do is open my zipper a couple inches and I can pee straight out of my tent," Will bragged.

Sydney and I rolled our eyes and laughed. "One of the many ways you men have it easier than us," Sydney bantered.

"Sleep well," I offered through my anxiety and exhaustion.

"I'll try my best," Will sighed in reply.

"Goodnight," Sydney said, and Will and I echoed her.

Sydney and I nestled ourselves deep in our sleeping bags. My anxious thoughts spiraled for a moment.

I can't imagine what the reality of a rattlesnake bite would look like for us at this hour, this far into the Grand Canyon. There are only a few other campers here besides us that I know of. We're four and a half miles and 3,060 feet of elevation down from the rim. Who would we call? How would we get help? Would we know what to do?

I pulled my sleeping bag a little tighter over my chest, hoping that it would provide more comfort than the pounding of my chest which had only slightly lessened in the moments since we first saw the snake. I decided that I would never look for a rattlesnake again and that I would actually be quite happy if they kept their distance from me for the rest of the trip. I no longer had any desire to lay eyes on one in the wild, and if I had to face one in the wild again, I hoped that I would at least see it somewhere other than my sleeping quarters.

Eventually my own reptile brain's strong desire for sleep and survival was more powerful than my escalated heart rate, anxiety, and fear. I drifted into a sleep that lasted through the night without any more scary, sudden, waking moments.

{22}

UP

M Y EYES FLUTTERED OPEN AS MY WATCH ALARM PIERCED
the silence. The sun was up, but the air clung to a slight
chill, as if it didn't want to wake up yet either. We weren't
in a huge rush to leave, so I had a few minutes to lay there and soak in
my last morning waking up in the canyon. I thought about how weird
it might be when I stay in the same place for more than a couple days
again, and even more so, the oddity of staying in a house, with a bed,
bathroom, shower, kitchen, and air conditioning. It had been three
weeks living on the road, and whatever normal life was supposed to be
was a foreign concept to me now. I felt like I was always supposed to
live this way.

"How much do we have left?" Will asked when he joined Sydney
and I to stretch once our tents were packed.

I pulled out the trail guide. "From here to the rim is 3,060 feet of
climbing in only four and a half miles, which I am assuming is going
to feel like it is basically straight up." I balanced on one leg to stretch
my aching quad.

"Dang. That is like hiking six Devil's Corkscrews in a row," Will
huffed, referencing the terrible switchbacks from yesterday that felt like
they would never end.

"Great," Sydney said. "Just six Devil's Corkscrews. With giant packs that are way too heavy for us. Solid." I could tell she was not amused.

"Well, I'm definitely not sleeping here another night with that snake lurking about," I said as I looked behind me to make sure it hadn't snuck up on us again.

"I still can't believe that happened," Will laughed. "Well," he looked around, "it looks like we're the last ones out of camp again." He raised his chin to gesture toward the empty site which used to hold the one other tent besides ours.

"Amateurs for the win?" Sydney joked.

"Yeah, let's hope we still feel confident about that in a couple hours. Ready?" asked Will.

"As I'll ever be," I said. We hoisted our packs onto our backs and limped toward the trail.

The hike up from Indian Gardens was much more challenging than I expected. My body had a hard time thermoregulating, and I was overheated within thirty minutes of walking up the first section of the trail. I thought it was steep until we got to the three-mile rest house, and then the trail shot up even more steeply. I sat in the shade at the rest house for a couple minutes trying to cool off. Since there was a water spicket there, I poured an entire liter of water on my head, cherished the delight of each cold droplet trickling down my hot skin, chugged another liter, filled up my water bottle again, and put it back in my pack. We began our last three miles, which in the Grand Canyon world, feels a lot more like thirty.

Will was leading per usual. Originally, I tried to keep up with him and Sydney, but once I got overheated it was game over. I longed for a reality where I could throw my pack on the ground and leave it there to rot forever, but I knew that was not an option. Even though we only had three miles left, we still had 2,100 feet to climb vertically, mostly in the form of switchbacks so steep that my stiff boots made it hard to take normal steps.

My clunky, heavy hiking boots, which had no breathability and were much more suited for trekking through two feet of snow than navigating a sweltering desert canyon, now made it quite clear that they were out of their element. I hadn't noticed them bothering me too much on the way down besides how much my feet were sweating and how hard the soles were. However, hiking up after the three mile rest house I noticed that their stiffness and height above my ankle kept my foot in a constant flexed position. I couldn't point my toes to fully engage my calves to help me walk, which made for an even more awkward climb.

My pace slowed tremendously as I inched my way up the switchbacks, and by the time I caught up to Sydney and Will at the mile and a half rest house I was nauseous and light-headed from heat exhaustion. I was drenched in sweat, and my mouth was dry. I felt terrible, and it was hard to find the mental stamina to continue walking. It seemed that Sydney and Will were navigating the heat much better than I was, and my slight embarrassment for being so slow did not help my morale.

I was miserable every step of the last mile and a half and 1,100 feet of ascent. I looked up to see that Will was multiple switchbacks above me, and I figured I would just see him at the rim. Sydney waited for me to catch up every once in a while to make sure I was okay, and I tried my best to hold it together and keep walking. My face was beet red. All of my body heat felt like it was concentrated in my head which made it hard to think straight, and the sun was so hot on my back that it felt violating. Unfortunately for me, there was no other option but to keep walking.

During the last mile or so, day hikers started to come down the trail dressed to the nines and recently showered and pampered. One guy was even wearing a tie. I felt defensive, like I had to make sure they knew that this was not all of the Grand Canyon. Underneath feeling defensive, I felt sad about leaving the wilderness and re-entering society.

I guess I looked pretty pitiful because most of the people I passed going the opposite direction met me with sympathetic "bless your heart" or "you poor thing" expressions or forced consolations such as, "Hang in there! You're almost there! Just a little bit further!" These were all exclamations which, to someone that had been hiking for hours in the heat and was on the verge of passing out, just pissed me off. I didn't want anyone to talk to me or look at me, especially if they were wearing a tie in the wilderness like they had a business meeting with a damn rattlesnake or something. I just wanted to be at the rim.

I never understood why people cried when they finished running marathons until I saw the top of the switchbacks, which meant the end of the trail. I had tears in my eyes before I even got to the top. My time in the Grand Canyon, though it was short, had been an intensely emotional and physical experience for me, and I was grateful for the wild space of solitude that it provided. Even though it had only been two nights, I'd found more significant breakthrough and healing in the Grand Canyon than any other experience thus far on the trip, and being able to share the grueling experience with Sydney and Will made it that much more meaningful—tears, blisters, rattlesnakes, sweat, blood, and all.

The triumph increased when I got to the trailhead. I finally could peel my pack from the ruts it had made on the tops of my shoulders, and ecstasy filled my being as I laid down on the concrete in the shade. Will and Sydney walked up to me and gave me high fives, but I just extended my hands from the ground to meet theirs. It would be a while before I could be convinced to stand again.

"Yowza, that was hard! I don't know if I've ever been so physically uncomfortable." I sighed and chuckled. "We did it, y'all. Barely. But we did it." I smiled, my cheeks still burning with heat even in the shade.

"We should seriously be proud of ourselves and our bodies," Will emphasized. "There's like five million people that visit this place every year, and only a tiny percentage of those people experience the Grand Canyon like we did. That's pretty special."

"It is pretty special," Sydney agreed, "but I'm probably good to not do that again for a couple years at least."

"Same," I choked, and we all laughed. I winced as I tried to sit up and stretch.

"What's up dudes?" someone called from behind us.

I recognize that voice. I turned around and met eyes with Ethan. He bounced across the sidewalk in his normal goofy, lanky walk, sporting his high-top Vans.

"Oh my gosh! Hi!" I peeled myself up off the ground to give him a hug, only slightly aware of the fire in my thighs.

"You smell terrible," he said as he immediately pulled away from me, and we all laughed.

"What a warm way to welcome your sister back from the depths of the Grand Canyon!" Sydney encouraged sarcastically.

"Well, this is day seven of no shower," I pointed out, "and I don't think I've ever sweat this much in my entire life, so it would make sense."

"Are y'all ready to get out of here?" asked Ethan. "I found a parking spot pretty close."

"Yes!" Our voices echoed in one communal hoot.

We grabbed a quick group photo at the rim, and then we limped to the car to find some clothes that were not soaked in sweat.

"So what did you do for the past two days?" I asked Ethan at the car as I slowly took off my left boot to examine the status of my throbbing wound.

"Well the first afternoon after I hiked back up, I was sweaty and starving so I thought it would be nice to get some real food instead of tortillas and peanut butter for the four hundred and sixty-eighth time. But I went into the McDonalds near the park and a Big Mac meal was like eighteen dollars!"

"Seriously?" I quickly raised my eyebrows.

"Okay, maybe not eighteen dollars, but it was way more expensive than a normal McDonalds."

"Bummer. I guess they can jack up the prices since there's nothing else around." I grunted as I peeled my bandage off.

"Um, well that's disgusting," Ethan turned his nose up at my foot. To give him credit, the oozy, slimy hole in my foot was anything but pretty after three days of rubbing and pounding in my hot boots.

"Still not infected though! So I'm still winning in the wilderness First Aid challenge as far as I know," I shrugged.

"Anyway," Ethan continued, "So I went to the Wendy's instead and got the cheapest thing on their menu. It was gross, but it was better than another freaking tortilla. After that I decided that I would go to Flagstaff."

"You went to Flagstaff?" I asked, shocked. "Wow, I didn't think you would go quite that far away!" I immediately thought of Jake, and I died inside thinking about what my brother would think if I told him about spending the night with Jake, or if somehow Ethan happened to meet him while he was there. That night felt like years before now.

"It's only an hour and a half away, and I figured since I had two days I had time."

"Well, what did you think? Flagstaff is a cool town, right? Meet any cool people?" *Please don't say Jake.*

"Nah, I pretty much kept to myself." Oh thank God. "On the way I passed this Flintstones Bedrock City place on the side of the road, and they had re-made a lot of the things from the Flintstones movie set, like the houses and Fred Flinstone's car. Remember the live action movie we watched when we were kids?"

"Wow yeah, I haven't thought about that movie in ages. That's so random."

"Yeah, I wouldn't have known about it, but since I didn't have anything to do I walked around there for a while."

"That's what I love about road trips," I said. "You find so many things while driving across the country that you didn't even know existed, and you actually have time to stop."

"Exactly," Ethan nodded.

"And after the random Flintstones place?" Sydney asked.

"I hung out in a library," he answered.

"Wow, to read?" Will asked, seemingly impressed.

"Nope. To watch The Office. Free WiFi," Ethan shrugged.

"That sounds more like you," I said, and we all laughed.

"Hmm, I've never thought about libraries being places to hang out with free internet. I'll have to remember that next trip," Will noted.

"Yup. Then I parked in a random hotel parking lot that night, did the normal sleep in the front seat thing, woke up, walked around some shops, bought this sweet pullover on sale, and then headed back up to the Grand Canyon."

"So that was yesterday, when we hiked to Indian Gardens," observed Sydney.

"Yep. And, hmm, what did I do yesterday? Oh yeah," he giggled. "I went to an informational video presentation on frogs."

"What?" I cackled. "This story continues to unfold in the most random unpredictable events. Flintstones, library, frogs?"

"Yeah the rangers were doing a presentation on the amphibians and reptiles of the park. Where they live and what they eat and stuff. It was actually pretty cool."

"Wow you really got around," Will laughed.

"Oh that's not all. After that I made friends with a librarian in the Grand Canyon library and talked to her for three hours. I was going in to watch more of The Office, but when I walked in the librarian, Susan, asked me to help her change one of those big water jugs in the spicket machines because she couldn't lift it, and then we just talked all afternoon, about traveling, life, how she got here. Cool lady. Then I just drove back here late and slept here at the trailhead. I was hanging out at the car until I noticed you come up."

"Aw look at you, you little man living on the road by yourself! I'm so proud of you," I nudged him. "Was this the first time you've traveled alone? Even for a night?"

"Yeah it was," he affirmed.

"Welcome to the club. You beat me by two years."

"Ha. Yeah we all know I'm the real traveler here," Ethan boasted. "Come on, let's get you guys some food."

"Yes, please." I nodded. "My post-3,060-feet-of-ascent hunger is no joke."

07/24/15, Day 22 -

We have set up camp just outside of Zion National Park in southwest Utah. It has been 22 days since I left Boone, but I felt like I have lived a whole other life since I've been gone. I have just taken my first shower in eight days, which is my new personal record of supposed grossness. The water that washed off of my body was dark brown, which surprised me because I honestly didn't feel that dirty. Even though I slept outside and at some point my hair was completely sweat-soaked every day, I didn't really think I smelled that bad, but maybe I have just gotten used to my own stench.

My gratitude for my time in the Grand Canyon continues to permeate my being with reverence. For what? For life? For the Grand Canyon? For whatever remaining concept I still hold wrapped up in the word, God? What is this reverence? This state which, if we breathe deep and slow down enough, brings us to feel a part of something bigger than ourselves. Something beyond our understanding. Something completely out of our grasp.

Maybe this is what I am able to call God. That which calls me forth, further into who I am. Further into love, further into becoming, further into existence, further into being. Life is returning to me with each passing day, and something in me is drawn to my knees. I used to be able to worship, to sing songs with certain language to celebrate my gratitude to God when I felt this way. What does worship look like now, in the middle of deconstruction, when there is no longer concrete language for who or what I am thanking? For now, I don't know.

Anyway, in the meantime, we decided that tomorrow we would try to hike as much as we have energy for. Even though the Grand Canyon was a lot of physical suffering, part of me already kind of misses it. I have done no research about Zion (surprise), and I don't really even know if there are mountains inside the park or if there are just rocks. Will mentioned something about a famous hike called the Narrows, but I guess we'll see when we go into the park tomorrow.

{23}

LOST

"AH, FINALLY JOINING US IN THE WAKING WORLD I SEE," I called out when Ethan poked his head out of the tent. His curly locks still tightly framed his face and ears.

"Yeah, whatever," he mumbled, smiling. He quickly buried his head back in his sleeping bag.

"Hey, I'm serious. It really is time to get up." My tone was firm. "The three of us have been talking and we're going to try to do Angels Landing and the Narrows today, so we have to pack up now and get moving if we're going to have enough time to hike both. Start getting your stuff together." Ethan gave an annoyed huff, but he complied and began to shake himself out of his sleeping bag.

I didn't like feeling like a mom. If it were just the two of us it wouldn't have been a big deal, but with Will and Sydney there I felt like making sure Ethan was up and ready in time was my responsibility. I figured they probably didn't mind, but I didn't want it to fall back on me if Ethan slowed the group down with his hibernation habits.

We spent an hour packing up the entire campsite and organizing the car in its typical tetris fashion only to find out from the camp warden that the campground had a last minute cancellation, and we could stay another night. Though we were relieved to have secured a place to sleep that night, it felt incredibly inconvenient to have to drive back to the exact same spot and set everything up again before going into the park, so we decided that we would just do it once we got back that evening. We sped on giddily toward the Zion National Park entrance.

"How can the rock out here look so similar to the rock in the Grand Canyon, but so different at the same time?" Sydney asked as we wound our way through bright orange rock that rose up in distorted pillars and clusters above the road.

"Yeah, it's the same color in a lot of places, but it's weird seeing desert-like rock formations intermingled with evergreens that give off a forest feel," Will said. "I can't wait to capture some footage here! I'm going to need a couple of hours to record today. I was thinking after dinner, close to sunset. Is that okay?"

The rest of us gave him affirming nods and shrugs. "From the looks of it there's not a lack of beautiful places where we could hang out while you shoot." I added. "I can't get over how gorgeous this is!" I hung my head out the window and let the wind whip through my hair as we snaked our way further into the heart of Zion. My eyes were having a hard time adjusting to yet another new form of natural beauty unlike any I'd ever seen.

By the time we parked the car, it was already close to 11:00 a.m. The heat of the sun had burned through the morning mist and clouds, and the intense reds in the rock layers shone passionately in the light. Though it was a Saturday in Zion National Park in July, the parking area was not overwhelmingly crowded as we expected. We scarfed down a small lunch of bars and nuts by the car before it was time to catch the shuttle. I groaned when it was time to put on my hiking boots. After how uncomfortable and inhibiting my boots were while hiking out of the Grand Canyon, they looked like torture devices to me now. I tried to get over it, laced up quickly, and hobbled myself to the shuttle behind the rest of the group.

I had heard rumors that the Angels Landing hike was not for the faint of heart. There was talk of thousand-foot drop offs and stretches of trail so thin and dangerous that you had to hold on to chains bolted into the rock to make it across safely. I wasn't sure if the rumors were exaggerated or not, but I did notice a vague sense of intimidation pulsing in my gut as I approached the trailhead. I didn't know what to expect.

The four of us inched our way to the top slowly because the trail was so crowded, which I was annoyed by at first. However, I eventually found gratitude for the traffic because moving more slowly gave me time to really take in how high up we were and how far we would fall if we slipped off the edge. Maybe some people wouldn't want the extra time to stand and ponder the level of danger involved in their daring actions, but something about teetering on a thin ridgeline the last half-mile, looking down a thousand-foot sheer drop on my left while holding onto a thick metal chain on my right made me more invigorated and present in my body. Inching our way up made the experience feel even more extreme than if we had just rushed straight to the top. I powered through my lingering fear with some deep breaths in order to complete the last scrambled climb to the top Angels Landing. The flat rock finally expanded to around twenty feet in width, which felt massive compared to the thinnest part of the ridgeline we'd just come up from. My heart rate began to slow, but that didn't last long.

Soon after we reached the top, I noticed that Ethan had left the group. I scanned the crowd of people standing on the summit, and then I saw him waving to me as he stepped over a large orange sign that said, "DANGER. DO NOT CROSS."

I sighed. "Hold on," I interrupted Sydney shortly after I'd asked her what her experience on the ridgeline was like, "I have to go convince my brother that dying is not on the agenda for today."

"Ethan! What the heck are you thinking? Get down!" I urged once I stopped at the danger sign.

"Chill!" He trotted over to me and held his camera out like he wanted me to take it.

"Nope. Not happening."

"What? It will be fine! I just want you to take a quick picture of me on that ledge over there!" His expression communicated that he thought I was the lamest person ever.

"Ethan. This sign you climbed over? It's here for a reason. Someone probably died falling off the cliff edge, or maybe that rock up there is unstable! The ledge you're talking about is literally only a foot wide, and if you fall, you're dead."

"I'm not going to fall," he pleaded.

"Dude, I'm sorry, but I'm not going to be the one to have to call mom and dad and tell them that I let you go out on a sketchy ledge and watched you slip and fall to your death!" I was feeling angry now, but I was mostly scared for him because his body language made it seem seem like he was going to turn around and do it anyway. "E, just, please don't be stubborn right now. Something in my gut is telling me this is a bad idea!" I tried to keep my voice at a normal volume so people wouldn't stare at us fighting, but I wanted to scream at him.

"God, you're so annoying!" Ethan muttered harshly. "Why are you making this such a big deal? It's just a quick picture!"

I shook my head. "Instagram likes aren't worth dying for. I'm not taking it. Find someone else to take it."

I walked away frustrated, but when I turned my head to look back at him, he had come down off the step where he stood and hung out in another place he found. My anger was flooded by relief.

We got off Angel's Landing to find that the Saturday crowds had swarmed in at full capacity. We got back on the park shuttle and rode it to its last stop. We arrived at the Narrows trailhead at the Virgin River where we planned to begin hiking upstream to experience the renowned cave-like feel created by the tall canyon walls that stood in place of what would normally be a river bank. The first fifty yards of the shallow, clear water was dotted with what seemed like hundreds of loud tourists with their selfie sticks, wafers, and cool sunglasses. I was over-whelmed by the people, and I had a hard time being present until we had walked far enough upstream to get away from the crowds. Once we passed the dozens of folks only there to dip their toes in the river, I had space to think straight and could see more of the river beyond the backs of the people in front of me, the experience totally changed.

Hundreds of feet of rock now towered on both sides of us, smoothed by millions of years of water flowing through the narrow canyon. There were some moments where we could walk on stretches of sand or rocks, but for the most part, the river was the trail, and we trudged through the water the whole way. I was worried about my foot since my bandage was starting to saturate with water and slip off. My running shoes were rubbing against it as I walked which hurt, but the water was so cold that it numbed my foot slightly which helped keep my mind off the discomfort.

Thankfully Sydney offered to let me use the hiking poles her mom gave her to use for the trip. They turned out to be a life saver because I could put my weight on them when I had to consistently walk on unstable rock with my hurt foot in two to three feet of rushing water. We eventually came to a section of the river that decreased to only about twenty feet wide.

"There it is!" Will hollered with a giant grin as we came around a bend in the river canyon. Ahead of us, the river narrowed to only about fifteen feet wide. Will, who was leading as always, turned around to face us with a glimmer in his eye. "This is it. This is Wall Street."

We all excitedly walked forward through the river, trying to keep our balance. We followed the contour of the cliff which seemed even more steep now that the river had shrunk so much in width.

"I just want to remind you that we are currently experiencing one of the top ten rated hikes in the world," Will stated.

"Really? It's that famous?" I asked. I hadn't done any research then, but I now know that I was one of roughly 480,000 people that visited the park in that month of July alone.

"I honestly didn't realize that this hike was such a big deal. I had never even heard of it before coming here," said Ethan.

"It's pretty surreal if you think about how many epic adventures we have crammed into the same week," I said as I stopped and looked up at the sunlight which only reached a third of the way down the canyon walls, leaving us and the river in shadow. There were only a few other people in the river around us, and it seemed that everyone was feeling the same reverence that I felt, for everyone, including myself, spoke in hushed voices. "Four days in Yosemite. Then straight into hiking in and out of the Grand Canyon. Then straight into doing Angels Landing and the Narrows in the same day? You can't get much more extreme than that."

"Doing so many things in so many extremely beautiful places back to back has made it almost harder to appreciate how significant each place is," Sydney pointed out. "I haven't been able to process our time in Yosemite, much less our time in the Grand Canyon or the fact that we are in the middle of the Narrows right now!"

"I totally identify with that," Will agreed. "I've felt like my brain has needed way more time to take in the places we've been. Although staying in just one of these places the whole time would be cool, I am grateful that we've been able to do as much as we have, even with so little planning upfront."

"And the weather!" exclaimed Ethan. "The only rain we've had so far was in Yosemite."

"Yeah, we've been pretty lucky." I took a deep breath, raised my hands and hiking poles above my head, and exhaled as I bent over and let my hands rest in the water below my knees. As I watched the river water rush past my hands and shins, I remembered the lyrics from the Benjamin James song I listened to the day I left Boone. *Come back to the river, I will take you to the sea.* I still didn't know exactly what those words meant to me, but I could feel that I was coming back to something. If nothing else, I was coming back to myself, and that was enough for me.

"Hey guys," Will called," I am loving this and wish we could stay longer, but we should turn around soon. I'm running out of daylight to shoot video."

Sydney, Ethan, and I set up our camping stoves on a picnic table at the visitor's center to make dinner while Will took the shuttle to go record footage. Before he left Will mentioned he hadn't decided exactly what his plan was or how long he would be out, so we told him to just meet us at the visitor's center whenever he was done. Sydney and I cooked instant Thai rice noodles with a red curry sauce, quite a gourmet camp dinner compared to the average tuna or beans, and Ethan had Ramen for the sixth night in a row. Then we waited. I journaled for a while. And we waited. Sydney and I did yoga for a bit. And we waited. Ethan played games on his phone. And we waited.

An hour after we finished dinner, when the sun started to approach the horizon, the anxiety began.

Sydney was the first one to name it aloud. "He should be back by now, right?" she asked with concern in her voice. "I don't remember… Did we agree on a time to meet?"

"No time," I answered. "We just said meet back here when he was done."

"Well, the sun is going down, and surely he can't record past dark," Ethan added.

"He's probably wrapping up and will be on one of the next shuttles," I hoped, though I still worried something bad had happened, and I could tell that Sydney was becoming more nervous too.

Five buses and two more hours later Will still hadn't arrived back at the visitor's center. It had been completely dark for almost an hour, and we were running out of safe explanations for why Will hadn't returned. When the next empty shuttle arrived, I walked over to ask the shuttle driver when the last shuttle bus was.

"He said there's only two more shuttles running this last hour," I said once I had returned to sit with Sydney and Ethan at the picnic table, "and then they're done for the night. I think Sydney and I should take the car and drive around and look for Will, and Ethan, you should stay here and call us if you hear of anything or find him."

"Where are you going to look though?" Ethan asked. "It's pitch black outside of this parking lot, and we don't even know where he went to shoot footage. After this much time, he could be anywhere."

"Yeah, let's go," Sydney quickly agreed, slapped her hands on the table, and stood up. "I can't stand sitting here anymore. I don't know what else to do besides try to look ourselves. I'm just worried because it would be like Will to think that he had enough time to hike up some hard trail with all his heavy gear to get footage and make it back before dark, and I don't think he brought his headlamp with him."

I sighed, not knowing what to say to make things any better. "E, call us immediately if you find him, okay?" I urged.

"Yeah, I got you. Okay."

Sydney asked if she could drive, and we drove down into the darkness in silence. There were no streetlights in the park besides in the parking lot and far off in the distance where there was a small hotel, so Sydney turned on the brights to increase chances of seeing Will if he was walking on the side of the road. I didn't say any of my thoughts aloud because I figured Sydney was in the same place, but by this point I had started to consider extreme situations that would have caused him to lose his phone or get injured or knocked unconscious, or heaven forbid, bitten by a rattlesnake on some remote trail, and it wasn't helping my nerves in the slightest.

Being in the car made us feel at least a little more proactive and a little less helpless in the situation, but we had no luck. There was no sign of Will anywhere. We had no phone service, but even if we did, we didn't know who we needed to call for help. After the third time driving up and down the entire road, Sydney pulled over in the small parking lot of the hotel, and we both just looked straight ahead without saying anything.

My phone started buzzing and broke the silence. My heart pounded when I saw it was Ethan. I took a deep breath and answered it, hoping to hear good news. "Did you find him?" I put the call on speaker phone, and Sydney looked at me expectantly.

"What? Oh, no," Ethan replied. "I just wanted to tell you that I'm literally three feet away from four deer right now and it's so freaking cool!"

"Oh my gosh," Sydney huffed and rolled her eyes.

"Ethan! Seriously?" I sighed. "Okay, cool bro that you're near some cute deer, but in case you forgot, our friend is missing and that is a little more important than making sure the world knows that you are a deer whisperer right now."

"Dang, chill! I just thought it would lighten the mood!" Ethan replied. "I do have bad news though." His tone became more serious. "The last shuttle bus just came, and Will wasn't on it."

"Shit," whispered Sydney harshly, and she took a deep breath.

I sighed. "Okay. We'll head back that way." I hung up the phone.

"God I'm so frustrated!" Sydney exploded and threw her hands up. "This doesn't make any sense! I've been trying to come up with scenarios that would explain this, but I don't understand. Will is smart and knows how to communicate and would know what to do to get help if he needed it. I don't get it. Where is he?" She looked out the window.

I wanted to tell her that it was going to be fine, but I didn't want to lie. I had no idea, and now wasn't the time for fake consolation. I was scared, too.

Sydney was the first one to speak again. "I'm just going to pull in back in that lot where we originally parked this morning. At first I didn't think it was necessary to check there because we clearly told him to meet us at the visitor's center, but I guess there is a chance there was a miscommunication and for some reason Will might have ended up there."

She turned the car around and we pulled into the parking lot a few moments later. We didn't see anything as our headlights swept the first half of the empty parking lot, but as we drove across to the far side, we saw the silhouette of a person sitting on the sidewalk down the way.

"Oh my God. There he is. Ugh! I'm so pissed! Why would he come here? We never even talked about this parking lot!" Sydney grumbled and sighed as we drove up to him. Will stood up slowly as she got out of the car.

"What happened? You scared the hell out of us!" she sounded angry, almost on the verge of tears, but she walked up to him and immediately embraced him.

He sighed. "I thought we said this parking lot, and I didn't want to leave and go somewhere else to try to find you or we might have missed each other over and over again. I figured you had the car, so it made more sense that you would try to come to me instead of expecting me to walk around in the dark trying to find you, so I just stayed here and waited." I could hear the frustration in his voice.

"How long have you been here?" I asked, also feeling a little angry myself that we had been so worked up for so long for nothing.

"I got here right as the sun went down, so like two hours. Can we just go? I've got to get food in me ASAP. I'm starving and low blood sugar." Will was angry. Sydney was angry. I was angry. We didn't really know what else to say except that we were just glad he was okay.

We picked Ethan up from the visitor's center lot, and after riding in silence for a while, Ethan interjected, "Well, I mean at least he's not dead." He shrugged and laughed, but we didn't join him.

"Not now, Ethan." I tried to say it gently because I knew he was just trying to lighten the mood, but it was not the time.

Not only were we all on edge from losing Will and thinking for hours that he might have been dead, we'd also forgotten that we'd chosen to not re-set up camp that morning and still had all of our tents packed away in the car. So, on top of being frustrated, sore, and exhausted, we arrived back at the campground and had to set up camp in total darkness in the cold at 11:00 p.m. The four of us pitched our tents in complete silence, and none of us said anything else about the matter until morning.

{24}

MOUNTAIN OF MYSTERY

W E ALLOWED OURSELVES TO SLEEP IN, AND WE AWOKE to another sunny day. Once we were all up and had dragged ourselves to the picnic table, I still felt tension lingering in the air from the night before. Sydney finally named it, and we were all able to give our apologies to each other for the chaos, miscommunication, and hurt feelings involved in losing Will now that we were all less exhausted and angry.

Getting separated from Will was the first big hiccup in our trip that brought conflict, and I was grateful that we were able to communicate and resolve the tension almost right away. I told them I thought it was impressive that even with spending so much time with each other, especially considering all of the confined space in the car, that it took us this long to get in a fight, if one could even call it a fight. Everyone else laughed and agreed.

Taking two showers within the span of two days felt entirely excessive to me now, but we all took advantage of the bathroom facilities one last time. Over breakfasts of oatmeal, bananas, and peanut butter, we decided to drive to Moab, Utah next to visit Arches National Park, and per usual, we figured we would just find somewhere to sleep once we got there.

Will took the driver's seat to Moab, and I claimed a spot in the back seat opposite of Sydney for most of the drive so I could put my headphones in and not talk to anyone. I hadn't had much space to check in with myself since our night at Indian Gardens. I grabbed my journal and made an attempt to scrawl some thoughts in between the bumps and curves of the road.

07/26/15, Day 24 -

Most of the mountains in Zion National Park have spiritual and religious language in their names, and I wonder why that is. The East Temple, The West Temple, Angel's Landing, Mount Majestic, Church Mesa, Cathedral Mountain, The Great White Throne, Inclined Temple, and Mountain of Mystery. Seeing these names held me in a state of reflection about the idea of church going forward. Though it was more in the back of my mind while we were in the park, I have more time to sit with it now.

Many Christian churches seem like the roof needs to fall down so that sunlight may come in and expose the death and decay that many Christian communities have been neglecting for too long. The tame, safe, Americanized white Jesus presented in many churches doesn't actually save people. Jesus becomes a marketed product or a buzzword used to justify hoarding power and achieving economic gain for both churches and for America as a country instead of a way of life that actually leads people to freedom and liberation from the very "powers and principalities" that Christians claim to be against.

I've seen that being faithful to a specific form of church often gets blended and blurred with being faithful to a specific ideal for the country. Then eventually, some churchgoers make idols out of themselves and out of their country, blindly following a supposed "one right way" without critiquing the gap between what they claim to believe and how they choose to live. Finally, instead of being on the frontlines fighting for liberty, freedom, and justice for ALL as Jesus did, many churches in America become institutions that do nothing but perpetuate sexism, patriarchy, white supremacy, racism, ableism, homophobia, and xenophobia. Why would I ever want to go back to a Church that seems to eventually push everyone out, including Jesus?

For now, I don't think I can grow inside of the current Church walls, at least not inside the Church walls I have experienced. It's possible that I will never be able to go back. Even though part of me wants to live a spiritual life, I don't know if I will ever be able to feel safe inside a cathedral, or a temple, or at a church again. It will only be possible for me to exist in a Christian community again if it has expanded to make room for an all-inclusive, affirming, loving, authentic, vulnerable, justice-seeking Christianity. I want the real Jesus without the bullshit.

I don't want an all-knowing faith again. I don't want an answer to everything, with a cherry-picked Bible verse to back it up. I don't want to judge all people, thoughts, and ideas outside of Christianity to be "of the Devil" like I was taught. I don't want a religion that separates me from the neighbor that the Christ calls me to love. I don't want to cram God into such a tight box that it keeps me from being able to experience God in the world, and in other people, even people who use a different language to talk about God than I do. I know before I deconstructed, my strict idea of God was the idol that kept me from seeing the Christ, the Spirit, the Universal Love that is in all beings. I don't want to carry around that God anymore. Right now, I'm feeling more liberated and open than I've ever felt in my life.

In the meantime, there's no way I'll ever reconcile my relationship with Christianity unless I name what I'm feeling. Right now, I'm pissed. Most Christians make me angry, and I don't feel safe around them. I don't really want much to do with the Christian community, and I honestly have little hope that the Church will remain alive. It seems like it is dying, and I don't know if I have the energy to stay in it and help expose the decay so it might recover. Do I stay inside the old thing and try to heal it from the inside out, or do I leave it behind and try to make a new thing? I can't say any of this in a church community because it would just make people angry and feel personally attacked, but I don't know if people outside of Christian contexts will care to *listen either. Where does one go to find a safe community in the middle of deconstruction?*

We're stopping for gas. I'll end with this thought. There was a mountain in Zion called Mountain of Mystery. As I try to reimagine spiritual language that works for me, maybe I can start with calling God a Mountain of Mystery.

Oh Mountain of Mystery, who are you?
How tall are you?
What are you made of?
Do you go on forever?
Is there language big enough to hold you?
How do we seek you?
Do you speak to us?
Do you control us?
Or do we control you?
How do we reach you?
Is there only one path to your summit,
Or are the paths to you limitless?

Somehow, I hadn't noticed that my car was 3,000 miles past the need for an oil change until we got gas right outside of Moab. I guess I was used to only having to get oil changes two or three times a year because I didn't usually drive much. I did the math on the last bit of the drive to Moab, and in my twenty-four days since leaving Boone, my car had driven roughly 4,900 miles in around seventy-eight hours of driving, not including the miles and time spent driving around in each national park. Once I got cell service again I made sure to make an appointment for an oil change right away. Depending on which route we took back to Boone, we still had upwards of 2,000 miles left to drive, and I needed my car to make it.

After nine nights sleeping outside, we decided to completely defy our tight trip budgets and splurge on a cheap motel room for our night in Moab. Sometimes you just need a night to be a diva. That night, being a diva looked to us like walking down a smoky smelling, faded, red carpet hallway to a room with basic electricity and the now foreign concepts of air conditioning, beds with real mattresses more than an inch think, a full bathroom, a flushable toilet, a mirror, and no mosquitoes.

I don't know how he did it, but somehow within thirty seconds of stepping foot in the motel lobby Ethan was gone and back with a banana in his mouth, and four more in his hand.

"Ethan, what the heck? Where did you get those?" I shook my head in disbelief. "Did you make friends with a monkey in the bathroom or something?"

"Oh no, I just walked into the complimentary breakfast room, and the pantry door was open, so I took that as a sign that I was free to help myself."

I put my palm to my forehead. "Ethan. It's six o'clock in the evening. You can't just go into the motel breakfast pantry and take whatever you want! Even if it is unlocked!" I was beside myself, but I couldn't help but laugh.

He shrugged his shoulders nonchalantly as he tended to do and took another giant bite of banana. "Too late. You want one?" He held out a banana to me, smiling with banana-filled cheeks. "Come on, you know you want one," he teased.

I wanted to say no, but even though we just ate, I was already hungry again. My body was trying to make up for all the thousands of calories I had burned during all of our hiking excursions. I rolled my eyes, looked behind my shoulder to make sure the coast was clear, and snatched one from his hand. It was gone before I reached the motel room.

After relaxing for a while in our foreign beds, we peeled our dusty bodies from the stark white bedsheets and piled into the car to catch the sunset at Arches National Park down the road. Again, I had no idea what to expect and when we drove in; I was completely shocked.

We parked at the Windows area, which was the most concentrated area of natural sandstone arches in the park. We finished our short exploration by climbing up to the famous Double Arch, where two insect-like legs of sandstone stretch out from the same stone, creating two separate arch bridges right next to each other. Standing there, looking around at all of the rock, I understood why Arches National Park would be a rock climber's paradise. The sandstone was rough, perfect for a solid grip. I wanted to climb everything, but I was tired, and my ankle ached from twisting it on a slippery rock in the Narrows the day before, so I figured I would just have to train and get really good at rock climbing and come back.

"I feel like this could be one of the planets in Star Wars or something," I said to Ethan as we walked behind Will and Sydney.

"Yeah, the rock formations are so random. Some of them look like they defy gravity," said Ethan.

"The Double Arch is actually in the opening scene of *Indiana Jones and the Last Crusade,*" Will called back to us. "Did you know that?"

"Whoa, no way!" Ethan exclaimed. "Emily and I watched those movies like a thousand times growing up!"

Will chuckled. "Same. Hey, when we get back to the car I think I'm going to set up my gear down on those big flat rocks on the right to get some footage of Sydney walking as the sun sets for the music video I'm working on. I don't know how long it will take. Are y'all okay with hanging out until we're done?"

"Yeah, no worries," I replied. "We'll probably just grab a seat on a rock off to the side and watch the sunset."

When we got back near the car, Ethan and I sat down as the sky began to fade from an orange to pink to purple haze over the mountains in the distance.

"Did you watch the sunset the two days you were apart from us?" I asked, wondering if Ethan had kept the pact.

"Yep, once at an overlook in Flagstaff and once at the Grand Canyon."

I smiled. "You know, it's been really special to share this experience with you, E. It's been the first time we have actually hung out as adults. I can't believe you're eighteen now."

"Yeah, I know. I've felt eighteen for a while though," he said. "I'm tired of being around kids from high school, and just people in Athens in general. Everyone's the same and wears the same stuff and does the same things. It's so boring."

"I felt like that too senior year. That's why I defied everyone's expectations for me to go to some fancy Ivy League university and chose to go to App State—to get away from it all." I paused for a moment to look back at the horizon. "Do you think you'll go to college in the fall? You got accepted to North Georgia right?" I asked.

"Yeah, I've been thinking about it, but everyone from our high school goes there, and I want something different. Part of me just wants to work for a while. I feel like I've been in school my whole life, you know? I've never had a chance to just work and figure out what I want to do or what I care about. All I've done with my time in high school is play basketball, trying to get a scholarship, but now that that's not happening anymore, I don't know what I should do instead."

"I think it's important to have a season away from school for some self-discovery. I think its stupid that society puts so much pressure on us to know what we want to do with our lives at eighteen, like we should be able to choose a major right away that we know we are good at and love, and we should immediately go into a career that we will work for the rest of our lives," I said. "Yet people rarely question it, and that is what's scary to me." I shook my head. "I don't think I want that kind of life. I told you I'm taking the fall off, and honestly, I haven't told mom and dad this, but since being away on this trip and realizing how much I want to do before I'm locked down in a career, I don't know if I'm going to go back to school in the spring either… Part of me just wants to work and travel for as long as I can."

"I'd do it if I were you," Ethan agreed.

"I don't want to live my life just waiting for retirement. I'm terrified of becoming the person that always pushes my dreams aside so that I can be a workhorse playing the game of the system."

"How will you afford it though? I mean, if you don't have a degree, and you want to travel? It's not like traveling is cheap."

"Well, you really don't need that much money to live if you're fine not buying beyond what you absolutely need. I think if you prioritize the right things, anyone can make traveling work. I made minimum wage at App, was fully paying all of my own bills, minus my phone bill and health insurance since that was included in my college loans, and still saved up enough to travel for a month. You just have to be okay with not buying so much excess stuff. No new clothes unless something breaks, not going out to eat all the time just because you don't want to cook, not spending a ton of money on stuff you don't need. Minimalism has really changed how accessible travel feels to me."

"If you can make it work, I don't see why not," Ethan shrugged.

"Have you thought about taking a semester off?" I asked.

"A couple times, but I don't know what I would do. I don't want to be just living in Athens while all of my other friends are in class at community college or UGA."

"You could move to Boone," I blurted out. I hadn't even thought of it until I said it.

He paused and raised his eyebrows. "Well, I mean, Boone is great. And after being in Colorado at camp in June and now out here with you guys, getting to stay in the mountains would be awesome."

"You should do it!" I got excited. "E, oh my gosh, please move to Boone! It would be way better than staying in Athens. There are always jobs opening up with students changing their class schedules. You know me, and now you know Will and Sydney. And you would love all of my friends!" I felt a slight prick of pain when the last statement flowed out of my mouth. It was true. Ethan would love all of my friends, but it hurt to be reminded that my relationship with them might never be the same, especially after this trip.

"I'll think about it," Ethan trailed off.

"Well, I'm really glad you came out here, E. This trip wouldn't have been the same without you. I've missed spending time with you. I haven't known how to bridge the gap once I became," I paused for a second, "distant. I was scared you would be mad at me."

Ethan raised one questioning eyebrow. "Why would I be mad at you? I'm glad I came too."

"I don't know. I guess I've never really been able to say it before. But I thought you might be mad at me for not being there for you like I should have been when things got really bad with mom and dad. I know I kind of just went to college and pretended like everything was fine because I was distracted. I wasn't surrounded by it all the time anymore, but you were still in it, and I never asked you how you were doing. Then everything with Cam happened, and I've been wrapped up in that. I just felt like I didn't know what to say, so I didn't say anything. And I'm sorry. I should have."

He sighed and nodded. "Yeah, I mean it was hard, but it was manageable. Basketball kept me busy, and once I could drive, I would just hang out with friends a lot, so it wasn't too bad. But thanks for saying that, Em. I never was mad at you or anything. I just figured you had your new college life, and I had mine at home with mom and dad. But it did suck for a while."

"Yeah, it did. I felt like I had to be strong for you while I was home, so I never was open about how mom and dad were affecting me. You seemed like you were doing okay, and I was scared to bring it up with you and make things harder than they already were. After their big fights mom would come into my room and ask me not to talk about it with anyone, and I assumed that meant you, too. I see that I was wrong now, but I couldn't see it then. And I'm sorry. Are things still bad at home?" I asked.

"It's not your fault. It was hard on all of us, and I don't think anyone knew how to handle it, including mom and dad. It's not terrible, but they definitely still are always in a fight it seems like."

"Do you think they'll ever split up?" I asked.

"No." He shook his head. "I used to. But they seem pretty committed to figuring it out. That's what they always say, at least."

I sighed. "I wish it was easier. For you. For me. For all of us. But family is hard. Love is hard. Humans are hard. And sometimes choosing to love family in the midst of each other's pain and give grace for each other's shortcomings is the hardest. Know that I'm always here for you, E. I want to be more present in your life, especially as you make this fun transition into adulthood. A lot of things are going to change for both of us these next couple years, and I want to stay close through it all, okay? I'm just really grateful for you, and I'm really proud of you. I don't tell you that enough."

"Aw come here." He leaned over and gave me a side hug. "Thanks, Em." Ethan had never been one to have long emotional conversations, and that was okay with me. I could tell that he heard me out, and he genuinely appreciated the fact that we could both name it. I was thankful, too. Part of this giant weight I'd carried by believing I was a terrible sister just slipped off my shoulders.

Ethan looked over to Sydney and Will. Sydney was twirling, and her hair flowed as gracefully as her arms in the wind. Will was crouched with the camera, moving along with her.

"So, are they gonna date or what?" Ethan blurted out.

"Ha!" I cackled. "That's hilarious. I've been wondering the same thing," I admitted. "I'm surprised you picked up on it honestly."

"Well, you said she's modeled for him for years, right? So, they spend a lot of time together. And he's cool. And she's cool. She's close to his family. And they obviously have a lot in common if they both wanted to do an extreme trip like this."

I nodded. "My thoughts exactly. I've been tempted to ask Sydney about it, but I feel like we're still getting to know each other, and I don't know if that would be too forward."

"I'll ask her," he said confidently.

"Oh my gosh. Um, no. You absolutely will not. Please don't!" I nudged his arm lightly with my fist. "You're going to do it so bluntly like you always do and it's going to be so awkward! I'll ask her before the end of the trip."

"Promise?" Ethan stared at me expectantly.

"Promise," I affirmed, though I wasn't excited about what I just signed up for.

"Okay. Then I won't," said Ethan. "But they're totally into each other."

"I agree. It's been really funny trying to be okay with the fact that I've had to watch my travel companions fall in love literally before my eyes this entire trip while I'm over here trying to grieve, process, and heal from a really toxic relationship and break-up," I emphasized dramatically, and we both chuckled. "No, I'm happy for them, really. They seem like they would be really great together, though I have been super thankful that you are here to balance the group out. It would probably be pretty hard if it was just me alone with Will and Sydney the whole time. Plus, your extroversion and humor helps bring us introverts out of our fantasy lands in our heads."

"Oh my gosh don't get me started! You guys literally never talk! I don't understand it. You're always contemplating some deep, complex thing, and I can do that sometimes, but jeez I can't do that all day, every day! Y'all are so weird!" We both laughed.

"Weird is one way to put it," I grinned.

I watched Sydney and Will laughing as they finished the last shot and smiled softly. I was grateful that I picked up on their vibes early in the trip because it saved me from feeling any sort of competition with Sydney. I'd been more present with where I was and able to grieve the things I needed to grieve.

{25}

ME TOO

E THAN AND I TOLD WILL AND SYDNEY BEFORE WE WENT to bed that we might watch the sunrise with them inside the park. When their alarms went off at 5:15 a.m., I could barely make myself get up, and Ethan didn't budge, so I told them to just go ahead without us. Plus, if they actually were a thing, having some alone time to watch a romantic sunrise might be nice for them.

Sydney and Will came back to the motel around 8:30 and joined Ethan and I at our table in the continental breakfast room. We were eating some legally acquired bananas along with other average motel eats that seemed gourmet to us after camping.

As Will and Sydney sat down, I asked, "So, how was the sun—"

Before I could even finish the sentence, water suddenly erupted from Sydney's mouth and spewed all over the table. It barely missed my face, but some sprinkles settled on my arms resting on the table. All four of us were caught off guard, even Sydney. She looked up afterward, her eyes wide and her mouth open. She blushed and quickly wiped the water dribbling from her chin, half coughing, half choking, while the rest of us sat in a brief moment of silent shock. Then, all at the same time, we lost it, laughing hysterically until our stomachs hurt. Everyone in the room stared at us.

"Aah, gross!" Ethan scrunched his nose up.

"Jeez, maybe I shouldn't have asked," I muttered, faking dramatic concern. "Maybe the sunrise wasn't so great. Did I hit a nerve and your bodily response was to spit your water all over the table? Is that what just happened?" I asked, still cackling.

"No! I seriously have no idea!" she squealed, still laughing between her coughs. "It was one of those instances where water hit that specific spot in the back of my throat in the wrong way and it was an automatic reflex to spit it out! I'm so sorry! There was no way I could keep it in, and I couldn't grab my cup fast enough!" We all laughed harder.

"Well, *I* thought the sunrise was great, but apparently Sydney thought otherwise," Will joked. "The truth comes out, I guess."

"Oh stop," she nudged him, and the pink hue in her cheeks deepened slightly. "It didn't have anything to do with the sunrise. Anyway, to answer your question, Em, the sunrise was beautiful, and Will got some really good footage."

"Yeah, the light was *perfect*, and it was nice to be outside without it being blazing hot," Will nodded.

I was scared Ethan was going to take the opportunity to ask some over-the-top question like 'did you guys make out or something, so I changed the subject. "Good! I'm glad. So, the plan for today is to get an oil change on our way out and drive to Brekenridge?"

"Yeah," Will answered, "there's a free wilderness campsite not too far from Brekenridge that I've been to before. We can hike the backside of Grays Peak from there."

"Oh, cool. I didn't realize you'd been before," said Sydney.

"Yeah. I did it a couple years ago," Will replied. "The summit is a little under 14,300 feet I think."

"They call mountains over 14,000 feet '14'ers,' right?" I asked.

"Yep," Will answered.

"Sweet. My first 14'er!" Ethan grinned.

"Mine too," I nodded.

"Same," Sydney said.

"Oh man. Y'all are going to love it," Will smiled. "The view from the summit is like you're on another planet."

"You're sure you don't want to go to one you haven't hiked before?" I asked.

"No." Will shook his head and took a swig of orange juice. "It's spectacular. The campsite is in complete wilderness, and few people are ever there. It will be worth it. I'd love to go back. Plus, it saves us a ton of research because there are over fifty 14'ers in Colorado, so knowing where we are going and where we can sleep for free is better than picking one at random not knowing if there's any camping around."

"I agree with that. Grays peak sounds good to me," Sydney confirmed. "Does anyone need anything? I'm going to get another bagel."

Will and I said no thanks, but Ethan took her up on her offer and asked for a toasted bagel with extra cream cheese.

"I guess all of this hiking has probably been good training for us," I noted. "I've heard hiking at that elevation can be hard on your body."

"For sure. We'll still need to get to Breckenridge with enough time to acclimatize to keep ourselves from getting altitude sickness," Will warned. "And we need to pound water today and tomorrow to help our bodies adjust."

"That means Emily and Sydney are going to have to stop and pee a million times on the drive though," Ethan whined.

"Oh hush." I made a face at him.

"We all probably will," Will laughed, "but it will be worth it. Altitude sickness is not something you want to mess with."

"Shall we pack and head out?" I asked once Sydney came back with the bagels. We packed our freshly washed clothes into our stinky backpacks, performed trunk tetris at lightning speed, and tried our best to get to our oil change appointment on time.

"I missed this so much!" I stretched my arms up high when I got out of the car at our campsite that night. We had driven up a long, steep gravel road which ran next to the most bright turquoise mountain stream I had ever seen. When the road leveled out slightly, we started seeing clearings for campsites and chose one of the first ones. We feared that my Jeep without four-wheel drive would be out of its element if we pushed further.

Will wanted to get footage of Sydney in the valley before sunset, so we set up camp quickly and drove further up the road to the Grays Peak trailhead. Ethan walked down to the right to explore a small side stream, and Will and Sydney walked off the trail into the longer grasses of the field to set up.

"Watch out for rattlesnakes!" I called after them as I turned to find a boulder where I could sit, following my own advice.

"Oh my God. Don't even say that!" Sydney squealed, and Will and I laughed. I took a moment to take in the sweeping valley filled with a rainbow of wildflowers and the towering, spiked mountains reflecting the soft, golden hour light off their snowy peaks above me. I opened my journal.

07/27/15, Day 25 -

I wouldn't have changed anything about this trip, but I am noticing my fatigue and know that the time for the trip to end is soon. My body is tired, and I find myself craving physical rest, though I notice that my mind is oddly much more at rest than it was when I left—almost four weeks ago. I wonder what life will be back in Boone. I assume we will be back within a week. Part of me feels sad that it is almost over, but an equal part of me can feel in my gut that whatever time we have left will be enough.

I know there will still be days going forward where I feel trapped in toxic thought cycles and overwhelmed with spiraling thoughts, but I must continue to learn how to find my way to the still, safe space at the middle of the storm in my mind, where I can exist in a state of peace without always having to be lost somewhere in a rabbit hole of existential angst. I must learn to come and go, not letting myself be bothered by the tornado of thoughts that often shows up unannounced. I must learn how to sit and observe the tornado without being sucked up into it and identifying with it, knowing that it will pass eventually.

For so long I've made my mind the enemy. I resented it being a part of me, but the more I push down and sit with the ugliest and scariest parts of myself at my rock bottom, the less anxiety I feel in solitude. I can say to my thoughts, I love you, and you are welcome here. Though I might not enjoy all of the thoughts and emotions that show up inside of me, I know they will eventually pass. Maybe not today, or tomorrow, or next month, or maybe not even next year, but they will pass and peace will come again.

I wonder if the cloud of emotion from my nightmare that I feared so much doesn't actually have much to do with Cam at all. I wonder if the cloud was just my own darkness, the shadows of my life that I didn't have the courage to face. For so many months I have been running away from the cloud because I believed if I actually turned around and looked at it in the face, it would consume me. I had it all wrong.

Throughout this trip I have been finding the courage to face the cloud for the first time, to ask it what it wants to tell me. I have started to listen, and though it has been so hard, I am still here. My darkness is a part of me, but it is not all of me. Facing the cloud and giving the darkness permission to take up space does not mean giving it power to define my reality. It means telling the truth and giving those parts of me a safe place to have a voice so that they might be heard instead of being repressed and turning into the ghosts that haunt me.

I think all of our clouds, our darkness, our demons, our shadows want us to do is to tell the truth. They need us to put language to them so that they can show us that they're not as ugly as we think them to be, that they're just the parts of us who have been rejected, denied love, kicked out, traumatized, ostracised by whatever system we have let define who we can and cannot be. It is the resisting them that allows them to haunt us. It is the repressing them that gives them power over our joy. It is running away from them that suffocates us, not the co-existing with them.

Facing the clouds of our lives, our systems, our institutions might be the most intimidating and scary thing that we ever do, but it might be the only way to live in integrated freedom and wholeness, where we can use the darkness to inform and show us where light needs to be let in.

I heard the crunch of Ethan's footsteps on the gravel behind me. "Find anything interesting at the stream?" I asked as he sat down next to me.

"Nah, just skipped some rocks for a bit. And I tried to see how long I could leave my hand in the water. I only lasted twenty-two seconds before I thought I was going to have to stick my hand in a fire to get blood to return to it."

"Wow, sounds *really* fun," I said sarcastically, and we both laughed.

He looked over at Will trailing behind Sydney with the camera as she twirled in the meadow. It appeared as though she sculpted the wind with her hands.

"So, are you gonna ask Sydney about Will or what?" he pressed. "You're running out of time!"

I sighed. "I know. I thought about asking her on the hike tomorrow. I think it's funny that you are so invested in the romantic drama of our group dynamics."

"I mean hey, if they get married one day at least you can take the credit for inviting them on the trip that made them fall in love." He raised his eyebrows.

"Uh, I think that's jumping a little ahead of ourselves," I laughed. "Come on. I think they're wrapping up."

Will and Ethan joined Sydney and I at the fire to make dinner.

"Wow, lasagna! Going all out today I see?" I joked when I saw their freeze-dried backpacking meals which were much more expensive than our average beans and rice.

"I figured since I barely absorbed any of the calories of that burger at lunch today before it exploded out of me I might need some extra calories before our big hike tomorrow," Will shrugged. (We had grabbed burgers on our drive from Moab, and none of our digestive systems handled the sudden grease well.) "And I saw this at the gear shop we walked through today, and I was like yep," he nodded and grinned, "this is the night."

"And once I saw him grab it off the shelf, I couldn't say no either," Ethan said.

Sydney and I made more instant rice noodles with a green Thai curry sauce that was warmed and ready to eat within minutes, and we teased Will and Ethan while they had to wait an eternity of fifteen minutes for their backpacking meal to be ready.

As Will and Ethan scarfed down their pouches of lasagna, Sydney and I boiled water for tea. We finished our evening by the fire as the last bit of daylight faded away.

"What's our game plan tomorrow?" Sydney asked.

"We should wake up as early as possible and take it as slow as we can to avoid getting altitude sickness," Will replied.

"How early?" Ethan asked reluctantly.

"We should be on the trail within an hour of sunrise," answered Will, and Ethan groaned.

"We have to seize the day!" I encouraged. "It's the grand finale of our adventure! Grays Peak is probably the last big hike we'll do before we are mostly just driving home our last couple days, right?"

"Yeah, that's what I was thinking too," agreed Sydney. "This is the last thing that I had in mind as far as intense physical activity goes. I don't think I have much left in me."

"My body is wiped, too," Will said.

"I'm a little sad that we're already near the end," Sydney sighed. "I feel like we have been out here for months, but at the same time I feel like Will and I just got to San Diego yesterday. I don't know if I'm ready to go home," she sighed. "This trip has been everything I needed and more."

"Me too," I said. "I'm glad you were bold and asked to come with even though we barely knew each other when I left. And somehow we all still haven't killed each other!"

"There's still time," Ethan noted nonchalantly, and we all laughed.

"Ethan, you have definitely been the comic relief on this trip," Will said and took another sip of tea.

"Well yeah, I had to because you guys sure as heck weren't going to speak! I have literally never met more quiet people in my life. I don't know how the three of you do it." Ethan shook his head, and we all laughed.

"You know you love us. It was good practice for you to be around introverts! Everyone needs silence, we just need much more of it than most people." *And my internal space has been a little more occupied than normal.* I paused for a moment. "Oh yeah! Ethan, are you going to tell Will and Sydney your big news?"

Ethan looked confused. "What are you talking about?"

"Your move." I smiled and raised my eyebrows up and down.

"Oh," he chuckled. "Em thinks I should take a gap semester and move to Boone."

"Oh my gosh. Yes!" Sydney got excited.

"Dude. You should *totally* move to Boone. You would love it!" Will urged.

"We know a lot of people that might be able to get you a place to stay, and we're like, your favorite people now, so you'll also be close to us. Even better," Sydney joked and giggled.

Ethan laughed. "Yeah, well Em and I were talking, and I think it could be really good for me to just have some time to work and think about what I actually might want to study without this huge pressure to decide and pay a lot of money for college right away. I have no idea what I want to do."

"I still have no idea what I want to do, and I'm twenty-five and already graduated from college," noted Sydney. "I wished I would have taken time off before college. College will always be there. Living in an amazing mountain town with a really great community won't be. You won't regret taking time off. Don't let anyone scare you into thinking that you absolutely have to go to college right away to be successful. You have so much time."

"I'm becoming pretty persuaded honestly. You might have a new neighbor, as long as y'all aren't too tired of me yet," Ethan grinned. "Well," he stood up and stretched, "I don't know how you want to be awake right now. I'm exhausted. I'm going to call it a night." He started cleaning up his dinner mess. "Are y'all going to stay up for a bit?"

"For a little bit, I think," I answered.

"Well, goodnight," Ethan called as he walked toward the car. "Beat on the window when it's time to get up. My phone is dead so I can't set an alarm."

"Goodnight!" I called.

Once Ethan shut the passenger door, Will asked, "Do you know what you're going to do when you get back to Boone, Emily?"

"Nope. Not at all. I assume I'll get a random job for the fall— something that will pay the bills and give me enough time to read all of the books I've been wanting to read and listen to the hours of podcast interviews I have saved."

"What books have you been into lately?" Will asked.

I was scared to be honest, but I just decided to go for it. The trip was nearing an end, and if they didn't take it well, we only had a few days left for things to be awkward. My heart rate increased. I looked toward the car to make sure Ethan was inside with the door closed.

"Actually, most of the stuff I've been into lately is within the genres of religion, philosophy, and psychology," I began. "I haven't really said it explicitly with you both yet, but I've been in a pretty intense head-space the past couple months, beyond what happened with Cam. Most of it has been trying to process that I don't really think I believe in Christianity anymore. Well, at least not in the same way as I used to. My old Christian language doesn't work for me anymore, so I guess I'm searching to see if I can find a new language that does."

I took a deep breath and anxiously braced myself for rebuke. Would they think I was a demon-inhabited crazy person?

Will smirked like he had a secret. "Me too."

I didn't realize how much I had been longing to hear someone say those two words until he said them.

"Wait. Really?" *Holy shit. I was right.* "That's why you quit worship team?"

"I should have way before I did. I started deconstructing my faith two years ago, but after spending my whole life in that church, with constant pressure from my parents who have always been in leadership roles, and with the added community expectations that came with my position as a worship leader, it took me that long to work up the cour-age to be honest with myself. I don't know what my view of God is now, but it definitely is not from an evangelical Christian place where Jesus is the only right way to *"go to heaven."* I have only told my parents the tip of the iceberg, but it has been a huge deal in my family."

"Wow." I took a deep breath. I was still a little shocked. "I've want-ed to ask you so badly, but I didn't know how to bring it up. What has it been like with your parents?"

"It's been hard recently. My dad doesn't really know how to re-spond. I mean, him and my mom both say they still love me, and they're praying for me, but it's become this giant elephant in the room that no one in my family knows how to acknowledge, so for now, we just aren't. I was a little on edge around Keith and Heather since they're close to my parents. I know they've talked about it with them. Mom and dad don't confront me about it anymore. I'm not remotely interested in debating the literal meaning of Bible verses, and it is hard to want to talk to them about what I think when they think that it's something that can just be prayed out of me, like I have a disease or something," Will sighed.

"I think I have written that exact line in my journal!" I exclaimed. "Telling my parents I didn't believe in Christianity anymore was one of the hardest days of my life. I feel like it changed everything. I don't know if there's something harder than looking into the eyes of the people that raised you and telling them that you are turning away from the life they want for you, and they feel like you are betraying them when you're just following the way you feel led to go."

Will was nodding his head. "I know how that is, for sure. I feel like I'm under a giant spotlight in my family now, like everyone is tip-toeing around me, like my thoughts are contagious and if they get too close, the demonic, as they call it, will jump on to them too."

"Yep. I know that all too well." Tears welled in my eyes. Between the sudden feeling of solidarity and the sudden reminder of the pain of isolation, I couldn't say much more without crying. I looked across the fire at Sydney, who wasn't saying much. I felt worried not knowing what that meant. She didn't seem angry per se, but her facial expression was still hard for me to interpret.

"I haven't told Ethan yet," I warned them. "I don't want it to change our relationship too. I don't want to scare him. I don't want him to think that I'm crazy or that he should keep his distance from me. I could have brought it up with you when Ethan wasn't with us in the Grand Canyon, but I was dealing with other stuff then."

"You've said some things in our conversations in the past that have made me wonder where you were at with religion, but I didn't know how to bring it up either," Will admitted. "It's hard in tight-knit Christian communities where opening up to the wrong people can mean risking social exile, being labeled as dangerous, losing friends, or all of those things together. I didn't expect you to respond in any of those ways, but it's still hard for me to bring up too, so I get it. Sydney and I have briefly talked about our changing perspectives on Christianity as a whole, but like you said, it's hard having a concrete conversation about God when your old spiritual language doesn't mean anything to you anymore, but you haven't constructed new ways of expressing what you believe or think now."

"Yeah, that's the main thing that I was going to say," Sydney chimed in, and I felt more relieved knowing that she hadn't been sitting there waiting to spew judgement on us. Even though she and I had built a significant amount of trust over the course of the trip, I was scared of losing love by being honest.

Sydney continued, "I haven't talked much about it either, mostly because I really don't know what to say yet. I don't know how to describe where I'm at. I just know that there's a lot about church that makes me angry, and there's a lot that I don't know, and I don't know how to have helpful conversations when all of my answers are just that I don't know."

"I think being able to acknowledge that you don't know is the right place to be," Will urged. "I think that's where all healthy spiritual transformation begins."

"It's a foreign place to be," Sydney replied, "and an uncomfortable place to be when your entire life you falsely believed that you had all of the answers, and that they were the only ones that could be right and true."

"Exactly," I sighed. "I just can't believe that I've existed around you both for months, and we've all been hiding, not knowing that we've been in similar places. I thought for sure I was the only one in our community that felt this way."

"Same," Will nodded and chuckled.

"Me too. Though I think you guys are further along in your questioning than me," Sydney said. "I've only begun to dig deeper in the past couple months. Right now I'm mostly just overwhelmed and angry."

I nodded in solidarity. "I feel that. Especially the anger. I'm scared if I talk to Christians right now, I'll just spew rage, so I feel like it might be some time before I'm ready to have a productive conversation with anyone who still identifies as a fundamentalist, evangelical Christian without it turning into an angry debate. What do we do in the meantime though? I've been thinking about the community I want to be a part of, one that is inclusive and not exclusively Christian, open to discussion about anything, and intellectually honest without claiming to have all of the answers."

"I don't see it happening in the Church," Sydney replied. "I find myself constantly going back and forth between wanting to try to keep church as a part of my life even amidst the anger or just leaving it all together."

I nodded. "Deconstruction will continue to happen, and probably for a while before reconstruction begins. Now that I'm fully in the midst of analyzing religion and spirituality, it's led me to realize that I have so many other perceptions about the world, outside of religion, that need to be deconstructed and analyzed—many of which have been handed to me by my family, or my school, or by my status in society. The more that I realize I was handed a biased and limited story of my religion, the more I realize that my entire narrative of the world is biased and limited," I admitted. "I don't even know the full story of the history of this country except from the one, white, colonialist, European meta-narrative of history that we learn in school. It feels like there are now a dozen different things I need to analyze and critique in myself—my religion, my idea of race, my perceptions of gender and sexuality, and what it means to be a privileged white person who was born in America. Getting slapped in the face with all of that for the first time at twenty years-old, when I am trying to figure out how to pursue life as an adult is so damn confusing. I don't know where to start. There is so much that I have to re-learn about reality and my position in it before I can commit to a degree or a career or a specific way of life, but I don't know what to do in the meantime while I learn on my own." I exhaled harshly. "Sorry for ranting. It's just a lot, and it has been bottled up inside of me for so long because I haven't had anyone in my life that was safe enough to talk to about all of this."

"Oh no, I totally agree with you," Will urged. "It's overwhelming and confusing, because once you no longer believe that there is one correct and exclusive voice of truth and wisdom, you suddenly have a lot of options for starting points of study, anywhere from philosophy to science to religion to anthropology to psychology to history, and each of those has a thousand subsets."

"Exactly," I nodded. "I know deconstruction is important, but I'm scared that it's never going to end." I paused and stared at the fire.

No one spoke for a few moments. I think we all shared the weight of that fear.

"If we didn't have to get up in seven hours to hike a giant mountain, I'd love to continue this conversation," Will began, "but we should probably go to sleep."

"Yeah, I agree." I nodded. "Soon my brain is going to be too tired to form concrete thoughts about anything."

"Yeah, I literally can't think anymore," Sydney chuckled. "Sorry I haven't said much. I'm really tired, but I definitely support the conversation. Honestly, just listening to you guys helps."

"Well, I can't tell you how much this conversation has meant to me. It's so easy when you're trapped in your head for too long to think that you will be alone and isolated forever."

"Yeah, the more I study and read, there seems to be a consciousness revolution right now," Will began, "in all sorts of traditions, even non-religious thinkers, as if a giant wave of people is waking up to the fact that the institutions we've centered life around, especially in the West, hurt more than help, and perpetuate systems of violence and oppression and tribal mentality that breeds hatred and fear. I don't know where all of this is going to lead, but with the world changing as rapidly as it is, it's an exciting time to be alive right now."

"I just know that I have to keep talking about this, and preferably with real humans outside of the voices in my head and the podcast hosts I listen to, which have been my only source of real conversation for way too long," I muttered, and we all laughed.

"We will," Will encouraged, and Sydney nodded. We made eye contact across the dancing flames between us and smiled. It was a gift to feel seen.

Though I couldn't have named it then, all I longed to hear throughout my deconstruction was that I wasn't the only one. I needed to hear confirmation that the path I'd taken was normal and good, and it was okay to feel how I felt. Hearing the simple phrase "me too" changed everything for me. I felt hope that I could have a sustainable community again one day. Even though I didn't know what that would look like long-term, I now knew that it began with Will and Sydney. After spending months feeling alone, this washed me in a wave of comfort, and my fear of being honest began to trickle out of my bones.

{26}

THE THINGS THAT
CHANGE US

I WOKE UP IN A DAZE. I HEARD A MUFFLED, STRANGE, DREAM-like voice saying something about spruce or juice or a goose. Or was it a guy named Bruce? As I opened my eyes, I realized the foggy voice was Will's, and what he was really whispering was, "Moose! Moose! Emily! Sydney! Get up! There's a moose!"

I moaned and looked at my watch. *6:08 a.m.*

"Oh, shut up Will! You just want us to come out of the tent so we can get ready and start hiking," I muttered and pulled my sleeping bag over my head to warm it again with my breath. I'd only slept in short stretches throughout the night because the cold Colorado air made it almost impossible to stay comfortable without shivering, and I was not ready to leave my cocoon yet.

"No. Seriously," he whispered harshly. "There's a giant, freaking moose right in our campsite! Hurry up! Look before it runs away!"

Will wasn't normally one to lie or be dramatic, so Sydney and I decided that we better wiggle out of our sleeping bags quickly in case he was actually serious. We unzipped the tent slowly, trying to make as little noise as possible. From the opening on Sydney's side of the tent, we looked through the soft pink light of dawn and saw the body of a dark brown giant in our midst. The bull moose easily stood at six feet tall. He was about fifteen yards away in the middle of the grassy clearing to the right of our campsite. His massive head was turned toward us, and a soft puff of steam floated up from his nostrils with every exhale. His antlers spread in a wide crown over his ears, and I was too captivated to think about counting the points. Beholding the gaze of a moose was slightly terrifying, but it was mostly magical and mesmerizing.

"Holy shit! That thing is huge," I gasped. "I've never seen one!" I looked over at Will, and he hadn't taken his eyes off the moose. A giant grin was still spread across his face.

"Oh my goodness," Sydney whispered reverently. "Me either. It's gorgeous."

I laughed. "Look at Ethan." I pointed to the passenger's side of the car, where Ethan had cleared a face-sized spot in the foggy window to observe the moose from. He looked over at us and made a face that expressed something along the lines of, "Can you believe this is happening right now?"

Our moose visitor stood there for only a brief moment before deciding he was done with his grass breakfast and uninterested in hanging out around us any longer. Though he weighed over a thousand pounds, he swung his giant rump around with ease and grace. He trotted through the tall grass and disappeared behind the tree line on the far side of the clearing. Though the moose was gone, the fluttering feeling in my chest lingered a few moments longer. Even looking back now, I still don't quite have words for it, but in that moment I was certain I'd experienced something holy.

Ethan opened the car door and got out. "Wow, that was insane!" he hollered as he walked over to us, his disheveled car bed head hair curls sticking straight out over his ears. "I woke up and that thing was basically in my face staring through the passenger's side window! It scared the hell out of me! It was as tall as the car at least!"

"That's a wild awakening for sure," Sydney chuckled.

"Good one," I giggled.

"I can't believe that just happened. I've always wanted to see a moose in the wild. And we got to see a male moose! He was giant! I wish y'all could have seen it when it was closer." Will's eyes were still wide with wonder.

"How did you know it was here? Were you still in your tent when you heard it?" Sydney asked.

"No, I walked down to the river once I woke up, and when I crested the hill on my way back to the campsite, I looked up from the ground and met the giant eyes of that thing, twenty feet away from me, literally in the middle of the campsite. So massive and beautiful. And also a little scary," Will admitted.

"Wow. I can't imagine," Sydney stammered. "I probably would have peed my pants. What was it like, to just casually walk up on giant moose first thing in the morning?"

"I froze in terror at first. But some awe eventually got mixed in when I was pretty sure it wasn't going to charge and trample me to death," Will laughed nervously. "I just stood completely still and tried to give off the least challenging or threatening body language I could, and after what felt like years it finally turned around. Once it seemed like he was going to continue walking away from me, I finally was able to breathe again. I think Ethan was up by that point, but I didn't start whispering to you and Emily until the moose was far enough away that I felt comfortable speaking," Will explained.

"Yeah, I was up by then. And I got the real front-row view," Ethan enthused, "but even though I was locked safely inside a thick wall of metal and glass it was still pretty intimidating. I didn't realize moose were so tall! Or is it meese? Mooses?" We all laughed.

"Yeah, that one always confused me in school, too," said Sydney.

"I think it's moose." Ethan shrugged. "Anyway, too bad you didn't sleep in the car, or you would have seen it," he bantered, rubbing it in my face after I gave him so much crap about choosing to sleep in the car instead of sleeping outside on a camping trip.

"Yeah, okay. There's your *one* perk for sleeping in the car," I nudged him playfully. "I am a little bummed that I didn't get to see it so close, but I do think a rare moose sighting first thing on the day that we climb the tallest mountain we've ever hiked before is a good sign!"

I shivered as another wave of chill bumps trickled down my arms. "Brr. It's so cold this morning! It has to be at least in the low forties, or maybe even thirties! I've got to put more clothes on." I was already wearing my wool base layers, but I ran over to my backpack to grab a jacket to go on top. I looked at the thermometer hanging from the shoulder strap. "No wonder, it's thirty-four degrees!" I shouted. "It's basically winter in July!"

Will laughed. "It will warm up once we get moving and the sun gets higher," he assured. "Let's get dressed and eat. We need to get on the trail soon."

The excitement and distraction of the moose wore off quickly. As I fixed my oatmeal, the cold air wrapped my stiff fingers in icy pain. I wasn't expecting winter temps during my middle-of-summer road trip, so I hadn't packed any gloves or hand warmers. By the time we all were finished with breakfast and ready to leave, my fingers were so frozen I could barely move them. I always had poor circulation, so I wasn't surprised, but I began to slip into a bad mood because of the pain.

Hiking a 14,278 foot mountain didn't sound appealing to me at that moment. I knew I had to find something to shield my hands from the whipping wind or there was a chance I wouldn't enjoy this day at all. The only thing I could think to use was a pair of my wool socks. Thankfully, I still had a pair left that I'd only worn once since we washed our clothes at the motel in Moab, so I didn't have to shove my clean hands into completely crusty, stench-filled socks. I walked with sock nubs for hands the first couple miles, keeping them stuffed in my rain jacket pockets both for another layer of protection from the wind and to keep the vague sweaty foot smell from floating up to my nose as I walked.

We slowed our hiking pace to half our normal speed to avoid altitude sickness. We'd consumed what seemed like a bathtub of water since we left Moab the day before, and considering the amount of urine I had excreted the past twenty-four hours, I didn't think I had ever been so hydrated.

The morning fog dissipated, and the sun soon peeked over the ridgeline and shone down on the glimmering dew-soaked grasses of the valley. Though it looked like we would avoid rain today, I was glad I wore my rain jacket because the wind still danced across the valley in strong gusts, and my jacket was doing a good job deflecting its chill.

Once the sun's warmth began to melt my ice box hands, the hike was a totally different experience for me. After walking the first hour with my head down to keep the harsh wind off my face and hide my tears of frustration from the rest of the group, I was able to look out from under my rain jacket hood to fully take in my surroundings for the first time that morning. I was still a few yards behind Sydney who was about fifteen yards behind Will and Ethan. Their heads bobbed in the distance as they walked. As far as I could tell, we were the only hikers in the valley, and that made me feel both small and large, significant and insignificant at the same time.

My eyes followed the rocky trail up the hill in front of them and around to the left, where it disappeared around a bend that reached some large clusters of boulders in the grass. I wondered how far we had left to hike before we were above the grassline where there was nothing to walk on but rock. We'd climbed to 13,000 feet, and I could already feel my breath getting shorter. It seemed that we still had a few miles before the climb along the ridgeline up to the summit. I hoped our bodies would make it.

The trail divided two slanted seas of wildflowers shaking the sleep off their yellow, pink, purple, and orange heads and stretching their arms up toward the sun which now beamed in full force. I smiled at them and decided I would do the same. I wiggled my hands free of the socks, stretched them high above my head, and took a deep breath. I tried to reground myself in my body, noticing the way the muscles in my back clenched and relaxed as I let my arms down, feeling the weight in my feet with each steady and strong step. I thanked her, my perfectly imperfect body, for carrying me up, over, down, around, and across the many miles of the past weeks, the miles that held and healed me.

I could feel myself expanding now that the hard, outer shell I left Boone with had melted away. I swore to myself that I would never stop expanding, and I welcomed the growth yet to come.

I am slowly becoming the person I have always wanted to be.

"Watch out for the lasagna!" Will called over his shoulder as he turned the corner ahead of us.

"Lasagna? Where?!" Ethan asked excitedly, as if he was expecting to find some wilderness street vendor selling lasagna, and we all cackled.

"I think he's referring to his lasagna-flavored farts that he has been letting out all morning as he's been walking in front of us." Sydney rolled her eyes.

"Oh." Ethan paused and scrunched his nose. "Gross," he muttered and continued on, though now obviously stepping off to the side instead of walking directly behind Will in the line of fire, and we laughed again.

"Dude did that backpacking meal not give you gas?" Will asked when Ethan caught up to him. "My stomach did not like it apparently."

"Maybe a little, but dang, not like that! Shoo wee! You need to move to the back and stop crop dusting us!" Ethan yelled.

"You guys sound like brothers arguing!" Sydney shouted toward them, and I smiled because it did feel like Will and Sydney had become family to us.

We had been above the tree line for a while, and at one point I stopped on the ridge to look back behind us at the turquoise alpine lake we passed earlier from above. As I looked, something dense and cold struck me hard in the middle of the back, completely catching me off guard. I quickly spun around to find Ethan bent over and laughing up the ridgeline from me. I'd just been hit with a giant snowball.

"Hey, stop it!" I screamed at him, laughing. I hadn't reached the snow patch yet, so I didn't have anything to fight back with besides rocks, and I figured hurling rocks toward his face wasn't a playful gesture. I ducked and dodged more snow grenades as he continued to launch them down the trail every few seconds.

"Can't say I've ever had a snowball fight in July before," I panted once I caught up to him and gave him a shove on the shoulder. We looked out above the valley below us. "Pretty beautiful, huh? I had no idea there were so many mountains around us until we got up here. You can see mountain ridges all the way to the horizon!"

"Yeah, besides a few ski resorts, there isn't much out here," said Ethan. We couldn't see a single building from where we stood.

"Should we summit this thing?" Will called down to us with a wide smile.

"Let's do it," said Sydney, and Ethan and I nodded in agreement.

The trail was extremely steep from there on, and I was having a hard time with the incline. I had to stop to catch my breath every twenty yards or so now that we were approaching 14,000 feet. None of us

had any other altitude sickness symptoms like headaches or feeling disoriented though, so we pressed through the last 250 feet of climbing.

My boots could no longer bend at the correct angle to step normally, which was the same problem I had hiking out of the Grand
Canyon. My pace slowed as I tried my best to scramble up the loose
rock nearing the summit. I had a few minor slips which almost gave
me a heart attack, but thankfully my boots would catch traction almost
immediately, and I wouldn't skid far. I knew if any of us took a hard fall
on a trail this steep and loose, there wouldn't be much to grab hold of
to slow the slide. I tried to keep my balance so that wouldn't happen,
trying not to look back at how far I might fall if I lost my footing. It
looked like Will had already reached the summit, and I directed all of
my attention on joining him.

We summited Grays Peak in three and a half hours. Once we were all
standing on the peak together, we gave each other high fives and let
out a loud, long, celebratory hoot. Our echoes went on forever in the
empty air and bounced back to us in staggered waves. Ridge after ridge
stretched out before us in a thousand horizontal shelves shoved together with jagged, snow-capped peaks sticking up at varying heights.
There were a few other folks at the summit who had hiked up from
the other side of the mountain on the more trafficked and established
trail up to Grays Peak. It was disorienting to see other people all of the
sudden on the cramped summit of a giant mountain after hiking completely alone in the opposite valley all day.

The wind at the top was relentless, even stronger than it was that
morning. Some gusts were so strong that it was hard to stay balanced.

"Hey," I called to the rest of the group, "I'm going to go sit down
against that rock face over there and journal for a couple minutes. Is
that okay?"

Everyone nodded. "Yeah sure. We're just going to eat our snacks
behind this boulder to get out of the wind," Will replied as he and
Sydney turned away, and Ethan walked to another viewpoint to take
some photos.

07/28/15, Day 26 -

Like avalanches falling off remote mountain peaks as the sun melts the snow's grip away, the parts of me which are not my true self are falling away, and I am finding little reminders of who I am. Something has lurched and given way, and I can feel old, familiar parts of me letting go as new, unfamiliar parts of me surface. Something about walking in the woods day after day has melted a layer of residue off of me. I feel clean, despite the dust that currently coats my skin; clear, despite the many things that still remain so up in the air. I am reminded that there is a way of being which, at its core, always resides in peace.

I know that it will take so long to portray all of the tiny details of this trip, externally, yes, but especially internally, to anyone that didn't experience it. It might be impossible. So many moments have changed me in both microscopic and colossal ways, and I can barely put language to them because I am still processing them myself.

Amidst the change, though, I find myself asking so many questions. How do we fully grasp the things that change us? How can we ever fully name the gratitude we have for our transformation? I can't place a direct finger on it, but I sense the subtle change in that secret place inside of me which I used to call Spirit, and maybe I still do. Spirit—that underlying, embodied place which forms the Ground of our being, from which the fruits of love and grace grow up and out.

How might we shout a praise of thankfulness that covers all of the ones that have taken part in saving us, when both human and mountain, bird and bee, sunrise and sunset, stranger and friend, light and dark, chaos and peace, grief and rejoicing, have all been the hands that have filled the empty space in our palms and taken part in walking us home? To whom do we direct our prayers and praise when we see that the Divine might just be everywhere, when we believe that there is a possibility that everything could be Sacred?

I think it is easy to miss moments of transcendence, not because we aren't paying attention, but because we are looking too hard. I used to strive to have these giant, sudden, world-shattering revelations, but I'm beginning to understand that transcendence often comes in whispers opposed to shouts. Sitting here on top of Grays Peak, looking out into wave after wave of an ocean of rock, I find it easier to believe in the possibility of God beyond the God I thought I knew, and I find myself humbled and reverent.

Maybe the wilderness always makes it a little easier for us to experience transcendence, but we must remember that transcendence is always available to us, even once we are off the highest and most exciting mountain in the adventure. The invitation is always there, calling us higher, calling us closer, calling us further into the process of becoming, calling us to join the Divine dance, calling us home.

I was losing body heat even in the sun, so once my hand started cramping from the cold, I had to quit writing. I walked back over to the others, and the four of us laid in a little rut created by some boulders for refuge from the brutal wind. I lavished every crumb of my protein bar and wished I had five more to follow it.

"Well, should we take a group photo and head down?" Will asked once we were too cold to sit anymore.

We crawled up off the hard ground, took a windy, triumphant group photo, and began our long descent. I thought my knees were surely going to give out at any moment, and I longed for flat ground. The four of us were scattered at different paces for the first half of our hike down, but once the trail incline lessened a little bit, Sydney and I ended up next to each other again.

She and I passed time on the long walk through the valley by making rainbow bouquets of lupines, columbine, fireweed, and alpine meadow greenery as we walked. I felt much more joyful than I felt at the beginning of the hike. I found myself unable to stop smiling, and I was tempted to just sprint all the way down the mountain, but for my knees' sake, I stayed with Sydney.

I debated it for a while, but eventually I worked up the courage to break the silence. It was time to ask the question.

"Hey Syd, I've been wanting to ask you for days, but I didn't really know if it was too forward. I didn't want to catch you off guard, but I've been wondering if you and Will are, like, a thing?" I started speaking faster because I was nervous. "Because I've noticed here and there that there seems to be something going on between you two, and, I mean, I guess I was just wanting to know, if you don't mind." I felt incredibly awkward.

Sydney chuckled and automatically blushed and smirked. She sighed. "Yes," she giggled and paused. I couldn't tell if she was going to say more or if she also felt awkward and her 'yes' was the end of the conversation. She started talking again, which helped me feel more at ease. "It's been something that has been building for years, I guess, but we finally acknowledged it verbally right before we left to come meet you in California."

"I knew it!" I shouted, laughing. "Ethan did too, and he threatened to ask you and Will in a really obnoxious and embarrassing way, so I told him I would save you from that and work up the courage to ask."

"Ha! That's hilarious. We wouldn't have minded if he asked. I thought about mentioning it to you when we first got to California, but I didn't want it to make the group dynamics weird since we weren't really a thing before you left. I didn't want you and Ethan to feel like the third and fourth wheel or anything."

"Oh, no. We haven't felt like that," I assured her. "The things I've picked up on are not obvious at all, which is why I waited so long to ask. I couldn't tell for sure. But aw, that makes me happy! I mean, I really only know you both from this trip, but it seems like you two would be really great together. Plus, you've spent so much time together and are so close already that if there's any attraction there, it makes sense." I shrugged and smiled.

"Yeah, it does," Sydney nodded. "I was scared to push into any sort of romantic space with him because it's super risky. I would never want to jeopardize my friendship with Will, but eventually it didn't make sense to just stay friends anymore. Another part of me waiting to say anything was that I didn't want you to feel like it was being rubbed in your face the whole trip if we were more open about it. I thought it might be hard to be around a new couple all the time when you're still processing so much after Cam."

"Thanks for saying that. It has been hard at times," I admitted, "but I can't just keep myself from ever being around couples again as if there aren't healthy ways to be in a loving relationship, though some days I'm tempted to retreat into eternal singleness." We both laughed.

"It will take time," she replied gently. "Like I said before, you can't rush your healing."

"Thanks, Syd." I picked another lupine and added it to my growing bouquet I clenched in my left hand. "Cheers to you and Will. To all of us. To this incredible road trip." I held out my bouquet like a champagne glass, and Sydney touched hers to mine, toasting to the beauty of change.

We took the back way along Colorado 9-South through the mountains to reach Colorado Springs, our last stop before heading due east. I reached out to Tyler, my best friend from high school, but never heard anything from him, and since we figured we couldn't park and sleep overnight in the city, our only idea was to look up free campsites. We found a website which had a list of potential free campsites in Colorado, and we took a risk and picked one within thirty minutes of the city, not knowing what to expect.

We arrived at a long dirt road, and though we didn't see any spaces that even remotely looked like established campsites, we decided to pull off about a mile into the woods and set up camp, hoping that we weren't on private land and that we wouldn't wake up to some angry man with a shotgun or something. I didn't even know if there were people like that out West, but growing up in Georgia trained me to know the risks of trespassing.

By the time we got out of the car and began setting up our tents, I noticed some tension in the group. It seemed like I wasn't the only one growing tired of the whole ordeal. We were tired of sleeping in a tent, tired of being dirty, tired of fixing every meal out of the back of our car. I think mentally we all had decided that Grays Peak was the finale, and now instead of feeling like an adventure that we were excited about, it felt more like killing time before we had to go home.

It was 7:00 p.m. Sydney and I squatted around our small cook stoves balanced on flat patches of grass between the knobby roots and bumps in the clearing. We cooked a quick pasta and spaghetti sauce dinner for the four of us while the boys finished setting up the tents.

No one talked. The only sound was the gas flame soaring out of our camping stoves.

As Sydney split the pasta into four even portions, Ethan finally broke the silence. "Am I the only one that noticed the fact that there is some sort of animal poop literally everywhere around this entire clearing?"

"I did notice," I confessed. "I've been trying to tell myself that it's just dog poop."

Will squatted down to investigate. "Oh no, it's definitely coyote scat," he warned, "and a lot of it."

"Oh, good," Sydney emphasized sarcastically. "Everything I want to hear right now."

"I think I'm going to sleep in the car tonight," Will admitted.

"What?" gasped Sydney. "And make the two women sleep out in the tent, exposed to the freezing temps and carnivores lurking in the darkness?"

"Yeah, chivalry is dead I guess." I rolled my eyes playfully. "They'll just have to watch us getting eaten alive from their safe window, and they'll have to pay for it by living with guilt for the rest of their lives. You guys sure you want that?" I gave them a judgmental look.

"Coyotes are omnivores, actually," Will interjected, "so as long as y'all leave some food out for them, they'll probably leave you alone." He smiled.

"Yeah, quit being a baby," Ethan bantered. "Nothing is going to kill you. Here." He opened the side door and extended his hand. "You can take your taser to protect you." We all laughed.

"Man, I honestly forgot about that thing." I shook my head. "I still can't believe our mother chose to purchase that. Did I even tell you that she shocked herself with it?"

"Oh my gosh. No. She would." He shook his head.

I lightened the mood by telling the story about my mom, the stun gun, and the awkwardness of receiving a weapon by mail unbeknownst to the stranger who owns the house you are staying in. It felt good to laugh in the midst of feeling tense and annoyed that our lack of plans after Grays Peak led us to a poop-covered clearing surrounded by red mud and straggly, half-dead trees. Though it was quite a lackluster evening compared to the consistently mind-blowing beauty of our other campsites the past couple weeks, it felt like it was just part of the deal. Some days, your epic road trip leads you to sleep by pristine alpine streams or on the edge of a cliff surrounded by mountain summits, and others, your epic road trip leaves you with no other option but to sleep in a big pile of literal shit.

{27}

THE FEAR OF STARTING OVER

07/29/15, Day 27 -

I *hate to buy into stereotypes, but Kansas is the least enthralling landscape I have ever encountered. It seems like clones of the same plot of land are lined up in a straight, flat eternity, like every five minutes we hit rewind on reality and play the same clip over and over again. We are four hours into our drive from Colorado Springs, and we are officially driving due east for the first time since I left Boone, 27 days ago.*

Garden of the Gods stood up to its reputation of beauty, with great thrones of red rock jutting out of the dark evergreens in a massive palace-looking array. I think it would have been more impressive though if we weren't coming from two weeks of experiencing the most epic places this country has within its borders back-to-back. Like Sydney said a couple days ago, there was barely enough time to process any of them individually before we rushed off to the next one. Garden of the Gods was also packed with people, more of a drive-up tourist attraction than a grueling hike with a view, which made it hard to want to stay much longer than an hour.

I wasn't expecting to hear from Tyler, but on our way to lunch I got a text from him asking if we were still around. I told him which restaurant we were going to eat lunch at, and he replied, "Okay. About to jump out of a plane. Be right there." Tyler has always been one to live on the edge, and skydiving is his new adventure hobby. I was not even surprised that he would just casually text me moments away from hurling himself out of an airplane for fun.

It was really good to see Ty, but his visit left me feeling angsty, even though we had a connected, insightful conversation like we have had any time we've talked in the past eight years. We talked about the direction he was heading with his job and his doubts about his ability to choose a career path he felt confident in, which was something I could relate to. I told him some of my ideas about what I might want to do with my life outside of the one-right-way-to-be-an-adult-in-America. He asked how I was dealing with the effects of the breakup with Cam, and I was honest about how hard it has been but how much this trip has helped me heal. When he asked me what ways God has been speaking to me throughout my trip though, I couldn't bring myself to tell him the truth. I hid. I gave a bullshit answer, using safe, edited, old, familiar Christian language that I knew would make him feel comfortable and save me from having to be honest about my deconstruction and my lack of answers.

How do I find the courage to be myself when so much is at risk?

I not only feel angst about my relationship with Tyler specifically, but I also feel angst about community going forward in general. Will I ever be able to be a part of a spiritual community again? Even if it's not Christian? How will I be able to have an open, authentic, honest friendship with anyone from church again if they're always going to think that I need to be re-convinced, that I'm just a lost sheep that needs to come back home? How can I have relationships with Christians if I don't always believe that God is conscious? When I don't know that I care much about what the Bible says literally? When I don't think that people that aren't Christians are going to hell? When I no longer believe that my mission in life is to get as many people as possible to "come to Jesus" or "get saved" or say the "sinner's prayer?" How do I interact with the Church as a whole when a good portion of people in the Church would view me as a heretic and discredit everything I have to say? How do I explain to people in the Church why I and so many others like me needed to leave, why being in the Church is harmful for me right now?

Despite the fear of starting over, I know that coming back and finding sustainable community, even outside of the Church, will require vulnerability. It will require opening up, being transparent, and inviting people into my pain and longing and questions.

It's scary thinking about telling the truth, just being Emily for the first time. I had to cut the roots of a part of me that was dying and let her go back to the earth. But what is this tree that now stands in its place, and in what direction will it grow?

{28}

THE COURAGE TO GO

07/30/15, Day 28 -

*A*fter some consideration of possible routes, we decided we are going to stop at Lynn and Chip's to stay the night when we drive through Nashville this evening, which means that our sketchy campsite in rural Kansas last night was our last time sleeping outside before we're back in Boone. Though I am excited to sleep in a bed and have a shower, part of me felt sad when Sydney and I rolled up our tent together for the last time this morning. We made a promise that we would sleep in it together again soon, though. Maybe in Iceland. Ethan said he was down. Will has always wanted to go. We told Ethan if he moves to Boone we'll make it work out to go to Iceland together next summer for road trip round two.

We have been on the road for about two hours so far, which means we have about eight hours left until Nashville. We are in Missouri now, which is slightly more interesting than Kansas, but not much.

It's been a weird morning filled with a lot of reflection. I dreamed about Cam last night, but the interesting thing about *this dream is that it was the first dream I have had about him since we ended things that was not a nightmare.*

I was inside of a room, in what I assumed to be my house, and I got up to answer a knock at the front door. It was a weird time of night for someone to be coming by, so I opened the door hesitantly to find Cam standing there. His expression was calm, and his eyes held a gentleness and clarity I hadn't seen since before he went into the military. There was a group of people behind him. When I asked him what this was about, he said, "I brought these people to you, because they are in the same place as you."

I knew in my dream that the place he was referring to was the place of deconstruction and isolation I felt in my experience with leaving my fundamentalist, evangelical Christian community and not knowing where home was anymore. I didn't recognize any of their faces, but they were all smiling. I immediately had this overwhelming feeling that there was a reason for everything I'd been through, and being honest and talking about my experience would lead me to the next right step in my life, even though I had no idea what that step was yet. I began to cry and embraced Cam, thanking him for knowing me, for seeing me, and for bringing me the kind of community I have been searching for.

And then I woke up.

What does it mean?

Seeing Cam in my dream reminded me of my scars, but I think the nature of soul-deep scars might be ultimately life-giving. They might actually be our portal to being able to understand the sacred in the raw and deep trough of suffering we experience. Through these scars, we might be able to push through into the real mystery, the mystery of "God," aside from religion, and legalism, anger, and hypocrisy.

Our sacred scars are our source of inspiration, the things or events that break us open so intensely that our lives will never be the same. They are the things that force us to change everything, to leave something, or to maybe start speaking up for the first time. Maybe it's a relationship ending, maybe it's a radical change in your beliefs, maybe it's a loved one dying, maybe it's a medical diagnosis, maybe it's being marginalized and oppressed for the color of your skin, maybe it's exclusion and rebuke for your gender identity or sexual orientation, maybe it's coming out as gay to unsupportive parents, maybe it's mental illness, maybe it's the loss of a job, maybe it's a natural disaster, maybe it's healing from an eating disorder, maybe it's a miscarriage, or one of so many other things that break us open. We all carry these with us, our sacred scars, which we thought very well might be the end of us, which we didn't believe we would be able to ever heal from and push through, which we thought would make us walk with a limp forever.

But I want to believe that my trauma, loss, grief, and pain aren't scars to resist or run away from. They are the scars that open me up to the sacred. They bring me into the possibility of understanding redemption, the possibility of experiencing grace, the possibility of actually being set free, of resurrecting, of being born again, of experiencing the reality of what Jesus might have meant when he talked about new birth.

Going home, I don't want to be scared back into dormancy, where I don't feel anything. I want to relearn how to fully feel, for emotion is a gift. It makes this life mean something, and even moreso, hard emotions I don't want to feel enable me to notice and be thankful for the easy ones. Contrast is necessary for joy to be differentiated from the pain.

I realize I must continue to know myself, which will take careful attention and time before I am grounded in a self-identity not rooted in my trauma, and though I would like to one day make something of all of this God mess, I still feel like a young vine that needs some sort of wire structure to grip as I grow and as my roots become more stable.

Going back, I can't commit to much. I can't commit to believing in God all the time. I can't commit to ever being a "Christian" again, at least not in the way I used to embrace that label. I can't commit to being able to be a part of a church community in the current model of church I have seen.

But I can commit to showing up. Showing up to the things going on inside of myself and tending to them, exploring them, holding them with open hands, including all of the grief and pain and insecurity and fear. I can commit to learning self-compassion, so that my self-love would give me the ability to authentically love my neighbors--my human neighbors, and my neighbors the honeybee, the spruce, the cardinal, the mushroom. I can commit to giving myself grace when my healing work takes longer than I expect or want it to, for like Sydney said, I can't rush my healing. I can commit to press into the unknown, to create space for wonder, to seek peace in ambiguity, to surrender to what is. Going back, I can commit to telling the truth.

The end goal doesn't really matter to me. I don't know who I will be, or what I will do. I don't really think arriving somewhere is the point. It is what happens to us and what we learn and how we change as we go that we must hold close. That is the point of living. The being. The going. Not the arriving. Arriving at the California coast, or to the campsite at Snow Creek, or to the river at the bottom of the Grand Canyon, or at the top of Angels Landing, or to any destination this past month would mean nothing if I was asleep the whole way there, if I didn't pay attention to what the soil sounded like crunching under my boots, or how much my knees hurt, or how much I wanted to quit, or how the desert smelled when it rained, or how sad I was some days, or how beautifully the land threw itself up into a mountain from the valley, or how I changed along the way. It is the going that changes us.

Going forward, in every single second I have on this tiny blue dot hurling its way through an ever-expanding universe, I want to be in constant acknowledgement of the reverence humming within me that tells of a universal love, a slice of Divinity that resides within me, and within all of us, and in every atom of this incredible universe, which leads us further closer into wholeness, healing, reconciliation, and love.

And it starts with breathing. Being. Now. Here.

Because this is all we have.

I find myself wondering how I was able to leave my house four weeks ago. I was so scared of what this trip would lead to. I honestly don't know how I found the courage to go, but somehow, I did, and here I am, barely recognizable compared to the shell of a human that walked out of my house four weeks ago.

I think at some point in all of our lives we have to find the courage to go. No matter how we are raised or what we experience, a time comes when we have to leave something, and even though leaving is the scariest thing we've ever done, it's the only thing that will keep us alive. Leaving was the best decision I ever made. Doing the scary thing was the only right next step for me. I had to make peace with the shadows in my life, and I thank the part of myself that resisted all of those voices in my head screaming for me to stay and got in the car anyway.

I had to give myself permission to say no to other people's expectations of who I should be. I had to do the hard work of slowing down enough to hear the still, small voice inside of me again. I had to give myself permission to grieve the loss of a partner, with all of his goodness and all of his own pain and trauma, as well as the loss of my evangelical upbringing. I had to give myself permission to be honest, to tell the truth, to name my emotions and feel them no matter how many tears came. I had to give myself permission to inhabit my body, to feel the flesh on my bones and claim my womanhood, my beauty, my body being inherently good. I had to give myself permission to be angry, to let the rage I had put in a box fill my chest so that I might be able to breathe it out and fill my lungs with life again. I had to give myself permission to be in process, to not know, and to be fine with not knowing.

Leaving was making a peace accord with myself. It was a promise to seek an end to the battle inside of my head, to open my hands to hold all parts of me, no matter how incongruent. The brokenhearted romantic. The raging skeptic. The angry atheist. The Spirit-seeking mystic. I've realized that the only way forward is finding a way to integrate all of those parts of me. Instead of fighting against each other, they must be able to have the courage to sit down together, shake each other's hands, and say, "Welcome. I am glad you are here. Who are you, what truth do you need to speak, and what gifts do we have to give each other?"

This trip has taught me that before we can truly come to the table with others, we must first figure out how to come around the table with ourselves, in radical acceptance and love. There's no forcing yourself into loving yourself. I've tried, and I know it doesn't work that way. I must start small by paying attention to the ways that my ability to love myself as I am is often hindered by my trauma. I must learn and observe my triggers, as well as my emotional and psychological responses to different stimuli, so that I can help myself form new synapses in my brain which tell a new story—a story which says that I am good at my core, a story which says that I matter, a story which says that I belong.

———

7/30/15, Day 28, Pt. 2 -

I am laying in a bed! A real bed! With a real pillow instead of a sack of dirty, sweaty, smelly clothes! And my hair is washed! And my pits don't stink! What is this foreign state of being?

We arrived at Lynn and Chip's to a giant dish of homemade lasagna on the middle of the table, not without a good laugh and a joke about Will's lasagna gas on the hike to Grays Peak. There was cheese bread, salad, and sweet tea, the perfect feast to welcome us back to Southern living. We sat around the table and told stories for what felt like hours. Stolen stray dogs, tasers, seagulls, injuries, good meals, bad meals, hot days, cold nights, good campsites, bad campsites, majestic mountains, rattlesnakes, losing Will, a moose, and hard hikes…Lynn and Chip couldn't believe any of it. They couldn't stop saying how blown away they were by how much we crammed in, and looking back, I'm pretty blown away myself.

After dinner, once Will, Sydney, and Ethan had gone upstairs, Lynn got to talking about church stories, and I was too timid to interrupt her and leave.

She told me something else, though, that I don't know what to do with. Lynn said she has had dreams about me since I was a little girl. She told me that I was a writer, and that she always knew I was going to be a writer, because "the Lord" told her in her dreams. I don't even know if she has read anything I've written, and the fact that she said God had told her that I was going to be a writer was a little too freaky for my liking, but I can't help but admit that it prodded something in me. I can't stop thinking about it and I feel some strange but familiar nudge inside of my gut that tells me it is somehow the next right step.

I didn't tell Lynn that I was mostly terrified of writing because if I shared anything publicly, it would mean I would have to tell the truth. What will that mean, to tell the truth, especially telling the truth through writing? Will it be worth it? Will I be rejected? Will people be angry with me? Will it be hurtful for my Christian friends? What will my family think? Writing truthfully feels so difficult and intimidating, but I think I have to. Not any time soon because I have a lot of healing to do, and I barely even have language for my experience right now. But eventually, I will.

This is the last night of the trip. After our six hours and 350 miles on the road tomorrow back to Boone, I will have reached roughly 115 hours and around 7,000 miles on the road in the month of July. Seeing those numbers written out makes it harder to justify that it was a rational idea to cram that much traveling into a month, but I stand by my decision. I needed every town, every mile, every day, every moment of this trip. I reach the end wiped of energy but full of life—a new kind of life. Hope, I might even call it, that this meaning I have found out here will last the rest of my life. These seven thousand miles have healed me in ways I'm sure I will still be discovering years down the road. This trip has been both the hardest and greatest teacher I've ever experienced. I hope I never take its lessons for granted.

I will sleep in my own bed tomorrow. I am pulled in a thousand different directions as I wonder how to feel about going home, whatever home means to me now. I never know how to close out sections of my journal after traveling. How do you confidently say goodbye to something you are only beginning to get to know? Sigh. Almost one month ago, I started this trip with an attempt at prayer. I guess after this trip taking quite an unexpected spiritual turn despite all of my efforts in the beginning to stubbornly avoid it, I think it makes sense to end with an intention.

Oh, hell. Fine. I guess I can call it a prayer.

God, Divine, Universe, Ground of Being, Ultimate Reality, Collective Consciousness, Spirit, whatever he/she/it/they/you might be,

May I carry the gifts of this trip forward into every day I am given in this precious life. May I be reminded of the Divine that whispers in all things. May my ears hear the heart-song of my Spirit that comes into frequency and resonates with the Spirit of the world around me. May I fall in love with life, over and over again, proclaiming that it is full, even when I feel empty. May I let the canvas be painted black, no matter how scary giving up the paintbrush is. May I recognize and welcome love and grace when they are given. May I allow myself to be brought to my knees in gratitude, over and over and over again. May I always show up to seek God, seek the Divine, seek the Source from which all things flow, the Ground of Being, the Reverence that hums within me, the All.

There is a fire in my soul. It is raging with anger and frustration and grief, but there is still a passion there. A passion to live, to love, to show up. May I find the courage, the truth, the people, the healing, the life that will fan the flame and keep it alive. May the fire burn, and may it light the Way that will take me where I need to go.

AFTERWORD

Though still to this day I do not know what to think about my conversation with Lynn in her living room that last night, I cannot deny that it was the first nudge that sent me into exploring the craft of writing. Many years later, that nudge, combined with many others that followed it, developed into my decision to write and publish this book. There is mystery wrapped up in it all, and though some days my inner critic still tries to strip my experience of wonder and explain it away with reason, something deep in me knows there was something divine about the seed my conversation with Lynn planted inside of me.

It seems as if many lifetimes of growth and change have somehow taken place in these five years since I left that first sunny July morning. Leaving was always the only way I could ever return, and it is only through the process of writing this book that I have been able to fully understand that. Even five years later, I am still discovering daily what it is that I am returning to. I don't know if it will ever be defined by consistent language again, and I have arrived at a place where I am okay with that. Though I no longer identify fully with the version of myself in this story and now understand ways in which some of her thoughts and questions were limited, I stand by the questions she needed to ask and the feelings she needed to name in this narrative. I remain passionate about the conversation she started, and I felt it my duty to give this story space to do whatever work it needs to do in the world, even if that work is nothing but sending me, and hopefully a few of you, further along the beautiful Way of becoming.

As I release this book, I find myself still asking the same questions I asked in my last journal entry. I don't think telling the truth in our lives ever stops being scary, but I believe it is important Work, and we must do it over and over and over again. Telling the truth opens us up for rejection, yes, but more importantly, it creates space to open up our deepest dark and let the light in, and that is the Work I feel called to. The conversations in this book are only a portion of that Work, but we all have to start somewhere. I don't know where I will end up, but I do know that along the Way, asking the hard questions and exposing the darkness instead of repressing it will always be at the center of the Work I commit myself to, whether that be in my life or in the institutions and systems of power that govern this world. I personally believe it is the only way toward lasting reconciliation, healing, justice, and change.

May it be.

ACKNOWLEDGEMENTS

I have found myself on my knees many times throughout this multi-year labor of love. Sometimes it was out of anguish because there were many moments where finishing this book seemed too great a task, but most of the time, it was out of immense gratitude for the beautiful humans who have held me, healed me, encouraged me, loved me, and given me unwavering support these past five years of re-discovering life.

To my wonderful parents, brother, grandmother, and family for graciously making space for the person I continue to become, willingly trusting my judgement in times when they didn't understand, and thoroughly loving and supporting me every step of the way.

To my life partner, Peter, for being the safe place I returned to after the many hard and long days involved in this process, the mirror I sought when I lost sight of what was important, and the cheerleader I needed on the days I didn't believe I could become an author.

To Jordan Glover, for insisting that I accept myself as a writer for over a decade now, for affirming me as I slowly began to believe him, and for being my most constant friend through these many years of change.

To Mr. Van Wyk, for being the English teacher this science and math nerd needed, for encouraging me to push into my abstract ideas instead of conforming to the "one right way" to think, and for planting a seed so many years ago which grew into a craft that has saved my life.

To Julia Zaleski, for pushing agasint my walls relentlessly until I let you in, for teaching me how to trust people again, and for being my forever person.

To Danielle Kovasckitz, Lucas Kovasckitz, Ben Roberts, and Lydia Roberts, for being the family I have chosen, for giving me space to be myself, and for all of the ways you have walked me home.

To Mike Morrell, for giving your time to a beginner with a dream, for answering my never-ending questions, and for helping this book get off the ground.

To Jasmin Morrell, my most incredible and talented editor, for your dedication and hard work in the midst of such a turbulent season, for your patience with the monster of a manuscript this book was in the beginning, for your gracious critique when I had blind spots I was not aware of, and for your commitment to making my vision into a reality. This book would not have been possible (or short enough for someone to want to read) without you.

To the Appalachian Mountains, my beautiful home, for being my place of rest no matter how long I have been away, for being my teacher when I haven't known what questions to ask, and for being my healer on days when I don't know what I need.

And finally to you, dear friend, for picking up this book, for holding space for vulnerability, and for allowing me to tell the truth, even when it is uncomfortable. May it encourage you to do the same.

I carry parts of each of you within me, and it is a profound honor. I extend my deepest and most humble gratitude to you all.

Grace and Peace.

ABOUT THE AUTHOR

EMILY DOBBERSTEIN is a writer, community organizer, backpacker, and world traveler based in Asheville, North Carolina. Emily is an advocate of radical vulnerability and authenticity, and she is dedicated to fostering spaces where all are welcome at the table. *The Courage to Go* is her first book.

emilydobberstein.com
instagram: emdobberstein
facebook.com/emily.dobberstein
emily@emilydobberstein.com

Emily Dobberstein is available for speaking engagements. To inquire about a possible appearance, please send an email to emily@emilydobberstein.com